"This is a travel book in the truest, deepest sense. In describing her sojourns on the luminous Scottish island of Iona, Clare Marcus also moves us to journey into our own inner world. There we discover, as she does, the importance of place: how we have been altered and enriched by the landscapes of our lives. Draws from archetypal psychology and her love for this living Earth, the author's personal story becomes the most trustworthy of guides."
—Joanna Macy, author, *World as Lover, World as Self.*

"Both personal and professional experience illuminate Clare Cooper Marcus's deep understanding of an important, over-looked truth: the quality of our lives depends on our relationships not only with people, but also with places. On her journey from her childhood's English countryside, to healing gardens in America, to the magical island of Iona, she shows us how to look past our own fragile boundaries to the great world outside, where we can find unsuspected strength, wisdom, and joy."
—Winifred Gallagher, author of *The Power of Place: How Our Surroundings Shape Our Thoughts, Emotions and Actions,* and *Rapt: Attention and Focused Life.*

"Clare Marcus's prose lifts us beyond intimate contact with this magical island into the spaces in our own hearts that we have closed off. Her touch, her eye for light, her honest memories of old pain, her joy in birdsong and small woodland plants—these open us to the power of place and we are healed too."
—Louise Dunlap, author of *Undoing the Silence: Six Tools for Social Change Writing.*

"Do you wish for a special place that is a wise and loving friend that empowers you, heals your illness, soothes your worst fears and disappointments? A place that holds you in its embrace and makes you whole? Clare Cooper Marcus writes of her such place and in so doing instructs us to discover places where we can be fully alive. In turns literary and primal, *Iona Dreaming* will imbue you with sensuous reasoning and change you forever."
—Randolph T. Hester, Professor, Department of Landscape Architecture and Environmental Planning, University of California, Berkeley; author of *Design for Ecological Democracy,* and *Cultivating Sacredness in the Everyday Landscape.*

"This is an enchanting book about geographies of the heart, sacred landscapes of desire, longing and memory. Clare Cooper Marcus invites us to accompany her to many landscapes of her remarkable life's journey—from the childhood terrors of wartime England, to hippie California, and finally the rugged solitudes of the Scottish island of Iona. Clare's acute perceptions balance her warmth and compassion as she describes Nature's many healing qualities in facing life-threatening illness and the many challenges experienced in a life well lived."
—Wendy Sarkissian PhD, author of *Kitchen Table Sustainability.*

"In this hauntingly beautiful memoir, Clare Cooper Marcus traverses the liminal spaces of the landscape of Iona and the inner terrain of the soul with a sensual eloquence. Through this pioneer in the field of therapeutic landscapes, we encounter a personal story of transformation and healing that points beyond itself to the numinous power of place, unfolding through memory, insightful reflection, and a rich tapestry of dreams."
—Susan Williams. Jungian Analyst, Teaching faculty at C.G.Jung Institute, San Francisco.

"Clare Cooper Marcus was the first person to alert me to the emotional meaning of our environment. In this moving memoir, she turns her writerly eye to the power of place in our spiritual, emotional and physical healing. Eloquent, evocative, and original."
—MJ Ryan, author of *Attitudes of Gratitude* and *This Year I Will…*

"This is a fascinating book about an impressive woman who 'turns within' after retirement from a prestigious academic career and life threatening bouts with cancer to make peace with herself, nature and, yes, even God. Exquisitely written and self-revealing, Clare Cooper Marcus' chronicle of her journey to the Scottish Isle of Iona provides real insight into what 'inner life' means and what rewards await those who cultivate it."
—Roger Doudna, PhD, Findhorn Foundation Fellowship Coordinator

"Through Clare Cooper Marcus's poetic landscapes we are transported to Iona on a journey of transformation and healing. Mythology, dreams, the wisdom of rock, tree, and sea all weave a fabric of inspiration and guidance, where at the end we meet ourselves and become whole. Magical, poetic, and uplifting, this book will sneak into your dreams and beckon you to set out on your own path of inner exploration. Clare is a talented, intelligent, and lyrical writer."
—Linda Joy Myers, Ph.D., president of the National Association of Memoir Writers, author of *The Power of Memoir: How to Write Your Healing Story,* and *Don't Call Me Mother.*

"Clare Marcus' poetic prose draws us gently into the widening circles around the human heart, in this deep journey of personal healing. We go with her, to the sacred landscape of the remote Isle of Iona to discover that it is through her experience of profound identification with the natural world in this particular place that she can rediscover her own authentic heart and, in resonance with the sea and sky and spirit there, be healed. This is a beautiful book of discovery by a remarkable and brave woman."
—Carolyn North, Author of *Ecstatic Relations* and *Voices out of Stone*

"These days, when we are so aware of how we have wounded the earth, it is a treat to read a book that reminds us that the earth can heal us. Marcus' journey to Iona is an inward and outward voyage of the soul, a contemplative adventure triggered by the tender presence of Iona's shores and windswept plains. Marcus' fine-grained prose sings and dances the reader toward a full embrace of what that time and place meant to her, and what a heartfelt return to landscape could mean for us."
—Norman Fischer, Zen priest and poet, author of *Sailing Home: Using the Wisdom of Homer's Odyssey to Navigate Life's Perils and Pitfalls.*

"Clare Marcus has given us a pilgrim's way, an invitation to take the deepest hero's journey – to go into the unknown landscape of nature and of memory, and to return home healed, and whole. Marcus' own memories take her back to displacement in wartime and to unresolved relationships, and yet in remembering there is also resolution: a field of daffodils in childhood, she writes, "pulls at me like a favorite love song." Marcus finds peace on a remote island, and charts the course for us, if we dare to go in search of our own solitude, our own love songs."
—Pat Schneider, author: *Writing Alone & With Others* and founder, Amherst Writers & Artists.

Iona Dreaming

The Healing Power of Place

CLARE COOPER MARCUS

*For Karen,
with warm wishes,
Clare Cooper Marcus*

Nicolas Hays, Inc.
Lake Worth, FL

Published in 2010 by Nicolas-Hays, Inc.
P. O. Box 540206
Lake Worth, FL 33454-0206
www.nicolashays.com

Distributed to the trade by
Red Wheel/Weiser, LLC
65 Parker St. • Ste. 7
Newburyport, MA 01950
www.redwheelweiser.com

First Edition 2010

Library of Congress Cataloging-in-Publication Data

Marcus, Clare Cooper.
  Iona dreaming : the healing power of place / Clare Cooper Marcus.
— 1st ed.
      p. cm.
  Includes bibliographical references.
  ISBN 978-0-89254-157-7 (alk. paper)
  1. Iona (Scotland)—Description and travel. 2. Marcus, Clare Cooper—
Homes and haunts—Scotland—Iona. 3. Healing—Scotland—Iona.
4. Sacred space—Scotland. 5. Environmental psychology. I. Title.
  DA880.I7M143 2010
  941.4'2--dc22   2010002970

ISBN 978-0-89254-157-7

Book design and production by Studio 31
www.studio31.com

Printed in the U.S.A.

View from My Window

Layer upon layer, the scene
like a silken scroll unfolds.
First the field, shadows of grassy mounds
cast by a low-slung winter sun.
A fence row, simple boundary of stakes
stitching the window frame
together.
A gravel track's gray scar
its voice released as
booted feet pass by.
Beyond the track, a feathered
belt of dune grass holding tight
the belly of the sea.
The tide has turned.
A crumpled tapestry revealed,
a fabricated strand,
gray strata woven tight with olive weed,
jagged rocks black as jackdaw wings,
crystal pools where monuments of herons stand.
Quivering Chinese silk beyond the shore,
like the gift I gave my mother that she made into a shroud
salty water to embrace her aging frame.
Her ashes lie on the seabed now
sadness silenced by murmurings of sea life
and the sighing of a thousand winter waves.

—Clare Cooper Marcus (Isle of Iona, December, 2008)

For all my healers,
known and unknown.

Table of Contents

Acknowledgments

At the end of a long period of writing there are many people to thank. Several professional editors helped shape the book at different stages of its development: Mary Jane Ryan of Walnut Creek, CA; Renate Stendhal of Berkeley, CA; and Amanita Rosenbush of Oakland, CA. The wise and tactful advice of Sharon Butala of Eastend, Saskatchewan, Canada, and Laurel Warren Trufant, ProLogos Editorial Services of Durham, NH guided the final version of the book.

My thanks go to James Wasserman of Studio 31 for his professional skills in designing this book; to Lynne Elizabeth of Oakland, CA for the design of the front cover; and to Yvonne Paglia, publisher of Nicolas-Hays, for her support in bringing the finished manuscript to publication.

Many writer friends gave me editorial advice and invaluable feedback along the way: Wendy Sarkissian, Louise Dunlap, Carolyn North, Florence Ladd, and my niece, Sarah Godoy; Pat Schneider, Founder of Amherst Writers and Artists and participants in her writing workshops at the Pacific School of Religion, Berkeley, CA; Linda Joy Myers and members of the Memoir Writing Workshop in Albany, CA; and Joan Marie Wood and members of Temescal Writers in Oakland, CA.

I am grateful to friends and family who encouraged me on the long journey from inception to publication of this book, particularly my son and daughter, Jason and Lucy, and daughter-in-law Angela Laffan; and long time friends Al Baum, Sheila Madden, Jane Engel, Phyllis Greenwood, Susan Williams, Victoria and Alistair Jack, and the late Frances de Silva. I am thankful to Jill Black of Clachan Corrach, Isle of Iona, who read the manuscript and alerted me to some errors of fact about the island. To Elinore Detiger, who gave me a place to live on Iona in 1999; and to Barbara Hellenschmidt, who has provided a home away from home on the island every year since, I am eternally grateful.

I owe a huge debt of gratitude to the many people who guided and supported me during a long period of illness reported in the middle section of this book: Dr. Frances Tobriner, Jungian analyst of Berkeley, CA; psychologist Dr. Deehana Lorenz of Berkeley, CA who taught me healing imagery; Susan Wallace, acupuncturist of Albany, CA; Bonnie Maeda and the late Katie Allen, teachers of restorative yoga at the Yoga Room, Berkeley, CA; Priscilla Thomas, massage therapist, of Berkeley, CA; Greg Schelkun, psychic healer, of San Raphael, CA; the late Douglas Johnson, spiritual healer, of Silver Lake, CA; Jack von Dornum of Berkeley, CA, practitioner of plant-spirit medicine; Dr. Sarah Ferguson of Avenues for Health, Danville, CA; Dr. Gabrielle Levine, surgeon at Kaiser Permanente Medical Center, Walnut Creek, CA; Dr. Michael Jensen-Akula, oncologist at Kaiser Permanente Medical Center, Hayward, CA.; Marv and Nancy Hiles whose silent retreats at Santa Sabina in San Raphael, CA provided much needed respites of calm; and friend Sara Jaffe who faithfully accompanied me to many medical appointments.

Jungian analyst, Dr. Barry Williams of Taos, NM, interpreted the dreams recounted in this book (and many more), and to him I am eternally grateful for his wise insights and continuous support. I am thankful for the priests at the Zen Center, Green Gulch Farm, Marin County, CA, and in particular Norman Fischer, Reb Anderson, and Fu Schroeder, whose Sunday morning dharma talks provided me with spiritual sustenance in good times and bad.

Since I always write longhand, sometimes outdoors with a lined pad propped on my knees, I am indebted to those professionals who transformed my scrawl into a neat word-processed manuscript, notably the late Kaye Bock of El Cerrito, CA; Kathleen Kline of Oakland, CA; and Janine Baer of El Cerrito, CA. Victoria Jack assited me in ensuring the accuracy of the map of Iona, and Darin Jensen, Department of Geography, University of California, Berkeley patiently produced several iterations of the maps until we both felt they were right. I am grateful for his professional skills.

Finally, to the staff at Iona Abbey and the St Columba Hotel, and to the residents of Iona—some who know me and some who do not

—your smiles, greetings and very presence helped me feel a part of the community that makes up the population of this very special place.

ᴥ ᴥ

This memoir records events and feelings as I remember them. Certainly those of recent years are completely accurate, summarized from journals kept at the time. However, memories of childhood are, for most of us, probably skewed—sometimes recalled as more painful than they actually were, sometimes as more rosy. Who is to say on which side of this divide mine fall? All I know is, they are the memories that remain.

Brief facts about the World War Two appear in sections about my childhood in order to place the period in context, and to provide readers with information about that conflict with which they may be unfamiliar.

This is not an autobiography. I have written little of my professional life for this is covered elsewhere. I say little about my siblings or my children as theirs are other and different stories.

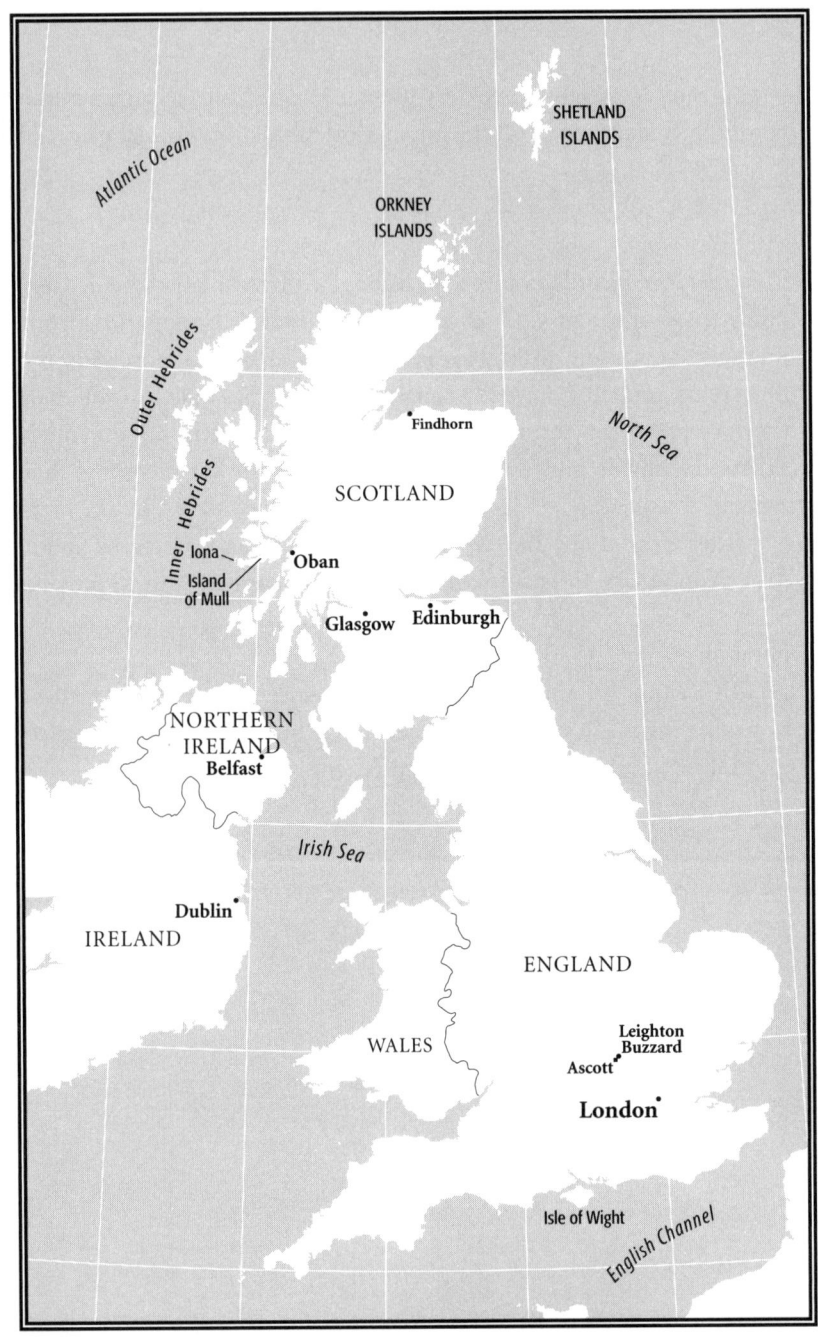

Figure 1. Location of Iona in the British Isles.

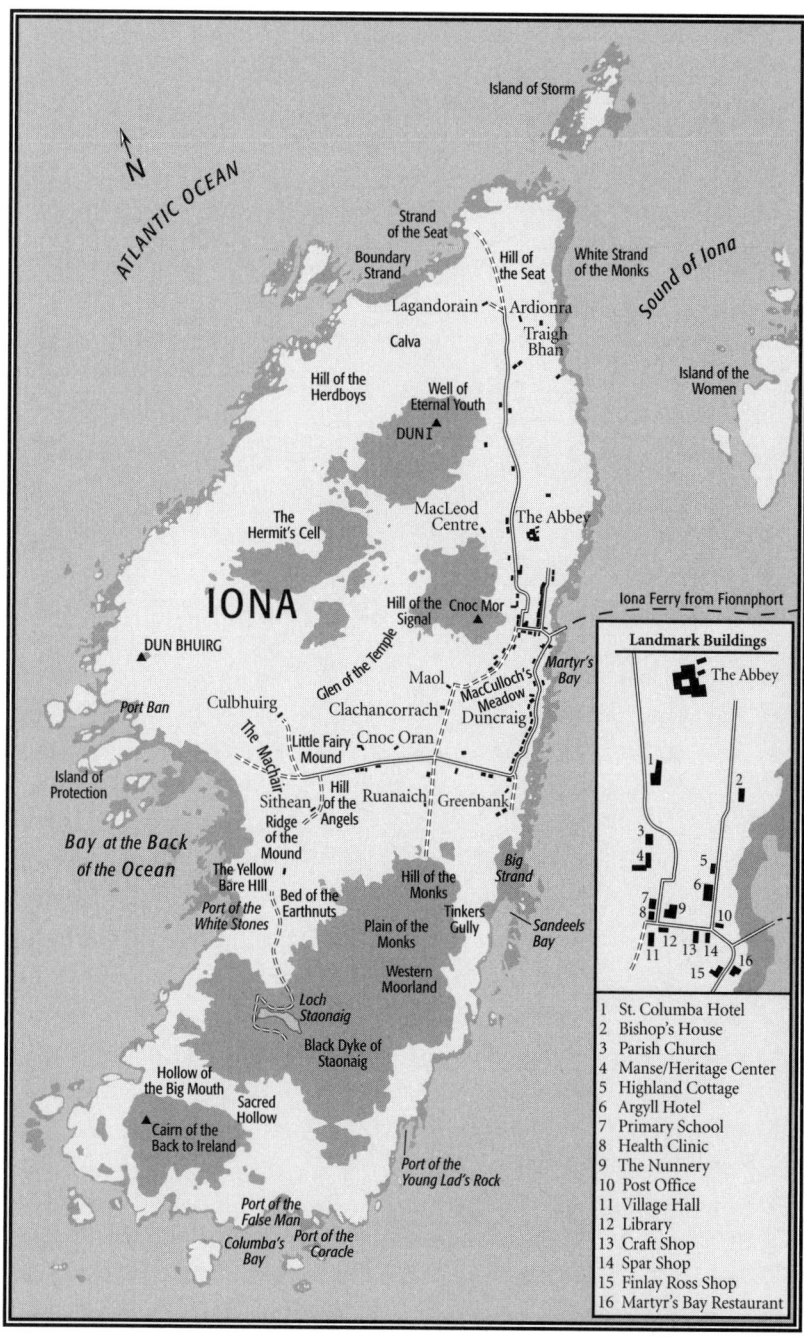

PART I

~

Journey to the Island

CHAPTER 1

❦

Coming to Iona

In the process of writing, of discovering our story, we restore those parts of ourselves that have been scattered, hidden, suppressed, denied, distorted, forbidden, and we come to understand that stories heal. As in the word "remember," we re-member, we bring together the parts, we integrate that which has been alienated or separated out ... self-discovery is more than gathering information about oneself.... It alters us. We re-store, re-member, re-vitalize ... Writing our story takes us back to some moment of origin when everything was whole ...
—Deena Metzger[1]

She turned and spoke to me in a firm but quiet voice: "I own a house on Iona." I did not know this woman. She was gray-haired, in her sixties perhaps—about my age. We were standing in line for lunch at a conference in Scotland in the fall of 1998. My surprise at her statement—which had come out of the blue—must have shown on my face.

"I have a house in the village. I am often away traveling. I like people to use it." She fingered a stray blue thread on the arm of her embroidered jacket, then brushed a strand of hair away from her eyes.

"There's some building work going on. It should be done by next April. I don't want any rent." We both moved forward in the lunch line. She turned to face me once more. "It's yours," she said as she briefly touched my right shoulder. Then she walked away.

I was dumbfounded. Who was this woman? Had she seen me on one of my many visits to the island? Even if she had (which I doubted), how could she know that I yearned to return there for a long period of quiet? I had told no one—barely admitted it to myself. My dream was to live on Iona, reflect on a difficult period in my life, and write.

Later that week, I saw the woman again and asked her why she was offering me her house when she didn't know who I was, not even my name.

"You know how thoughts drift through your mind and most of them you don't say out loud? Well, I'm strange that way. Sometimes I have to say whatever is on my mind. I knew I had to tell you that I have a house on Iona."

At the time, I was living in California, retired from academia, recovered from a post-retirement bout of illness, and all too aware of an inner voice that kept nagging at me: "Now what? Are you ready to slow down and reflect on your life?"

Though part of me still yearned for the camaraderie of campus life, another part longed for an extended period of solitude away from familiar routines. My life was comfortable enough—movies and the theater with friends, restaurant meals, a book group, evening classes, visits with my adult children, listening to famous authors at Berkeley book shops, tending my garden, occasional out-of-town lectures—but it wasn't enough. Retirement had left me dangling.

Now comes the offer of a house on a remote Scottish island. It is an invitation both completely unexpected and perfect in its timing. On previous visits to Iona, I had felt a powerful attachment to the place, as if it were the home of my forebears, which—as far as I know—it isn't. I met people there, visitors like myself, who told me that, inexplicably, when stepping ashore, they had found themselves in tears or had the feeling that they had at last come home. This mysterious attraction of Iona is strangely echoed by this offer of a place to live there that has fallen unbidden into my lap.

In the six months following my meeting with Elinore (for that, I discovered, is her name), I made the necessary arrangements for my move to Scotland. I booked a flight to Glasgow, said good-bye to my children and friends, and packed what I needed for the vagaries of weather at a latitude comparable to Hudson Bay and Siberia. Leaving my California home in April 1999, I had no idea what was about to happen.

At last I am on my way. Flying east across the United States, I look down from 30,000 feet onto a snowy landscape in Montana. I see river meanders, ox-bow lakes, dendritic drainage, deltas, peneplains— vocabulary from fifty years ago and my first scholastic passion, geomorphology, the study of the physical features that make up the crust of the earth. That discipline now seems as remote as the landscape beneath me: those years of high school field trips to the Yorkshire Dales, pouring over ordnance survey maps, the excitement of seeing in the real world what I had only seen, until then, in dog-eared high school textbooks.

Flying over the Midwest: long straight roads; township lines; a mosaic of square and rectangular fields in beige, brown, and dusty green; the glint of farm ponds catching the sun like tiny mirrors. A landscape etched with human imprints. As my youthful passion for geomorphology faded, my interest turned to how people mold the landscape to their needs. The study of historical geography led me to archaeological digs—to archives, rare books, and yellowing maps. I was inching my way toward looking at real live people in the present moment—including myself. But back then, I said: "No, no, not that. Not too close." Better to look at the landscape than what may be lurking beneath the surface. Safer to follow my fascination with the outer world than to delve into the murky dimensions of the inner.

We land at Glasgow airport. It has been an overnight flight of fitful sleeping. I board the train that will take me on the West Highland Line from Glasgow to Oban, from whence I will travel by boat and bus to Iona. My body feels pregnant with yearning. Heavy eyelids. Staccato chatter of wheels on iron rails leading north and west. At Helensburgh Upper, spring growth of clover and buttercup pierce through the red gravel of a platform rarely trod upon. In close-cropped fields, tufts of sheep's wool festoon the grass like flickers of late-winter snow. We stop at Ardlui. Mountaintops across the loch are hazy, cloud-covered; hillsides are patched with hummocks of last year's dead bracken. We rattle past the carcasses of two sheep, their ribs showing bare through grimy wool. Trees beside the tracks—oak, birch, alder—stand still and leafless in the mock death of winter.

We stop at a station that has no name. No one gets on or off. Moss invades the platform through jagged green cracks in the asphalt. A mother and son seated across the aisle hold hands in sweet embrace. The boy sits up excitedly, pointing as two shadowy deer leap away from the track and into the mist.

We draw into Oban. The train slows down as it follows a wide curve above the town and finally stops at the terminus near the harbor. I swing a small pack onto my shoulders and pull my suitcase the short distance along Shore Street to Harbour View Guest House.

At last, a bed. I sleep without stirring for eleven hours and wake to the sound of a clock striking somewhere nearby. I lie in bed thinking about the complicated journey I am on: shuttle, plane, bus, train, ferry, bus, ferry. Lots of stops and starts. Iona is so remote that there is no easy way to get there. Maybe that is the point. Although it was the physical landscape of the island that first entranced me, now I sense it is something deeper that draws me back. Something deep inside *me* that I do and don't want to acknowledge. I pull the bed clothes up to my chin. What if I don't like what I find? Perhaps it is better left undiscovered.

I am hungry. Mrs. MacDougall serves me a breakfast of fried egg, bacon, tomato, mushrooms, toast, and tea in her cozy front room. The TV news drones on at low volume and seagulls glide by the window in graceful white arcs.

The next stage of my journey—a ferry to the island of Mull— doesn't begin until noon. I walk to Tesco, the local supermarket, to pick up items I may not find on Iona (my favorite dark-chocolate digestive biscuits, soy sausages, organic rolled oats) and then wander along the main street of town. I stop at the windows of the Edinburgh Woolen Mills store. There are thick knitted sweaters and tartan kilts, Celtic-style earrings, and beer mugs decorated with the crests of Scottish clans. I start to move away, but then see a reflection of the harbor behind me. There is the ferry coming in from the Isle of Colonsay; fishing boats bob at anchor and herring gulls whirl about, hungry for scraps. There is a smell of ozone in the air.

I turn to take a look at the real scene instead of its reflection and catch sight of myself amid the sweaters, the kilts, the Celtic-style earrings. There is a gilt-framed mirror in the window display, the glass slightly tarnished with tiny gold explosions. I turn to see if anyone is watching me—watching me looking at myself—but no one is. People hurry past on their way to do the weekend shopping, chatting about last night's episode of *Big Brother*. I look back at the mirror.

Who is this woman, on her way to spend six months alone on a small rugged island? She is wearing black stretch pants, sensible walking shoes, a burgundy parka zippered shut with a gray-green sweater just showing at the neck. Her hair is nondescript, mousy with hints of gray. She lifts her hair, exposing where it is white beneath, and quickly arranges it back into place. Deep lines angle down from nose to mouth; more lines from each end of the mouth furrow down to her chin. Lines of aging, signs of having lived; skin rumpled like sod furrowing down hillsides, unable to resist the pull of gravity, unable to hold tight to the smooth softness of youth.

I look back at the mirror, startled. *I* am the woman I see in the mirror, not someone else I am dissecting. I smile as I push my glasses onto the bridge of my nose, smooth down my hair disarrayed by a sea breeze, and taste a hint of salt on my lips. Not bad for sixty-five—still some traces of the attractiveness that brought many men into my life. For an instant, familiar, long-ago names and faces cascade through my mind. I sigh and turn away. Retracing my steps to the guest house, I collect my luggage and make my way to the ferry bound for Mull.

A young man in a navy-blue sweater casts us off and the "Isle of Mull" slips slowly out of Oban—past the shops and hotels on the Esplanade, past rocks painted olive green and black with seaweed and a million breathing tides. Stone houses with sharp-peaked gables and white trim step up the hillsides around the harbor. The gray-green sea is wrinkled like the back of an old watery hand. As the mainland recedes, green transmutes to deep blue, to dark gray, to paler gray—as if gossamer curtains are slowly being drawn across the past. Ten oyster catchers skim across the stern of the boat, black-and-white commas punctuating the vast blank page of the sea.

The prospect of six months alone on a remote island, away from the usual demands of life, fills me with deep contentment. No more calls on the answering machine—no more junk mail, appointments in my calendar, getting the car fixed, days frittered away in a dozen necessary but unfulfilling tasks. After years as a single-parent full-time academic, each day a logistical nightmare, I am ready to sink into a life where no one needs me except myself.

I look forward with relish to exploring the island on foot, beach-combing, finding half-hidden ravines, watching families of eider ducks, bending to examine the blooms of sea thrift, bog asphodel, and heath-spotted orchid. A country childhood spent largely alone has primed me to enjoy the outdoors without fear or hesitation. But sleeping in a house alone? That is a different matter. A wartime childhood punctu-ated by fears of air raids and enemy invasion has left me anxious at night if no one else is near. I tell myself that it will be different on Iona, an island with barely 100 inhabitants, no police, no crime. I will be able to live there without fear.

I return from my daydreaming, draw in a deep breath, and look around me. No place to be but here, anonymous among jacketed men with glinting binoculars, boys below decks playing video games, elderly couples dozing in tipped-back chairs. The comforting pulse of the ship's engine throbs through the soles of my feet.

I enter the brightly lit cafeteria and am momentarily caught off-guard by the choice of tea-time goodies from my childhood: Genoa fruitcake, buttery shortbread, flapjacks, Bakewell tarts. Shades of Proust. For an instant, I am back at Sunday tea in Grandma Cooper's formal dining room at 2 Parkside in north London, arrays of home-made cakes on three-tier silver platters and steam rising from delicate, gold-rimmed teacups decorated with flowers.

The ferry judders to a stop against the dock at Craignure. Children are plucked from high chairs; the cafeteria quickly empties. People find their luggage and the crowd shuffles awkwardly down the long ramp, pulling suitcases and carrying bags of groceries. Dogs strain at their leashes, thankful to be on land once more. Several buses stand waiting, their drivers in a convivial cluster, smoking and talking. I board the bus bound for Fionnphort. The door closes with a gasp-like hiss. Our driver, alternately whistling and coughing, starts the engine and we are on our way, following a narrow winding road across the island of Mull.

I stare out of the window at the passing landscape. When did I first visit Iona? It must have been in 1979 or 1980. It was a convoluted journey that, strangely enough, began on another island on the opposite side of the world.

It was 1976 and my husband, Stephen, and I were on holiday on Maui, in Hawaii, with our two young children. One morning, Stephen handed me a book. "I found this—*The Findhorn Garden*. I think you would enjoy it." I thumbed through beautiful photographs of vegetables and flowers, skimmed the first few pages, and motioned to Stephen. "Take the children to the beach—*please*. I want to read."

I settled onto a comfortable chaise longue in the lush courtyard of the Pioneer Hotel and read the book from cover to cover. I was enchanted. The book told the story of a spiritual/ecological community that had grown up around a garden in the unprepossessing setting of a trailer park set in sand dunes at a place called Findhorn in the far northeast of Scotland. "I must go to this place!" I told Stephen excitedly when he returned hours later with two sand-covered and slightly sunburned children.

It was several years, however, before I did go to Findhorn.[2] Eventually, I attended a workshop there, and afterward traveled by mini bus across Scotland to the west coast to spend a week on the Isle of Erraid, where some people from Findhorn had established a small offshoot community. It was from Erraid, across a mile-wide stretch of sea, that I first saw the island of Iona.

One day that week, four of us journeyed by small motor boat to spend an hour at Traigh Bhan, a cottage on the eastern shore of Iona that had been given to the Findhorn community as a retreat house. Elizabeth, the custodian of the house, led us upstairs to a room known as the sanctuary. Here, under a raftered roof, with views of the white-flecked sea, we sat in a semi-circle of chairs and meditated for half an hour. By the time we filed downstairs for tea and biscuits, I had a headache pounding behind my eyes like the throb of a jackhammer. I almost never have headaches. I mentioned this to Elizabeth. She smiled sympathetically as she poured steaming tea into a deep-blue ceramic mug.

"Yes, sometimes people who come here get headaches, or colds, or feel immensely tired, or cannot sleep, or want to leave immediately." She finished pouring my tea. "Or never want to leave," she added. Her eyes closed for an instant before she turned away.

Two years later, I returned to Iona to stay for a week at Traigh Bhan. I hiked along rugged tracks, lay on white-sand beaches, took in the view of other distant islands, and began to fall in love with the place. No more headaches, just a quiet, contented sinking-in to some kind of mystery lurking beneath the surface of the land. I returned several more times, but, each time, a week seemed too short a stay. Now I will stay for six whole months.

As we approach Iona, I feel an immense upwelling of happiness, as if I were coming home from a long involuntary exile. Leaning against the window, I find myself smiling at the familiar olive-green seaweed along the shores of Mull, at daffodils bending in the wind, at a blue heron standing knee-deep in water. Pale yellow blooms of primrose (my birth flower) are visible as the bus slows down to allow vehicles to pass on the single-track roadway.

We round a bend in the road and, suddenly, there is Iona lying along the horizon like the body of a sleeping woman, with head and breasts and trailing rocky hair. Off to my right, I see the sun lighting up white-sand beaches, the roof of Traigh Bhan, and a few other houses at the north end of the island. To my left is the rugged, uninhabited south of the island, water breaking at the foot of steep cliffs slashed with the shadows of darkening gullies. Straight ahead, I can just make out the village—a row of stone houses near the shore, protected from the prevailing westerly winds by the rocky bulk of the island. And just north of the village stands the abbey, the largest and most imposing structure on the island.

Our bus arrives at Fionnphort. I buy a one-way ticket to Iona at a tiny office and haul my case along the road and down a concrete ramp onto the waiting ferry. Its engine purrs softly as gannets dive off-shore for fish. A small vehicle maneuvers slowly into the yawning hull of the ferry hauling a trailer of plaintively calling sheep. A bell rings; the steel ferry ramp rises and clangs shut. I stow my luggage in a secure place and, holding tight to cold hand rails, climb the narrow steps to the deck. Pulling the hood of my parka around my ears, I breathe deeply as we slowly approach the island.

CHAPTER 2

∽

Surrender

The spontaneous return of a utopian place and time to our nodding daydreams may be preparation for leaving for soul country. Whether there is such a place, whether there is even a soul, or a home that is its source and destination, no one will ever prove or know ... Evidence is not the point; desire is. Maybe the desire is the evidence.
—James Hillman[3]

Sunday morning. Blessed silence. The sun casts leaf shadows on the curtains; no demands to be anywhere at any time. I unpack my few possessions. Elinore has guests, but will soon leave for a long trip abroad. Before moving into her home, I will spend my first two weeks on Iona in a tiny room near the Iona Craft Shop, steps from the ferry landing. It is basically one room—ten feet square—with a bed, a dresser, a chair and table, a corner closed off with a drape for hanging clothes, a heater, and a window looking out to the Sound of Iona, the mile-wide expanse of sea that separates Iona from the island of Mull. Along a short corridor is a pantry with shelves for dishes and food, a small fridge, a bathroom with toilet and sink (but no shower or bath), and two gas burners in front of a window looking out to the rocky eminence of Cnoc Mor, Big Hill.

I feel liberated to have so few possessions: for clothing, just a choice between two sweaters and three pairs of pants; for shoes, one of three pairs—heavy hiking boots, solid walking shoes, and sandals. My one indulgence: books. I can see eight from where I sit: several brought with me, three borrowed en route from the public library in Oban, and two bought yesterday at a used-book sale in the island library (open for half an hour on Saturday mornings). And soon to arrive from California, parcels containing eight more. Letting go of possessions, distractions, luxuries, and entertainment is easy; letting go of reading—impossible!

It is a good day to do some washing. As I hang a few clothes out on a line in the garden, two large rams (*tups,* they are called here) come up to the fence. I stretch over the wire and rub their foreheads. One, with black bowed legs, stands immobile, head down, one leg slightly raised as if he were in pain; the other, with corkscrew curly wool like a Wensleydale, crops the grass while kneeling. Are these the only male sheep on the island? Scanning the rocky landscape beyond the village, I see nothing but ewes and lambs. The rams appear exhausted, drained. Has all that fathering brought them to this? As I return inside, I find some mint growing around the doorway and make tea in a small ceramic pot. I settle down to read, the sounds of seagulls calling as the ferry slips away, bound for Mull.

The next day is gusty and cold, but I feel impatient to be out on the island. I pull on boots and padded jacket and set off across the island to the cove of Port Ban, where a tongue of white sand stretches inland between high rocky headlands. I hunker down against the rocks, seeking shelter from the cold.

I prop a lined pad against my knees, holding the pages down with my left hand. Clenching my shoulders against the cold, I feel an urge to write, to acknowledge and greet this place, to open myself to its voice. What do I have to say? What am I doing here? I suddenly feel very alone. The excitement of preparing to leave and a journey full of expectations are over. I am well and truly here. I start to shiver.

Strong sea wind whips sand grains against my jacket. A dried mermaid's purse rattles past my boots like a black-legged spider on a mission. Waves break in a line of foaming surf against the shore; farther out to sea, they surge against the rocks in cascades of white mist. Four seagulls glide over the green-and-black expanse of the Island of Protection just off-shore and disappear from sight. Skeins of beige seaweed race toward the sea like small rodents pursued by the wind. Sand skitters over the page on which I write and nestles into the laces of my boots. A small thread of fresh water trickles down the beach, divides

into a tree-like pattern, and merges with the incoming tide. Tiny fragments of grass, kelp, seeds, and a feather are swirled by the wind into a whirlpool of sudden movement at my feet—and then are gone. Clouds pass over the sun and a pale gray shadow scuds across the bright sand and disappears out to sea.

All is movement—waves, sand, birds, seaweed, clouds, dune grass—all except the rock beneath my thighs and at my back. I feel it, cold and hard, yet reassuring. Experiences, feelings, memories jostle for my attention like unruly children. The rocks beneath and behind me are still and silent. They have eroded over time. Cracks have appeared and sand grains have smoothed surfaces. But in my lifetime, a mere blink of the eye, nothing has changed. That thought is oddly comforting. These rocks will be a solid anchor for my journey—whatever events skitter like grains of sand across the pages of my life, whatever wind blows me off my course, whatever clouds dim the warmth of the sun.

I stand up. My legs feel stiff. Time to go home for tea. I bought some bannock bread this morning at the Spar shop near the ferry landing. I am anxious to try it.

❧ ❧

The next morning, I delve into one of the books I brought with me: James Hillman's *The Soul's Code.* We each enter this life, says Hillman, accompanied by what the ancient Greeks called our *daimon,* an invisible, indefinable essence that carries our soul's purpose, our reason for being alive. Part of our consciousness in childhood, the daimon may assert itself through unusual gifts, obsessions, or inexplicable longing. Often, however, it is silenced—by parental demands, schooling, or our own perverse natures—and must be reclaimed in adulthood. "... What is lost in so many lives and what must be recovered," Hillman asserts, "is a sense of personal calling, that there is a reason I am alive...."[4]

There is a reason I am alive. It is hard to wrap my mind around that thought. I wrap my hands around a hot mug of tea and stare out of the window. The day is calm, blessedly calm after recent gale-force winds and snow. The Sound of Iona glistens, hazy sunlight transforming its surface to molten pewter. The ferry from Mull carves a gentle silver trail like a slow-moving snail. In the leafless trees behind the parish church, the rooks are still and voiceless, their nests like smudges of brown ink in the calligraphy of growth.

Hillman writes that the daimon seeks to awaken us, to keep us on our soul-path through any means—synchronicities, dreams, accidents, illness. Something—perhaps my daimon—has drawn me to Iona. I need to meet it, confront it; I must hear what it is trying to tell me, even if, at times, I grow fearful of what I may learn.

I pull on my boots and jacket and walk across the island to the wide crescent that forms the western shore, the Bay at the Back of the Ocean. I lean against a sandbank known as Druim na Cruaiche, Ridge of the Mound. It is low tide; sand, rocks, and seaweed are exposed in the bay. Inland, on the grass of the Machair—the traditional common grazing land—a flock of oyster catchers are feeding. They are such striking birds—black-and-white plumage, red legs and beaks. They are spread out, silent, heads down, industrious. Over the gentle rise of the Machair, the gray slate roofs and white chimneys of the crofts known as Culbhuirg, Back of the Fort, and Sithean, Fairy Mound, are just visible. Beyond is the rocky eminence of Dun I, the highest point on the island. When I close my eyes, I hear, to my left, the soft swoosh-swoosh-swoosh of an almost wave-less sea; to my right, the distant cries of lambs. I am content to be in this place. It is a relief to be where words are few, but sounds are many. I feel as if my life has been overwhelmed with words—writing them, reading them, speaking them. Perhaps on Iona I can find contentment in not-knowing, not-thinking. Perhaps I can learn just to be.

❧ ❧

I wake up to the sound of the ferry leaving on its first trip of the day across to Mull. Seagulls are crying, their calls a strange mixture of plaintiveness and aggression. I turn over in bed and push one foot into a corner where the sheets are refreshingly cool to the touch.

Images of family flow through my mind: Paul, my brother, at his farm in Canada, out checking on his cows ("my girls," he calls them); Jason, my son, probably at his computer planning his next business venture; Lucy, somewhere on a chilly slope in Colorado teaching snowboarding. How did I, totally uninterested in sport, spawn a professional athlete for a daughter? I guess that's about as far from academia as you can get.

After breakfast, I step outside to feel the temperature. It is sunny and a little warmer than yesterday. It feels as if spring were breathing down the neck of winter. I pack a picnic lunch, fill my thermos with green tea, and set off to walk the two miles or so to Columba's Bay.

I take the longer but easier route, first along a road that stretches from the village to the western shore; then across the springy green of the Machair, the path faintly visible where booted feet and sheep's hooves have trodden a slight depression in the sod; then up a rocky track down which water from recent rains trickles in glinting trails. At the top of the hill, a small lake comes into view. It is Loch Staonaig, formerly the source of Iona's drinking water. I stop to catch my breath and think of friends at home who might be afraid to do what I am doing now: hiking alone all day in a place where I will probably see no other person. But then, I would certainly not feel comfortable or competent doing what some of them may be doing right now: Phyllis, counseling troubled clients; Al, cheerfully greeting strangers at a cocktail party; Sarah, taking tango lessons; Sheila, going to morning mass. No, I find my greatest degree of comfort in being alone, outdoors in nature. I have a country childhood to thank for that.

As I follow a steep path, Columba's Bay comes into view. Sheep and lambs graze quietly on a wide grassy expanse. They scatter, lambs calling out to temporarily lost mothers as I walk among them. This is the bay where St. Columba, who founded Iona's abbey, is reputed to have landed with a party of monks when he fled from Ireland in 563 A.D. An auspicious place.

I sit at the base of a cliff, shielded from the north wind. The sun warms my face and strikes a silver path across the sea. Sounds of waves breaking, surging, crashing, receding through beds of glistening olive kelp. Heartbeat of the world—regular, dependable.

Under my outstretched legs, hundreds of rounded rocks and pebbles bear witness to the sea's persistent action. Smooth, gray flecked with white; rosy pink with veins of green; large, palm-sized with concentric swirls of glistening mica. I pick up a smooth green-and-white rock. It feels as soft as the skin of my cheek. A white vein bisects it like the line of the horizon on a clear day. A trace of gray forms the silhouette of a mountain range with parallel lines where forest turns to grass, turns to alpine plants, turn to bare rock. Deep green clouds form to the left of a mountain peak; a white channel like lightning reaches from heaven to earth. I turn the rock over and see seaweed and coral, and a clear night sky, with stars glinting like small notes from a lone flute. Pale striations tell of geological ages long past—or yet to come. I stroke the rock and feel its smoothness against my lips. I hold it against my heart and it becomes part of my body, rising and falling with each breath.

This rock has been pounded and smoothed, has had its roughness worn off by the storms and tidal flow of life. It has not resisted, cannot resist. Perhaps that is what I have come here to learn: to surrender. Yes, that feels like the right word, "surrender." Not as in admitting defeat and showing the white flag, but as in sinking into the inevitable passing of life.

I put the rock into my pack and start for home.

❧ ❧

It is still early spring and the weather veers without warning from storm to calm. After hours (or days) of cold slanting rain, it is tempting to stay inside, but that doesn't feel right for the body or for the soul. I put on boots and waterproofed jacket and pants, and set off along the east shore. There is water everywhere: cascading down ditches; gurgling through culverts; clinging to the coats of black-faced lambs that crouch for shelter against walls and fence posts; standing in muddy pools on farm tracks; resting in silvery parallel lines in a recently ploughed field. I stop to watch a herring gull that has lost its left foot pace awkwardly in the wet grass. On taking off, it curves gracefully in the wind, its wings white against the rain-laden sky. A woman garbed in a worn green rain jacket comes into a field with a shepherd's crook made of aluminum. She approaches a cluster of sheep and lambs and, catching one lamb around the neck, pulls a blue plastic baby bottle out of her pocket and begins to feed it. The lamb sucks noisily at the nipple and drinks in the warm milk its mother, dead or indifferent, cannot provide.

I feel cold. I walk briskly home, shed my wet clothes, turn on the gas heater, and put some milk in a saucepan. I make a cup of hot chocolate, butter a scone, and relax into the one easy chair in my tiny room. It would be good to talk with a friend right now. Everyone I care about is so far away.

I stare down at the hot chocolate. Tiny bubbles coat its surface. It feels comforting against my tongue, my throat, down into the yawning crevasse of my body. I wish I had a piece of my mother's chocolate shortbread. Not her, just the shortbread.

It must have been in the mid 1950s, after wartime (and postwartime) rationing had ended, when my mother invented that "secret recipe." She always made cakes for the weekend on Fridays: rock cakes, jam tarts, flap-jacks made with golden syrup, sometimes a Victoria sponge, and shortbread. One week, tired of the same old recipes (which she knew by heart), she threw some cocoa into the shortbread mix.

"This is good!" we all raved the next day at tea time. Thus it was that chocolate shortbread became a family tradition, its recipe handed down to children and grandchildren, but never to anyone outside the family. I take the last sip of cocoa. I wish I had a piece of chocolate shortbread now.

The next day is gloriously sunny; the sea is the color of Waterman's royal-blue ink, the kind I used in my fountain pen before the days of throw-away ballpoints. I walk toward the south end of the island and sit on a bench with a little plaque affixed to its back: "In memory of Malcolm Macleod. Born on Iona, 1922. Died at Glasgow, 1982." Born on Iona—born on Mull—born on Skye—born on the Isle of Man— but not born on England. When does an island become so large that we no longer say "born on," but "born in"? Certainly Iona is small enough to be born "on." Its smallness is why I feel so comfortable here. When the last ferry leaves at 6:45 in the evening and the "Loch Buie" chugs to its nighttime resting place behind the Island of the Women, it is as if a drawbridge to the world were raised. The sheep and the islanders settle into the evening shadows and even the rooks in the sycamores behind the Heritage Centre fall silent. Slowly, I am sinking into the natural rhythm of the island.

I decide to follow a circular route back to the village: along the road to the west, turning right along the track to Maol, and thence to home. I look up and the clouds stop me in my tracks. A string of cirrus range across an otherwise cloudless sky, each with a long feathery tail, as if winds were blowing straight from heaven to earth. White balloons on frayed strings; elephant heads with long dangling trunks.

I walk past the house named Clachancorrach ("rough stones" in Gaelic) and stop to speak to a woman digging in her garden.

"Good day for digging. Are you putting in potatoes?"

"Aye. It's a wee bit late, but we've had so much rain."

"You have a nice bed of rhubarb."

"Aye. Rhubarb and kittens; we always have plenty of both."

Rhubarb and kitten pie? I quickly suppress the thought and say good-bye as a flock of purple-black starlings wheels overhead. I make my way down the rocky track back to the village.

What is it about Iona that so affects me? Perhaps it is the rocks, among the most ancient in the world. Perhaps the sound of the sea, never far away. Perhaps it is the island's remoteness and the effort it takes to journey here, or the magical quality of light that has drawn so many painters to its shores. But I sense that the mystery of Iona will not reveal itself to my questioning intellect. I have to experience it in my sinews, breathe it into my body, absorb it through my eyes and ears. See ocean, feel wind, hear seagull, smell seaweed, look over distant horizon. Iona has to be lived.

CHAPTER 3

ℰ℈

Waitress Practice

The breeze at dawn has secrets to tell you.
Don't go back to sleep.
You must ask for what you really want.
Don't go back to sleep.
People are going back and forth across the doorsill
Where the two worlds touch.
The door is round and open.
Don't go back to sleep. —Jelaluddin Rumi[5]

On a blustery morning, clouds scudding low over the hills of Mull, Elinore calls to say she will be leaving the next day. And so I depart the cozy room near the Craft Shop and move into Highland Cottage. It is one of a long line of stone-built houses that form the village, the only clustered settlement on the island. Each house faces the Sound of Iona and its own walled garden. Some gardens, like Mrs. Kirkpatrick's, are neatly ordered with mown lawns, a gravel path, spring flowers, and an old anchor propped against a wall. Others, like the garden of Highland Cottage, are rambling and overgrown with brambles and weeds. At dusk, a speckle-breasted thrush perches on rowan tree or rooftop and sings exuberantly to the lengthening evening shadows.

"Choose any one of the three bedrooms," Elinore says. "My arthritis is so bad I can no longer manage the stairs. When I'm here, I sleep in a room near the kitchen. I'll be traveling abroad for several months."

I choose a room with a view out to the rocky beach at the end of the garden and the stretch of sea separating Iona from the island of Mull.

I can see the ferry going to and fro, hear the abbey bell and the cries of herring gulls, smell the salty tang of the sea. Not for me Peter Mayle's cottage in Provence, or Frances Mayes' Tuscan farmhouse. Something in my genes or in my psyche has drawn me to the Celtic north. This first morning in the cottage, I look out of my bedroom window and see the sun glinting off the waves in a billion sparkling lights, as if a far galaxy has fallen in the night into the soft embrace of the sea.

The front door of Highland Cottage opens onto a cluttered porch. A second door opens from the porch into a hallway filled with boxes of books, umbrellas and beach toys, rain jackets and rubber boots. On either side of the hallway is a room with mullioned windows looking out to the village street and the sea. In one of these, there is a small dining table and upright chairs, an easy chair and footstool, walls lined with shelves of books. The other room has a settee piled with books, some arm chairs, a fireplace, and the bust of a bearded man whose lined face is creased with dust. The sound of waves breaking on rocks permeates the house. As I find my way around the kitchen, I soon have a favorite mug; it is decorated with a scene of a beach, rocks, seaweed, and a distant horizon. I feel as if I were drinking in Iona itself.

Almost every electrical appliance in the house is broken or mal-functioning—a large photocopying machine, a washing machine, a TV. The plates on the electric stove have only two positions—off or red-hot. No matter; the two most critical systems, central heating and hot water, work perfectly. It is a joy to come in from a wind-swept hike to the cozy warmth of this cottage or to luxuriate in a six-foot-long bathtub and endless hot water. To be warm, to have enough to eat and interesting books to stimulate the mind, that is enough. I have always been something of a Luddite. I didn't own a car or learn to drive until I was in my thirties; at this point in my life, I still didn't own a microwave, a dishwasher, a computer, a mobile phone, or a washing machine. Life in a remote place with minimum technology suited me just fine.

One day after I move into the cottage, a cold wind is blowing and, as evening falls, the slopes of Ben More on Mull are clouded in mist. I eat lentil soup for dinner, an apple, a chocolate biscuit, and decide to go to bed early. Elinore has left and the house feels empty.

After reading for a while, I turn out the light and curl up under the bed clothes. Just as I am dropping off to sleep, I hear a creak on the stair. I hold my breath. It's just the wood contracting as the temperature drops. Nothing to worry about; no crime on this island; no one locks their doors.

Then ... I am back in the house of my childhood. "I'm just going next door to hear the nine o'clock news," my mother calls up the stairs. "Our wireless is acting up. I'll be back soon; go to sleep now." I hear the back door shut.

Silence. No sound of Churchill's latest speech filtering through the floorboards. No sounds of my mother playing the piano. "I'll be back soon." How long will that be? She never leaves me in the house alone at night.

I study the cracks in the ceiling above, just visible in the dim light. I listen for the door to open again, for her footsteps moving down the passage to put the kettle on, put the dishes away.

My eyelids droop. On the BBC news, they said the invasion might happen at night, that they will come in planes, drop by parachute. I pull the bedclothes up under my chin and curl my knees toward my face. My breath comes in shallow pants: "Not tonight. They won't come tonight. Mum will be here with me. Please come home ... Please come home soon ... Please ..."

And then I hear them. Booted footsteps on the stairs. They have come; this is the night. I lie rigid in my bed, scarcely breathing. The door opens. I hold my breath. It is a German soldier with polished boots, a steel helmet, a rifle with a bayonet fixed to the end. I stop breathing. Pretend to be dead, then he'll go away.

"This one looks dead," I hear him say. "Better make sure." He raises his bayonet high above my rigid body, then plunges it into my stomach …

I wake up with a start. A nightmare. Where is my mother?

A recurring childhood dream. This is the first indication that I will have to face up to memories much older and more damaging than retirement and a recent experience with illness: a wartime childhood, my father's absence, my mother's depression and narcissism, a life-long feeling that I'm not quite worthy of love.

❧ ❧

I open the first of three parcels of books I sent myself from Berkeley. Do all writers get mildly panicked at the thought of being somewhere without a single interesting thing to read? Several years ago, when walking the Cornish Coastal Path in southwest England, I was so concerned about not having enough evening reading that I sent myself parcels of books *poste restante,* at various rural post offices along the way. But I over-estimated my speed of reading or under-estimated my speed of walking, or both. I ended up with six books in my backpack, much to the amusement of Carolyn N., my fellow walker, who leapt ahead like a mountain goat, a few pairs of underpants and not much else in her child-sized pack.

I tell myself I'll open just one parcel at a time and I'll read whatever is in it before I open another. I've forgotten what I chose to send myself, what I thought would be "suitable reading." The first parcel contains *An Interrupted Life: The Diaries of Etty Hillesum,* a book by Thomas Merton, Sharon Butala's *The Perfection of the Morning,* and Doris Grumbach's *Life in a Day.* I settle for the last and am not disappointed.

How is it that an account of an ordinary, uneventful day in the life of a seventy-seven-year-old writer in rural Maine can be so fascinating? Of course, her mind is not ordinary, nor are the many books she picks up and muses about in the course of the day. She quotes author Margaret Walker speaking about her craft: "A writer needs certain conditions in which to work and create. She needs a piece of time; a peace of mind; a quiet place; and a private life."[6] Indeed, and that is what I have.

For the next two days, the rain barely stops. I settle down for a long read, my feet resting on an ottoman, a cup of tea at my side. Canadian writer Sharon Butala believes it is particularly the task of women at this time to record their experiences in nature, to attempt to find words to express the ineffable mystery. Nature is the feminine; the earth is the Great Mother. Butala discovered a healing for her soul through a deepening relationship with nature and the landscape when she left behind her life as an academic in Saskatoon and married a rancher in a remote area of the Saskatchewan prairie.

> I was discovering something about living in Nature that I had never heard anyone speak of or read in any books … I think we have so allowed the scientific approach to the world to take over our perceptions that we are afraid to mention such experiences for fear of being laughed at or vilified. When we do, we find ourselves stammering, struggling for words, never being able to convey in language to our own satisfaction exactly what it felt like or looked like or what sensations it evoked in us. We struggle against skepticism, our own as much as anyone else's, and in time lapse into silence about them and a whole, valuable dimension of human experience remains unsung and unvalidated.[7]

"Yes, yes!" I want to cry out as I read this. As difficult as it is to find the words for something beyond words, as skeptical as others may be, I will not lapse into silence. I cannot. I have come here to explore and write about some unnameable connection with the land that is essential for my survival and for the survival of all sentient beings.

It feels as if this island has entered my life as might a wise and loving friend, urging me to look at critical relationships past and present, what I have embraced in life, and what I have unconsciously rejected. Iona is whispering to me in countless different ways, reminding me, sometimes commanding me in a firm but loving voice: "Don't go back to sleep." Indeed, I will not.

※ ※

Soon after moving into Highland Cottage, I start working part-time at the St. Columba Hotel—not because I need the money (in fact, I am not paid, but work as a volunteer), not because I need something to do, but because my days of reading, writing, and contemplating the landscape need to be balanced by a sense of community and "down-to-earthness." I feel a need to anchor myself more firmly in ordinary life, to balance my meandering thoughts with companionship and physical work.

The St. Columba is one of two small hotels on the island. The older of the two, the Argyll Hotel, faces the village street and has an elegant wood-paneled dining room and gable windows that look out to sea. The St. Columba Hotel sits on a slight rise above the village near the abbey, and has a cheerful light dining room, a luxurious lounge

with comfortable easy chairs, and an expansive view of the Sound of Iona and Mull.

I met Peter, the manager of the St. Columba Hotel, soon after I arrived and learned that they were short-staffed. Much as I relish my time alone, it occurs to me that if I slip and am hurt or fall off a cliff, no one will ever know. No one is expecting me home at any time.

I call in at the hotel and am informally interviewed by Peter and the deputy manager, Richard. I like them both, as well as the relaxed and cozy atmosphere of the hotel. They seem delighted that I can start right away, three hours a day (noon to 3:00 PM), to help with the lunchtime crowd.

I work in the servery putting dishes and silverware through a noisy commercial dishwasher. I serve tea and coffee to guests who come in to help themselves to a soup-and-salad lunch, make out checks and wipe down tables. I love it. I have never waited on tables before. Well, of course, I *have* waited on tables; every mother has. I find myself saying under my breath, "Good girl, you finished up all your lunch!" as I retrieve the empty plate from a sweet-smiling, white-haired Scottish lady who has ordered a Highland Fling (scrambled egg and smoked salmon on toast). Thank heavens to be back on this side of the Atlantic, I think, where people know how to make scrambled eggs that are smooth and creamy, and have the good sense to serve hot food on hot plates.

The head waiter, Robbie, who comes from the Isle of Arran and rides his motorcycle up and down the two miles of Iona's roads in between shifts, shows me how to set the tables for dinner. "Line the silverware up completely straight, their ends just one thumb-nail in from the edge of the table...."

Guests thank me as they leave. "You're welcome," I stumble in reply. What *do* wait-persons say when they are thanked?

"Good-bye. It was lovely," says a trio of white-haired ladies. "Compliments to the chef—or is it a chef-ette?"

"No, a chef. I'll tell him. Thank you. Have a nice day." I cringe as I say this.

There is little to do before the lunchtime rush each day, so I wander the garden picking bluebells, cowslips, and yellow-flowered euphorbia and arrange them in liqueur glasses on each table. After the rush, I help myself to lentil soup, hot homemade rolls, and salad, and sit in the garden watching the lambs play king-of-the-castle on some rocks in a neighboring field. Ian, a stone-craftsman, is rebuilding the steps that lead down from the road to the hotel entrance. His old Labrador, Blackberry, dozes in the sun. A carpenter from Mull arrives with a handsome new pair of gates made of honey-colored, unpainted wood that he sets in place at the top of the steps. On the back of one is a tiny shelf and miniature bench.

"What is that?" I ask the carpenter.

"Oh—it's a wee bench, so the fairies have some place to sit and look at the view."

I am happy in this place.

❦ ❦

Working at the hotel becomes an almost Zen-like practice. Rinsing off dishes before stacking them in the dishwasher; drying the hot and steamy glasses after the washing cycle is over; greeting guests; taking them tea or coffee; writing bills; re-setting tables. I seem to do all this in a state of quiet, non-cerebral awareness. It seems sufficient to be doing just what I am doing: waitress practice.

Peter comes into the servery one morning, his blond hair wind-blown, his slightly lined face ruddy with exposure to the weather. He was a farmer in Denmark before he took on this very different job—running a hotel. Today, he looks less worried with his manager duties than he sometimes does. "I spent the morning with Jane MacFadyen, helping her with the lambs. She is bottle-feeding twelve of them in the barn." Jane's only son, Logie, drowned in a tragic accident just before Christmas. Peter and others on the island are helping her out in the lambing season. Peter bends down as I reach out my arms to hug him. I feel his ear, cold and damp against my cheek.

On chilly days, I eat my lunch (often a big baked potato stuffed with tuna) in the staff dining room. I chat with Amy, who makes all the bread, rolls, cakes, and biscuits for the hotel. She has a degree in anatomy, but her real passion is basket-making. She has just come back from a course in the Shetland Islands where she learned to make baskets out of straw. Elizabeth joins us for a quick lunch break. She works the reception desk in stylish clothes, was married to a Member of Parliament, and clearly comes from upper-class English society. "I've never had a job before in my life," she tells me.

Lucky you, I think. Well, perhaps not "lucky you." I muse on the many jobs I've had and how much I've learned from each of them: working behind the counter at a Woolworth's store and at a plant nursery in north London on Saturdays in high school; cleaning houses one summer holiday; being a bus conductor on the Number 13 bus (Golder's Green to London Bridge) one hot summer on vacation from college; working as a counselor at a California camp for rich kids from Beverly Hills; doing research at the Ministry of Housing and London County Council; teaching cartography at the University of Sheffield; writing encyclopedia entries in New York City; working as a planner in Puerto Rico; cleaning hotel bathrooms while living in the Findhorn community; becoming an academic in California. Now, a waitress. In slow periods, I re-do the flowers on the tables. The dining room looks so pretty and welcoming; I am getting quite territorial about it, as though preparing for guests to enter my home.

Sophia, an Australian who has lived in Scotland for two years, is often my co-worker in the servery. She has a beautiful voice and can sing in Gaelic. She is tall with long black hair and swims most days in the sea at Port Ban. "A nosy neighbor once asked me why she never sees my swim suit drying on the line. 'Because I don't wear one,' I told her. That shut her up!"

One day, Sophia notices a spiral silver ring on my right hand.

"Oh yes. I bought that on a trip to Australia, at a gift shop at Uluru."

"I have exactly the same ring!" Sophia says in an excited voice, lifting a stack of bowls up onto an empty shelf. "They're made by Kevin, an Irish silversmith I know back home. What a coincidence."

I think about favorite necklaces and earrings, most of them hanging, gathering dust, on a wooden rack in my bedroom in Berkeley.

"I have such a lovely necklace at home," I tell Sophia as I lean against a counter, wiping my damp hands on my apron. "It's made of pieces of beach-washed glass strung on a fine leather thong. My friend Wendy sent it to me from Australia several years ago."

Sophia turns around from the sink, her face lit up.

"I *made* that necklace!"

"No! Wendy bought it at a farmer's market in Fremantle."

"That's where I sold them! I *come* from Fremantle!"

We stop work and stare at each other, half-smiling, astonished. Later, sitting in the hotel lounge sipping green tea and eating a buttered scone, I ponder this synchronicity. Such coincidences are said to point to the rightness of your path. It feels as if I am exactly where I need to be.

⅌ ⅌

The hotel provides me with more than a pragmatic routine to balance my meditative rambling through the landscape. What I find there is a sense of community. The staff at a hotel, just like the crew of a boat, are under pressure to work closely together to get things right. Crises happen, tempers fray; everyone pulls together to get the job done.

"Alistair has threatened to quit!"

"What? Oh my God—how will we get dinner on the table tonight?"

"Michael has been fired!"

"No—what happened?"

"He's acting too sexy with the women guests."

"Old-timers are asking for meat, gravy, and two veg; the chef is refusing to change the menu."

"We've run out of whiskey and there won't be another delivery until Tuesday."

Not surprisingly, all those who work at the hotel are younger than me. I love their energy and humor, the fact that they come from so many different countries: Denmark, Germany, Canada, Australia, Italy, England, Scotland. Off duty, we greet each other warmly at the grocery store, the post office, or on the ferry heading for a day of hiking on Mull. I am grateful to this group of people who feel like my extended family on the island.

The islanders themselves—the farmers, boatmen, shopkeepers, bed-and-breakfast owners —are more of a mystery. In any place that attracts tourists, the long-term residents tend to remain somewhat detached. Add to this the natural reserve of the Scots and the unwillingness to embrace newcomers that is true of any small rural community, and you have a situation, as on Iona, where the islanders form one social group, the short-term residents—the hotel and abbey staff— form another, and the tourists form a third. A few of the tourists who come to the island every year have formed close, almost family-like bonds with the owners of the bed and breakfasts where they always stay. But most tourists are day-trippers, alighting from their tour buses at Fionnphort, riding the ferry to Iona, and spending two hours visiting the abbey and buying postcards. The island residents, whether long- or short-term, experience some sense of relief when the last ferryload of tourists leaves at the end of each day and the island settles again into its quiet routine.

ჰ ჰ

A group of elderly day-trippers has come to the hotel for lunch. As I serve them tea and coffee, I catch a whiff of a smell I can't quite name. Of course—it smells like the foot lineament that Grandma Duncan— or Nana, as we called her—used to rub into her bunions when they were giving her trouble. I haven't thought of her for years, with her white hair tied back in a tight bun, her long somber dresses of brown and dark lavender, and her mostly unsmiling face. I felt envious when other children spoke of visiting grandmothers who taught them how to play card games, how to knit; grandmothers who held them tight to their bosoms and smelt of apple-blossom talcum powder. Nana did none of those things, but she did make delicious lemon-curd tarts (my favorite), the smell of buttery pastry escaping from the oven door when we sometimes went to her house for Sunday tea. Apart from that, I remember little about her. My mother, Christine, was the ninth and last of her children. Soon after that, Grandpa died of cancer and Nana retreated into a world of sad reminiscence.

As difficult as it is to imagine your parents having sex, it is even more difficult to envision sex between grandparents during the supposedly staid and virtuous days of Victoria's reign. But with nine children, spaced closely together, at least one of them must have enjoyed sex. My hope is that they both did and that that big double bed with the polished mahogany bed posts rocked with animal desire and the deep moaning of coital pleasure. Is that why she looked so sad in later years? Young love and youthful passion long spent. Only the smell of lemon-curd tarts baking for her granddaughter bringing a gleam to her eye. That and the pleasure of rubbing Sloane's lineament into her aching bunions, and settling to sleep and dreaming again on the sagging mattress of the marital bed.

"Could we have more hot water?" A woman's voice wakes me abruptly from my daydreaming. I walk briskly into the servery, fill a pot from the large bubbling urn, and return to the sun-lit dining room. Through the windows, I see the ferry from Mull plowing a watery furrow on its passage to Iona.

❧ ❧

One afternoon, my work shift over, I settle into a deep armchair in the hotel lounge, a cup of tea and a piece of Amy's shortbread at my side. Hanne, a young woman from Denmark, is weeding a flower bed in the garden. A thrush, hungry for worms, waits in anticipation on a bush nearby. For no apparent reason (does the unconscious need a reason?), a memory of two dreams emerges in my mind. Five years ago, soon after retiring from academic life, I attended a seminar in Switzerland on "The Voice of the Soul." Jet-lagged and tired, I quickly fell asleep and had two disturbing dreams. In the first, my mother is dying of cancer. I sit by her bed sewing, not knowing what to say. She seems quite philosophical about the situation. In the dream that followed, a bull rampages down the main street of a town. Bleeding, wounded, and dying people litter the ground. I view this from a window and am afraid and horrified.

A few days later at the same seminar, strong images of the bull returned as I listened to a lecture on "The Celtic Soul." The speaker was recounting an Irish myth in which the hero, feeling the power of his animal strength, goes berserk, but is tamed by women who approach him with bared breasts. It is a story of the balance of masculine and feminine. The wounded and dying people in my dream floated behind my eyes. Tempted to give them a voice, I started to write a dialogue as the lecture continued in the background.

"I am aggression and anger," says the bull. "I like to rampage and roar and kick and fight. I am uncontrollable animal power. I don't care who is injured and killed. I am that I am."

A wounded figure quivering with fear cries out: "I am bleeding. I'm afraid this bull will kill me. Why are you doing this? I didn't do anything to deserve this."

"Deserve—not deserve. It doesn't matter to me. I am power; I am your inner voice, which is growing impatient. I've been waiting long enough. If I have to rampage down the street causing bloodshed to get your attention, then that's what I'll do."

Another bleeding figure moans: "Let him speak, for God's sake. We're in pain; we're dying." I ask these figures who they are, why they were being trampled.

"We are the parts of you that are wounded and dying when you don't allow your power a voice. This is not a time to hold back. We and the world are in pain. Say what you have to say with conviction. Go on writing. The bull is your creative muse. Let it express itself and it will be as gentle as Ferdinand, with a flower in its mouth. Keep it chained up and it will rampage in anger." I was afraid. Now I am afraid again.

Why have I come to Iona? Initially, I thought it was to reflect on retirement and a post-retirement shock of illness. Now I am not so sure. Sometimes, I think it is to face my disappointment that I did not have a long-term, happy marriage. But increasingly, that also seems of little importance. I just know that I have to be here, that the means to be here arrived like a miracle, and that I will have to live with uncertainty. This stay on Iona is offering me permission to look deeply within at what was always present but unacknowledged in the onrush of my all-too-busy life.

"Are you done with your tea things?" Amy comes into the lounge and stands in front of me with a tray, smiling.

"Oh yes. Thank you."

I place the cup, saucer, and plate on the tray, get up from the comfortable chair I have sunk into for over an hour, and walk the short distance home to Highland Cottage.

⁂

Despite my new friends at the hotel, I sometimes feel enormously lonely. It is such a blessing that I can speak once a week on the phone with Barry, a psychoanalyst friend in New Mexico, to talk about what is going on in my heart. Late one Tuesday afternoon, I dial Barry's number in Taos. A brisk easterly wind moans around the gables of Highland Cottage; a beaded curtain of raindrops clings to the window and I watch droplets slither down the glass as I wait for Barry to answer the phone.

We talk about the bull dream of five years ago and then I tell him about a recent dream that has me puzzled. "In the dream, I go into my kitchen and there is a pet rat in a cage, racing around on a wheel. I have forgotten it is there and press some bread through the bars of the cage. I try to fix a faulty latch, but the rat escapes. I know I'll never catch it and I have to go out; Elaine T. is waiting to go out to dinner with me. So I close a cat in the kitchen hoping it will kill the rat, cleanly and quickly. But I can't leave; I'm worried about what's happening. I go back into the house and am amazed to find the cat has taken the rat by the hand and is helping it get a drink at the sink."

"What do you associate with rats?" Barry asks.

"They seem like symbols of ill-health, carriers of disease." I pause, sigh, and run my fingers down the window pane. I think about rats. "They disrupt and damage things; they work behind the scenes. In the dream, I have a rat caged, shut away, just as my cancer is in remission. But it escapes—threatens to recur?"

"You set a cat to kill it, to obliterate the cancer completely, but the cat knows better and befriends it, offering it a drink. The rat is invited to be part of the household. Whatever caused the cancer in you has to be befriended."

During these conversations, I feel truly listened to, totally supported in trying to understand my life at a deeper level. But once I put the phone down, I am flooded with loneliness. I long for a human companion, someone to touch, someone who will call out from the warmth of the cottage as I open the front door: "How was your day?"

I pull on my boots and walk north past the St. Columba Hotel, past the abbey, past the crofts at the northern end of the island, and out to Cnoc an Suidhe, Hill of the Seat, where, reputedly, St. Columba used to sit and pray. Leaning against the rock, I stare out to sea and start to cry. I feel so distant from friends and family; I have no one with whom to share my writing. All writers must feel this, but since I am writing in a vein so different from previous academic and professional work, I have no yardstick by which to judge it.

Is my stay here nothing more than a self-indulgent retreat from the world? Is there a place at this time for the contemplative nature writer? I think of colleagues in academe, still teaching and inspiring young minds, conducting original research. I think of people working for the environment, for change in the world.

But I'm not a political activist, nor any longer the scholarly academic I once was. I seem to have been drawn here simply to wander through this landscape, to contemplate what I see and experience— and to write. The map of my world was disrupted by retirement and illness; I am seeking a new destination.

The outlines of distant islands, Staffa and Dutchman's Cap, become blurry. I rub my eyes with the back of my hand and pull my jacket more tightly around me. I hear the distant call of a gull and then watch as it arcs effortlessly down toward the beach. Is it an act of supreme narcissism to write about myself, love of nature, the power of place? Virginia Woolf shuddered at the "egotistical" self-exposure of some of her contemporaries, yet most of her novels are thinly veiled re-workings of her childhood and family dilemmas. Perhaps, in this era of self-analysis, we have gone overboard in the other direction. But I feel it would be an act of cowardice to disguise what I have to say within the cloak of fiction— apart from the fact that I don't have the ability to do so. I think it was the British poet Kathleen Raine who wrote that she never felt that her life was her own property. Since it was all she had to offer, and since, she argued, we are all numberless expressions of the one Self, she could do no less than make her contribution to the whole.

A stiff breeze blows the hood of my jacket across my face. I pull it back and look off to the west. Low hazy clouds half obscure the sun. Then, to my surprise, I see that on either side of it are rainbow fragments—two short pieces that, if joined, would form a rainbow circle, a ring of colors around the sun. The wonder of it changes my mood. I feel the sadness lift. (Later, I learn, it is a meteorological phenomenon called a halo, caused by the sun's rays passing through ice crystals in the clouds.)

It is cold. I start for home. In a field just beyond the hotel, a herd of cows grazes peacefully in the evening light. I don't remember seeing them when I walked by earlier. One enormous bull with a rich brown coat ambles up to a cow whose calf is suckling and lays its muzzle on her haunches, a touching family group. Can I befriend the bull in me and let it have its voice? *That* is why I have come to Iona.

CHAPTER 4

ఐ

The Power of Place

*Do you want a long life? Well you will need to have
wisdom. You will need to think about your own mind.
You will need to work on it.... How will you walk along
this trail of wisdom? Well, you will go to many places.
You must look at them closely. You must remember all of
them. You must remember everything they tell you. You
must think about it, and keep on thinking about it, and
keep on thinking about it. You must do this because no
one can help you but yourself ... Wisdom sits in places.
It's like water that never dries up. You need to drink water
to stay alive, don't you? Well you also need to drink from
places.* —Keith H. Basso[8]

I wake up to the sound of rain on the roof. As I drift between sleep
and wakefulness, an image of daffodils floats into my mind. Yellow
blooms nodding gracefully, their fragrance unmistakable—not strong
and sweet like hyacinths or freesias, but indescribable and subtle. A
field of daffodils near our home remains an archetypal memory of my
childhood. As I see it now, from the vantage point of old age, it pulls at
me like a favorite love song.

Do we all yearn for that time when, anchored in place, our child-
self first experienced a sense of fusion with the environing world? I
think about people still alive who were born in Britain in the 1920s,
1930s, and 1940s for whom—as for me—World War II became the
preeminent watershed in their lives. So many of our reflections on
events, places, and memories are prefaced by "before the war," or "after

the war." With a pang of guilt, I reflect that, in some ways, the war, for me, was a gift. But for this momentous event, I would never have experienced the deep childhood connection with nature that has echoed down the decades of my life and profoundly shaped who I am. This must have been true for many of my generation. John Fowles wrote, of his evacuation with his family to a Devonshire village:

> Despite the horrors and deprivations of the time, they were for me fertile and green-golden years. I learnt nature for the first time in a true countryside among true countrymen, and from then on I was irredeemable lost as a townsman. [9]

As Graham Greene observed: "There is always one moment in childhood when the door opens and lets the future in."

My mother, my brother Paul, and I were evacuated from London in 1940. There had been government plans for the mass evacuation of people from the main urban areas of Britain dating as far back as the 1920s. German bombing of London in World War I, with the loss of more than 1000 lives, had prompted serious discussion of how to relocate millions of people to the safety of the countryside in the event of another war, in which loss of life from more sophisticated bombing techniques was likely to be far more disastrous. In the final days of peace, before Britain declared war on Germany on September 3, 1939, a massive exodus took place throughout the country.

> Nearly two million civilians, most of them children, were taken from the cities, industrial towns and ports of Britain to the relative safety of the countryside, using trains, buses, trams, coaches, even pleasure steamers. For many of the children it was the first time away from their families, for some the first time outside their town. They went carrying few belongings (each was allowed a small suitcase and one toy), not knowing where they would end up ... For some it was the beginning of a great adventure, for others a nightmare. This was the first great evacuation, but not the last. During the course of the war there were to be two more, and in between, a constant flow of individuals and groups both in and out of danger. [10]

While most of those evacuated—sometimes referred to by less-than-happy recipient households as "Bloody Vackees"—were part of a massively organized government program, for others there were private evacuations to homes of relatives or friends in the countryside. We were part of the latter group, moving as a family to live in relative safety in a cottage at Ascott, the Rothschild country estate. My father was employed in the Rothschild bank. We were forty miles northwest of London, just far enough to be safe from the blitz, but, later in the war, on the path of unmanned rockets that occasionally overshot the capital. Here at Ascott, amid overgrown formal gardens, farmland, woods, streambeds, and meadows, I discovered an environment that richly engaged my senses and offered me a level of emotional sustenance lacking at home. My father volunteered before he was conscripted and left to serve in the Intelligence Corps. My mother, lonely and depressed, left me and Paul to our own devices. When not at school, we spent most of our time outdoors, playing tracking games and building tree houses in the woods. I collected berries and mushrooms, grew vegetables, raised chickens and rabbits to supplement our rations, and learned the names of wildflowers from a precious book—C. A. Johns' *Flowers of the Field*—awarded to my mother as a prize for French in 1918. I became bonded to the landscape as if to a loving being: it was my home, my teacher, my substitute mother.

Thinking back to that time, I can remember almost every tree within a half-mile radius of our house: the feel of its bark, the smell of its leaves, whether or not it was easy to climb. But I don't remember anything about the room where I slept.

I can remember the hide-outs we built and found: a big old basket in a yew tree where we hid and spied on grown-ups; the hut that Paul and his friend Burt made of flattened army petrol tins; a tunnel we started to dig with plans for many rooms and a goal of reaching China; the overgrown quarry where my best friend, Mary, and I lit fires and ate stolen potatoes roasted in the ashes. But I don't remember any details of the house where I lived.

I did not think of this as a deprived childhood. My friends and I could wander safely far from home through farmland and small, cool woods; through formal gardens overgrown with weeds and spiders' webs; along the banks of a shallow brook where we once found a kingfisher's nest and Burt put his hand in the hole and pulled it out with a kingfisher clinging, terrified, to his index finger. Compared to the territorial restrictions and meager choices of children raised in contemporary suburbia, ours was an idyllic environment. What I missed in terms of family togetherness or maternal care I made up for in my passion for exploring the landscape, identifying wildflowers, scavenging food, gardening, and caring for animals. I learned about resilience and independence, curiosity and resourcefulness. I learned about survival. It was W. H. Auden who wrote: "The so-called traumatic experience is not an accident, but the opportunity for which the child has patiently been waiting—had it not occurred, it would have found another, equally trivial—in order to find a necessity and direction for its existence, in order that its life may become a serious matter"[11]

My first love was for flowers: the field of daffodils near our house, each year more and more of them, nodding to the springtime sun; tall magenta blooms of primula candelabra growing beside a lily pond; scillas, snowdrops, bluebells, and aconites blossoming each spring in the overgrown reaches of the neglected gardens at Ascott. In May, it was as if airy white foam drifted across the landscape: the white and creamy blossoms of hawthorn and mountain ash, horse chestnut and lilac; the white hooded flowers of dead nettle; Jack-by-the-hedge and cow parsley; stitchwort, chickweed, shepherd's purse, and daisies; creamy coronets of nodding plantain; fields of dandelion clocks that we blew to tell the time—"one o'clock, two o'clock, three o'clock, four …"—counting as we blew the seeds into the summer air. When there were none left, that was the time.

By June, the white haze over the landscape gave way to yellow: toadflax and cinquefoil; bird's-foot trefoil and buttercup. "Hold it under her chin. See if she likes butter." Of course, we all liked butter.

Auntie Jean, my mother's sister, taught me how to press wild flowers between sheets of blotting paper under a heavy pile of encyclopedias and then mount them with glue in a scrapbook. At the little school I attended in Leighton Buzzard, tall and humorless Miss Walker, her gray hair pulled back in a tight bun, made us dissect flowers and draw meticulous renderings labeled with words describing botanical anatomy that sound to me now like poetry: calix, corolla, sepal, stamen, anther, filament, inflorescence, and petiole. One by one, we studied each family—*Rosaceae, Leguminosae, Compositae, Primulaceae, Liliaceae, Umbelliferae*—the whole range of the flower kingdom was analyzed, ordered, and neatly tied down in our blue-covered school exercise books.

But that analytical approach to the world was not my way. Flowers and trees, birds and mushrooms, the whole cast of characters in the rich drama of nature became my close childhood companions as I learned to explore the world on my own. I needed to know their names to greet and caress them. Walking through the bluebell wood at Ascott one spring, on a hillside beneath gray-barked beech trees, my breath was taken away by a shawl of blue-like-the-sky. I knelt down, cupping one flower in my hand. "Look at you! Look at you! You're so beautiful," I whispered, and started to cry. The rich, encompassing arms of nature became a substitute for the nurturing family I so longed for.

A stabbing hunger for breakfast pulls me back to the present moment. I have been daydreaming about my childhood for too long. I am here. I am on Iona. Time to let go of the past. Was it really as I remember it?

❧ ❧

The next day on Iona, gale-force winds carve the sea into deep furrows and rattle the windows of Highland Cottage. I open another parcel of books I sent myself from Berkeley and pull out *Placeways: A Theory of the Human Environment.* The author, E. V. Walter, discusses the hero's predicament in so many Greek tragedies as one that relates to place. The hero is frequently described as a man of no city, a person without a place where he belongs. Something stops me in my mental tracks as I read this: the crisis of the placeless self. I think of people I know who were recently diagnosed with cancer: Kirsten never quite at home in California compared to her native Norway; Linda losing everything in a house fire just after a major move; Marv buying a house and finding major septic tank problems; Anita moving across country—did she ever feel at home in California?

I read that Sigmund Freud, who died of cancer, was also afflicted with a sense of placelessness. Although he lived and worked in the same house in Vienna for forty-six years, he confided: "I hate Vienna with a positively personal hatred, and … I draw fresh breath whenever I remove my feet from the soil of the city which is my home." Apparently he never felt free of a longing for the woods he knew in his childhood. According to a psychoanalytic biographer, the move away from Freiberg (now in the Czech Republic) when he was a child "was a catastrophe for Freud and he spent the next forty years of his life trying to undo it. The loss created long-lasting mourning."[12]

A longing for a childhood landscape. Why now, why here, do memories of those years between five and eleven keep surfacing in my mind? I look out of my bedroom window on Iona and see clusters of brown and golden seaweed throbbing in the waves. A couple walks by along the village street, laughing and calling out to their children who are lagging behind.

My mind wanders back to Buckinghamshire, to the landscape of my wartime childhood. "You were always there to meet my loneliness," I think, "to hold me tight in your green arms. Daffodil-splattered field of grass; pink-white candelabra of horse chestnut flowers; scent of violets, yellow bells of cowslips. You never failed me; never judged me or talked down to me: 'Don't be afraid, little girl.' No—you never said that. You just were—beech-tree home, yew-tree embrace, pine-tree spine. You were strong when I needed you most."

No house ever felt as safe to me as the green quilt of my childhood. Lying paralyzed in bed, waiting for the enemy to float down like white moths on their parachutes; lying awake on a bunk bed in the cold cellar as V1 rockets droned overhead. When I returned to that familiar landscape a few years ago, I found the place where one rocket had landed harmlessly in a field. The site is now marked by a mere ripple in the grass-skin of the meadow, cows softly munching, buttercups turning sunward. As children, we had raced there to salvage pieces of shrapnel before the Home Guard roped off the crater. Shrapnel was our trading currency—no foreign stamps or coins or matchbox labels to collect and swap. My brother had a piece of the tail of a Messerschmitt in his collection. It was shot down somewhere nearby. He charged our friends a penny a time to look at it. We gave the money to the Spitfire Fund, where it went toward building the fighter planes that would save our island home in the Battle of Britain. A few years ago, I experienced a heart-wrenching *déjà vu* as I watched the film *Hope and Glory,* which tells the story of the filmmaker's wartime childhood in England. There is a scene where a bomb has killed the mother of a little girl. Another little girl, not knowing how to express condolences, approaches her awkwardly and offers her the only thing she has of value—a piece of twisted shrapnel. My eyes filled with tears.

❧ ❧

I sit with my back to Cnoc na Maoile Buidhe, the Yellow Bare Hill, looking across the Bay at the Back of the Ocean to the headland of Dun Bhuirg, Hill of the Fort. I never tire of this view. The green of the sheep-cropped grazing land; the white of the beach sand; the blue wrinkled skin of the sea below me; the dark brown of seaweed-draped boulders; the sulphur-yellow lichen on rocks above sea level; the tiny pink flowers of sea thrift in crevices. Two lambs cry piteously for their temporarily mislaid mother. A flock of eider ducks in the quiet waters below me make sounds like owls—woo-woo-woo—as they paddle about, not diving, not ducking for food, apparently just drifting, perhaps for the sheer joy of being alive on this sunny spring afternoon.

I climb the rocky track from the Machair to Loch Staonaig and follow a narrow path I've never noticed before to the west end of the lake. In re-reading my journals from my time of illness, I am reminded of how many times in my imagination I came to this particular place on Iona for solace, seeking answers, seeking healing. It is both a bleak and a gentle place. It is surrounded by hills—dun-colored where hummocks of heather lie dormant before their summer blooming, and splashed with white where the rocks that are the ancient backbone of this island crest like foam on a tawny sea. This is the rugged cradle in which the lake rests. A strong wind blows from the southwest, ruffling the water's surface and creating long streamers of a paler color across the deep-blue, sky-facing eye of the lake.

A seagull gliding on the wind wheels up over the hillside that separates this place from the Bay at the Back of the Ocean. Its shadow-twin crests the landscape, until the two meet on the surface of the water. This seems to be their favorite bathing place. Seven birds flap, duck, preen in the waters at the far end of the lake. To my right, a skylark starts to sing exuberantly, its tiny fluttering body silhouetted against fast-moving clouds.

There is something magical, elemental about a tiny island poised in a salty ocean with a pool of fresh water on its upper flanks held up by rock: the microcosm in the macrocosm. I stare at the lake as I eat my lunch, chewing slowly, but not really tasting the food. Loch Staonaig is glinting blue, a soft place of inner and outer reflection. It is stroked by the wind; it does not resist. It doesn't rise and fall in moon-drawn tides like the sea. It is and will be. Why did I find such comfort, transporting myself here in my imagination during those fearful days of cancer treatment? Why to this particular place? It is a mystery. I stand up and swing my pack onto my back. Some mysteries are best left unanswered.

I retrace my steps and, when I come close to the seagulls bathing, I stop to watch. Half submerged, they stretch out their wings, then thrusting skyward, quivering with spray, they utter cries quite unlike their usual plaintive calls. One lifts completely out of the water, then returns to its splashing and preening. I imagine their muted cries to be expressions of sheer delight in the sensuousness of the moment. Perhaps that is my answer.

I return down the rocky track to the Machair and feel somehow lighter, less burdened. And it isn't only that, having eaten my lunch and drunk a flask of tea, my pack is less heavy. On the far horizon, I see the Treshnish Islands, the outline of Coll, the hills of Skye. As I approach Cnoc nan Aingeal, Hill of the Angels, where St. Columba is said to have had a vision, ten lambs appear, running. They are led by one lamb that is completely white; the others have black faces and legs. The leader occasionally leaps in the air with mad delight. They disappear round the back of the hill, appear again, disappear; one lone horned ewe grazes, seemingly oblivious to these juvenile antics.

I recall my daughter, Lucy, telling me once, "You're too analytical. Don't try and figure everything out." Perhaps she is right.

⁂

The next day is gusty and cold. I make a pot of tea, settle into the most comfortable chair in the house, and start to leaf through a thin paperback I have found among Elinore's books. It is by Philip Sheldrake and the title intrigues me: *Living Between Worlds: Place and Journey in Celtic Christianity.* Celtic Christianity was one distinctive strand among many that emerged in the Western Catholic tradition. Since the Celtic lands were on the far northwest edge of the known European world, the church there developed differently from the settled and more urbanized world of Rome. "Celtic Christians had—and even today have—a strong sense of living on 'edges' or 'boundary places' between the material world and the other world," Sheldrake observes. "The natural landscape was both a concrete reality where people lived and, at the same time, a doorway into another spiritual world.... This sense of living in a 'between place' enabled Celtic Christians to make connections between the physical and the intangible, the seen and the unseen, this world and a permanently present 'other' world."[13]

"Inherent in Celtic Christian spirituality," Sheldrake claims, "were the twin values of 'place' and 'journey.' The journey was a search for the ultimate *place,* a place of harmony and the unity of all things in the Absolute.... An engagement with 'place' ... may enable a spiritual, inner journey.... Both the pilgrimage journey and the sacred place encapsulate a here-and-now experience of 'transitus'—the conclusive 'passing over' to the other world that is ultimately brought about by death."[14]

I find that the day I am reading this book—May 24th—is the feast of St. Brendan, famous in Celtic lore for his voyage to and among many islands of western Britain and perhaps even to North America. Scholars now suggest this was less an actual voyage than a parable of an inner spiritual journey. Sheldrake tells of a constant theme from the fifth to the eighth centuries in which the wandering ascetic banished himself in self-imposed exile from a loved homeland and went on a journey, usually by sea in a frail craft, in search of the ultimate place of harmony. "Celtic ascetics," Sheldrake writes, "sought out places where, in some special way, heaven appeared to meet earth ... not just *any* place in the landscape would do.... There was ... a belief that there was one precise location in the sacred landscape of the world that was particularly potent for their spiritual destiny.... The ultimate point of spiritual wandering was to 'seek the place of one's resurrection.'"[15]

I lay the book down and go for a walk. It is early evening. The sun has returned and transformed the waters of the Sound of Iona into a channel of shimmering blue silk. Beyond the landscapes of Mull and Erraid, the Paps of Jura are faintly outlined on the horizon. There is a seagull perched on each one of the seven chimneys of Bishop's House. A thrush sings sweetly to the lengthening shadows. Surely this is my place of pilgrimage and of re-birth.

❧ ❧

I have not come to Iona to study its natural history or its geology, though there is a thread of that in how I look at things, in what I do. I need to know the names of unfamiliar wildflowers and birds, not to place them, as a scientist, at a distance in some Linnean system, but rather to relate to them as other living beings with whom, albeit briefly, I share this complex habitat.

If there is a modicum of the curious observer in me (What are those small coils of mud that appear at low tide?), there is also a questing woman in me who needs to look outside myself into the myriad interconnected patterns of nature in order to seek—what? The divine? Buddha-mind? The mysterious unknowable? When I find myself

engaged in dialog with some aspect of the natural world—a tree, a lake, a rock—I am not partaking of some sentimental anthropomorphizing of nature, but attempting to comprehend our mutual interdependence. The only way to develop an ecological worldview is to become deeply, passionately knowledgeable about one small portion of the planet. Iona is that portion for me. And although it is not where I currently live full-time, it is the place to which I am drawn again and again, with a deep, magnetic attraction. Iona is my lover, my teacher, my place of balance and deep joy. It is my *axis mundi,* the place on earth where I feel a profound connection between the life of my earthbound body and the aspirations of my heaven-seeking spirit. As Gary Snyder, California poet, has written: "It is not enough just to 'love nature' or to want to 'be in harmony with Gaia.' Our relation to the natural world takes place in a place."[16]

Above all, living in one small place is teaching me to pay close attention. I learn to read the clouds and wind direction to determine what clothes to take on a hike, to be aware of the state of the tide, to recognize which grasses indicate a boggy footfall, to respect the sheep grazing on a rocky ledge by announcing my approach with a discreet cough lest I startle them and they accidentally fall.

By paying close attention, I am becoming more and more aware of my surroundings: clusters of sea thrift buffeted by the wind, the vibrant colors of pebbles as they are washed into luminosity by the incoming tide, minute shells that I can only see when I get down on my knees. As I quiet the chatter of my mind, I hear the subtle sounds of this island—not just the calls of gulls and oyster catchers, but the gentle pull-and-munch of sheep grazing, the distant engine purr of the ferry from Mull, the different tones of boots impacting dry sand, damp sand, wet seaweed, and rounded, sea-washed rocks. I am conscious of the smell of rain evaporating from hot tarmac, of banks of rotting seaweed, of bread baking in the village, of a salty wind blowing in from the Atlantic. I feel the wood of a fence post in my palm as I grasp it to climb over a stile, shell sand slipping through my fingers, the raspy texture of dune grass as I grip it to keep my balance, the shock of cold water as I wade into the sea. To live in such a way is to overcome that disconnect from the natural world that I often feel living in a city. On Iona, I am acutely aware, encircled, enmeshed—sometimes threatened—by the myriad sensations, smells, sights, sounds, and tastes of a real earthy, living, pulsing, breathing *place.* Here, at last, I feel fully alive. Describing his feelings for the Shiants—uninhabited islands in the Outer Hebrides—Adam Nicolson wrote: "I have felt at times … no gap between me and the place. I have absorbed it and been absorbed by it, as if I have had no existence apart from it.… The place has entered me. It has coloured my life like a stain. Almost everything else feels less dense and less intense than those moments of exposure. The social world, the political world, the world of getting on with work and a career—all those have been cast in shadow by the scale and sensuousness of my brief moments of island life."[17]

CHAPTER 5

え⌇

Facing Up to Prejudice

*When you see a worthy person, endeavor to emulate him.
When you see an unworthy person, then examine your
inner self.* —Confucius[18]

Iona not only provides me with moments of deep contentment, it also pushes my face into half-forgotten prejudices I would rather not revisit. If I have come here looking for healing, it is much more than physical healing that I need to embrace.

The moment I first become aware of Elizabeth greeting guests in her capacity as receptionist at the St. Columba Hotel, I am acutely aware of her unmistakable upper-class accent. Accents immediately place us— either by geographic location or, in the case of the English, by social class. Elizabeth always dresses in neat cashmere twin sets, keeps her hair beautifully coiffed, and wears jewelry that is discreet, not too flashy. In her presence, I feel not quite appropriately dressed, not quite of the "right" social class. As I hear her clipped Oxford-English accent, I am swept back to my childhood and something in me freezes.

Living on the Rothschild estate in the war, we were treated with patronizing condescension—*noblesse oblige*. The social hierarchy there comprised the Rothschild family, military officers occasionally billeted in our homes, the few elderly servants who remained at Ascott (butler, handyman, gamekeeper, groom), and those of us who didn't quite "fit"—the evacuees from London. The Rothschilds were *nouveaux riche* compared to the traditional landed gentry and, though they were more than generous, offering us a rent-free cottage and vegetables from their

gardens for the duration of the war, they represented in my child's mind something superior that I resented.

They lived in an immense mock-Tudor mansion. We children were told never to set foot on the wide terraced lawns and gravel paths from which the Rothschilds could look out to the Vale of Aylesbury and the distant Chiltern Hills. We crawled under bushes and stared up at the forbidden house with its multiple mullioned windows. We dared each other to step out onto the lawn and whispered about these distant beings who seemed to be so different that they might be another species.

Wartime evacuation caused enormous ruptures in the class system. Some children from inner-city slums encountered indoor toilets and bathtubs for the first time in the houses where they were billeted. Some from middle-class homes had to get used to using an outhouse. Others, sent to live in the palatial homes of the aristocracy, were relegated to the servants' quarters. Some couldn't understand the thick accents of their new "Aunties" in rural Devon or Glasgow; some sent to Wales had to learn a whole new language. There were new regional foods to get used to, different social customs. Many were bitterly homesick, couldn't stand the quietness of the countryside, and pleaded to be allowed to return home. Others took to country life, were excited about helping with farm and garden work. One of my distant cousins became so attached to the farm family with whom he was billeted that he didn't want to return to London after the war.

At some point during the war, the government commandeered the huge Rothschild house for use as a convalescent hospital for wounded troops. The Rothschild family moved into a modest flat over some garages, formerly the home of their chauffeur, who was now serving in the RAF. Upstairs-Downstairs reversed. I often wondered how it felt to them living in the "cramped" quarters of one of their former servants. Certainly for me, occasionally asked there to tea with the Rothschild children in the company of their French governess, Mademoiselle Donet, visiting them in a home not unlike our own was vastly more comfortable than the few times I entered the Big House, intimidated by its gloomy oak-paneled corridors, walls of 17th-century landscape paintings, and priceless collections of Chinese porcelain in locked glass cases.

One day, unaware of the correct social niceties, I asked if the Rothschild children could come with us to the Odeon Cinema in Leighton Buzzard to see the latest Abbot and Costello film. Their mother—a tall, forbidding woman who was French, and therefore doubly strange to us—visibly shuddered. "Oh no. The children never go to the cinema," she said. "With the common folk," I later added as I recalled this embarrassing meeting. I had stepped over the line.

Living on the Rothschild estate was only one of the ways in which I was initiated into the class system. There, I felt low on the totem pole, though the Rothschilds probably had no conscious intention of eliciting this response. At school, on the other hand, I was clearly instructed that I was better than some others and should not mix with them. This was the attitude of our teachers at The Gables, a small private school evacuated from north London that I attended between the ages of five and eleven. Here, we were educated by four "maiden-lady" teachers— Miss Thomas, Miss Walker, Miss Barker, and Miss Smith—who taught us geography, history, arithmetic, geometry, algebra, Latin, French, botany, and current affairs. They believed that children of seven, eight, and nine were quite capable of writing an essay every week and learning irregular French verbs, details of the mountain ranges of Central Europe, and the history of the Roman invasion of Britain—and we were. There were just three of us in my class: Mary, Brenda, and myself. It was like having private tutors.

But we were taught something beyond the set curriculum. We were told in no uncertain terms that we were never, *ever* to play after school in the "Rec"—the Linslade Recreation Ground—an area between the parish church and the railway lines where there were lawns, trees, a soccer field, and, most tempting of all, a playground with a slide, swings, a merry-go-round, and a maypole. Why we were not supposed to play there puzzled me at the time. Was it that we might have an accident? Or was it that it was inappropriate for us to mix with children of lesser means who went to the local primary school? Years later, I realized it was, of course, the latter.

Once a week, I went home to tea with my friend Mary prior to our Girl Guide meeting in a church hall on Lake Street. We walked away from school past the neat terraced houses on Waterloo Road, turned into the Rec (Mary's normal route home), and, when we were out of sight of The Gables, gleefully took off our school hats and satchels and rode on the maypole. To ride the maypole, you had to hook your right arm through a wooden fixture at the end of a long chain, then start running in circles round the central pole until, miraculously, your whole body was lifted in the air and swung higher and higher in delicious, stomach-churning, gravity-defying flight. It was one of the most thrilling kinesthetic experiences of my childhood, far surpassing the more somber excitement of climbing a tall tree or running alone through darkening woodland. We seized the chance to swing hatless on the Rec's maypole whenever we could.

But one spring day, disaster struck. Flying up in the air in breathless rebellion, I caught sight of Miss Barker entering the Rec from Waterloo Road. No escape; she was on to us. We dropped to the ground as she approached.

"Clare—Mary—what on earth do you think you are doing?"

"We're not on earth," I wanted to say. "That's the whole point." We looked at the ground and our dusty shoes in a gesture of mock contrition. From under my downcast eyes, I could see a prominent vein on Miss Barker's stiff neck throbbing with anger.

"Put on your hats and go home at once!" she thundered. "And come to me tomorrow. You will both have to write a hundred lines: I must not play in the Recreation Ground."

We retrieved our school hats and satchels and shuffled away, feeling equally humiliated and defiant. Once Miss Barker was out of sight, we engaged in our second-most-favorite thrill-seeking after-school activity—standing on a footbridge that passed over the London and Midland railway lines at Leighton Buzzard station and letting smoke from passing trains hide and engulf us. As the sooty cloud billowed along the footbridge, we ran to stay in the heart of it—existing, just for a moment, in a hidden, magical world where we could see nothing and no one could see us. Least of all, Miss Barker.

I'm sure Miss Barker would have deemed this behavior shocking for nice little girls in their Gables school uniforms, but she never did find out, any more than Madame Rothschild ever allowed her children to accompany us to the cinema in Leighton Buzzard. Such are the ways in which a culture conveys its prejudices to the next generation.

Sixty years later, living on Iona, I am confronted with these prejudices and confusions from childhood. Elizabeth walks into the staff room at the hotel one day, her high heels click-clicking on the recently mopped tile floor. She screws up her face as she lowers herself into a seat across from me.

"What an awful smell. I hate that floor cleanser, it smells so ... so ... well, lower-class, don't you think?"

I mumble something inaudible through my mouthful of baked potato.

Elizabeth takes out her make-up from a stylish leather purse and re-applies dark red lipstick in a neat bow, then pats her nose and cheeks with face powder. She sighs, fingering her pearls.

"I've never had to work before," she confides. "Though it's not so bad—answering the phone, greeting guests. Sometimes I imagine this hotel is my home and the guests are people I've invited for the weekend. That makes it a little easier." She pauses, absentmindedly sweeping some crumbs from the table onto the floor with the back of her fingers, her ring scraping across the wood.

"Of course, some of the people who come here are not the kind of people I would invite to *my* home as guests. Do you know what I mean?"

I squirm inside, feeling coerced into agreeing with her.

"Have you tried Alistair's new salad made with walnuts and apples?" I ask brightly, trying to change the subject.

"Yes … lovely," she answers distractedly, her face, just for a moment, displaying a flicker of loneliness.

"Well, back to the grind." She gets up from the table, a weak smile on her face. I sigh and feel a mix of emotions as she leaves the room.

As we work together at the hotel, I find myself avoiding Elizabeth as much as I can, chatting only briefly in the lunch room, cringing at her upper-class accent, watching her take her dog for a walk in her hours off. Then one warm evening, she calls out to me from the hotel garden as I return from a walk to the north end. She offers me a glass of sherry and asks if I'd like to go with her to Mull the next day; we could drive to Ben More and go for a hike. She keeps her car at Fionnphort, near the ferry landing.

A whole day with this woman? What would we talk about: holidays on the Riviera? Coming-out balls in Chelsea? But, she has a car; I would see parts of Mull I'd never visited before. For all the wrong reasons, I accept her invitation.

It is a glorious day, the sun at this high latitude drenching the hills with color. We drive through dramatic landscapes and hike up the lower slopes of Ben More, lifting Elizabeth's tiny West Highland terrier over the stiles. We eat our picnic lunch looking over Loch Scridain. Elizabeth starts to tell me about her life: a failed marriage, a painful divorce, grown children she rarely sees, no financial support. That is why she is now working. I sense her loneliness. I start to share something of my own story. She listens sympathetically. My awareness of her accent and all the prejudice it arouses in me starts to fade. We listen to each other; we laugh at little incidents we have witnessed at the hotel. And through it all, I begin to appreciate Elizabeth as a unique and interesting person, not just an accent I have branded as "bad" since childhood. What are the chances of such a meeting happening on a remote Scottish island? It feels like something the fates have orchestrated. I am grateful for this encounter and what it has taught me.

A few days later, I chat with Robbie as we prepare the tables for the evening meal. I listen to his Scottish burr with pleasure, and then an unwanted question insinuates its way into my mind. What of the prejudice felt toward *me*—an English woman, living in this country where my forebears caused endless misery? I remember one of my teachers recounting a childhood move from England to Scotland and how she was picked on in the schoolyard. "Remember Bannockburn!" the Scottish children hissed at her, running away laughing at her bewilderment. Guiltily, I hope that Robbie and other people on the island will assume I am American, not English. My mid-Atlantic accent does not quite place me squarely in either country.

⁂ ⁂

Meeting Barbara, who sometimes works in the dining room of the hotel, seems like another of these serendipitous happenings forcing me to confront a prejudice from the past. Barbara is German. Needless to say, childhood fears of German air raids and the dreaded enemy invasion set me up for a seemingly life-long prejudice against "The Germans." Yet I have felt a special affinity for every individual German I have ever met—hardly surprising, considering our common Anglo-Saxon background. I think of Ute, whom I met on an archaeological dig in Denmark; Eva, a fellow foreign student in the United States; Christa, a former Lufthansa flight attendant who became part of the community at Findhorn. During the war, one of my mother's few women friends was Hilde Woodman, a German woman married to an Englishman who lived near us when we were evacuated to the country. Hilde had the unenviable experience of living among people who, I imagine, secretly suspected she was a spy.

One day at the St. Columba Hotel, Barbara and I start to talk as we eat lunch together at a table in the garden. It is an unusually warm day in May. A blackbird sings in a sycamore somewhere nearby. As we ask each other about the years before coming to Iona, we realize we are not far apart in age and spent our childhoods on opposite sides of a momentous conflict. Our conversation turns to the war. Barbara's father was in the army, as was mine. Her mother's "nervous disposition" in the war, like my mother's isolation and depression, caused her to withdraw. Barbara's fondest memories are of her grandparents, in whose house they lived. Barbara's fears of "The Enemy" were not directed at the Americans or the British, but at the Russians who occupied their town in 1945, pillaging, raping women, breaking up her mother's beloved piano for firewood, and forcing the family into a cellar as prisoners for many weeks while troops took over their house. Bravely, as an adult, Barbara forced herself to go to Russia to confront her fears and seek healing. I have not been so courageous. I have never been to Germany. Just once, I passed through on a train from Holland to Copenhagen. When German customs officials came on board with their neat buttoned uniforms and polished boots, I sweated with fear.

I find myself warming to Barbara. We are both temporary workers at the hotel; we often meet and chat briefly in the dining room, in the servery, in the staff room. Then one day, Barbara invites me to her house, Greenbank, a ten-minute walk from the village. We stop to watch her neighbor, Colin. One of his ewes, pregnant long after the others, is having difficulty giving birth. She is too exhausted to push the second of her twin lambs out of the heaving, bloody opening in her body. Colin pulls gently and, finally, a lamb covered in yellow mucus falls onto the damp grass. He carefully picks it up and places it close to the mother's face. The lamb attempts to stand, but falls back to the ground. The mother starts to lick it clean.

I feel tears as I remember the births of my children. "Push, honey, push," the doctor urged me. (Who is he calling "honey"?) I started to scream as ten-pound Lucy forced her head out into the waiting world.

We enter a glass-enclosed porch at Greenbank that smells of geraniums and basil. Barbara takes off a worn padded jacket. Underneath, she is wearing a turquoise sweater with a soft, white chiffon scarf tied loosely at her neck. Her hair is mousey blond, pepper-and-salt, just like mine. A small Celtic triune symbol on a fine silver chain hangs round her neck. Barbara makes tea in a brown ceramic pot that glints in the sunlight as she carries it into the porch. We settle at the table and sit for a while in silence, watching the twin lambs now licked white by their mother, heads butting into her bulging udder. I turn to look at Barbara, and smile. We pick up our cups and drink as a breeze whips the surface of the sea into a mosaic of green, gray, blue, and white.

For years, indeed decades, after the war, I wouldn't buy anything "Made in Germany," but I won't mention this to Barbara. A Volkswagen was out of the question; shopping for my children, I turned over every toy and, if I saw the dreaded words "Made in Germany," I put it back on the shelf. Finally, I convinced myself this was ridiculous. How long do you hold on to fears and prejudices dating back to childhood? In my case, a long time. How long will it be for the children of Israel and Palestine, Iraq, Northern Ireland, and Afghanistan?

CHAPTER 6

✌

Survivor Guilt

*People say that what we're all seeking is the meaning of
life. I don't think that's what we're really seeking. I think
that what we're seeking is the rapture of being alive.*
—Joseph Campbell[19]

It is surprising to me that I have started to go each week to the Sunday
morning service at the abbey. I don't think of myself as a practicing
Christian. At first, it is just another setting on the island—like the
hotel—where I look for a vicarious sense of community. But slowly, it
is becoming more than that, something I cannot quite grasp or name.

I sit in the southern choir stalls so I have a good view of the person
giving the sermon. I arrive early and watch the quiet preparations for
the service: a man lighting tall white candles; a young woman rehearsing a small group who will sing while the collection is taken; guests
at the abbey—men and women, young and old—being instructed in
how to pass the communion bread and wine along the rows of seats.

I stare across at a stone wall: black, gray, dull white, muted pink.
Stones from this island of many colors; stones within, stones without.
The inside of the abbey is spare, even stark, with arches of palest beige.
A barn-like roof covers the choir, which is reassuringly warm in its
wooden trusses. The windows are mostly of plain glass. High up in the
choir, there are four small stained-glass panels of the saints connected
to this abbey: Columba, Patrick, Bridget, and Margaret.

One morning, a blackbird flies into the abbey through an open
door. It wings back and forth, agitated to be inside a building. Finally,
it settles on the capital of a column close to the altar and quietly preens
its feathers. People nearby watch, as the lesson is read from the Gos-

pel according to John. "In the beginning was the Word ..." The bird remains atop the column for much of the service. Then, as the preparations are taking place at the altar for communion, the blackbird bursts into song. My eyes burn with tears.

After the service, I often walk down the road to the St. Columba Hotel for lunch. By June, the hotel is fully staffed, so my stint as a waitress has ended. I sit in the light-filled lounge in a deep armchair watching gannets dive for fish in the waters between Iona and Mull. There is something deeply comforting about a hotel lounge—people writing postcards, reading the Sunday paper, dozing over a book on a rainy afternoon. The contrast between brilliantly sunny days and rainy stay-at-home days that is typical of the weather in this part of the world provides a pleasing rhythm to my life. In California, there are months on end of sunny hot weather and months on end of wet gloomy weather. On Iona, daily, sometimes hourly, the island decides whether you are welcome to tread its beaches or whether you need to seek shelter indoors.

A vague memory surfaces of a geographer who maintained that people in regions characterized by rapid and unpredictable changes of weather experience stimulation of the brain and its creative centers.

Test scores from different climatic regions of North America support his argument. Whether or not this is true, I find my own patterns of thought strongly affected by the weather. When it is overcast or rainy, I am more prone to introspection. I seek stimulus from reading, staring out the window, and letting my eyes graze over water, sky, fields, and sheep in a dreamy state of consciousness.

But when the sun returns and shadows sharpen the reality of the outer world, when colors spring to life and silhouettes become clearly articulated landscapes, then my mind, it seems, is similarly alert and attentive to detail. Not only am I drawn outside to walk, hear skylark, smell seaweed, and feel the sun warming my limbs, I want to converse with the world and explore its mysteries. These unpredictable swings from introspection to exploration feel as if they inject my body and my psyche with aliveness after a long, somnolent sojourn in my head.

❧ ❧

At Highland Cottage, I live in a house full of someone else's books. I scan the shelves, pulling out likely titles: *The Birds of Britain, Buddhist Women on the Edge, Scottish Fairy Tales, The Celtic Year.* I feel as if I were living in a slightly chaotic used-book store that is open at all times and has no proprietor.

I pull out a thin volume whose title appeals to me: *A Thousand Reasons for Living.* It is a collection of poems by Dom Helder Camara, Archbishop of Olinda and Recife in northeast Brazil. The book is dusty and I clean it off with the side of my hand, the better to see the face of the author—a short tanned man standing in a doorway in white priestly garb, his face creased in a smile, his thinning gray hair catching the sunlight. His poems are brief—and poignant.

> *I love flowers more and more*
> *They speak to me*
> *of how ephemeral life is*
> *and make me face up*
> *to eternity.   (11 July 1956)*

If you have a thousand reasons for living,
if you never feel alone,
if you wake up wanting to sing,
if everything speaks to you,
from the stone in the road
to the star in the sky,
from the loitering lizard
to the fish, lord of the sea,
if you understand the winds
and listen to the silence,
rejoice,
for love walks with you,
he is your comrade,
is your brother! [20]   *(28 January 1973)*

Camara's poems are a reminder of the joy of a place speaking to you. I lay the book down and set off for a walk. When the sun is out, the island calls. I start up the rocky track that leads from the village to Maol and stop just to look, to take in everything I can see. MacCulloch's Meadow, sloping down to Martyr's Bay, is alive with countless daisies, as if the Milky Way had poured itself onto the land in an act of celestial exuberance. Out to sea, the wind carves white caps on the waves; a fishing boat passes, leaving a creamy trail in its wake.

I take a route that I haven't walked before, south past the croft named Ruanaich, Place of the Red Flowers, then east following a valley between two rocky hills—Hill of the Narrow Flank and Hill of the Monks. I cross a fence by a stile and walk down a wide valley to Sandeel's Bay.

I hear children's voices before I come over a grassy bank and see them playing rounders on the sand; perhaps it is a group staying at the Macleod Centre near the abbey. Off to my right, four young girls climb over rocks to reach a narrow cleft in the sea-facing flank of the bay. They disappear from view. Instantly, I am drawn back to the scene from the Australian movie *Picnic at Hanging Rock* in which four schoolgirls leave a picnic to explore the heat-buzzing interior of an ancient aboriginal sacred place—and are never seen again. I see myself a few years ago in Australia, walking the base of Uluru (Ayer's Rock) and peering into the areas labeled "Place of Special Ritual: Keep Out." I felt like a tourist-intruder at Uluru. The rock, the desert surface, the birds and plants—everything spoke to me of an ancient culture with which I had no connection. Iona feels different. The rocks and landscape feel benign. I do not feel like an intruder. Though I have no proof of names and genealogy, it feels as if it could be the home of my ancestors. I sigh with relief as the four girls re-emerge from the rocks and run out onto the sand to join their friends.

❧ ❧

During two days when the rain barely lets up, I read *An Interrupted Life: The Diaries of Etty Hillesum 1941-43*, an extraordinarily moving account by a 27-year-old Jewish woman of her daily life and spiritual growth in Nazi-occupied Amsterdam. Despite all that was happening around her, she retained a deep inner strength and a remarkable lack of fear or anger or a need for vengeance.

The last few pages are letters that Etty wrote to friends just before being put on a transport train to Auschwitz, where she, her mother and father, and her two brothers all died in 1943. I cannot get this extraordinary woman's strength and luminous being out of my mind. Thankfully, she had the foresight to give her diaries—"eight exercise books closely written in a small hard-to-decipher hand"—to a friend in Amsterdam for safekeeping in case she did not return. In a matter of two years, her diary entries changed from those of a confused adolescent to those of a mature, wise woman of almost saintly qualities.

Her last entry, for October 11, 1942, reads:

> I always return to Rilke. It is strange to think that someone so frail and who did most of his writing within protective castle walls, would perhaps have been broken by the circumstances in which we now live. Is that not further evidence that life is finely balanced? Evidence that, in peaceful times and under favorable circumstances, sensitive artists may search for the

purest and most fitting expression of their deepest insights so that, during more turbulent and debilitating times, others can turn to them for support and a ready response to their bewildered questions? A response they are unable to formulate for themselves since all their energies are taken up in looking after the bare necessities. Sadly, in difficult times we tend to shrug off the spiritual heritage of artists from an "easier" age, with what use is that sort of thing for us now?

It is an understandable but shortsighted reaction. And utterly impoverishing. We should be willing to act as a balm for all wounds.[21]

I weep for this woman and her interrupted life.

Why are we born when we are born, in the place where we are born? Every time I read a book like *An Interrupted Life,* or see a movie or TV documentary about World War II, I am overcome with survivor guilt. When so many died in the camps and on the battlefields, why was I spending my childhood in rural England almost untouched by these horrors? Of course as children, we were aware there was a war going on, but we hardly comprehended what that meant. We counted the bombers—Lancasters, Wellingtons—that took off from Wing Airfield and noted some were missing on their return. Seventy thousand British airmen died in the war, including, I learned later, three distant relatives of mine.

The grounds of Ascott were often commandeered for maneuvers. We sat in the sweet-smelling grass of the daffodil field and watched young soldiers engaged in bayonet practice, racing toward sacks of straw hung from the branches of a copper-beech tree, yelling as steel pierced burlap, spilling yellowing entrails onto the ground. In the current era of smart bombs and guided missiles, such training seems almost medieval.

Once when soldiers were practicing war games in the woods around us, some officers took over the living room of our house to hold an enquiry. I sat crouched in the corner of the room, unnoticed.

"He is dead," protested a ruddy-faced private. "I definitely shot him."

"No, you didn't," argued the "dead" man. "I was shielded by a wall when you crept up. You couldn't have killed me!" Grown-ups arguing about which one was "dead"? War was puzzling.

There was fear as well, but we understood relatively little of what was happening. As children living safely in the countryside, we were unaware of the start of the "blitz" (from the German *blitzkrieg*, or "lightning war"). On the evening of September 7, 1940, an aerial bombardment from almost 1000 German and Italian planes dropped 600 tons of high explosives and 17,000 incendiary bombs on the East End of London. This first big attack was the start of a relentless assault on London that continued for fifty-seven nights of fear and destruction. On the night of December 29, 1940, German planes dropped 24,000 incendiary bombs, starting an inferno that lit the way for the second wave of planes carrying high-explosive bombs. The fires were concentrated around St. Paul's Cathedral in the City of London. It was Hitler's intent to shock Britain into surrender by destroying this sacred and symbolic building. Word came from Churchill to the firefighters: "Whatever you do, save St. Paul's." Fires destroyed an entire square mile of the City and came within twenty-five feet of the cathedral walls, but it survived—as if by a miracle. Photographs of the cathedral dome, floating like an island in an ocean of fire, became a potent symbol of Britain's determination to survive.

I remember that photo and the newsreels we saw at the cinema, but, from where we lived, it seemed like a distant event—though certainly not to our mothers. On May 10 and 11, 1941, we children were probably climbing trees or playing in the fields and knew nothing of the fact that, on those spring days, less than forty miles away in London, air raids killed 1,500 people, destroyed 11,000 houses, burned a quarter of a million books at the British Museum, and set the Houses of Parliament on fire.

American journalists in London sent home detailed accounts of bombing raids and British civilian casualties. Britain hoped that these would prompt the United States to join the war, but that didn't happen until a year later when, in December 1941, the Japanese bombed Pearl Harbor.

Away from the scenes of bombing, we children regarded some aspects of the war as exciting rather than frightening. My brother, Paul, and his friend Burt found a book on Ju-Jitsu and started practicing

self-defense in case the Germans arrived. They taught me how to dis-
arm someone coming at me with a knife. (I can still do it, but only if
my assailant is "thoughtful" enough to come at me with the knife in a
particular position.) They practiced a technique for securing a prisoner
to a pole or thin-trunked tree without a rope or anything with which
to tie them by forcing them to the ground with their arms and legs
wrapped around the pole in an intricate pattern. It was called, I think,
the Grapevine Lock (or that is my childhood memory of its name).
One day, they decided to try it out on me, and ran away leaving me
crying and sweating with fear after assuring me that, if I tried to stand
up, I would break my back. I suppose they came back eventually to
rescue me; at least I am still here, with back intact.

Sometimes, German bombers that had overshot London dumped
incendiary bombs in the fields near where we lived. Paul and I and our
friends collected shrapnel to trade with other children; we raised money
for the Spitfire Fund by loaning our books to friends at a penny a time.
Once, when troops in training were on iron rations, two wily corporals
paid us sixpence each to go buy fresh-baked bread from Bonhams the
Bakers in Wing and bring it back to them at a secret rendezvous. And
while all that was going on, across the English Channel, unimagina-
ble horrors were taking place of which we knew almost nothing. That
stretch of sea, just twenty-one miles across, was what saved us. Perhaps
that's why I'm so attracted to islands, with their watery boundaries
that provide a sense of refuge and separation, the distinction between
here—and there.

Walking home one day on Iona, I stop at the war memorial near
the Martyr's Bay Restaurant. I had glanced at it many times before, but
never really stopped to read the names inscribed in black on the gray-
flecked granite column.

Hugh MacDonald. John MacFarlane. Neil MacFarlane. What
madness took you from the shores of Iona to the bloody battlefields
of Mons and Ypres? Duncan Campbell. Hector MacLean Lee. Dugald
Black. Did you dream of blue seas and Hebridean skies when you slept
fitfully in the muddy trenches of France? John MacDonald. Lachlan
MacDonald. Alfred Macarthur Williams. Who tended your sheep, who
hauled in the crabs while shells whined at the Somme and you went
over the top into a hail of machine-gun fire? William Black. Angus
MacPhail Mackecnie. When the shells found their mark and blackness

exploded, who took the news to your mothers and sisters in the crofts of Iona? Who lifted your bodies from the mud amid shattered trees and scurrying vermin in the No Man's Land of Verdun? Meanwhile, in London, aging generals safely sipped sherry in their clubs, thankful that it was you, not they, making the ultimate sacrifice.

Robert Campbell. Dugald MacArthur. John MacFarlane. War came again. You left the island, as did your fathers. Donald MacDonald. Colin MacDonald. Donald C. MacDonald. Were you brothers or cousins? Did you comb the hills in spring, looking for lambs abandoned by their mothers? Who came looking for you when you fell on the beaches of Normandy? Anthony McAllister. Colin MacColl. John Patterson. We counted the planes; some didn't return. Did you feel the bullets ripping through fuselage and flesh? Did you see the green fields racing up to meet you? Neil Black. George Dougal. Neil MacLachlan. Did you man the ships that brought us food? Fragile convoy, torpedo, explosion, frigid Atlantic water filling your lungs, memories of Iona's beaches. John MacGregor. Gregor MacDonald. Did your spirits return? Can you smell the salt air? Are you present in the wind, the call of the corncrake? John MacInnes. Donald Black. I am here on your island in evening warmth, safe and at peace. There is no justice.

One side of the memorial obelisk is white and empty. Whose names wait to be written on the cold blank stone facing the sea?

༨ ༨

I wake up with a start from a dream. I am in the woods. I am in the woods and I hear footsteps approaching. Not so much footsteps as boot steps, breaking dry twigs like brittle infant bones, striding closer in a fearless military memory. A soldier appears. His uniform is flecked with mud; his black helmet has a hole in it that appears to go through his head. I see light from the other side. I crouch low; perhaps he won't see me. Perhaps he'll march on to some magnetic destination beyond the wood. But he does see me. He stops, smiles, and comes closer. I quiver with fear, unable to flee, like a rabbit caught in the headlights. I see he is dragging a parachute, its harness caught up with bright spring leaves and purple flowers, as if he has just emerged mermaid-like from the sea draped in seaweed. But he has come from the sky, not from the sea. We were warned they might come at night, falling like 1000 ghostly moths from silent gliders slicing the icy clouds. They have come. He is one of them. The invasion has begun.

"What's your name little girl?" the soldier asks in a guttural accent. "I'm not going to hurt you." My eyes fix on the shine of his bayonet. I do not believe him. He holds out his hand and, suddenly, my feet disengage from the ground and I flee on whirring feet, brambles tearing at my cheeks, drops of blood welling up like jewels, like sacred scars of initiation. The booted feet follow, loud and insistent, long strides catching up with my cat-like leaping body. He is getting closer. My feet sink into a lake of molasses. I am sucked under, unable to breathe. The soldier grabs my shoulders and spins me around. I shriek abuse into his blue eyes and see that the face is my own. I cannot speak. The soldier falls onto me and we both sink, unbelieving, into the ghostly quagmire, clinging to each other for safety, fighting each other off in anguish. We disappear beneath the surface and all is silent in the tearing, blood-flecked wood. Together at last.

༨ ༨

I stop to watch the rooks in the sycamores behind the Heritage Centre; they cry noisily to each other. Or are they protesting the wind tossing their nests to and fro in the highest branches? A parliament of rooks. Yes, that is an apt word for this raucous, bickering community. Perhaps they are arguing about territory. Even male and female pairs creating nests together confront each other noisily. One brings a stick for building; the other tosses it out. "Not good enough. Go find another."

Cuckoos have returned to the island from their winter lodgings. I hear one calling from behind the parish church. The cuckoo lays an egg that mimics the color and patterning of the host bird's eggs. It hatches first, ready to nudge its rivals out of the nest as they emerge from their shells, while the foster parents frantically hunt for food to feed the hungry interloper. What quirk of evolutionary zeal brought about this cunning arrangement? Which unfortunate bird will have its eggs tossed out and unknowingly raise the cuckoo's young?

I walk north to the White Strand of the Monks and settle my back against rocks encrusted with tiny acorn barnacles. I look across the stretch of blue-green water to the Island of Storm. It is a calm day, small ripples breaking rhythmically, like the quiet, untroubled breathing of a child.

Why was I spared when so many others died? I picked up a book in the abbey gift shop—*Before I Say Goodbye,* by Ruth Picardie. She had cancer and did not survive. I haven't had the courage to open it. Another NATO "mistake" in Kosovo; many die in a village that was not supposed to be bombed. Picking up a magazine, I read of a terrible massacre at a school in Colorado that happened a month ago. It seems almost obscene that I am on this peaceful island with no responsibilities in a world of so much suffering. Yet this is where I am.

In the piercing evening light, the world is vibrant with life—the waves more noisily insistent, the sea a deeper blue, the shadows on Mull and Staffa more sharp-edged and black than the sun-bleached landscape of noon. Three seagulls glide by, wings still, balanced on an invisible ribbon of wind. Don't be concerned with survivor guilt, Iona seems to say. Be here, be present, be thankful that you are in this place—breathing, healthy, alive. That is enough.

PART II

༄

Looking Back

CHAPTER 7

 co

Invasion of the Crabs

Critical illness offers the experience of being taken to the threshold of life, from which you can see how your life could end. From that vantage point you are both forced and allowed to think in new ways about the value of your life.... Illness takes away parts of your life, but in doing so it gives you the opportunity to choose the life you will lead, as opposed to living out the one you have simply accumulated over the years. —Arthur W. Frank[22]

Five years ago, when undergoing cancer treatment, I certainly had no feelings of survivor guilt—far from it. I was determined to survive, no matter what the statistics predicted, no matter what gloomy outcomes were dumped on me by pessimistic specialists.

Though scarcely aware of it during the shock of diagnosis and treatment, cancer came as a gift, forcing me to look at my lived and unlived life and to choose a direction close to my heart instead of proceeding in a manner I had "simply accumulated over the years."

I find a lump in my right breast in August, 1994. My doctor quickly arranges an ultrasound test. If there is liquid inside the lump, it is likely to be a cyst, probably benign. If it is solid, the prognosis is more ominous. I know from an expression that flickers across the face of the technician that it is cancer.

They need to remove a piece for a biopsy. Though sedated, I can feel an instrument poking around inside my breast. I try to extract myself by imagining I am in my garden, but the imagery is interrupted by jabs of pain, followed by another injection and the chatter of two nurses and a surgeon as they work on my body. I resent their laughter and banter about work schedules while I lie white-draped on the table, half-drugged and terrified.

That night, I have trouble sleeping; catastrophic outcomes keep intruding. Faced with mortality, my alarmed ego goes into double time, stroking itself with the nice things people will say at the memorial service when I am no more. I need to take myself to a place of calm, far from biopsies and medical tests. I find myself retreating, in my imagination, to Loch Staonaig on the upper slopes of Iona. Out of nowhere, a helicopter appears; its noise frightens the seagulls; its whirring blades create a wind that sets the bog cotton scudding across the landscape.

"What do you want from me?" I beg.

"I want your *attention*!!" the helicopter yells, lights flashing, rotor blades spinning madly.

As I give it my full attention, the helicopter appears to grow smaller and quieter. Tears drip from its front windows. "What do you want from me?" I implore. "What can I do to heal myself?"

"Love yourself," the helicopter answers gently. "You have directed attention out, not because you are a saint or a selfless being, but because you imagine that paying attention to yourself is selfish. It is not. It is what you must do right now. It is your path to healing. Do what makes you happy: water the house plants, tend the garden, pick and arrange flowers, sit and write. These are the ways to love yourself."

A few days later, I hear the official diagnosis: infiltrating ductal carcinoma in the right breast. It is hard to embrace this news fully when I feel so healthy. I am two months into retirement and my life is less stressed than it has been in the last thirty years. Is that why this has happened now, when I have the time and energy to focus on healing?

A friend loans me a book about healing imagery and I start to do the suggested exercises. One day, when the instructions are to imagine the tumor in symbolic form, to my surprise I see a small iron ball with spikes on it. Is this what a sea-mine looks like?

Instantly, I am drawn back to a beach on the east coast of England. It is the summer of 1945 and I am eleven. The war has just ended and my best friend, Mary, her Aunt Margaret, Great-uncle Tom, Great-uncle Welburn, and I are having a picnic on the beach at Felixstowe. I don't remember ever having been on a beach before; most beaches were off limits during the five years of the war. We went on seaside holidays before the war; there are photographs in the family album to prove it. But everything before 1940, the year of our evacuation from London, has been erased from my memory.

After eating a lunch of sandwiches and fruitcake (a rare treat), I leave the group—the uncles are tossing pebbles into an empty can—and walk off down the beach alone. It is a heady experience: the sound of waves, seagulls gliding by, a gray stretch of sea separating us from France and Holland, the moat that protected us from invasion. A strand of barbed wire stretches from somewhere inland down to the sea. I crawl under it and continue walking, rounded pebbles squeaking underfoot. After fifteen minutes or so, I come to another strand of wire with a wooden notice on top of a pole facing away from me. I crawl under the wire and look up at a rough wooden sign with words spelled out in red capital letters: "Beware! Unexploded mines. Keep out!"

My lunch turns over in my stomach. Sweating with fear, I stumble away, walking quickly, looping inland far from the mined beach, until I come back to the picnic group. Nobody asks me where I've been. I say nothing—neither then, nor at any time since. But the mine must have stayed there, buried somewhere in my unconscious.

Fifty years later, in my imagination, I ask the spiky iron object what it wants. "To be touched," it says. I stroke its surface and begin to cry. Despite its outer form, there seems to be something of a baby in this symbol. I dress it in a pink bonnet.

❧ ❧

I am to lose my right breast. "Sit in here and watch this video," a nurse instructs me, patting my shoulder in a manner that is both intimate and perfunctory. She places a box of Kleenex beside me, switches on the VCR, and leaves the room.

The video is of women who have had mastectomies. It is a shock to see so much one-breastedness. Thoughts of freaks at fairgrounds and body parts in formaldehyde pass through my mind.

"You can always have reconstructive surgery," a doctor has reassured me. Would I want to go through that? I wonder if it would be worth it at my age. If another man appears in my life, will one breast be enough?

As the video ends, I blow my nose and gather up my things. It's not so bad. I can live with it. How ironic that this should happen just as I have become totally at home with my body image. To look in the mirror at sixty and like what you see is something of an achievement. For many years, I carried the memory of a conversation between my brother, Paul, and his best friend. I was sixteen at the time; we were walking across Hampstead Heath on a Sunday afternoon. "Well, Clare will never be another Marilyn Monroe!" one of them quipped and they both laughed. I blushed and turned my head away, feeling a mix of anger and shame.

For years after that, the relatively small size of my breasts worried me greatly. It was the era of Monroe, Jayne Mansfield, Diana Dors. I wonder how many adolescent girls like me must have felt painfully inadequate. Who was the first person who touched my breasts? Probably the spotty-faced medical student who took me to a formal ball and fumbled with my bra straps in a steamy parked car in Regents Park in 1952. No, I don't think he made it. I had stuffed falsies into my bra cups and squirmed away from his clammy, searching fingers, terrified that he would find out the dreadful truth: my satin-clad curves were not all that they seemed.

When I was eighteen, I found a small lump in my left breast. It was assumed to be benign, but just in case, I was admitted to Guys Hospital in London to have it removed. The day before the surgery, a group of medical students (all male) gathered round my bed with their professor and were invited, one by one, to examine and feel the lump. I was acutely embarrassed, all the more so when the doctor-professor cracked a joke in a low voice. Although I didn't hear what he said, I imagined it was about the small size of my breasts. The students dutifully laughed, then moved on to the next bed. Ashamed of my body and in awe of medical authority, I shrank under the stiff hospital sheets in a pool of humiliation. These were the first males to whom I had fully exposed my breasts and they had laughed.

It was David who helped me to see myself as beautiful and sexy. We met in graduate school at Berkeley in the early 1960s and had a long, on-again, off-again relationship for almost five years. One spring, before a vacation trip to Mexico, he took me to Mrs. Bentley's lingerie shop on Shattuck Avenue (now a shop for buying glasses) and had me fitted with a blue-and-white spotted bikini. "There you are, my darling," said Mrs. Bentley in her thick, Central European accent, her expert hands cupping the bikini professionally over my breasts and doing up the clasp on my back.

I looked in the mirror. Amazing! Mrs. Bentley and David stood beside me, glanced at each other, and then smiled broadly at me. I was beginning to feel good about my body.

At the start of our relationship, I wanted to make love in the dark so David couldn't see that I didn't have the kind of voluptuous breasts deemed sexy at the time. Who was I kidding? David was fondling and kissing those breasts. He knew what size and shape they were. One day, David gently persuaded me to pose on the bed naked while he took photos. When the prints came back, I was stunned.

"That's me?" I asked incredulously, pride and disbelief mixed in that rhetorical question.

"Yes, honey. That's you, as I've been telling you." I looked like a Playboy centerfold. Now, thirty years later, I look at my breasts and they seem just right. Not too large, not too small; just the way they are and beautiful.

I think of the babies who have suckled at this breast that will soon be gone; the lovers whose hands and lips have caressed its soft skin, its upright rosy nipple. It feels inconceivable that a surgeon—a woman at that—will skillfully remove this most precious part of my body. I am sick with fear—not at the immediate outcome of the operation, for I know the body can survive without a breast, as it cannot without a heart or liver, but at this violent intrusion into the core of my femininity.

What will they do with my breast once it is removed and the pathology lab has done its tests? Will they just put it in the medical garbage along with used needles and soiled dressings? Will they provide it a dignified cremation?

ᘒᘒ ᘒᘒ

I am aware of sunlight on red leaves outside the window, shadows of birds, the whoosh of distant freeway traffic.

My breast is gone. I feel exhausted, relieved it is all over. Waiting for surgery, I space out on Halcyon, listen to a Bernie Siegel meditation tape, doze, and float. Then I am on a gurney being wheeled by a sandy-haired man, lights flashing by overhead. I cover my eyes. The anesthetist looks down, smiling. She asks me something. I am g - o - n - e …

A wretched night after I wake up—heaving, vomiting. Lying still, trying not to move, sucking ice cubes. More heaving. Sun glinting behind long drapes.

By breakfast time, I feel almost normal again. A blah meal of cream of wheat and orange juice, but at least something in me that stays down. There is surprisingly little pain around the incision. I am hooked up to an IV drip to give myself morphine. A nurse in a flowery cotton jacket breezes into the room and adjusts my pillows.

"Don't forget, honey, if you're in pain, press the blue knob."

"I don't feel any pain."

By mid-morning, they unhook me and I go for a walk up and down the corridor. My body feels slowed down, but strong.

Visitors come after lunch; friends phone. Lucy and Sara walk with me into the hospital garden. No smell of disinfectant here; no rattle of trolleys. Just the sweet smell of grass, starlings chirping, a squirrel collecting acorns. Figures move quietly between buildings. Shadows of olive and maple cast patterns on the ground. Later, I do the same walk with Carolyn and, after dark, when it is still balmy-warm, with Frances and Stephen. The garden is such a welcome contrast to the hospital interior. I feel my body relax as I step outdoors, coming alive again.

My daughter Lucy arrives to take me home. She has put plants and flowers in my bedroom ; a spiral of stones from Iona on my dresser and on the largest stone, a tiny figure of White Tara, the Buddhist bodhisattva of compassion who brings healing to those who are hurt or wounded. Sunlight falls on the quilt. Pushkin, our cat, sits on my lap and stares at me through yellow slit eyes: "Where have you been?"

Before cancer, I was always robustly healthy. I rarely had colds, never had flu, and in twenty-five years of teaching, only once took a day off sick. I rarely thought about my body. It was something I walked around in, like my clothes. As to thinking about inevitable decay and death, that was out of the question, banished from consciousness like some unruly child ejected from the quiet order of a Victorian sitting room.

Wth a diagnosis of cancer I can no longer live with the myth that I alone, by some miracle of heaven, am immortal. Before, I had totally ignored my body; now, it becomes, reluctantly, my total focus.

❧ ❧

The pathology report shows six out of seventeen lymph nodes are cancerous. After hearing the news, I sit in the hospital garden feeling both stunned and surprisingly calm. A breeze blows hair over my eyes. People are moving along the paths: a pink-coated volunteer pushes an empty wheelchair; a woman dressed in purple sits pensively in the shade and stares across the garden in my direction. The top branches of an olive sway gently, as if breathing.

Write myself into hope, that's what I have to do. I always feel nurtured in this place—birds, shadows, breeze, solid tree trunks. The natural world continues, ever-changing, merging, molding, emerging, singing, urging me to reach deeply into my own inner nature where all is well. All is very, very well.

I meet the oncologist who is to oversee my chemo treatments. Dr. S. strides into the little white holding cell where I sit cold and terrified in my paper hospital gown, and I am initially impressed. He is tall and distinguished looking; he shakes my hand firmly. My friend Sara, who faithfully comes with me to most of my appointments, feeds him a set of questions I have prepared and writes down the answers. Dr. S. tears a strip of paper from the examination table and proceeds to draw the tumor and various key organs with a fat, black magic marker.

"You know you have a very aggressive type of tumor, don't you?" he inquires brusquely.

"Yes," I reply meekly, feeling like a child being admonished for coming late to school.

"Good. Some people just won't accept it, you know. They go into total denial. You'd be surprised."

He proceeds to talk in a loud, authoritative voice while recording cancer types, tumor sizes, average survival rates, and levels of chemo doses with his magic marker. "You'll need adriamycin cytoxine. Four doses. That's the limit we can give you or it weakens the muscles of your heart."

I shrink into my skimpy hospital garb and want to vomit.

"It's in your lymph nodes ... Hmm ... six out of seventeen. With this aggressive a tumor, that's like a truck barreling down a freeway out of control. I recommend you go home, make your will, and get your affairs in order. Make an appointment at reception for your first chemo dose next week." And with that, he is gone.

Sara helps me into my clothes and I cry all the way home. After she leaves, I lie sobbing on the living room floor, hysterical with fear and digging my nails angrily into the soft beige pile of the carpet. The next day, I call oncology and ask to be transferred to the only woman in the department.

A week later, I fly down to Los Angeles to see Doug Johnson, a healer who once cured a friend of mine of uterine cancer. Doug is in his fifties, with a ruddy face and curly reddish hair; he lives in Silver Lake, a modest neighborhood of small detached houses. Silver Lake. I like that name.

I sit in a straight-backed chair in a low-lit room full of funky furniture and dusty ornaments. He sits at a right angle to me, holding his hands an inch or so from my back and chest, and later, over my stomach. Doug is a psychic healer.

"How did you become a healer?" I ask.

"Oh, it goes way back. I was born in Minneapolis. My grandparents had emigrated from Sweden. They loved the forests in Minnesota."

Doug shifts his chair to the other side. A fluffy orange cat wanders in from the garden through a door left ajar, and curls up on a chair covered in faded purple velvet.

"My mother had a heart problem. She died when I was only nine. I have the same problem; I take care of my health."

A clock strikes somewhere. I sink deeper into my chair.

"Does it matter that we're talking?" I ask. "I mean, does it interfere with the healing?"

"Oh no! It doesn't help for me to concentrate. In fact, I'm less effective. Yes, well, when I was a young man, I worked at Dayton's, a department store in Minneapolis. One day, an older colleague of mine had a stroke and I went to visit her at the hospital. Impulsively, I laid my hands on her. The next day she was a whole lot better. That's how it all started."

Doug asks me some questions about my life. We chat; I feel very relaxed in his presence. I start to yawn a lot.

"That's good ... good! It feels like something is lifting. You'll begin to feel lighter."

The orange cat stretches, then settles back, watching us through half-closed eyes.

"You have a long life ahead of you," Doug reassures me as I prepare to leave. "The most important thing is to ask yourself the question: What is my purpose in life?"

After the second and last treatment with Doug, I sit and write in a sunny café courtyard in Pacific Palisades and feel as calm and happy as I have in the past two months. Bernie Siegel, in *Love, Medicine and Miracles,* writes of people finding lucky pennies when they make an important and correct decision on their healing path. I glance under the table and see a shiny penny on the brick floor. A good omen.

A few days later, I am at the Zen Center at Green Gulch Farm in Marin County near San Francisco, a place I go to almost every Sunday morning. Tenshin Reb Anderson sits cross-legged before us, his brown Buddhist robes draped over his upright body. As if reiterating Doug's suggestion, Reb urges us to ask ourselves: What is my ultimate concern? Then he urges us to let go of those things that don't support that concern. "Every waking moment can be seen as a garbage dump or a treasure of many jewels. Every person you meet, every place you are, is a source of light. Enlightenment is inherent in everything, yet it is important not to envisage it as some 'thing,' or as no 'thing.' Enlightenment can come to you in worry or anxiety, as much as in calmness and non-grasping. The light that shows you the way to go is in the darkness as well as in the sky."

What is my ultimate concern? To stay alive, in good health, and to relish each moment as a gift.

ॐ ॐ

Through a friend, I discover Deeahna, a psychologist in Berkeley who uses healing imagery to work with people who have life-threatening illnesses. She focuses on the emotions that are aroused by illness and medical treatment—panic, anger, bewilderment, exhaustion—emotions with which medical personnel have neither the ability nor the inclination to cope. As soon as I see the amenities she provides in her waiting room—hot water and a dozen varieties of herbal and black teas—I know that I will like her.

I am calmed by her presence, by the view of a large tree behind her house and the incongruous sounds, somewhere in the neighborhood, of chickens. I bring her up to date on the prognosis, the surgery, the plans for chemotherapy. Soon, I am talking about "doing too much," a problem throughout my single-parent and professional life and something I am repeating even now—reading books on cancer, seeking out healers, going to medical libraries, and on and on. Given my personality and the fear that my days are numbered, I don't know what else to do.

"On hearing they have cancer," Deeahna remarks, "some people go into complete denial and carry on as if nothing has happened."

I laugh. That is *not* my problem.

The next time I see Deeahna, she asks me: "What place would be the most healing place for you to be right now?" I see my garden: the avocado tree with glossy leaves; the orange tree bending over the fence from a neighbor's yard; birds perched on the feeder outside my kitchen window. Then instantly, in my imagination, I am on Iona. I sigh deeply. Yes, *this* is my healing place, my place of calm and inner peace.

I describe it to Deeahna and she invites me to sit back, relax, close my eyes, and imagine returning there. I see myself on the ferry approaching the island; I see the familiar undulating topography, the village, the abbey, and the roofs of distant dwellings. The ferry docks. I walk down the steel ramp of the boat and up the concrete ferry slip. I see myself walking past the ruins of the nunnery, the parish church, the St. Columba Hotel, and the abbey. There are sheep and lambs on the hillsides; seagulls drift overhead. I come to a gate, turn off the road onto a track, and clamber my way between exposed rocks to the summit of Dun I, the highest point on the island.

I lie down on the short-cropped grass and, in my imagination, relax and melt into the landscape. My body and the island become one. Am I on Iona or in a chair in Deeahna's office, imagining I am there? Time and space collapse. I hear Deeahna's distant voice asking quietly: "And if you were to imagine the cancer cells right now, what would they look like?" I see small, worm-like creatures under the surface of the landscape, under the surface of my skin. They can do me harm; they need to be extracted, to be rendered harmless.

"Your immune system, the white blood cells in your body, are ready to assist you. What do you imagine they look like?"

The worm-like creatures seem to be like maggots now: white, secret, cut off from the light. Then, out of the sky, seagulls swoop down. They alight on the greensward of the island, my body, and start to move around rhythmically on their feet.

Suddenly, I am swept back in time to a visit to the island sometime in the 1980s. I am leaning on a gate watching ewes and lambs graze when a lone gull appears. It seems to dance on the grass, moving in a small circle, tapping its feet, stopping to eye the grass, then moving sideways and tapping again. Swiftly, it pecks an earthworm out of the sod, swallows it, and taps again. Can this bird be simulating the rain in order to draw worms to the surface? It seems unlikely.

That night on Iona, Christa and I, staying with others at Traigh Bhan, treat ourselves to dinner at the St. Columba Hotel. There is an exhibit of paintings on the walls of the sea-facing dining room. While we wait for the food to arrive, I am drawn across the room to look at a small watercolor. When close enough, I am startled to see its title: "Seagull Dancing for Worms."

I hear a rooster crow. For an instant, I am back in the comfortable, tipped-back chair in Deeahna's office in Berkeley. Then, in a flash, I once again imagine myself on Iona, with seagulls, my white blood cells, dancing on the grass. The worm-like cancer cells come inching to the surface and are immediately eaten by the powerful gray-and-white birds waiting expectantly for them. The cancer cells are numberless, but so are the seagulls, their strong orange beaks poised hungrily, their eyes alert for any unusual movement amid the grass stems at their feet.

After some time immersed in these imaginings and talking to Deeahna in a low, far-away voice, I slowly extract myself from the landscape of Iona and am drawn back to the present moment, to the room in Berkeley where we both sit. A chicken cackles somewhere nearby, exuberant at the appearance of an egg. Deeahna hands me the relaxation tape of our session and, with an encouraging smile, urges me to listen to it at least once a day until I come back for my next appointment. Sunlight caresses gently moving red leaves outside her office window as I leave.

ॐ ॐ

As the appointment for my first chemo infusion draws closer, I grow more and more fearful. On the day itself, I count down the hours: eight hours from now, four hours, three hours. Sara arrives to drive me to the hospital in Walnut Creek. I sit tense in the passenger seat and try to make conversation.

Joanne, the oncology nurse, exudes quiet reassurance and sits me in a comfortable infusion chair with wide arms and support for my legs. I put on headphones and start listening to a relaxation tape, trying to ignore the activity around me. An IV pole is positioned next to my chair and a plastic bag containing red liquid is hung from its metal arm like a body from a lynching tree. I flinch as Joanne inserts a needle into a vein in my left arm. She starts the flow of red liquid into my body. I close my eyes and focus on the soft voice on the relaxation tape, which takes me to a forest, a lake, birdsong—far, far away.

I feel wretched for the next two days: vomiting, retching, dozing. Jason and Lucy come up from Santa Cruz where they are both at university. They bring me some marijuana and a bubble pipe. "Try it, Mom. Try it! It will stop you feeling nauseous." I try it, but since I've never smoked and don't know how to inhale, I'm not sure it does much good. But it is a kind gesture. The next day, I go for a short walk, admire the flowers in a neighbor's garden, and feel my strength returning.

ཿ ཿ

A silent contemplative retreat led by Marv Hiles, a former Presbyterian minister, and his wife, Nancy, comes at a perfect time. I need to get away from home, from phone calls and get-well cards, and just *be*. I sit in the cloister at Santa Sabina Retreat Center in San Rafael and cannot imagine a better place to be than this garden with its encircling brick-paved pathway. I hear the gentle sound of the fountain in the center of the garden; I see a swarm of gnats hovering in the sunlight.

The sword-like leaves of a Douglas iris move in the breeze; from the tip of one leaf, the shimmering remains of a spider's web waves like a tiny silken banner.

One morning on the retreat, we listen to a tape of a Romanian folktale read by Clarissa Pinkola-Estes. An old, weary man staggers through the forest to a cottage where an old woman rocks him by the fire saying, "There, there … there, there," through the night. During the night, he becomes a young man and, by morning, he is an infant. She plucks three golden hairs from his head just before he walks out of the cottage and flies up to become the sun.

As I listen, I see myself as the old man lost in the forest. The old woman beckons me in and takes me, exhausted, into her arms. "There, there," she croons as she rocks me before the fire. "There, there," she comforts me. "I am here—now and always—ready to welcome and comfort you. I am the loving mother who can hold and nurture you."

I see myself becoming young and whole and radiant as the man in the story did. And just before I leave as an infant to become the sun, the old woman plucks three golden hairs from my head—three things that I no longer need to complete my journey. They are busy-ness, control, and self-pity. All I need to do when I am lost or fearful is to sit very still, do nothing, and comfort myself: "There, there … There, there... There, there...."

The next day, I awake early to the sounds of a squirrel chattering in alarm. Hazily, I recall a dream in which I encounter a long line of children walking on their knees in some kind of ritual pilgrimage. They look so sad; I feel badly for them. One stops and raises her knee for me to pat. Later, in my imagination, I continue the story of the dream. The long line of children is all of us who have cancer. We have lost our innocence; we have been brought to our knees. The line is endless. We are on a painful journey. One child raises her bloody knee for me to pat. I ask her name. It is Clare. I start to cry. I pick up the child and gather her in my arms to comfort her. "There, there," I croon. "There, there."

I imagine carrying the child until we come to a barren place where we find a dragon and a female raven. They invite us to stay with them. The dragon lights a fire with his fiery tongue and the four of us settle down for the night, forming a circle around the flames. It feels comforting, peaceful, as though the dragon and the raven are also parts of me. The dragon is my restless, sometimes passionate, creative side, my fast-paced academic past; the raven—also creative, in a softer, more reflective vein—is my slower, more spiritual nature, which now has time to flower. At the end of my extended dream, we form a quaternity, a balanced whole: wounded child, caring adult, passionate professional, spiritual soul-searcher. I feel deeply comforted by this image.

❧ ❧

Whenever I have the energy, I go to the Zen Center on Sunday mornings. On this morning, I drive the hour or so from my home in Berkeley and park at Muir Beach. Fog is lifting in a long sigh over Green Gulch Valley. Ducks feed greedily on the muddy grass where water from recent Pacific storms is receding. A horse stands awkwardly on a steep slope by Redwood Creek, its muzzle in the water: no sloppy lapping of a thirsty dog, no delicate tongue twists of a cat at its bowl. Horses drink silently, their soft lips immersed in water, low ripples furrowing the surface in a mandala-like circle round the point where animal and element meet.

At the Zen Center, Abbot Norman Fischer reminds us that spiritual practice is not another thing to do, but the underlying philosophy of *everything* we do. It doesn't take time; it *is* time. When I garden, I take care of my body. When I remember painful rejections in academia, it is an opportunity to practice forgiveness. That is hard for me to do. When I recall hurtful things I have done to others, it is an opportunity to practice forgiving myself. That is also hard to do. When I visit a friend with problems, I practice compassionate listening. When I drive in the rush hour, I learn to practice patience. Spiritual practice is the horse's muzzle in Redwood Creek—absorbing what flows into our lives without grasping, without rejecting, without making noise or impeding the flow. Observing the natural world, we receive teachings on the path.

One Sunday, I arrive at the Zen Center too late to go in for meditation, so I settle onto a warm, sunny bench in the garden. Meditation seems so much easier, so much deeper, outdoors. The sounds of birdsong and distant voices float in and out of my consciousness with barely a ripple. I feel calm, detached, centered. When the deep-throated bell rings to mark the end of meditation, I notice a branch of bamboo bending low over the grass, extending almost horizontally out from the hedge that bounds the garden. Though perhaps in danger of breaking off, its leaves are thrust out into a blaze of sunlight; they shine and quiver like golden banners, while the leaves of its vertical brothers stand in deep shade. It seems to speak of flexibility, of the benefits of a vulnerable position, of the need to surrender in order to feel the healing rays of insight.

⁂

A few days later, my hair starts to fall out. At first, there are just a few more hairs than usual in my brush; then I notice a soft haze of hairs on my pillow. Finally, I stand over the compost heap at the bottom of the garden and comb vigorously. My hair comes out in great clumps until I am well and truly bald. It seems an appropriate place for my hair to rest, returning eventually to the soil in my garden, nurturing new growth. Ashes to ashes; dust to dust.

I can barely look at myself in the mirror before I pull on a colorful babushka-like scarf to cover my nakedness. There seems something shameful about losing your hair. Maybe it is the photos I remember from soon after the war when French women accused of collaborating with the Germans had their heads shaved and were paraded in town squares to be jeered at by former neighbors.

Our hair is such an intrinsic part of who we are. Born in the era of cute, curly-haired, blonde Shirley Temple, I was raised to feel that my straight, mousey hair was—well—unfortunate. In the 1940s, my mother experimented on me with do-it-yourself home perms, and the resultant frizziness didn't seem much better than what had come before. By the time I was in high school, I was going to bed with large, uncomfortable rollers in my hair, trying to coax the dreaded straightness into sexy curls.

Finally, in the Sixties in Berkeley, my then-boyfriend David persuaded me to have my hair cut into bangs (strange American word for fringe), and styled to hang straight. I was amazed. I looked good and the style was in keeping with the pervasive straight-hair-no-make-up fashion of those times.

Now, even that hair is gone. It seems almost worse than losing a breast; that I can disguise with a squishy, plastic "Nearly Me" prosthesis tucked in my bra. But wearing a wig, could I do that? Would it fool anyone? Ortha, a friend and former student who has gone through chemo, gives me her collection of hats, and I choose a beige beret with a peak that looks quite chic and French. I start to feel better about my baldness.

❧ ❧

Sessions of healing imagery with Deeahna become part of my weekly routine. I talk about what I am feeling, the reactions (helpful and otherwise) of friends, my energy level. I relax into the tipped-back chair and close my eyes. I describe my now-familiar arrival on Iona in a low voice. I can hear the waves; I can smell the salt air.

"What about the maggots?" Deeahna enquires. "Can you see them?"

In my mind's eye, I walk down to the beach below Traigh Bhan, the White Strand of the Monks, where monks from the abbey were once slaughtered by marauding Vikings.

"No, I can't see any maggots, but I can see crabs," I murmur. "Yes! Dozens, hundreds of crabs! They're coming out of the sea. They're crawling up onto the dunes. Oh—there are so many, so many!"

I watch them in silence, partly fascinated, partly horrified.

"What's happening now?" Deeahna asks quietly.

"They've reached the grazing land above the beach. They're eating the grass. The sheep are running away; the crabs are advancing." I stop speaking and observe the scene unfolding as if in a movie. I breathe deeply. "They are eating the grass down to the roots. They're destroying the island!"

"Where are the seagulls? Can they help?"

Suddenly, they are there—swarms of them. They start to dive, plucking up crabs and flying off with them toward the west, out into the Atlantic, dropping them into deep water and returning for more. The seagulls seem to be winning, but more crabs emerge from the sea.

Prior to my third chemo infusion, they take the usual blood test at the hospital and inform me that my white-blood-cell count is too low to continue. At my next appointment with Deeahna, she encourages me to imagine more helpers ridding the island of crabs.

In my imagination, I watch the seagulls, dependable as always. "I can see people coming to help!" I tell Deeahna excitedly. "Oh—they are in boats. There are lots and lots of small boats coming across from Mull. They are soldiers! They have swords!"

I watch with fascination as the soldiers disembark and start to spear the crabs, which are coming ashore all along the eastern edge of the island.

"They are killing them! They are killing the crabs!" I say out loud, gripping the arms of my chair. "And now I see dolphins. *Lots* of dolphins swimming just off-shore. They are eating the crabs, swallowing them whole before they can get to the beach."

I let out a long sigh.

"You have reinforcements," says Deeahna. "They have come to assist you."

I feel my energy slowly returning. A few days later, after listening to my seagulls/soldiers/dolphins tape twice each day and going to the hospital for several injections of Neupogen, my white-blood-cell count is deemed high enough for chemo to recommence—something I hope for and dread in equal measure.

CHAPTER 8

ℰↄ

A Second Warning

*Stories have to repair the damage that illness has done
to the ill person's sense of where she is in life, and where
she may be going ... People tell stories not just to work
out their own changing identities, but also to guide others
who will follow them. They seek not to provide a map that
can guide others—each must create his own—but rather
to witness the experience of reconstructing one's own
map.* —Arthur W. Frank[23]

Four months after finding the lump in my breast, I feel as if I have turned a subtle corner. I stop reading books about cancer and start to read novels, autobiography, and humor. My days follow a quiet routine: a healthy breakfast, vitamins, reading. A hot lunch, perhaps a half-hour walk or some gardening, a nap listening to one of my relaxation tapes, reading. Then dinner and TV, or talking to friends on the phone. To bed at ten. Not long ago, all this seemed narcissistic and boring. Now, it feels comfortable; just what I have to do.

I do not think of cancer as something to be "fought," as something with which I am "at war." Militaristic analogies seem counterproductive. Having weathered the first few months of fear and panic surrounding surgery and chemotherapy, the word "surrender" keeps re-appearing in my mind. I am willing to accept what is.

I start to focus more on my work: doing final editing of the book I have now entitled *House as a Mirror of Self*; meeting with the publishers; talking with an ex-student, Carolyn F., about a paper we are completing on children's outdoor play in housing projects. People tell me how relaxed I look. I feel relaxed. With no major stress in my life, I decide each day what I will do, where I will go. I practice mindfulness. I listen to my body: eat when I feel hungry, rest when I feel tired. This is my work, what I have to do to heal.

The trouble with looking so well is that family and friends think everything is normal. They want to believe everything is normal, as do I. But everything isn't normal. My body is replenishing, healing, learning to recognize irregular cells and to banish them. Illness is a fine spiritual teacher, demanding attention in the moment, requiring that the body be heard.

I remember thankfully the words of Fritz Perls, gestalt therapy guru of the Sixties and the early days of the Esalen Institute in California. "There can be no anxiety in the present moment," he growled in his guttural German accent, holding his cigarette between nicotine-stained fingers. "Anxiety comes from looking back with regret, or looking forward with apprehension. Stay grounded in the present moment … breathing in, sound of a bird, stomach full, smoke curling from cigarette … that is all there is—yah? No anxiety; just what is. Anxiety is the gap between the 'now' and the 'then.'" Stroking his beard, he tapped his cigarette ash into an ashtray and challenged us to Be Here Now.

As the day of my last chemo treatment approaches, images laced with anxiety pollute my thoughts: the red bag hanging from the IV pole, the needle going into my vein, the face across the room of a young man who looks so ill, so sad, so alone.

"But that is not now," I admonish myself, picturing these fear-inducing thoughts as a kite, which I haul in, pulling the string hand over hand until the sky is empty and I am totally aware of the steam rising from a cup of tea on the table in front of me—the cat purring on my lap, laughter from children in the street. This is now. This is all there is. Be Here Now.

❧ ❧

Sometimes, I arrive for my appointment with Deeahna so tired I can barely talk. I hold my head in my hands, weeping. "I feel so useless, so useless," is all I can manage to say. It is hard enough to have just taken early retirement, to have little contact with former colleagues, but to have to cajole myself into doing nothing—to rest and recuperate—is almost too much to bear.

Over the years, scarcely realizing it, I fully embraced the notion that to be worthy in society is to be productive. The "publish or perish" mantra of academia impelled me into a mindset in which I evaluated each day in terms of how much I had accomplished. Work became all important to me. My marriage crumbled. Single-parent life became a logistical nightmare as I juggled work, mothering, house-care, and what little remained of my social life. And now my body, my caregivers, my family, and my friends are all demanding that I slow down. This transformation is almost as painful as the disease that has prompted the change.

Driving home from Deeahna's one day in January, my attention is drawn to a striking row of leafless London plane trees on Hopkins Street. I stop the car to look at them more closely. I am beginning to understand that, when something pulls at my attention, it is likely to hold an important message. Stand firm as we do, the trees seem to say. We are resting now—no leaves, no growth. It's a time to hibernate and recoup; without this time of non-doing, we would not be able to form buds in the spring and draw on our sap to feed summer's growth. Let yourself rest and be. You are gathering strength for a new role that awaits you.

❦ ❦

As I wait to give a guest lecture in a course I created twenty-five years ago at Berkeley (now taught by two former students, Louise M. and Carolyn F.), I realize I don't really miss teaching any more. Once, I cared about inspiring young students to think about how the physical environment affects people's lives. What I want to communicate now is something totally different. It is personal, spiritual, emotional. And the people I want to hear me are middle-aged and beyond—people, particularly women, who are looking closely at their lives; people who want to explore their own inner truth.

I have a dream in which I find myself cast as Lady Macbeth in a play. It is opening night, but I haven't learned my lines. I am terrified and confused. What should I do? Perhaps I can fake it, make up the lines as I go along. Shakespeare? Perhaps not. If I go ahead and appear, I'll embarrass the cast and the director. If I don't show up, I'll ruin the play; they won't be able to open. Curtain time gets closer and closer. Eventually, in a phone booth, struggling with books, papers, change, and phone numbers, I call and leave a message on the director's answering machine. I am sick; I cannot appear in the play.

This dream is a perfect metaphor for what has happened to me. I think I need to perform (work, teach, lecture), but I've lost the energy and will-power to do it. I don't know my lines; I feel badly, guilty about it. I am going to let people down—the students, my peers. I can't think of a way out. I start to empty my office (papers and books in the phone booth), and then I'm diagnosed with cancer. I call in sick. I've found the perfect excuse for not performing.

꙰ ꙰

I start attending a support group for women with cancer. We meet in an over-heated upper room at Alta Bates Hospital; a social worker is there to guide us. Nine women with breast cancer, erratic cells eating away at the tissue of that most precious part of the female body: pink globes of milky nurturance, raised red nipples of sexual desire, curved silhouettes beneath stretched silk blouses.

Janice speaks first. She starts chemo next week and her voice quavers, the fingers of her right hand plucking nervously at the stitching in her fluffy black sweater. I pick up her anxiety and begin to pick at my nails until one is sharp and jagged. I rub it against my lower lip. It gives me a curious kind of pleasure, of reassurance.

"It won't be so bad," Roberta assures Janice. "I hardly had any nausea; just increasing tiredness."

Janice doesn't look reassured. "Your hair looks great!" someone says in an upbeat tone of voice. I am still picking at my nails, looking down at my lap, wondering why there is a long silence. Then I realize the remark is directed at me.

"Oh—my hair. Isn't it strange? My hair is normally straight and mousy, but it's growing back dark and curly. My mother felt so bad that

I was born with straight hair and kept telling me I'd be a lot prettier if it were curly. Well—now it is!"

The other women beam and smile. Lucille, who lives in the Berkeley hills and is usually silent throughout our meeting, tells of her normally curly hair that has grown back straight. Chemo does strange things to the body.

"Does anyone have any issues or questions they want to raise?" asks Jane the social worker, smiling in a slightly forced kind of way.

"Yes, I do." We focus our attention on Deborah, a young woman who recently joined the group. "I have two small children and I'm a single parent. I have to keep working, but sometimes I need to take half a day off to go to the cancer clinic. Should I tell my boss? Will he fire me?" She starts to cry softly and Jane hands her the box of tissues.

"No, don't tell him," I say, surprised at my vehemence. "It's none of his business."

The other women agree and start a debate on whether it's legal to fire people because they have cancer.

As the discussion rambles on in the background, I reflect on how lucky I am to have cancer when I am older, retired with a decent pension, my children grown, good friends. I look across the room at Deborah, who is staring at the linoleum floor, dabbing her eyes occasionally with a wadded-up piece of tissue. Yes, I am lucky. I can't imagine how I would cope if I were in Deborah's shoes. I want to cross the room and put my arms around her, but I don't. I am afraid.

❧ ❧

One week in our support group, someone recommends a yoga class she is attending. Why not, I think. I want to pull out all the stops, try everything. I am taking extra vitamins, meditating, having acupuncture treatments, buying only organic food. Yoga sounds like a good idea. The class meets not far from my home in a community center that offers yoga and ballet classes, and houses a pre-school and a theatre.

I am in yoga class lying prone on the floor. I can hear piano music floating up through the floorboards; the notes seep into my ears like honey, like the purring of a contented cat. It is so delicious to be given permission to relax, to do nothing but experience my breath pouring in and pouring out. It isn't even the kind of yoga I have heard about—standing on your head, that kind of stuff. It is restorative yoga for people who have back problems or are recovering from cancer. The music from the ballet class below lulls me into a state of almost-sleep. Images drift in and out of my mind—clouds, waves, flowers, grasses, waterfalls. Nothing to do but be prone and silent as a corpse—like a body ready for burial, like a baby sleeping.

The class is over. I pull on my shoes and jacket, ready for the walk home. Underneath the yoga room is another studio where a ballet class is in progress. As I walk by, I stop at a window where a piece of paper covering the glass has been scratched away. I bend down and squint to see what is happening inside. I can just see the masculine hands of the pianist running expertly over the keys, but not his torso or face. Then three young girls come into view, leaping like pink gazelles in time with the music, their taut legs outstretched, their firm arms flung sideways in unison. They disappear from view, then three more girls appear, repeating the leaping movements so effortlessly it seems as if they have been wound up like dancing dolls.

I sigh, stand up clutching my back, and continue on my walk home. I can no longer leap like a gazelle. In fact, sometimes it is an effort even to walk a short distance. I realize that, now, I often hold onto banisters, fearful that I may trip; that I get breathless walking along College Avenue, which had, in my younger days, seemed perfectly flat, but now appears to be tilting slightly uphill.

This is what it is like to grow old, I think. This is what it is like to slow down, to feel cautious, to lose energy. Does it matter that I can no longer leap like a gazelle? Am I jealous of those girls in the ballet class, glimpsed through the window where the paper has been scratched away? No, I can honestly say there is no jealousy—just a slow, peaceful sinking into an old age where lying prone on the floor with music pouring into my ears is the most delicious of feelings. Perhaps one day, I will welcome lying prone and never moving again with as much deep contentment as the little girls experience waiting their quivering turns to leap like pink gazelles across the shiny, polished studio floor to the lyrical strains of Strauss and the melodies of Debussy.

※ ※

It is January 1995. Chemo finished, I begin to have radiation treatments every day at a hospital only ten minutes from home. I enjoy the walk there and back, looking at people's gardens, taking a different zigzag route each day. There is a house on Russell Street where narcissi bloom in a strip beneath a retaining wall beside the sidewalk. It is always a shock that spring comes so early in California. One day I stop there, look nervously up and down the street, bend down quickly to pick some flowers, take in their sweet perfume, and then walk home purposefully, pretending I have bought them at the florist's. Stealing flowers—it is a weakness of mine, though I only do it where the boundary between private and public space is, shall we say, ambiguous. Not so in my childhood.

It is 1943 in southern England and I am nine years old. Ronnie Land and I have decided to run away from home—not because we're particularly unhappy, but just because it seems like an exciting thing to do. Ronnie says the railway lines that run through Leighton Buzzard go all the way to Scotland where his granny lives. We don't stop to think how long it will take us or how we'll find his granny when we get there. "I bet my mother will be happy I've run away," I whisper to Ronnie. "She has to pay half a crown for my dancing lesson at Miss Cook's on Saturday mornings and I hate dancing. I know she'll be glad of the money."

Ronnie and I start to prepare secretly for our great adventure. In a wood near our adjacent homes, we hide our bikes (we are planning to cycle beside the railway tracks) and start to secrete scraps of food in our saddle bags. "We mustn't forget our gas masks," I remind Ronnie. Even in this moment of childhood rebellion, we remember the rules: Take your gas mask with you wherever you go. There was an intense fear that Hitler would use gas in this war. Thirty-eight million gas masks were issued in 1938. Ronnie and I had two of them.

What will we do for money on our trip? That's where the stolen flowers come in. We have access to the extensive grounds of the Rothschild estate where we both live. The seventy gardeners employed before the war to tend the formal landscape around the Big House— herbaceous borders, rock gardens, ponds, statuary—are now reduced to three elderly men too old to serve in the army. Ronnie and I sneak through the large hillside rock garden and pick bunches of exotic Alpine flowers peeking out between dandelions, sow thistle, and hogweed. Then we go from house to house on the estate offering them for "six-pence a bunch ... it's for the Red Cross." (We not only steal; we sell what we've stolen under false pretences!) That evening when my mother returns from her job at a nearby munitions factory, Mrs. Maynard (wife of the Rothschild butler) stops by for a chat. "How nice of Ronnie and Clare to be raising money for the Red Cross." I shrink into my chair and hold my breath. Later, in an unaccustomed display of warmth, my mother takes me on her knee and gently explains that what Ronnie and I did was wrong. I cry with shame and embarrassment, but don't tell her why we needed the money. Our plans for running away next Saturday are still "on."

The day arrives and we wheel our bikes up the driveway, past the cricket field. A game is in full-swing: an RAF team from Wing Airfield versus a team from the village. There may be a war on, but cricket must continue! Ronnie wants to watch, so we settle down on the grass and he patiently explains the game to me. An hour later, we're feeling hungry and decide to go home for lunch. "We'll run away tomorrow instead," suggests Ronnie, and I readily agree. The next day, we say nothing to each other, or the next day. Our plans for running away to Scotland drift away, eventually forgotten, until ... lying on a gurney half a lifetime later, staring up at white ceiling tiles as radiation machinery zaps me where little blue "Xs" mark the spot, I think of stolen flowers and the narcissi I will pick on my walk home along Russell Street, and the many times I have "run away" to Scotland in my imagination.

⁂

Lucy is home from college and I ask her to help me by clearing some brambles beyond the compost pile. Soon, she comes running back to the house with a beautifully formed empty bird's nest she has found. Its outer structure is made from thick dried grasses woven together in a basket form more than an inch thick. The soft, hollowed inner void is lined with hair. As I pull out a strand, I realize it is human hair, some blonde, some gray. Then, with a jolt, I realize that it is *my* hair, combed

in long, straight strands into the compost last October. I cry as I touch the nest—a perfect gift from nature, from the garden, from spirit-birds back to me. It feels like a symbol of re-birth, just as my new hair, surprisingly curly, starts to re-adorn my head.

❧ ❧

"The obstacles in our path are not obstacles, they *are* the path." Deena Metzger, the poet, is addressing a conference for people dealing with cancer—Cancer as a Turning point: From Surviving to Thriving. I start to take notes.

> The onset of cancer rivets us and awakes us deeply to the sacredness of the body. It provides an extraordinary opportunity to make a shift. Illness in individuals, and in society, is a sign of imbalance. We're in a culture of imbalance. Healing at this time is a political act. We all have a responsibility to fight for our own lives. "To cure" may be easy; "to heal" takes much greater strength and commitment. In a struggle for a life that

feels right, you are working for everyone. The task is to lead an authentic life. Heal your life and then your life heals you.

I look around the large auditorium. I feel a surge of compassion for these people, young and old, their faces revealing fear and hope. Deena continues:

> The life force breaks through in our spirit as the cancer breaks through our cell walls. It is the life force that is not being heard. Cancer is the silence breaking out. Ask yourself: Who inside, or out, wants me to be silent? We must speak out, because society is killing us. What matters is finding what is true, what is passionate for *you*.

Metzger had breast cancer and started to write about all the truth she knew, looking for what she had silenced in her life. She chose not to have reconstructive surgery after a power failure occurred in the hospital just prior to the procedure. The photo she subsequently had taken of herself, "Determined Joy," is the image she wants to convey. In the picture, she is standing naked on a hilltop, arms flung wide, with a tree tattooed on the scar across her flat chest. "I never look in the mirror and forget I have cancer.... I never forget the changes I've made in my life. Cancer kicked me into my own life."

I drive home inspired by her words. What is it in me that has been silenced?

⁂

Nearing the end of six weeks of radiation treatment, I drive up to visit my friend Louise D. at her family home hidden on a hillside of California live oaks above the Napa Valley vineyards. In a break between February showers, I go for a walk. Winter woodland. Colors and sounds are muted, as if in the pause between in-breath and out-breath. Fallen leaves from a live oak form cups of copper-brown liquid. No sounds in this place of unmoving tree trunks gently embraced by moss. Then—a flock of wild turkeys appear, their bodies brushing the dead grasses with a soft whirring breath. They stop. I stop. Slowly, one, then two, then most of the flock move cautiously toward me. I let my feet grow roots; my hanging arms become dead tree limbs. The turkeys come closer. I dissolve into tree-ness. Then, one of the turkeys that has remained motionless, suspicious, during this tremulous encounter, takes off with racing feet up the hillside. The others quickly follow its lead, their tan-colored tail feathers splaying out like rudders as they wheel away under the trees and out of sight.

A wind blows up. The last remaining leaves on a skeletal oak quiver and fall, silhouetted against the colorless winter sky like soft brown butterflies. Childhood memories of scavenging cloud my eyes. I start to see the woodland for what it has to offer, what I can take away with me. Firewood, kindling; toyon berries and shriveled grapes to put on the bird feeder, a feast for city birds; moss for making a miniature landscape in a bowl, as Auntie Jean taught me long ago. Tree gifts.

I return to the house and pick up a book—John Fowles' and Frank Horvat's *The Tree*. Its message is a challenge: Science has separated us almost inexorably from the experience of nature; attempting to communicate the essence of that experience via words or photography or painting is vain self-indulgence. Nature is being. Our experience in it is to be felt, not analyzed or recorded.

How can I hope to remind myself and others of the healing qualities in nature, of the ineffable connection with our environing world that is beyond description, infinitely more complex and subtle than words or pictures can convey? Despite Fowles' pessimism, I feel an urgency to continue with this task. "There is something in the nature of nature," Fowles writes, "in its presentness, its seeming transience, its creative ferment and hidden potential, that corresponds very closely with the wild, or green [wo]man in our psyches ..."[24] Yes, I have succeeded in using my love of nature, my fascination with the physical environment, to provide the impetus for an academic career, but it is this "hidden" aspect of nature that Fowles writes of that now fills me with deep yearning. This is what I want to explore—nature as a mirror of my essential nature, that which I have all but lost in academia and the material busy-ness of my life. The part of me I have silenced.

❧ ❧

The first, hot-off-the-press copy of my book *House as a Mirror of Self* is delivered to my Berkeley home and I feel a surge of pride that I didn't give up through all those years of single-parenthood and publishers' rejections. I smile to myself as I recall a quote from the novelist Saul Bellow that I came across the other day: "I discovered that rejections are not altogether a bad thing. They teach a writer to rely on his own judgment, and to say in his heart of hearts, 'To hell with you.'"[25] Indeed.

I never did get any financial support. Foundations funding architectural research thought my book too weird ("People talking to their houses?"). Those funding the social sciences didn't see the value of exploring our relationship to house and home. So I soldiered on over summer vacations and weekends when the children were with their father. And now it is finished, edited, proof-read, illustrated, printed, bound—and ready to meet the world.

It is ironic that, after searching for some years for a method to probe deeply into people's relationship to home, I found it in a gestalt therapy group I had joined to deal with the pain of my divorce and potential loss of my own home. One evening, Pat, a Catholic sister, spoke of her yearning for the Arizona desert she had left when she moved to California. Anita F.-C., the therapist who guided our group invited Pat to speak to the desert as if it were animate, to tell it of her feelings, and then "become" the desert speaking back to her. Listening to this moving and poetic dialog was a pivotal point in my research. If Pat could conduct a conversation with the desert, why could I not have people engage in dialogs with their houses?

Shortly after that, I joined Anita in a training group in gestalt therapy so that I could learn enough about this powerful role-playing technique to use it responsibly as a research tool. Pat became my first subject, followed by other women in the group, and then by a widening circle of men and women, young and old—people living in places as diverse as up-scale mansions, modest bungalows, rented apartments, houseboats, and illegal hippie domes in the forest. Their stories of homes loved and hated, grasped and rejected, remembered and forgotten, became the rich ingredients of my book. And now it is done.

For most of us, home expresses who we think we are. How far my home was from my own essential wholeness came home to me (no pun intended) when one of my students, Kim D., offered to interview me in the same way that I had interviewed the sixty-plus people whose stories formed the core of my book. I spoke about the choices I'd made in terms of neighborhood, type of house, decor and art work, colors and mementos, and what they seemed to express of my values and preferences. Kim noted all this down and then said quietly: "And what about your garden?" Suddenly, I was in tears, sobbing and unable to say much more that was coherent.

The garden, that small portion of the natural world I can nurture and tend, is a symbol of my soul, of the higher Self (with a capital S); the inside of my house is a symbol of the personal self (with a small s), molded by experience, history, family, society, and education. My tears that day were an expression of how far, how dangerously far, I had allowed my life to become unbalanced. My soul was crying out for recognition and nurture in the one-sided intellectual pressure-cooker of academia. I needed to get away—from my job, from my home, from all the familiar support structures of my life. As Alain de Bolton writes in *The Art of Travel:* "It is not necessarily at home that we best encounter our true selves. The furniture insists that we cannot change because it does not; the domestic setting keeps us tethered to the person we are in ordinary life, but who may not be who we essentially are."[26]

Ironically, it is the book I have written that enables me to "get away," but not in quite the way I had imagined. The publishers arrange for me to go on a promotional tour. When I show the schedule to Deeahna at my next appointment, she is mildly appalled: New York, Boston, Philadelphia, Washington DC, Chicago, Minneapolis, Miami, Dallas, Los Angeles, Seattle. "Even for someone in full health, this would be a challenge. Can you look at this and cut some corners? Smooth it out? Make it easier on yourself? I need to remind you that, when you first came to see me, you told me your primary problem was doing too much." It seems ironic that, now that the book on which I'd worked, on and off, for twenty years is finally out, my journey to publicize it may compromise my health.

About to plunge into book signings and media interviews, I am confused and ambivalent. The hectic last week as I juggle buying clothes, packing, and local interviews, I feel like a puppet with the publishers pulling my strings: "Dance for the people and they'll shell out some money." I know they mean well, but every additional interview they plug into my schedule, every phone call from the Oprah show or the Los Angeles Times or public radio, makes me feel like bowing out, sending someone else on the tour, and retreating to clear up summer growth in my neglected garden. This is not who I am—someone in smart, expensive suits, preparing for radio interviews and bookshop appearances. I feel as though I am playing a part.

On the eve of the tour, I have a poignant dream. I am in a prison. I work there as a woman preparing male prisoners for release. Four men are being discharged. I hand them each 500 dollars, but there is some sleight of hand and, though one of them says he doesn't have his money, I am sure he has. I search my bag as the men listen to a concert. I find a wad of 500 dollars and realize the man was speaking the truth. I find him in a park where people are waiting for their families to pick them up and I apologize. He is very gracious. He is one of my former students. He thanks me for being an inspiration to him. We talk about what he'll do when he's released. He seems happy and expectant. I am relieved he hasn't left and is not angry with me.

My creative, out-in-the-world-professional, masculine side had been closed down and in prison since my illness. Now, as I embark on this book tour, it is released. The feminine part of me, concerned with my health and well-being during recovery, is ready to give the masculine equal time, release, and money. But there is some ambivalence about this: Does this man have the money or not? Finally, masculine and feminine are in accord, in a state of mutual recognition and admiration; the masculine thanks the feminine for her inspiration.

Despite my concerns about overdoing it, I do go on a book tour that takes me across the United States and back. As I return, I settle into my window seat on the airplane and start to write in my journal:

I am so relieved to be on my way home. These past nineteen days have been like a frantic performance I never want to repeat: hotel rooms, airports, bookshop appearances, TV interviews, escorts waiting to drive me to my next appointment. Yet some of it was pleasurable: room service (at Oprah's expense) looking out from my hotel room onto Lake Michigan; a great interview on Minnesota Public Radio by a woman who had carefully read the book and had good questions; a wonderfully appreciative audience at *Books and Books* in Coral Gables, Florida; resting up in Miami Beach, watching bizarrely clad people glide past on roller blades, one with a green iguana draped across his shoulders; creeping through a greenhouse at a botanical garden between appearances in Minneapolis and "stealing" cleome seeds while the guard was reading a book of poetry.

Some of it was terrifying: appearing live on the Oprah show and feeling at my most uptight. The publishers were, of course, most excited about this event; mention of the book on this show will mean a huge boost to sales. But for me, the experience was quite an ordeal: being frisked as we entered the building where the show takes place in Chicago; the frenzy of backstage preparation—hair, make-up, tips from the producer; sitting on-stage before a live audience feeling self-conscious in my newly purchased, out-of-character, pink suit. All this as a panel of so-called experts—an eager designer, a quiet Canadian academic, a photographer of Hollywood homes, and I—are invited to answer the question: "What does your house say about you?"

"This won't be an English tea party," the publisher's business manager had warned me. "You have to grab every moment of air-time you can get. As soon as anyone draws a breath, jump in and mention the book."

But that wasn't how it turned out. The introvert academic that I am was no match for the publicity-hungry New York decorator, sitting on the edge of her seat in purple hose and royal blue mini-skirt. I had my little moments of success, however. When asked which of four couples who stood up in the audience lived in which of four houses that were flashed on the screen, I guessed all four correctly before mini-skirt could open her mouth. And then there was the piece we had taped several days before. Followed by a cameraman, we snooped around the house of an upscale Evanston family who had agreed to leave for the day. Speculating who someone is from what you see in his or her house: now *that* I can do. Something got into me that day. I hammed it up, commenting on junk food in their fridge, wondering why the husband had no suits, putting on the children's tiger bathrobes, holding up the wife's not-so-sexy nightdress. The studio audience laughed, but I felt ashamed as I saw the look on the faces of the couple whose house we had explored sitting in the front row. Show business can be cruel and I'd been part of it.

Now I'm on my way home, flying over the Gulf of Mexico. The surface of the sea 30,000 feet below is pitted with white specks, like stars, like the Milky Way, like a lost drowned galaxy. The world turned upside down.

In this brief flirtation with minor-celebrity status, I feel I've lost touch with my soul. It comes back to remind me in fleeting images of birds. Canada Geese preening on mud-flats between piers on the lower East Side, glimpsed from a taxi. A cacophony of starlings settling at dusk into the cornices of the National Gallery in Washington. Cormorants perched in neat lines on half-submerged buoys on the Intercoastal Waterway. Two turkey vultures landing on a directional sign spanning the freeway that leads to Miami Airport. Birds appear to remind me of spirit—free, soaring, unencumbered. I *will* feel that way again.

🐦 🐦

Back in California, my attention is drawn more and more to birds. Walking up Parker Street in the rain, I glance into a fenced yard and see what I take to be a life-sized sculpture of four geese, but then they move and come cackling toward me. I stand, fascinated, staring. Geese on Parker Street? Ten minutes later, rounding the corner from Telegraph Avenue to Bancroft Way, weaving between damp bodies and tugging umbrellas, I see five starlings in a maple tree. They seem more real, more present, than all the bustling street activity beneath them. What is the meaning of this "more real"? English poet Kathleen Raine writes of her experience with birds:

> To see the heron or the crow was in that remote world, an epiphany of indescribable mystery; not the mystery merely of the bird itself (although that was part of it) but of something that concerned also the seer of the bird, a confluence of our existence with the existence of the bird and of both with something else otherwise. [27]

I drive down the coast to visit my friend Frances in Morro Bay. In a neighbor's garden, two tethered wild birds sit on a perch. I stare at them, fascinated and sad. The red-tailed hawk grips his perch amid a wild garden of yellow oxalis and white alyssum. His claws are parchment-yellow, scaled like a lizard, with black curved claws. He leaps the two feet that his leather leash allows, stretches his ochre-red tail feathers, and hops back meekly onto his perch. His plight touches me deeply. In my imagination, I engage him in conversation.

"How do you feel, tethered, tamed—sitting passively in this garden in Morro Bay?"

"No different from you, tethered to old routines and beliefs; tied to home; tamed by society."

"Oh—I didn't expect you to answer that way."

"I'm used to this life. I've come as a teacher—a member of the wild come into the company of humans."

The hawk seems fascinated by two blue jays fluttering around the telephone wires.

"Do you wish you were free?" I ask.

"I'm as free as I want to be. In my dreams, I soar and glide high above the spring-green hills. Now, awake, I live a contemplative life, sitting, listening, observing."

"You are a magnificent creature. I've never been so close to such a large wild bird. But I feel sad for you. I'd rather see you free in the sky."

"I chose this life, to be here, quiet. It's hardest for Peregrine Falcon, my companion. He's impatient, impulsive."

The peregrine falcon pecks at his claws and flies off his perch, hobbled by his tether, his black-and-white-flecked under-wings stretched out in frustration.

"How do you feel?" I ask.

"I am angry, frustrated. Why am I chained like this? Why do I deserve this? I need to be free, soaring wild, instead of tethered like a dangerous dog."

"Your friend the hawk lives this life without rancor."

"He lives in the present moment. I can't do that. I keep remembering how life used to be, my wings free like the wind."

I drive home through the Salinas Valley. Vineyard rows flicker by in geometric patterns; above, a red-tailed hawk hovers expectantly. I think of the tethered hawk that belongs to the bird-trainer in Morro Bay. "He performs in school auditoriums," the trainer told me proudly. "He has no fear; he flies and returns at my command."

A performer in an auditorium; a role I know only too well. No fear; perfectly rehearsed; an appreciative audience. Who has tamed my wildness? Who gives the commands and tethers me between performances?

॰॰ ॰॰

I go for a routine medical check-up with Dr. F., a general practitioner I've been seeing for more than twenty years. A few days later, she calls to say my haemoccult test, which measures traces of blood in the stool, has come back positive and that I should have a sigmoidoscopy. Anxiety floods through my body. An hour later, I stop off at East Bay Nursery and lose myself reading labels, touching leaves, asking about fertilizer for my raspberries. Taking care of the garden, nurturing myself.

A few days before the scheduled procedure, I fly up to Vancouver to give a lecture in my friend Wendy's city planning class. I wander the unfamiliar campus at the University of British Columbia and come upon a Japanese garden: waterfall and soothing red rocks; lake rippling olive green; dry maple wings quivering on winter-bare tree; serrated reflection of a lantern in the lake; crows calling from tall pines; tiny shrill birds in a just-budding larch tree; shadows of cherry trees falling across a gravel pathway, dark gray on light gray.

I sit in the garden, feeling anxious about the exploration of my colon. My stomach turns, bowels grumble. I try to stay in the present moment. Green, brown, gray, beige, olive, white are all muted, compatible, not vying for attention. Body, mind, spirit all flow and caress each other. Each has its place, interweaving, forming a whole. Eyes follow lake ripples, ears drink in falling water, hands are stroked by sunlight, feet crunch on gravel. I am here, now, well, whole, healthy. I must not contaminate the present with what may be. Cherry blossom bends over lake in a sunlit moment. Crow wades into water from a white-pebble beach and takes a bath.

⁂

"Cancer in the colon." The gentle Chinese-American doctor shows me the picture of a pink, moon-shaped growth around my gut. He rubs my shoulder as I weep in disbelief. I am moved by his gesture of compassion. I don't recall any other doctor who has actually touched me in this way, acknowledging my feelings.

Again? I have to go through all this *again*? It is eighteen months since I found the lump in my breast. Acutely aware of the potential symptoms of breast cancer should it metastasize, it never entered my mind that a totally unrelated cancer might show up in a new, primary site. My body is reminding me in a cogent and frightening manner that, no matter the accomplishments of the mind or explorations of consciousness, the physicality of my being is a place of eating, digesting, excreting—and ultimately of decay and death. The existential paradox: We are individuals with names and life histories, but, ultimately, we are food for worms. If cancer has a symbolic meaning, as I think it does, then perhaps this second diagnosis is a reminder that I still haven't "got it," still haven't found that balance in my life that will support my continuing health. Cancer of the breast—the seat of motherly feeding; cancer of the colon—the place for preparation of excrement. The beginning and end of the cycle of nurturance of the physical body.

I meet with the surgeon, Dr. L., the same young woman who removed my breast, and feel 100 percent more optimistic. The surgery is relatively routine. The tumor is in an "ideal" place—lower down and I would need a colostomy; higher up and I'd lose more of the colon.

She will take out a portion of the colon, pull the rest around, stitch it up—and that's it!

"There's a slight risk of metastasis to the ovaries. Shall I take them out at the same time?"

"What are they doing for me now?"

"Not a whole lot."

"Go for it!"

I remember something I read about listening to music during surgery and ask the surgeon if I can listen to my tapes while I am unconscious.

"Sure," she says. "We'll put it on the loudspeakers so we can all listen, so we can be relaxed too."

"Fine," I reply. "Just don't get *too* relaxed!" We both laugh. I know I am in good hands.

I come home feeling almost elated, so full of energy that I don't want to go to my yoga class, to slow down and be passive. I change into old clothes and dig in the garden for two hours. I prepare an area where I'll grow tomatoes this year; I pull up last year's stakes; I yank up grass and weeds; I cut and compost the leaves of several massive acanthus plants; I dig out their roots, clearing out a "cancerous growth," down on my hands and knees in the earth, troweling deep to get every last fragment of root so they won't all be sprouting again in a trice. Terrible to hate a plant, but acanthus is the pits.

After a good dinner of pasta with pesto and broccoli, I sit—my muscles glowing, tingling—and feel centered, satisfied, exhilarated. I recall a story in Bernie Siegel's *Love, Medicine and Miracles* about a gardener with stomach cancer who said, "No time for an operation now—have to plant for the spring." Then months later: "Have to harvest now—no surgery yet." Then winter came, another excuse. Finally, Siegel examined him again. The tumor had entirely disappeared.

᯽ ᯽

My anxiety mounts as the surgery date draws close. The need to return to Iona in my imagination becomes more and more persistent. Sitting in meditation at the Zen Center one Sunday, my mind wanders and I see myself walking the trail to Loch Staonaig seeking help. I feel drawn to the edge of the water and, without hesitation, I plunge beneath the surface of the loch, falling, tumbling fearlessly over imaginary water-falls, carried down a swift river, until I come to a more gentle reach of the watercourse where an otter—sleek, brown, in his element—swims beside me.

"What do you have to tell me?"

"Follow me," the otter seems to say, and we start to swim upstream, pulling strenuously against the current. I am panting, pulling in gasps of air, feeling my arms and legs tire with all the effort. When I feel I can go no farther, the otter turns and I follow suit. Now we drift effortlessly downstream—resting, floating, observing.

"You have spent so much of your life swimming against the current—righting wrongs, being a maverick, finding strength to be an outsider, not exposing your needs, not demanding time and energy for yourself. Now is the time to turn around—to turn your life around—and let yourself be carried by the flow."

I let myself relax. The water holds me, enfolds me. The otter drifts by my side, his fur sleek, flattened by the river current. Presently, we come to a still pool where the river's flow is backed up by fallen logs. Our bodies circle around in a slow eddy.

"Look up and observe," says the otter.

I look up and see the tiny brown cones of an alder tree bending over the river; the iridescent blue of two dragonflies dancing; a petal falling.

"Sometimes you need to drift. At other times, in quiet places, you just need to observe what is. Most of all, you need to learn not to swim upstream."

With that, the otter dives underwater and disappears and I am back in my chair at morning meditation in the Zendo at Green Gulch Farm.

❧ ❧

I am driving home from a pre-surgery appointment when I see horse chestnut trees blooming on Spruce Street. I stop the car, walk to a pink-flowering chestnut, look around furtively, then snap off a low branch. If anyone were to ask me what I am doing, I'd just say—

What …? I put the branch in the car, then see a white-flowering chestnut across the street. White and pink would look so beautiful together. I cross the street. No one around. I pick a branch with two blooms on it and hurry back to the car. "I'm having surgery on Tuesday and these remind me of my childhood," I would have said.

Under the kitchen light that night, I look at the flowers more closely. Each cluster of white blossoms has two or three with pink accents and only one with yellow. Why? The leaves of the white chestnut are in clusters of five or seven, but never six. Why? The leaves of the pink blossom are all in clusters of five—never six, never seven. Why? Why am I writing all this down in my journal? To distract myself? To find order in an unpredictable world? Three blossoms fall onto the tablecloth. I feel so alone. I want someone to put their arms around me and tell me everything will be all right. I am afraid.

Pushkin, my cat, begins washing herself; I have woken her up. Mostly, I am afraid that I don't know any more how to live my life. What is essential? What extraneous? When should I say "No"? To what can I wholeheartedly say "Yes!"?

❧ ❧

As I am wheeled in for surgery, a robed figure bends over me: the anesthetist.

"You sound as if you're English too," I say in slurred tones.

"Yes, I'm from Gillingham near Salisbury." She smiles, her face circled by a blue paper halo.

"Do you miss it?" I ask, reassured by her presence.

"Oh yes—the flowers. They say the daffodils were very late this year … late this year … late…."

I lie in a dream-like state, waking from the anesthetic and fingering a comforting hot pack that rests on the incision. My mind wanders.

When we were evacuated at the start of the war, the field near our house appeared that first winter to be just another meadow of tall grasses interspersed with a few trees: horse chestnut, oak, copper beech. It lay beside the driveway to the Rothschild house, a driveway I cycled along on my way to school each day.

Snow came and covered the landscape; leafless trees cast spidery shadows. As the weather warmed (it was now the spring of 1940), something began to change in the meadow. Tall gray-green, spear-like leaves protruded from the flattened grasses. At first, I barely noticed them; then there were more and more. Tall buds began to appear between the clumps of leaves.

Finally, one sunny afternoon after a few days of unseasonably warm weather, I returned from school on my bicycle, turned off the road into the driveway and drew in a sharp breath of astonishment. The field had become a blaze of yellow where hundreds and hundreds of daffodils had opened their trumpet-like blossoms to the world. I stopped and stared, tears in my eyes. I had never seen anything so beautiful. It was my first experience of deep awe and I have never forgotten it. When, occasionally, I think about where I'd like my ashes scattered after death, it is always the daffodil field that comes to mind—a place of constant transformation from seeming death and buried dormancy into a glorious display of the continuing, unstoppable beauty of life.

I come to from my daydreaming as Dr. L. enters my room, green-garbed and smiling. "Everything went very well," she says, patting the end of my bed. "I can tell you are a quasi-vegetarian. Your colon looked shiny, healthy. It was very malleable. I just cut out a section, pulled the two ends together, and stitched them up. That was it! You were under anesthetic half an hour less than most people. Everything looked good inside: the liver, the stomach wall, the outer side of your colon. That's a good sign; no indication the tumor had broken through. But we have to wait for the pathology report next week." Medical caution; don't promise too much. I feel optimistic that I won't need any more treatment.

Phyllis brings me home. Home! It feels so good to be in my own bed, the sunlight setting the leaves of my plum tree aglow. There are flowers beside my bed: purple, white, mauve, with one pink rose. Priscilla comes by for a chat and tea. Sara brings homemade soup and strawberries for supper. I feel very cared for.

Reviewing my going-home instructions, a nurse remarks:

"Light activities, three or four rests each day, and strolling. You seem like a pretty independent, go-getter kind of woman."

"Who—me?" I interrupt. "How do you know that? I've been flat on my back."

"Not exactly. You've been walking around the corridors as we encourage people to do. But plenty of our patients don't do it and make more demands on us. So I want you to take this seriously—learn to stroll."

And so I do. And as I walk, I appreciate the beauty of my neighbors' gardens. I stroll, and I look. A block from my house, an older woman lives in an upstairs apartment without a garden. In the grass strip between the sidewalk and the curb, she has planted sunflowers. Around a telegraph pole, sweet peas cling to a fishnet. I stop, eyes closed, to press my nose into the heady perfume.

Between dozing and resting, I begin reading a magnificent book: Pat Barker's *Regeneration:* "Dr. Rivers knew only too well how often the early stages of change may mimic deterioration. Cut a chrysalis open, and you will find a rotting caterpillar. Why you will never find that mythical creature, half caterpillar, half butterfly, is a fit problem of the human soul.... No, the process of transformation consists almost entirely of decay."[28]

e9

Garden Healing

… One of the Navajo words for disease actually translates as "fragmentation and reassemblage." This is the sacred alchemy we witness every fall, in the dropping of sap, the moldering of leaves, and the scattering of seed, reminding us that life requires death … in the ongoing cycle of creation. The powers of decay, which operate with the ruthless detachment of all scavengers, do not care whether we are fat or skinny, good or bad, eating low fat yoghurt or steaks every night, they just do the work that is required—transformation—to restore equilibrium to an imbalanced system. Disease and death are not failures of life, they are part of the cycle of life, in fact, the very means of its continuation. —Kat Duff[29]

I am awakened by sunlight shining through the bedroom windows of Highland Cottage. It falls across a quilt decorated with flowers and fairy figures that I have taken to using. Perhaps it belongs to one of Elinore's grandchildren. I get up, arrange tea pot, bowl of porridge, buttered toast, and my favorite mug on a tray and carry it carefully into the dining room. I pull back the lace curtains. They have a slightly musty smell; definitely in need of a wash. Settling down to eat, I look out at the Sound of Iona and the cliffs of Mull, cast in shadow at this early morning hour.

Cancer is far behind me. I lift a spoonful of steaming porridge into my mouth. Then why do I keep recalling that period of my life? I suppose it is not as far "behind me" as I pretend.

Cancer carries a stigma in our society. We feel vaguely ashamed for mentioning this disease, for bringing up the dreaded word in conversation. After my second diagnosis, I was reluctant to tell people, as if the first diagnosis had been an unlucky break, but the second is a defect in my character, a personal failure.

I become acutely aware of how often the word cancer is used in the media to connote the worst that can happen, the dreaded other—and I resent it. Just as I am beginning to let go of the fears and relax back into a "normal" life, a newspaper story or radio report about "crime growing like a cancer," or "suburban sprawl spreading like cancer" brings me back painfully into identifying myself as a carrier of this feared disease. In her book *Illness as Metaphor,* Susan Sontag points out that cardiac disease implies a weakness that is mechanical and carries no disgrace, nothing of the taboo that once surrounded people afflicted with tuberculosis and that still surrounds those who have cancer. Indeed. When mentioning this second appearance of cancer, I sometimes make light of it, turn it into a joke so the recipient of this news will feel better. But it is no joke.

Ten days after the surgery, Dr. L. calls to say the pathology report indicates that the tumor has grown to the outer wall of the colon and that cancer has shown up microscopically in five out of seventeen lymph nodes. "I'm afraid this means you will probably have to do chemotherapy."

I am stunned. I lie in bed staring out at the garden—little feeling, just disbelief. Louise D. calls to ask if she can drop by. I am so happy to see her. I sit at the kitchen table, crying, as I vent my frustration and anger at the prospect of going to the hospital for a chemo injection once a week for a year. It is good to cry and have a sympathetic ear. After lunch in the garden, I feel a little better and, as the days pass, I am resigned, adjusting, calmer.

Nevertheless, I feel particularly frustrated that I can't go to a Jungian seminar in Switzerland. I have already put down my deposit. Dr. J.-A., my oncologist, agrees to let me take the chemotherapy drugs orally for the two weeks I'm away. The pharmacist goes through the instructions several times and hands me the vials in bulky plastic containers with warnings in large red letters.

I fly to Zurich, meet up with others attending the seminar, and travel by coach to Einsiedeln. After settling in at a rustic lodge, I take myself for a walk beside a nearby lake, Sihl See. The water is sculpted by a light breeze into a pattern of infinite images, infinite sameness. My senses are stimulated; my soul is soothed. I continue to seek both the stimulation of change and the peacefulness of the unchanged. Moving water provides me with both. Across the lake, huge cumulus clouds are banked up over the distant Alps. They seem as solid as ice, yet they will be gone by tomorrow. Others will take their place—other shapes, different shades of gray and white and blue. Nature provides us with boundless lessons on impermanence and the meaning of life, yet we prefer to look for answers in books, at conferences, in institutional religion, in the psychoanalyst's office. And here am I doing the same, anticipating stimulating lectures by eminent Jungians. We need to balance this quest for intellectual knowledge with insights that come to us from the natural world. As we learn to relate to the certainties of our senses, our intuitive imagination blossoms. That is why the existence of a path beside a lake and a bench in the shade of a birch with a view of water and clouds is so profoundly important.

It is through our projections—examined and re-integrated—that we come to know our true selves. Carl Jung wrote of a stone embedded in a slope of the garden of his family's house near Basel.

> Often when I was alone, I sat down on this stone and then began an imaginary game that went something like this: "I am sitting on top of this stone and it is underneath." But the stone could also say 'I' and think: 'I am lying here on this slope and he is sitting on top of me.' The question then arose: "Am I the one who is sitting on the stone, or am I the stone on which he is sitting?"

Later, he wrote of the brooding years of adolescence:

> It was strangely reassuring and calming to sit on my stone. Whenever I thought I was the stone the conflict ceased. "The stone has no uncertainties, no urge to communicate, and is eternally the same for thousands of years," I would think,

"while I am only a passing phenomenon, like a flame that flares up quickly and then goes out." I was but the sum of my emotions and the "Other" in me was the timeless, imperishable stone.[30]

After walking by the lake, I go into Einsiedeln to hear vespers at the monastery. I am reassured, if ever I doubted it, that this kind of institutional religion is not for me. The inside of the church is a gaudy, overblown Baroque-Rococo stage-set. Gilded, pink-and-white angels; painted ceilings; flourishes of ornament in every direction. The service seems to take place entirely among the monks and priests behind a scrolled metal screen at the far end of the chancel. There is no participation of the congregation, which sits and stands at various junctures like mute observers of a distant performance. Of course, I don't know what is going on in people's hearts, but for me, it is empty, boring, and almost offensive. I leave.

As the days go by, I feel some disappointment that the seminar I am attending has not addressed the issue of "Nature and the Psyche" in the way that I expected from its title. Most of the presenters either totally ignore the topic or translate it into a form they want to address. Is it because nature represents the dark feminine, a portion of the collective unconscious that many Jungians, as individuals, as men, do not want to address? Is it that the environmental crisis, the raping of nature, is so horrific, so threatening, that we cannot face bringing it into consciousness?

For the individual ego, as for society, change is threatening; we like to believe we have everything neatly under control. In India, the Goddess life force appears in two contrasting forms: Kali and Durga. Kali is the frightening Goddess with skulls around her neck and a bloody sword in her hand. Kali's function is to crush the ego, to force us to let go of whatever we cling to. And when we do let go, Kali is transformed into Durga, the Great Mother, the radiant Goddess. Only then do we experience the serenity that accompanies the acknowledgment of impermanence, the calm that comes with letting go. Kali came to me as cancer, and she comes to the world as pollution and global warming, acid rain and rising sea levels. Just as Kali-Durga is both destroyer and nurturer, so too is nature for us. She can kill us with earthquakes and floods. She can nurture us with food and flowers. We don't like to look at something—in the psyche or in the outer world—that can bring about both death and birth. No wonder many of the presenters in this symposium seem to sidestep the issue.

One morning, I look in the mirror and see that two large unsightly half-moons of red have appeared beneath my eyes. I am embarrassed by my appearance, but no one (out of politeness?) enquires as to what has happened. I talk to a pharmacist in our group and he suggests it is the chemotherapy drugs I am taking and that I should keep out of the sun. (Why did no one at the hospital tell me to keep out of the sun?) He kindly brings me calendula cream from a pharmacy in town and the red patches begin to fade. Calendula … marigold … the flower that bursts forth all over my garden in Berkeley, uninvited, radiant like the sun. Nature is both destroyer and nurturer.

I walk again beside Sihl See. It is glassy-white; reflections of the hills opposite ripple in gray, ghost-like images from the unconscious. Swallows dip to capture low-flying gnats. Distant sheep pierce the still air with their swinging bells. This lake seems like a well of wisdom, a third eye in the skull of the world.

It is a hot day. I lie down in the shade beside the lake, grass stems quivering around me. Invisible birds sing the song of the earth, weaving tones like a bright quilt of meaning. Aspen leaves whisper truths we can never know, but still must seek. The invisible is pregnant in the sounds around me. It seems as if the leaves are speaking: Be ever questing. The journey is endless, but must be undertaken. Never cease to ask questions, for under each question, the answer lurks, invisible, intangible. Your soul will hear the answer although it, too, lurks, invisible. We—aspen leaves on a summer afternoon—urge you not to stop. To look for answers in the humblest of places, the briefest of synchronicities. A butterfly, a leaf, a ripple on the lake, is all you need to know.

※ ※

Returning to Berkeley from Switzerland, I find solace again in my garden. The acts of digging, clipping, weeding, and watering lull me into a state of quiet concentration, of easy mindfulness, as fears and sadness melt away into the earth at my feet. I begin to go out into the garden before breakfast each day, a glass of juice in hand, to see how my plants are doing. Have the snails found the three hostas I planted a few days ago? Have the dahlia tubers sprouted, the cleome seeds germinated? As I go to sleep, I sometimes wander through the garden in my mind, checking on what I have planted. Do they like their new location? Will they flourish?

Leon Whiteson, in his book *A Garden Story,* talks of making a garden in the empty yard of a newly purchased house in Los Angeles as "writing a green novel." The white paper in the typewriter at which he was trying to write an actual novel remained unmarked. When inspiration dried up, he turned instead to the garden and composed with plants, vines, fountains, ferns.

In my Berkeley garden, I too am composing, though not a novel—more perhaps a mosaic or a movie. Plants evolve; colors emerge and fade; fruits ripen and are eaten. Unlike a novel, a garden doesn't end; it keeps emerging. The garden teaches us lessons about impermanence, about nurturance, about care, about interdependence—plants with other plants, flowers with insects, humans with the soil, the sun with the land, the body with food.

All over my garden, borage seedlings sprout among the vegetables and perennial beds. I pull most of them up to give the other plants a chance, but they persist and I always let a number grow to maturity. Their bright blue, star-like flowers are especially attractive to bees. Between my raised beds is a bushy profusion of French sorrel planted by Stephen, my ex-husband, twenty years ago. Despite considerable neglect (I don't do much to it or for it), the sorrel just keeps coming. That is persistence.

Plants have much to teach us about surrender as well. Annuals live out their cycle through spring bursting, summer flowering, autumn seeding, and then they quietly die, bending in winter rain, succumbing to gravity, back into the earth-womb to nurture another season's growth. The garden is a patient purveyor of silent wisdom.

One night as I lock the back door, I look out through the glass panes at the darkening garden and I am filled with a flush of warmth, as if seeing a dear friend after too long alone among strangers.

On Twelfth Night (January 6th), I take the leftover Christmas wine and, in midnight blackness, creep around the garden, pouring a token libation on the roots of each fruit tree, thanking them for last year's harvest and wishing them good health and bounty in the coming season. It is an old tradition I read about in a book of British folk customs. Although, according to the author, it is long forgotten in the British Isles, I now delight in this secret annual ritual in my Berkeley garden. Thanking the trees and plants that bring us food seems the least we can do to acknowledge our interdependence with the earth. I am immensely grateful for this patch of ground where I feel rooted in what seems a slightly foreign land.

I'm still attached in my body to the seasons in England. It always seems strange to see spring arrive in California in January and February. Hanging over the fence, my neighbor's trees stretch toward the winter sun: huge pink-white saucers of magnolia; tiny, rosy blooms of camellia; oranges I pluck for breakfast. Outside the bathroom window, there is a peach tree that just appeared one year and is now two stories high and covered each spring with glorious, deep-pink blossoms.

In my front garden (after thirty-five years of residence in the United States, I still cannot bring myself to call it, as Americans do, a yard), primulas bloom exuberantly in the cool, spring sunshine: magenta, pink, yellow, deep blue, white. Each morning as I step out to pick up the newspaper, I stoop to pinch off dead flowers and whisper to the new buds, telling them how beautiful they are.

Out by the road, in that strip of earth that seems to have no name (Parking strip? Verge? Tree-lawn? Nature strip? Space-between-sidewalk-and-curb?), a flowering quince is covered with deep pink, cup-shaped flowers. I bought it cheap at Payless and, for two years, it languished in its plastic pot while I, workaholic and single mother, found no time to plant it. All-forgiving, the quince, once planted, flourished and grew into a large, spiky bush whose leafless, angular branches bear a profusion of blooms in the cool February light. Cut for the house, one branch alone in a vase above my sink has all the stark elegance of a Japanese haiku.

Propped up against the redwood fence on the east side of my garden, a bunch of stakes stands ready to support tomatoes and beans when it is time to plant them. Some are bamboo stakes purchased at a nursery; some are produced in my own garden—the straight new shoots on plum trees known as water sprouts. Those that I can reach, I lop off as instructed in my pruning book. I am delighted by the economy of this act, which not only removes growth that saps the strength from fruit-bearing branches, but also provides sturdy, straight poles that will support food-producing plants in my vegetable garden.

This habit of saving things to use again dates from my childhood. We called it salvage in those days, not recycling. We threw nothing away: aluminum milk bottle tops were saved to melt down for fighter planes, for Spitfires; kitchen scraps went into the compost or were picked up for the pig farm; plastic had not yet been invented. "Halve the margins, children," Miss Smith would instruct us, "And rule extra lines at the top of the page." And we, little English children barely comprehending what the war was all about, did our bit to save paper and make our school books last that little bit longer.

Auntie Jean, my mother's sister, had a passion for gardening and it was during those wartime years that she passed it on to me. Her married sisters smiled behind her back. "Frustrated maternal feelings," they whispered, as if gardening were somehow an ignoble outlet for such

natural urges. Despite the fact that she never married or had children, Auntie Jean was more in touch with life than her more "fulfilled" siblings. She knew about nurturing. She pointed out edible plants and mushrooms in the hedgerows and fields. She took me for long walks in the country and taught me the names of wildflowers we saw along the way—figwort and ragged robin, bird's-foot trefoil and hedge parsley, self-heal and pink campion. She taught me how to look at the natural world and care for growing things and thus provided me a lifetime of quiet, fulfilling enjoyment in the garden. What better passion to pass on to a child?

Writing of his year-long experience creating a garden in southern France, Richard Goodman expressed the significance for men of sowing, nurturing, and tending a garden.

> I recommend that all bachelors have a garden. It will give them in some small way the experience of being a parent. I make analogies to sex and birth and children when I talk about a garden because they come naturally. In a garden, you put your seeds into the earth, into mother earth. They germinate; they

grow; they flower—like children. After they begin to grow, you worry about them; you tend them constantly; you fret over their maladies. Some are stronger, bigger and healthier than others. That concerns you. And mystifies you.[31]

Half the joy of gardening is planning, imagining. I look at the path, muddy and trampled, that leads from kitchen to compost pile and fantasize some stepping stones. Between the deck and the east fence— just room for a tiny pond and waterfall? I scan the local newspapers for ads of people who do garden clearance, excited about the potential of a patch of wilderness against the back fence. Once it is cleared—space for a longed-for greenhouse? A shade garden with ferns and azaleas?

It does not escape my attention that, just as I undergo chemotherapy again, I am un-cluttering my environment. Letting go of unwanted cells growing rampant in my body; letting go of papers and mail; clearing brambles and ivy that clog up my garden.

I finally let go of the old Toyota in the driveway. This station wagon, conveyor of small children and a dog, has stood there for several years, ever since its engine sputtered out, its upholstery splitting at the seams. Before it is towed off, I retrieve a stuffed animal from under the back seat—a puffin I gave Jason for his eighth birthday. When the car is removed, a gardener's treasure is revealed in the place where it stood: fine black earth, red worms, decaying leaves. I smile with satisfaction as I shovel this find into a wheelbarrow and add it to the compost pile. By letting go of something no longer needed, I uncover a rich source for growth.

❧ ❧

Each time I drive to the hospital in Hayward for my weekly chemo treatment, I pass a place where I can look down from the freeway onto row upon row of huge commercial greenhouses. The area seems to have been abandoned; the greenhouses are empty. I don't know why they intrigue me so; there is a melancholy hovering about the broken glass, the chipped paint. Someone's career and working life crumbling; perhaps a reflection of my own life.

One morning, I arrive at the hospital feeling exhausted, as I often do after the injection. "How are you doing, Clare?" Kathy asks cheerily. To my surprise (and Kathy's), I burst into tears. Tears come frequently, easily now, as if cancer has opened a rusty valve in my heart. Kathy tells me to take the week off. I sigh with relief and sit for a while in my parked car, weeping.

Since I have nothing planned, I decide to go look at the mysterious greenhouses. I figure out on the map roughly where they are and park nearby. Weeds sprout up in the gravel between the greenhouses. Shards of glass are scattered on slatted propagation benches. A slight wind sets up a low hissing sound as it passes through gaps in the greenhouse walls.

I flash back to my first job, when I was eleven, weeding pots in a greenhouse on Saturday mornings in a north-London nursery. The nursery owner was a neighbor of Grandma Cooper's. I loved the smell of that place—earthy, damp, like the rain forest, primeval.

Earlier, on the Rothschild estate, the greenhouses in the kitchen garden had been off-limits. We pressed our faces against the glass, looking in wonder at peach trees espaliered against warm brick walls. I had no memory of ever having tasted a peach. So, one day when the greenhouse door was propped open and the gardener was on his tea break, I crept in, heart pounding, and picked up a ripe peach that had fallen to the ground. I ran down to the lily pond and, hiding behind some bamboo, I bit into the slightly bruised peach, its sweet juice running down my chin and dripping onto the red-cherry pattern of my wool pullover. I stroked the juice from my chin onto a finger, sucked it, buried the stone, and ran home heady with excitement. Forbidden fruit, delicious fruit.

A blue jay squawks from a eucalyptus—and I am back in California. Exploring the paths between the broken greenhouses, I come across a little house with pansies, poppies, and primulas in the front yard. Someone still lives here. I walk a little farther and there, in a clearing where perhaps a greenhouse once stood, an elderly Asian woman in white clothes and a straw hat sits on a box hoeing the ground in front of her. A row of beans and some artichokes are growing nearby.

I fantasize the whole story: a family business, the couple ages, the husband dies, the wife is left alone, unable to keep up the business or maintain the property. All she has left is a patch of garden and a little white dog that I glimpse when I stand on tiptoe and squint through a broken window. The image of this elderly woman stays with me all day; something about her is infinitely sad and lonely. Does she have grown children? Does anyone call?

Several years later, driving to the hospital for a check-up, I see that all the greenhouses are gone and bulldozers are re-shaping the site. A large sign announces: "Condominiums for sale: coming soon!" Thus are dreams demolished, buried beneath concrete—the earth and all our lives a little diminished by their passing. I recall a poem by Dom Helder Camara.

> *Do you think land has no feelings?*
> *I saw a building-plot*
> *die of shame*
> *at being put up for sale*
> *like a slave*
> *with a price tied*
> *round his neck.* [32]

❧ ❧

There is a knock at the door of Highland Cottage. I jump in response, so deep am I in reminiscences about the past. It is Barbara, come to see if I want to walk over to the Bay at the Back of the Ocean to see the eider ducks. I pull on my walking shoes, drape a jacket around my shoulders in case it is cold on the other side of the island, close the front door to the cottage, and fall in step with Barbara as we walk past the Argyll Hotel. It is good to be back in the present moment, smelling the salt air and listening to the cries of gulls. We pass the village hall, open a rusty gate, and start up the rocky track that leads to the western ocean.

CHAPTER 10

❧

Healing Landscapes

*I only went out for a walk, and finally concluded to stay
out till sundown, for going out, I found, was really going
in.* — John Muir[33]

I hear the door open as I prepare a lunch of sardines on toast. It is
Mark, the postie (as the postman is known in Scotland), putting envelopes and packages on a bench in the enclosed front porch of Highland
Cottage. The mail arrives along with national newspapers on the 10:30
ferry from Mull.

I sort through the envelopes, all for Elinore. She has many friends
and contacts around the world. I pick up a parcel. It is for me. I look
at the return address—New York. I run to find scissors, cut open the
packaging, and there it is: *Healing Gardens*. I thumb through the pages.
The color illustrations look beautiful; we *did* choose the right picture
for the jacket. I smile, fingering the spine of the book. Finished at last!
How had it all started?

About the time of my first visit to Iona, in the early 1980s, a
researcher based in Texas who later became a friend and colleague conducted a small but pivotal study. Reviewing the medical records of
patients recovering from gall-bladder surgery in a Philadelphia hospital, he found that those who had a view from their beds onto trees
called the nurse less often, took fewer strong painkillers, and went home
sooner than those who looked out at a brick wall. It is something that
we might intuitively imagine to be so, but the medical world requires
scientific proof. With that study, Roger Ulrich helped establish a whole
new field of enquiry—the restorative power of nature, a field I found
myself drawn to as if to a friend I'd been seeking all my life.

How do beneficent synchronicities occur in our lives? The person we need to meet shows up at just the right time. A book falls open to just the passage we need to read. As I was finishing cancer treatment, one of my graduate students—Marni Barnes—suggested we apply for a research grant, just advertised, to study the restorative effects of gardens in hospitals. It seemed a long shot, but we got the grant and, with mounting excitement, selected our sites and began to develop a set of questions.

Back to work; it felt so good not just to be a passive patient waiting for blood to be drawn out or chemo drugs to be dripped in. I sat in the roof garden of Alta Bates Hospital in Berkeley, mapping where people walked, where they ate lunch, where they paused to look at the view. Even this garden on a rooftop—not actually on the earth, incapable of sustaining sizeable trees—even this small space open to the sky with views to San Francisco Bay and the Berkeley hills, even here, people found palpable relief from the stresses and anxieties within the hospital building.

A male nurse told us of bringing someone out to the garden to die; she wanted to see the clouds. A hospital office worker spoke of watching birds drink and bathe in a small central fountain, and her delight when a robin raised its young in the bougainvillea climbing the walls of the maternity wing. A man whose wife was in surgery reported how much more relaxed he felt outdoors compared with the fluorescent-lit waiting room. A nurse having lunch broke into a big smile: "I work underground in the Radiation Department; I feel like one of the Mole People! If it weren't for this garden—the sight of greenery, birdsong, the feel of the sun, the sound of the breeze—I think I'd go crazy!"

At another hospital, a surgeon told us she had taken a position there *because* of the garden, a place where she could relax from the stress of her job. A visitor with little money confessed to picking flowers surreptitiously to take to a dying friend. An office worker told of returning to work refreshed after eating lunch in the garden: "It feels like an oasis of peace and life in the midst of a city that feels dead."

The monograph that we wrote as a result of this work was published and received two awards. Then, out of the blue, a phone call came from a New York publisher to ask if I would write a whole book on healing gardens.

"Who, me?" I responded incredulously. "I've only co-authored one small study. That's all I know."

"But it's more than anyone else knows at this time. We think that healing gardens are the next 'hot item.'"

I was ecstatic! Being asked to write a book is a rare event. This request could not have come at a more opportune time: a phase of my treatment for breast cancer was over and my strength was returning. Retirement had left me with free time and a need for an intellectual focus. This would not seem like work, but therapy, something close to my heart. I called colleagues to ask if they would contribute chapters to the book, and all agreed.

Since there was little published on the topic, I didn't spend much time in the library. I hung out in hospital gardens instead, quietly watching, thinking, taking notes. One of my first field-work visits was to a hospice—an open ward for thirty terminally ill, indigent patients at Laguna Honda Hospital in San Francisco. Many of these people were dying of cancer. The atmosphere brought on heart palpitations and left me sick to my stomach with fear. Masking my feelings with an attentive demeanor and notebook at the ready, I listened to the attending physician, Dr. K., as he proudly showed me the garden he had helped create in a narrow courtyard next to the ward. "We placed sweet-smelling plants and a small Japanese water feature outside this window. Inside is the private room where we take people when they are about to die. Smell and sound are the last senses to leave us."

Later, more comfortable with the idea of dying, I visited the glorious garden of Trinity Hospice in London. Its gently undulating lawns, its lily pond, garden shelter, perennial borders, and winding paths seemed like subtle invitations to explore what is just around the corner, what is beyond. The gardener told me how important this garden is as a place of respite for family members who had been sitting all night beside the bed of a dying loved one. She showed me a garden shelter where staff members exhausted from the stress of work came outside to be alone.

In the garden of a hospice in Houston, Texas, I encountered a security guard and asked him if people who are bedridden have access to the garden.

"Oh yes, yes! We wheel their beds outside, and I can really see a difference when they come back in."

"In what way?" I asked.

"Oh, they seem much calmer, relaxed … happier, somehow."

Yes, I think. I would want to die in a garden—seeing clouds, hearing birds, feeling a breeze on my cheeks. Returning to the bosom of nature before drifting into oblivion. That seems the right way to die.

At a hospital in Farmington, New Mexico, where Marni and I were asked to conduct a workshop, there was nowhere to go outside except a meager plaza filled with people smoking cigarettes. We asked some of the staff what they did when stressed from work. Their answers brought tears to my eyes. The CEO of the hospital reported: "When I hit a brick wall, when I'm stuck with a problem and don't know which way to turn, I walk in circles around the building—through the parking lot, along the road, past the service driveway. It's hot out there, but at least I'm out of the office."

A nurse told how she went out and did exercises in the parking lot. A physical therapist responded: "Sometimes I'm so burned-out and stressed, I go and sit on the fire escape and cry. Yes—out there with all the dust and pigeon crap. At least it's outside." Caretakers of the sick and injured deserve better than this.

So do patients. How cogently does the juxtaposition of events in our lives startle us into deep awareness. Do we, at some level, "arrange" for this to happen? How else can I explain that it was just as I was co-authoring this book on healing gardens that I ended up being diagnosed with colon cancer and treated at a hospital where there was no garden, no place to sit outside. I deeply felt and resented its absence.

Waiting for chemo there one day, I started to write in my journal. The act of paying close attention to everything around me helped to calm my anxiety.

Pale, beige-flecked linoleum reflects the legs of a five-legged chemo chair. A low hum above in the ceiling vent; a distant voice calling for Doctor X. Scattered magazines on a table—*Reader's Digest, Woman's World*—do not tempt me. There is machinery clamped to the wall—black instruments to peer into ears and eyes, to register blood pressure. The examination table has fake wood-grained panels and lies white and expectant. Footsteps outside, voices. Nothing to look at but white walls, white ceiling, chrome legs, plastic wall rack holding forms, degree certificates in narrow black frames, gray plastic doorstop. Tall chrome IV pole, its empty hooks soon to dangle a plastic pouch of chemicals that drip into a tired vein on the back of my left hand.

I have come here thirty times for this encounter with the needle, only twenty more to go and I'll be free of Friday-morning treks to this little cell of fluorescent-lit fear. If only I could see a tree.

Martha comes in and thanks me for the homemade lemon marmalade I gave her at Christmas. She tries twice to insert the needle while I bite my thumb to distract myself from the pain. No luck; she can't find a vein. She tries twice more in my arm; the vein "plump and spongy" as she describes it. But after two more tries, she gives up. "I'm missing today," she sighs. "I'm sorry. Hold this cotton on your arm; I'll find Kathy."

Tears come to my eyes. I close them and focus on my breath. Door open, I hear conversation, laughter. I've been here an hour and a half. I feel hungry and tired. Low buzz of conversation. How do they tell people there's no hope? How do you break the news gently?

"I'll be with you in a moment, Clare," I hear as Kathy breezes in and leaves again. Sounds of a TV soap opera from the next room. I wish I could look outside. I wish I could see something green—a garden, or even a picture of one, a photo of running water, something beyond this place. Sounds of running water; I need to pee. The arms of the chair where I wait are made of wood—perhaps the only natural substance in the room.

Kathy returns, prepares the needle, and finds the vein easily. We chat as the chemicals go in. There is no garden where I can sit afterward and wish my body well. The chemo I am taking has a half-life of only fifteen minutes. I walk down the corridor toward the one bench in this whole wing of the hospital where I can rest and look out at a patch of lawn and a few trees around a busy entrance. At least it is a green view.

I arrive at the place and find that that one bench has been removed. Feeling quite distressed, I go instead to the cafeteria, the only other place to sit. Vending machines hum loudly, the cash register rings, an animated conversation in Spanish plays out behind me. Outside the window, the dark winter branches of a honey locust are etched against the parking garage. At its base, against the moss-flecked concrete pavement, magenta cyclamens shout their colors at the gray sky.

※ ※

The notion of creating healing outdoor spaces in hospitals slowly began to receive more attention. Serendipitously, my personal turning to nature for nurturance and the emerging discussion of restorative outdoor spaces fell comfortably into alignment. After the publication of our book on healing gardens, I began to be asked to write critical articles for a design magazine, *Landscape Architecture.* I felt blessed: to sit around in healing gardens and write about them, to be paid for what I most love to do, to find a focus again after retirement.

I wrote about a children's garden at Legacy Emanuel Hospital in Portland, Oregon with its Yellow Brick Road and Tin Man, its bird feeders and mosaic turtles, its winding paths through lush vegetation. I sat and wrote about the garden at a cancer clinic in San Francisco. It was created by artist Anne Chamberlain, who had to look out during chemo treatments at a bleak concrete courtyard when she was being treated there for breast cancer. "This ought to be a garden," she said to her breast surgeon, Dr. Laura Esserman. Together with garden designer Katsie Swann, they made it into one, adding a café to one side. Medical staff now come out to the garden to eat lunch or hold informal meetings; patients come early to sit and relax before appointments; family members wait for someone undergoing treatment. How could we have forgotten this most simple and natural component of healing, one embraced by the monks who ran medieval hospices and incorporated into 19th-century hospitals by public-health reformer Florence Nightingale? With modern medicine's emphasis on invasive surgery,

expensive drugs, and high-tech testing, we have lost touch with the body's need to find its own healing rhythm in nature.

At Good Samaritan Hospital in Portland, Oregon, the hospital staff worked with a landscape architect to create a garden where physical therapy can be conducted outdoors. At the Family Life Center in Grand Rapids, Michigan, staff at a day-center for patients with Alzheimer's disease provided input to the landscape architect to ensure that the garden, with its looped path, gazebos, and perennial flower borders, met the needs of its users.

As I sat in each of these places and watched how people used them, I relaxed into the sights, sounds, and aromas of the gardens, my body unconsciously becoming whole again. My own garden and the hospital garden; gardening and garden writing; the trowel and the pen; designed nature and wild nature; Berkeley and Iona. The world presented to me exactly what I needed, and I was deeply grateful. It was Van Gogh who wrote, in a letter to his brother Theo, that the nature we see and the nature we feel must permeate each other in order to last, to live. Yes.

CHAPTER 11

လ

Grasshopper Teaching

… little by little,
as you left their voices behind,
the stars began to burn
through the sheets of clouds,
and there was a new voice,
which you slowly
recognized as your own,
that kept you company
as you strode deeper and deeper
into the world,
determined to do
the only thing you could do—
determined to save
the only life you could save. —Mary Oliver[34]

I wake up in Highland Cottage dreaming about Barry. I try to recall some details of the dream, but the images fade just as the shores of Mull slowly disappear behind low-lying clouds. I think about Barry, so far away in New Mexico, and hope, for an instant, that he is thinking about me.

It was such a miracle that I met Barry. While still on chemo for colon cancer, I saw an ad for the Temagami Vision Quest in Canada and knew that I must go. Cancer had come as a shock and I sensed that, in part, it had entered my body to wake me up from a life lived on auto-pilot. A vision quest is based on a Native American ritual of seeking guidance in life by spending time alone in the wilderness. It seemed like the perfect thing to do at this time. I had seen the advertisement "by chance," but I knew by then that nothing in life really happens by chance.

My oncologist granted me a two-week reprieve from my weekly injections. I flew to Toronto and then traveled north in a rental car. A seaplane took us, six at a time, to Landskib Island in Lake Temagami in the wilderness of Northern Ontario. The island is uninhabited except in the summers, when youth camps and the Vision Quest take place in its forested and rocky landscape. The Vision Quest staff was on the wooden dock to meet us as the plane landed: Outward Bound leader David Knudsen and three Jungian analysts—Louise Mahdi from Chicago, Barry Williams from New Mexico, and Robert Johnson, noted author of such books as *He, She, We* and *Owning Your Shadow.* It was the latter's name that first attracted my attention in the Vision Quest brochure, but I had barely set foot on the island before my eyes, attracted by something more visceral, lit on Barry. Tall and slim, perhaps in his fifties, he stood a little apart from the group, smiling shyly.

The next morning, we were told that we would split into three groups for dream analysis and we could choose with whom to go:

Louise, Robert, or Barry. There was no doubt in my mind where I was going. For the next seven mornings, I sat entranced—"on the edge of your seat," a friend in the group later described it—as Barry listened intently, questioned, queried, and interpreted dreams in a manner I had never experienced before. We had all come seeking change in our lives. A week-long encounter was not the time for lengthy analysis. Barry cut to the chase. This man seemed to be peering into my soul and I was captivated—and frightened. How much did I want him to know? How much did I want to know?

What I did know was that I seemed to be falling in love, quite inappropriately: Barry was married (his wife and infant son attended each dream group) and was clearly "unavailable." But that didn't stop my feelings. Like an adolescent with her first crush, I was always acutely aware of his presence—in the group, during meals, at evening meetings. If he looked my way or smiled, I felt a rush of emotion through my body.

Midway through the week, we wandered as usual up to the lodge after breakfast. Some of the men had slept out on the landing dock and seen the aurora borealis. They described the colors excitedly as we settled down for the morning meeting.

After some routine remarks, David casually announced that, in a few minutes, we'd be walking to a site in the forest to do the ropes course. I drew in my breath audibly, as did several people sitting nearby. I eyed Peggy and Kris nervously. The ropes course? There was no mention of that in the Vision Quest brochure.

We followed David, single file, along a narrow pine-needle path until we came to a small clearing where the other staff waited. To one side, I saw a series of taut steel cables linking tall pine trees in what resembled a monster cat's cradle. My breathing became shallow. I moved to the edge of the group, contemplating a quick escape. Pictures of Marines on basic training flashed through my mind. "I am *not* going to do this," I said under my breath. "I am not a teenager on an Outward Bound course. I'm a woman in her sixties on chemo. This is way too dangerous."

I sat on a boulder rocking back and forth, tracing a finger around patches of lichen. David strode over with something in his hand.

"Come on, Clare! Let's get you up there first. Hold out your arms."

Too late to escape. David tightened a safety harness around my shoulders and chest and explained that I'd always be hooked to a safety wire and, if I should slip, I'd only fall two or three feet. I prayed this was a dream—a nightmare—and that I'd soon wake up.

The next moment—I don't know how I got there—I was on a taut steel cable thirty feet above the forest floor. Holding tight to the safety wire above me, I inched my way sideways along the cable, not looking down, eyes focused on the yellow-beige trunks of pine trees in the middle distance.

I arrived at the end of the cable, squeezed around a large tree, and felt a small rush of pride. I was doing "OK"; I was braver than I thought.

The next section of the course consisted of two cables, about three feet apart. The challenge here was to move sideways with a partner, each of us on one of the cables, each leaning into the other to form a triangle. I'd chosen Rick as my partner, a doctor from somewhere in the South; I found him attractive and he seemed stable, grounded.

But none of that helped us up on the cable, forty feet above the ground, with the rest of the Vision Quest crowd, their heads tilted back, calling out words of encouragement. "You're doing great, Clare!" "Go for it!" Rick urged me to lean onto his shoulders but I couldn't. I was terrified I'd push him off balance and he would go hurtling to the ground. No matter that we were both wearing safety harnesses; fear and survival instinct overwhelmed any semblance of logical thinking.

"I'm sorry, Rick. I'm sorry," I whispered, as tears started to stream down my face. I shuffled along the cable holding tightly to the safety wire. This was not how I was supposed to do it, but it felt to me like a matter of life and death.

The last section of the course consisted of a log, perhaps thirty feet long and six inches in diameter, slung between two immense pine trees to form a bridge sixty feet above the ground. The task was to walk across this log bridge, arms spread out in a T for balance, without holding on to the safety wire above. I stood on the cable, my arms tight around a tree—sturdy, dependable, grounded. "I can't do it … I can't do it," I sobbed, tears and snot smeared over my face, my legs quivering with fear.

"Let go of the tree!" David shouted up at me. "Let go of the wire. You need to do this. It's a metaphor for how you live your life. You must face this fear and go through it!"

"Fuck you, David," I said under my breath. "Don't talk to me about fear; I know all about fear. Ever been told by a doctor to go home and make your will?"

I held on to the tree and continued to sob. Suddenly, I was aware of one of the men in our group shimmying up a tree to my right. He handed me a large white handkerchief and I thankfully wiped my face clean.

"Keep going!" David yelled again. "You can do it!"

I felt like a failure, holding up the group. Then I was vaguely aware of a figure with a harness on climbing up a nearby tree. It was Barry. I felt the log move slightly as he climbed onto it beside me. I heard him breathing; quiet, steady breaths.

I looked into his eyes—blue, unblinking, encouraging. A shock of white hair (or was it blond?) fell over his forehead. Barry encouraged me to let go of the tree and, when I grabbed for the safety wire, to let go of it as well.

"Let go of the wire," he urged softly as he began to move slowly away from me, his hand outstretched. "Just touch my fingertips and let go—just for a second."

I let go and, barely touching his fingers, moved two steps toward him before I panicked and again grabbed the safety wire above my head.

"Good, good.... Now let go again—just for a second."

My eyes, fixed on his, filled with tears. I took two more steps along the log, our fingertips just touching. Then I grabbed the wire again.

"You're doing fine," Barry said quietly. "Let go again—just for a second."

And thus we inched across the log together, fingertips touching, Barry walking backward, one arm stretched sideways for balance, the other held out toward me. I forgot the chasm below, eyes watching, silent. I forgot the terror and kept focused on Barry's eyes. As we reached the far end of the log, the crowd below let out a great roar and I fell against Barry, shaking with relief and gratitude. "Thank you, thank you," I stammered as he steadied my body and, leaning into his arms, I smelled the sweat on his neck.

The last section of the course was a device that let you return to the ground down a long sloping cable. The group counted loudly to three. I let go and yelled with relief as I swung down through pine branches and gossamer spider webs, hitting the ground with a thud. The crowd let out a big cheer and David strode toward me as I lay exhausted on the soft pungent bed of the forest. Tall, macho David; his weathered face broke into a smile as he hauled me to my feet. He started to unhook my harness and I fell into his arms.

"I don't want to die ... I don't want to die." I sobbed into the rough wool fibers of his sweater. The terror of the last hour poured out of me.

"You faced your greatest fear today," David murmured. "This is how you need to face future fears."

I'm not going to die, I thought. Not just yet. I have so much to live for: places to see, books to write, maybe grandchildren to know and love. High up on that log, amid the trees, the fears I had hidden behind a stoic English façade came cascading out, like lava from a long dormant volcano.

The next day was the start of our two-day solo experience. Before leaving for this trip to Canada, I had explained to my oncologist what I would be doing (or the part I knew I would be doing). "Part of the week's experience is to go on a solo. We each go to a separate remote place and spend two days and nights alone there, without food or water."

"No, you can't do that. You're still on chemo; your platelet count is low. You need to have food and water. I'll let you take the chemo orally for that week—but take care, don't overdo it."

Everyone except me paddled in canoes across the lake to the opposite shore—rocky, forested, home to bears. Because I was on chemo, I stayed on the island on a rocky promontory a quarter mile from the lodge as a precaution. I took a bottle of water with me and a little food: an apple, an orange, a muffin, some nuts.

In the daytime of that two-day solo, I felt fine. I watched changing patterns of light on the lake; I listened to the muffled breathing of the forest. I wrote. But at night, deep in my sleeping bag, my fears came back: the enemy, wild animals, a painful death. As the sun rose on the last morning, I sat leaning against a rock, writing in my journal. Suddenly, a grasshopper landed on my leg. Keeping very still, I asked it to come closer. It didn't move. Then, shifting slightly, it left a minute turd on the black fabric of my pants. I smiled and returned to my writing. Within seconds, the grasshopper had leapt right onto the blank page in front of me, as if to say: "Pay attention to me!" With a sensuous movement, it stroked its right antenna with its right front leg. Then I saw that it had only one rear jumping leg—the left. "You think you're disfigured, disabled because you've lost your right breast? I've lost my right leg and look at me! I'm as good a jumper as ever." It leapt away. A wave of emotion rippled through me—part sadness, part wonder at this prescient message from the natural world. Why had this particular grasshopper landed on my leg? Was this a chance event? How often do elements of nature present themselves to us, while we, distracted by seemingly more important tasks, are oblivious to what they are trying to tell us.

I prepared to leave my solo spot and dragged a brush vigorously through my tangled hair. Pulling a bunch of loose hair from the brush, I was about to throw it on the ground when I remembered the bird's nest Lucy had found in my garden—the bird's nest softly lined with my own hair. I noticed a young pine tree with a hole in it; the perfect place for a nest. I put the hair into the hole and blessed it, hoping a bird of Lake Temagami would make its home there and bring forth new life next spring.

I walked over to a clearing where David and Barry were tending a fire to heat rocks for the sweat lodge. We would all take part in a closing ritual, stripped of our clothes, invoking prayers for our changed lives. Those who had spent their solo time on the opposite shore were arriving by canoe. Empowered by the message of the grasshopper, I undressed without a sense of shame. For the first time since my mastectomy, I felt unconcerned with my one-breastedness. I walked naked to the door of the sweat lodge and crawled into the dark, sweltering, womb-like, transformative heat. The legendary Amazons of Greek mythology are said to have burned off their right breasts, the better to draw their bows. What was the bow I had to draw? Where would I aim its arrow?

ᘐ ᘐ

It took me six months to pluck up the courage to call Barry at his New Mexico home and ask if he would be my analyst. We started to talk once a week over the phone and, periodically, I traveled to Taos to talk face to face in his professional office—a log cabin in the Sangre de Cristo Mountains with views out to a forest of pine and aspen and an occasional fearless deer wandering past the windows.

As the years passed, I slowly began to understand the deeper meaning of that prophetic meeting in the Canadian wilderness, why a feeling of "falling in love" had gripped me as powerfully as any comparable emotion in my life.

Barry had grown up near the Canadian border, in upstate New York. In his childhood, he spent summers beside a lake in the Ontario wilderness, a setting not unlike Lake Temagami. Numinous experiences in nature as a child led him, as an adult, to seek answers, first in the study of divinity and later in Jungian analysis, mountain climbing, leading vision quests in the wilderness, and as an analyst himself.

My initial attraction to Barry was mysteriously entangled with the power of the place where we met and the inner world of nature he seemed to embody. In metaphorical terms (though not in actual physical stature), he seemed like a Gnome of the Woods. I sensed he had some knowledge I wanted to access. My own childhood experiences finding solace in nature, though poignantly remembered, were barely understood at a deeper level and remained un-integrated in psychological terms. Attempting to understand them, I had followed the path of the intellect. But somewhere below, like precious jewels on the ocean floor, lay riches undreamed of. I needed to retrieve those jewels and to do so through a deep and intimate relationship with another human being. As the seaplane landed that hot August day and my eyes fixed on Barry standing on the dock, it was my unconscious that recognized in him the embodiment in the outer world of what was then unknown to me in the inner world, but which I valued profoundly. I saw in Barry my unlived life, the path not taken.

All my life, I had veered between trying to understand the landscape as an academic and permitting myself to sink unquestioning into its mystery. It took several years of talking with Barry before I understood the symbolism of seeking a precarious balance on the ropes course. The work of a lifetime: balancing intellect and emotion, logic and feeling, the masculine and the feminine, Berkeley and Iona. Our traverse of the log together—I precarious, terrified, needy; Barry calm, caring, offering guidance and encouragement—was a vibrant metaphor for the psychological work we subsequently did together. Though I didn't know it that day on Landskib Island, Barry would eventually accompany me into painful recesses of my psyche, a journey I sometimes wished to avoid, often resisted, but knew I must ultimately undertake.

CHAPTER 12

✑

Illness as Initiation

... [O]ne of the tasks of illness, and requirements of healing, is to reclaim one's soul—that vital essence that enables us to thrive ... calling up lost memories and reinhabiting them ... by listening to our dreams and intuitions, and by being honest with ourselves and others about our true feelings and desires, which the extremities of illness and the threat of death make so painfully evident. —Kat Duff[35]

As I live my quiet, sometimes lonely life on Iona, my weekly phone conversation with Barry is a dependable source of support. He is in his cabin in the woods in northern New Mexico; I am leaning against the window sill in Highland Cottage, the sound of passing seagulls sometimes miraculously flowing through the air waves to the American southwest. One week, after discussing a dream, Barry urges me to think about the archetypal meaning of cancer. "It's not just understanding, but insight—even revelation—you need to seek." Revelation. To draw back the veil.

As I return home from a walk to the north shore still pondering Barry's comment, I kick my boots against a fence post to knock off the sand and hear the crek-crek-crek of a nearby corncrake. It is an inconspicuous bird with a distinctive rasping cry; something about it has gripped me. When I first heard the sound it makes, like a thimble being dragged across a metal washboard, I thought it was a farmer sharpening a tool, but there was no one around. Then I met a couple who told me that the bird world is excited because more and more corncrakes are nesting on the island, and it is their un-birdlike cries that I have heard. The corncrake is virtually extinct in England, where the reduction of long-grass meadows and hay making have eliminated much of its natural habitat, but it is holding out in the Western Isles of Scotland.

I know there is at least one corncrake in the expanse of tall grass and thistles behind the parish church and another hiding amid the wild irises in a field near the abbey. They are very shy and nest on the ground. I hear them often. Then, one evening as I stop by the iris patch on my way home from Dun I, I see one clearly, and then a second. They are about the size of a partridge or grouse, buff with a flecked pattern of darker brown. One lets forth its grating cry, stretching its neck skyward to reveal a pink throat.

The corncrake is a short-lived bird. It lives only one or two years. To ensure the survival of the species, the females lay two clutches of ten or twelve eggs each season. Some are eaten by hawks; some don't make it to their winter habitats in Africa. The seagull, in contrast, has few predators, lives up to twenty years, and lays only one or two eggs each year.

Why does the corncrake keep showing up in my mind? According to the late-19th-century Roman Catholic priest and folklorist Father Allan McDonald, the corncrake and the stonechat were called *eoin shianta* in Gaelic. They were considered eerie, uncanny, enchanted, or blessed on account of their disappearance in winter. Before any observation or understanding of bird migration, the Celts believed that, when birds disappeared, they became dormant. That they could do so and not die rendered them enchanted, otherworldly. I feel some resonance with these shy, reclusive birds that ought to die—but don't.

The corncrake, like cancer, keeps itself hidden. But when it wants to announce its presence, its voice is jarring, ugly, and out of all proportion to its size. To survive, it has come to a rocky, remote place. The stress of exposure, of not finding tall grass, led to the corncrake's extinction in England. Farmers in Scotland are now compensated by the government to leave areas of grass un-mown till late summer so corncrakes can find hospitable places to live and breed. The nature preserves and healing gardens in our cities are the equivalent of these patches of un-mown grass for humans—places where people can go in times of stress to find the nurturance that nature offers. When Mayor Giuliani forced the closure of preciously tended community gardens in New York City, he did something far worse than merely reclaiming valuable pieces of real estate. He severed a connection with earth and the miracle of growth in a stressful environment of concrete, traffic, asphalt, and high-rise buildings.

❧ ❧

My days on the island follow a quiet routine of walking, reading, writing, thinking. But Barry's question keeps whispering in my mind, like a prompter reminding an actor of the next critical, but forgotten, lines in a play. What is the archetypal meaning of cancer? It is hard to articulate what is slowly seeping into my consciousness: perhaps cancer represents some kind of initiation.

Opening the next parcel of books I had sent myself as "suitable reading," I find—oh blessed synchronicity—a book that helps me

understand illness as metaphor. In *The Alchemy of Illness,* Kat Duff describes the many stories—of Ulysses, Aeneas, Inanna, Hercules, Psyche, Orpheus, Persephone, Dionysus—in which mythical figures descend into the underworld long before their bodily descent into the grave, and come back with knowledge that deepens their characters. Perhaps serious illness is a modern-day descent into the unconscious and that is its archetypal meaning: an encounter with mortality and a return with some element of wisdom that can be acquired in no other way.

Kat Duff recounts her journey through chronic fatigue and immune dysfunction syndrome, and discusses illness as having parallels with initiation rituals in many traditional societies. She writes: "I could not say that illness is equivalent to initiation … but I have observed that some illnesses, especially those that occur in midlife, serve initiatory functions, giving us the wisdom we need to assume the lion's mantle, the authority and creative power of age."[36]

The first stage of initiation in traditional societies entails the initiate being removed from family and familiar context, sometimes without warning. Yes, that sounds familiar: the shock of cancer diagnosis, the abrupt falling away of familiar routines, the forced entry into the depersonalized world of hospitals and medical rituals. In illness, we enter into a liminal world outside the spatial and temporal context of our previous, taken-for-granted, normal lives.

The second stage in traditional initiations—submergence—is accompanied by physical and psychological ordeals: fasting, purging, pain, fear, mutilation, isolation. It doesn't take much imagination to see the parallels in cancer treatment: surgery, removal of body parts, chemotherapy, nausea, terror, hair loss, radiation treatment, exhaustion, being told to "go home and get your affairs in order." For me, it seemed like a descent into the underworld, the symbolic tomb, the dark night of the soul. My social world shrank to close family and a few caring friends; my spatial world encompassed home, car, hospital, garden, and little else.

I re-wrote my will and slipped some notes regarding my wishes for a memorial event into a file. Though I prayed and called upon inner resources of hope and optimism, I had to face the distinct possibility that I might die. The word for initiation, Duff reminds us, actually means "to die." Carl Jung described the illness following his heart attack at sixty-nine as a process almost of defoliation, as if everything thought of or wished for were slowly stripped away.

The third stage of traditional initiation is metamorphosis, or the transformation from what we are into a being of greater knowing. The initiate understands, to a deeper degree, his or her place in the world and the interconnectedness of all life. A comparable change comes about for some through the rigors of serious illness. Certainly for me, dreams and waking fantasies, experiences in my garden, and—most of all—exploring the mystery of Iona have brought about a change of consciousness that I can only describe as transformative. I have let the old slip away, and am letting the new—always there, deep in my heart—begin to blossom and ripen into wholeness.

Finally, there is reemergence—reintegration into the community and traditional society, return to the "normal" world for the one who has been sick. I begin to see my sojourn on Iona as both a deepening of the descent into the mythic world initiated by the onset of cancer, and a preparation for a return to life. Illness is to health what dreams are to waking life.

Yes, it is unlikely that I would be here—sinking into the essence of this healing place, paying attention to dreams, reconsidering my relationship with significant people in my life—if it were not for the experience of a life-threatening illness. While by no means do I think that I caused my own cancer, it has certainly forced me to face questions so easily overlooked in the busy-ness of life, to embrace elements of wisdom that for me could be acquired in no other way.

The night after reading Duff's book, I have a dream. I am walking on a country road and encounter two men with pistols drawn. They push me into a house. I'm afraid they may come after me, so I lock myself in a toilet stall. I open a small window, pry open some mesh, and crawl out. With someone else, I paddle across a watery inlet in a boat; ahead, I see a trail through some mountains that will take us home. A few days later, I talk to Barry.

"Who do you think the two men threatening your life with pistols are?"

"My two bouts with cancer, I should think!"

"Yes! They scare you, but also save you by pushing you into a house. Sometimes the house represents the small self. Cancer has forced you to explore who you are."

"Why do you think I climb onto a toilet in the dream in order to escape?"

"What does a toilet do for us?"

"Helps us get rid of stuff we don't want?"

"Exactly! When the unwanted is eliminated, when you let go of what is no longer needed, you escape into the natural world and the Big Self."

"And the water in the dream, where I am paddling, is the unconscious?"

"Indeed. As you negotiate the unconscious with a helper—perhaps myself—you see a way to get back home, to return to wholeness."

ᚕ ᚕ

I browse the dusty bookshelves of Highland Cottage and pull out a slim paperback: Ian Bradley's *The Celtic Way*. It seems as if everything I need to know is contained in my dreams, in the landscape of this island, and on the dusty bookshelves of this house. I need to stop thinking about cancer, about what it may or may not have meant. It came; it went. I am here. Rain starts to chatter against the windows as I settle down to read.

The Celts, it appears, may first have emerged as a linguistic group in the area around the Black Sea around 1000 B.C. Having spread (or been driven) across Europe, they were well established in the British Isles by the time of the Roman invasion, around 50 A.D. While Roman influence was strong in England, they made little or no inroads into the tribal strongholds of Celtic society in Ireland, Scotland, north and west Wales, Devon, and Cornwall.

A key belief of the Celtic Christians was a profound sense of the immanence of God, in contrast to what later became the teachings of Roman Catholic and Protestant churches, which stressed the transcendence of God and his omnipotence and remoteness from the world. As

Christianity spread into Britain in the early fifth century, it seems to have been grafted smoothly onto the old religion of the Celts.

> To some extent this cosmic sense of God's presence through-
> out creation represented a Christianization of the religion
> of the pagan Celts. Their gods had dwelt within rivers and
> springs, mountains and woodland groves.... We are not in
> the world of pantheism here but in the much more subtle and
> suggestive realm of panentheism—the sense that God is to
> be found both within creation and outside it ... no worship of
> nature for its own sake but ... rather a wonderful sense that
> the whole cosmos is a theophany—a marvelous revelation of
> the goodness and wonder and creativity of God. Like Gerard
> Manley Hopkins, the Celts felt that "the world is charged with
> the grandeur of God."[37]

I read on and discover that Celtic monasteries tended to be established in remote and wild places, particularly on islands like Iona. The monks and lay people developed a deep love of nature, exemplified in some poetry that has survived, and in the incorporation of plants, animals, and birds on carved standing crosses and elaborate illuminated manuscripts like the *Book of Kells,* reputedly created on the island of Iona. St. Columba taught the monks on Iona to show hospitality, not just to human guests, but also to the birds that came to the island.

The more I read about Celtic Christianity, the more my heart opens. To be drawn to observe and write about nature is not a withdrawal from the world, but a coming to know the divinity in all matter—a belief that Christians share with Buddhists, who choose not to eat meat or kill a pesky fly because we are all one interconnected whole. Ian Bradley describes Celtic Christianity as the spirituality of a people who "perceive with their senses rather than their intellects or emotions.... The Celts were prime exponents of what is technically called natural theology, the idea that the existence of God can be confirmed, if not actually proved, through a contemplation of the beauty and order of the natural world."[38]

As a cold wind jabs at the windows, I sigh, put down the book, and go into the kitchen to make a hot drink—Barleycup, a coffee substitute. Definitely not coffee, but satisfying with a hot buttered scone. I take a bite of scone, relish the taste of butter on my tongue, and pick up the book again.

Although Celtic Christianity was gradually eclipsed by the form of Christianity flowing from Rome and by the Protestant Reformation, it never completely disappeared. It is heartening to read that there is, today, in Britain and Ireland a renewed interest in the traditions of Celtic Christianity. A parish priest in County Galway, John O'Donoghue, pleads for the recovery of the Celtic values of imagination, instinct, and identification with nature so that we may wake up from the alienation caused by technology and our belief that everything can be subordinated to human will. "As we walk through a landscape we may feel not that we are moving through a dead world of inanimate objects but that the landscape we are walking through is alive and that in a very intimate way it is our sister."[39]

More than anyone else in Scotland, it was George MacLeod, visionary minister in the Church of Scotland, who helped revive the values of the early Celtic church. He spearheaded the rebuilding of the ruined abbey on Iona by craftsmen recruited from among the urban unemployed. He was an environmentalist long before it was fashionable. "Pilgrim and poet, he tirelessly preached the oneness of creation and the thinness of the line that divides this world and the next ... In a talk given in 1955, he said: 'Follow truth wherever you find it. Even if it takes you outside your preconceived ideas of God and life. Even if it takes you outside your own country.... Be courageous. But concentrate on your search. Truth is one. All roads lead home.'"[40]

Bradley quotes another writer on the Celtic tradition, Robert Van der Weyer in *Celtic Fire.* "The British love of animals, gardens and nature and our whole tradition of pastoral poetry and landscape painting is another part of our Celtic tradition."[41] I feel a deep sense of satisfaction, of "coming home," as I read these words. My connection to the natural world finds its roots, not just in an evocation of a personal childhood spent largely outdoors, but also in a long-espoused philosophy of the immanence of the divine in nature in the culture into which I was born.

※ ※

The wind is blowing from the east, furrowing the Sound of Iona and urging foam-lipped waves onto the sandy shore at Traigh Ban nam Manach, White Strand of the Monks. Deep blue turns to aqua, and then to beige and white where water and sand meet, mingle, and separate. As each wet tongue recedes into the mouth of the sea, clusters of seaweed roll down toward the water and then are tossed onto the land again, forming a glistening brown arc close to the water's edge. Farther up the beach, a parallel band of seaweed, thrown there by some monstrous storm or high spring tide, crackles like fine dry twigs as I walk across it.

This is the beach where the Abbot and fifteen monks were slaughtered by marauding Vikings in 986. This is also one of the beaches where, in many healing visualizations, I saw cancer cells as crabs invading the island, crawling up over wet and dry seaweed, rounded pebbles, white sand, and dune grass, up onto the sheep pastures. This is where I saw seagulls—my white blood cells, my immune system—flocking down to protect the island.

There are no crabs here now, nor at the moment any seagulls. Just the sound of breaking waves and a lone woman walking toward me on the sand, her long evening shadow glancing over the foam like a ghost.

Yesterday, when I got off the ferry at Fionnphort to go hiking on the island of Mull, there was a large freezer lorry parked near the boat ramp. Young men in blue coveralls were loading crates of crab on board, bound for Spain. These crabs were five or six inches across, whereas the ones I had envisaged as cancer cells invading the island/my body were small, easily transported in seagull's claws. Maybe those now bound for Spain are the same ones the seagulls transported out into the Atlantic. Perhaps they returned to the waters around Iona and Mull plump and large, and are now bound for some café table in Barcelona, Malaga, or Madrid. Bon appétit!

PART III

❦

Approaching the Mystery

CHAPTER 13

❦

The Gift of Solitude

In the neglected crevices and corners of your evaded solitude, you will find the treasure that you have always sought elsewhere. —John O'Donahue[42]

I wake up with a start, the details of a dream clear in my mind. Something about it evokes a sense of panic. I talk with Barry and we discuss what it may mean. In the dream, I have a big argument with my daughter, Lucy, who has taken all my perennial seedlings and given them to a school or hospital. I want to get some back, but she can't remember the name of the place. We go to a train station and figure out the place where we have to go. Then I'm at a concert hall. People are finishing eating rich cake before going to a performance of Handel's *Messiah*. I have lost my ticket, but start climbing to the top floor, hoping they will let me in. On the way, I see Clem, a former colleague, who beckons to me. She keeps saying something I can't hear. Finally, I do hear: "The C is back."

"What do you mean?"

"The Death's Head Moth—the one that makes a C mark where it bites—someone on a ship has been bitten and has died. It caused an epidemic in 1890 and hasn't been seen since, but it's back."

My mother appears and asks, "Should I call the captain of my ship?"

"What ship …?" I reply. And wake up.

Barry points out that "perennial" conveys living year after year. Lucy, age twenty-five today, has that possibility before her; I don't. I gave my years away to institutions (schools, universities, hospitals).

I want them back. The dream states a problem: I won't live forever. This takes me to a performance of *The Messiah*—a story of incarnation, death, and redemption—victory over death. I hope I can get in to hear this story. On the way, a woman whom I remember in reality as a pleasant, efficient, slightly reserved dog-lover tells me (though I apparently don't want to hear): "The C is back." Cancer is back is the obvious interpretation; a frightening message.

"At the very least, you have to face your own mortality starkly," Barry says gently. "That's what you've taken on; that's what you've gone to Iona to do. From the psyche's point of view, it's irrelevant whether you live or die; the point is that you 'get it.' The small self has to face the Big Self."

Clem, in the dream, remarks: "Someone on a ship at sea has been bitten by a Death's Head Moth." I think there is such a moth, that my father had one in his collection, its body pierced by a long pin, dead and desiccated inside a glass-fronted case. Death's Head. Death of the head? Letting go of the intellect?

"It caused an epidemic in 1890, then disappeared and has now returned. What happened in 1890?" Barry asks.

My grandparents met, or married? The start of a chain of cancer in the family: my grandfather died of it two weeks after I was born (1934); my father died of it a month before my son, Jason, was conceived (1971). Is that the message of 1890 in the dream? It is also just over 100 years ago. In fairy tales, the princess falls asleep for 100 years, becomes unconscious. "The C is back" could mean cancer, or consciousness, or Clare, or Columba, or the Culdees—monks who followed the Columban tradition.

After talking with Barry, I walk toward the north end of the island thinking about our conversation and, on a whim, drop into the small secondhand bookshop near the abbey. I pull a book at random from a shelf: *A Historical Account of the Ancient Culdees of Iona* by John Jamieson—published in 1890! There are various interpretations of Culdee. *Cultores Dei,* worshipers of God. Or from the Irish, *Céile dé,* servant or companion of God. Or from the Gaelic, *cuil* or *ceal,* a retreat or sequestered corner. Those who retired to such a place were known as *cuildich.* Have I retired to this place to find God? I label that thought by turn pretentious, frightening, intriguing, tempting. Something is drawing me deeper into the mystery.

I return to Highland Cottage and sit staring out of an upstairs window. A fierce wind from the southeast is carving the surface of the sea into restless gray-green swells capped with white. A small dinghy moored near the ferry slip rocks back and forth, first exposing the underside of its hull and then its honey-colored ribbed interior. Herring gulls close to the shore float on the waves like gray-and-white corks.

It is time to stay indoors and appreciate roof, walls, warmth—and silence. In the words of the 13th-century mystic, Meister Eckhart: "We become a pure nothing by an unknowing knowledge which is emptiness, and solitude, and desert, and darkness, and remaining still."[43] It is said that our bodies reside in the soul and not the other way around. Silence enables us to expand through our senses and occupy the soul that is without. An environmental philosopher has noted:

> Nature's silence is felt not as an absence, a lack of communication, but as a powerful summons on the part of the natural world, a demand for attention to be paid. Obeying this command means shifting to a different kind of attention. ... We descend—really, we deepen—into a profound attention from which something can come to meet us.[44]

The Celtic Christian tradition emphasizes the immanence of God in the natural world. Nature is not something we go "into," as in modern parlance, but rather an encompassing element we are part of , that we live with. Nature is a second sacred book, parallel to the scriptures, revealing the immanence of the divine. God is close at hand, immediate and intimate.

I make a cup of tea and butter a slice of bannock, smearing it with Bruce's honey. The nectar from Iona's heather seduces my taste buds. Browsing the cluttered bookshelves of Highland Cottage, I finger the spines of paperbacks, turning my head sideways to read the titles. I pull out an anthology of poems; it falls open at a piece by R. S. Thomas, "Via Negativa":

… I never thought other than
That God is that great absence
In our lives, the empty silence
Within, the place where we go
Seeking, not in hope to
Arrive or find. He keeps the interstices
In our knowledge, the darkness
Between stars. His are the echoes
We follow, the footprints he has just
Left.…[45]

❧ ❧

The sun has broken through early-morning clouds and transformed the sea's surface into turbulent quicksilver. Gulls ride like princes on diamond-studded waters. I sit close to the wood-framed window, looking out at the wind-tossed world, grateful for solitude, grateful for silence.

In her beautiful memoir, *Fifty Days of Solitude,* Doris Grumbach waits early one morning for the sunrise. Growing impatient, she picks up a book and reads: "… the test of literature is, I suppose, whether we ourselves live more intensely for the reading of it." While doing this, she misses the sunrise, and makes this note in response to what she had just read. "No, I thought. At the moment I missed the sunrise by looking too closely at the printed page, I had diminished my life in a curious way. The intensity literature aroused in me, I believe, was often less than what happened when I listened to, felt, and saw the world around me."[46] "Yes, yes," I want to shout. Burying our heads in books, we miss the exquisite energy of life as it is around us, bursting out, invisible, silent, electrifying.

Yet even in the midst of entrancing landscapes, letting go of reading is almost impossible for me. I remember once, while walking alone the length of the Pennine Trail in England, I determined to wean myself from the written word, the better to take in the world around me. I lasted about a week. Then, hungry for the stimulation of reading, I left the trail and sought out a bookshop in a small Yorkshire town. I bought *Wuthering Heights* and read it as I continued on my way, thus absorbing the landscape of that moorland region both through my mind and through my senses.

Solitude permits each of us to go deeper into ourselves and into whatever is our calling, our passion in life. For Grumbach, it is writing fiction. And so, in solitude, her characters come more fully to life. For me, it is understanding our relationship to environment and place, and, since the jolt of serious illness, reflecting on the complex journey of my life. With advancing years, I have yearned for time to reflect on who I truly am. Now that the veils of daughter, wife, mother, professor have been lifted, I want to know my naked self before I die. Iona has given me the time and place to do just that.

≥ ≥

Brisk wind and bright sun; a good drying day. I fill the sink with hot water and soap flakes and start to knead my clothes: underwear, socks, T-shirts, nightdress. Squeeze, rub … squeeze, rub. I stare out at the garden as I work. It feels so good to have so few clothes to choose from; it is easy to wash them by hand, to fold and take care of them. My relationship to clothes has not been an easy one. Clothes rationing in the war meant that we had little choice. My mother knitted sweaters and advertised for a secondhand winter coat for me in the local paper. I don't remember feeling deprived; we were all in the same boat.

But adolescence was different. The war had ended, but clothes were still rationed. I was at high school in London. We were supposed to wear blue school uniform dresses bought at Pullen the Outfitter's on Finchley Road. The dresses had white collars and cuffs and white buttons down the front—not bad as uniforms go. But my mother, because of clothes rationing or lack of money, insisted on making my uniform. She was not a good seamstress: her seams were not entirely straight; her tucks were not neat. But worst of all, the material she bought was not quite the right shade of blue. I stood in the front row of the choir every morning at school prayers, facing hundreds of pairs of eyes in the auditorium, convinced as only adolescents can be that everyone was judging me. It was excruciating.

Years, perhaps lifetimes, later, I stood on a railroad platform in Moscow in an outfit that elicited envious glances from passersby, and I loved the attention. It was 1966 and, after living with my boyfriend, David, in Sweden for a year, I was returning to California the long way around, across Russia on the Trans–Siberian Railway. I was wearing tall white boots, a fake jaguar–spotted coat, and a genuine fox-fur hat—a present from David. The steam of two massive locomotives swirled around us. David and I, lovers for many years, were parting, perhaps forever. We stood on Platform 8, clinging to each other like Anna Karenina and … what's–his–name … and felt impossibly romantic. It was a time of austerity in Russia. Clothes like mine were a rarity. I felt both ashamed of my relative affluence and titillated by the sidelong glances of passersby. With a background of wartime rationing, my mother's inadequate dressmaking skills, and a lack of self–confidence about buying flattering clothes, I had never before experienced the secret exhilaration of having other women look at me with envy.

I finish the washing, hang my clothes out to dry, and explore the overgrown back garden of Highland Cottage. I come upon a black-and-white cat, and then—to my joy—a rhubarb patch. I pick a bunch of rosy-red stems, break off the leaves, and take them in to cook. From my wartime childhood days of scavenging, I get inordinate pleasure from finding food growing in the wild. In the 1940s in southern England, it was blackberries, rose hips, wild plums, mushrooms, and, occasionally, new potatoes dug up surreptitiously from Mr. Watson's fields. I look up "scavenger" in the Oxford English Dictionary and find it means: "Person employed to keep streets etc. clean by carrying away refuse; animal feeding on carrion, garbage, or any decaying organic matter." Not exactly how I would define it, but I love the sound of the word—scavenger. The very sound of it conjures up someone poking around and finding useful things, free, in unlikely places. My children probably wouldn't even know what it means.

I remember once using the word "glean" in a lecture at Berkeley and the students looked bewildered. I see my mother and myself gleaning at harvest time, following the reaping machine on a hot summer day, gathering up ears of wheat that had been dropped amid the stubble and taking them home to supplement the diet of our Rhode Island Red chickens, who, like us, were subject to wartime food rationing. I remember the time my brother and I found five pounds of butter left behind at the site of a field kitchen used by soldiers on field maneuvers. We were ecstatic! We'd never seen so much butter in our lives—our ration at the time was one ounce per person per week. The butter we found turned out to be rancid, but we ate it anyway.

❧ ❧

It's not only the solitude that I savor on Iona, but also the slow pace of my life. I smile to myself as I remember that the only race I ever won was a slow bicycle race on my childhood black-painted Raleigh. The point of the race was to get on your bike and, without ever putting your feet on the ground, come in last by wiggling your tires back and forth, barely moving. It was the summer of 1944. The end of the war was in sight. The government was sponsoring "Holidays at Home." They closed High Street in Leighton Buzzard to traffic—not that there was much traffic in those days, since only doctors and people on war work could buy petrol. Someone had decided the children needed a day of fun, so races and competitions were organized. I'm not sure why

I entered the slow bicycle race. Perhaps because I wasn't very athletic or fast or skillful at sports. Staying upright on a bike was something I thought I could do. I was so thrilled to win. It was the first and last such event I ever did win. What was the prize? I don't remember, but it set me off on a lifetime of reverence for slowness. I even eat slowly, carefully chewing broccoli or pieces of chicken breast when everyone else has placed their knives and forks neatly together and waits impatiently for dessert.

When I went skiing for the first (almost the last) time, I hated the trees rushing past my frozen ears and blue shadows on the snow melting away before I could examine them. What's the hurry? So much more pleasurable to take a walk in the snow, stopping to admire sparkling pillows of frost gleaming on pine cones, or the prints of a shy nocturnal animal disappearing into the underbrush like mirror-images of cirrus clouds.

I once went water skiing on a glittering lake in Tennessee. It was an outing for foreign students and I pretended I was thrilled at this opportunity for excitement, but actually I was terrified I would hit the water and it would feel like falling onto concrete. Later, I learned to kayak on flat water in British Columbia. I loved the lazy movement of the paddles, drifitng under the branches of alder trees and willows, hearing the sudden slap of a beaver's tail signaling alarm.

I like to move slowly through the world—to linger, to loiter, to wander, to ramble, to meander, to dawdle, to dally, to saunter. These are words we barely hear any more in these fast-paced times. I want to take in the world and its riches in small, slow encounters. Coming in last seems a good option if, along the way, you've had time to examine the patterns of rust on your bicycle handlebars and notice how much they resemble the shape of a butterfly resting lightly on the petals of a marigold.

❧ ❧

With a sore throat and a cold coming on, I sneak up to the staff room at the St. Columba Hotel to watch TV. It is the first time I've seen TV in months and I am mesmerized, particularly by the topic: the opening day of the Chelsea Flower Show in London. It is glorious: close-ups of flowers, interviews with designers and garden writers, prize-winning display gardens. "Mr. MacGregor's Garden" is based on Beatrix Potter's story, *The Tale of Peter Rabbit.* In order to propagate the plants that Potter depicted in her illustrations, the designer found a seed company that had been in business since the late 19th century. One woman is asked what she thinks about the gardens; she replies, "It's a treat to be here in a troubled world." I find myself in tears.

I am propelled back in time to my very first garden. The house where we lived during the war faced onto a cobbled courtyard that was bounded by houses and the stables for the Rothschild's hunting horses. We had no garden, front or back, but on the courtyard side, against the wall of our house, there were four small gaps where the lack of cobble-stones exposed patches of dark soil. It was here that I first learned to garden.

My Auntie Jean worked as a chemist at the Ovaltine factory in Kings Langley during the war, helping to develop Vitamin C out of rosehips as a substitute for citrus fruits that could no longer be imported. One spring day when I was perhaps six or seven, she came on a visit and brought me some pansy plants. She showed me how to plant them in those little square patches of soil in the courtyard, pouring water gently down the sides of each hole to settle the earth gently around the roots. Puddling in, she called it. I learned to water them and pinch off the dead flowers so the plant didn't use up energy making seeds. It was my first lesson in gardening.

A year or two later, the Rothschilds allowed a field near the cricket pitch to be ploughed up and subdivided into plots where residents on the estate could grow vegetables. The government was urging everyone to "Dig for Victory." I don't know how, at such a young age, I was permitted a plot; certainly my mother wasn't interested. But here, my love-affair with gardening progressed, fostered by Auntie Jean. I grew beans and potatoes, peas and spinach, and learned to distinguish weeds (shepherds purse, sow thistle, groundsel, dandelion) from the emerging seedlings. My only failure—mushroom spores ordered from an ad in the Sunday paper that, despite a carefully prepared bed of chicken manure, failed to germinate. When I was nine, I wrote my first "book," *The Joy of Gardening.* Carefully penned in a school exercise book, it is now sadly lost.

Germaine Greer, when interviewed on TV at the Chelsea Flower Show, referred to gardening jokingly (I think) as "a fascist activity.... Pulling out things that want to be there; forcing things to grow that don't want to be there...." I think of the wretched acanthus taking over parts of my garden in Berkeley, impossible to root out. If just a fragment of a root is left in the soil, it will spring back to life, just like cancer. I think of the pale yellow, delicate primroses that bloom on Iona, and how I've tried unsuccessfully to propagate and nurture them in my hot summer garden in California. Yes, in some ways, gardening is an unnatural act, justified because both the activity and the environments that result are healing for so many people.

When I speak to Lucy on the phone, all I want to hear, apart from news of her and Jason, is news of my garden. How are the tomatoes doing? The runner beans? Are the raspberries ripening? How are the orchids on the front porch? Is the garden thriving without me?

❧ ❧

Another day of rain. I stay indoors, sometimes reading, sometimes watching beads of water slide down the window panes, sometimes just staring into space, listening, not listening. What a gift it is to reach a state of mind, a time of life, where solitude is welcome, not feared as isolation or loneliness—a time when I can settle into it with gratitude, as if into a familiar and comfortable arm chair before a blazing fire.

CHAPTER 14

❧

Dreams and Synchronicities

… The dream is continually reminding us of the part which our conscious mind is forgetting … The unconscious may with infinite patience repeat a lesson over and over, trying with new images, new pictures, to show the truth…. The unconscious simply paints the picture, this picture, that picture, as the sea may cast up treasures on any shore; what use we make of these things is entirely our own affair…. If we will accept this inner event, experience it, make it part of our consciously lived life, then it becomes a potent factor, it produces change; we go from there to a new grasp, a deeper reality.
—Frances G. Wickes[47]

I sit at Columba's Bay for more than an hour—watching, listening, smelling. The waves are breaking onto a steeply banked beach fifteen feet below me. Above the water line is a shingle landscape of sun-baked, rounded rocks the size of oranges that make a muted pattern of grays, pinks, umber, white.

Why are we so endlessly fascinated by the meeting of land and water, the edge of things? River banks, lake shore, ocean beach; the end of land masses beyond which we cannot go—Land's End, North Cape, Cape Horn. I think of childhood history lessons and King Canute, the 11th-century Danish ruler of England who decided to show his courtiers the limits of kingly power. He had his throne carried to a beach where he commanded the waves to stop. As the tide advanced despite him, covering his feet, he is reputed to have said: "Let all men know how empty and worthless is the power of kings, for there is none worthy of the name, but He whom heaven, earth and sea obey by eternal laws."

At Columba's Bay, the waves are getting closer, the tide coming in. Like King Canute, I welcome its advance closer and closer to my feet. Is it something of the sea's danger, its potential killer quality that draws us mesmerized to its edge? How close will I let it come before I retrieve my pack and retreat higher up the beach? Only five feet from me now. Tangles of yellow-brown seaweed are caught among glistening pebbles, stroked landward and seaward with each breath of the sea. The salty smell engulfs me, reminding me of Jason's birth, briny womb-water running down my legs. It is time to move; time to go to the hospital. A tide turns abruptly in the fetal ocean, triggering an agonizing passage out into the light. Jason didn't cry when he was born. His face was composed, beatific, like a little Buddha.

The waves are now only three feet away. I begin to grow anxious. A freak wave could drag me out to sea, a brutal undertow hard to fight. The sun is clouded over; the water has changed to steely gray; the waves break with more force. It is time to move.

Higher up the steep shingle beach, above the high-water mark of stranded brittle seaweed, I lean against a mass of tilted rock streaked in pink, green, and gray. The rock in this part of the island—Lewissian gneiss—is 2.8 billion years old. Except for some places in Australia and the Canadian Shield, they are among the oldest rocks known on the planet. I feel secure in their embrace, supported, protected. They are as solid and unmoving as the sea is constantly changing. The juxtaposition of change and solidity, safety and danger, has a mesmerizing appeal. All my senses—vision, hearing, smell, taste—focus sharply on the present moment.

Contemplating his experience of the Shiants, uninhabited islands in the Outer Hebrides, Adam Nicolson writes: "Islands are made larger, paradoxically, by the scale of the sea that surrounds them ... The sea elevates these few acres into something that would never be if hidden in the mass of the mainland. The sea makes islands significant ... They are the not-sea within the sea, standing against the sea's chaos and erosive power, but framed by it, enshrined by it ... The state of siege is creative and an island, in short, is life set against death."[48]

I have always been fascinated with islands. In my childhood, I drew maps of imaginary islands; as an undergraduate, I went on a summer archaeological dig on the Danish island of Bornholm in the Baltic and took a bicycle trip to the Isle of Wight where my father's ancestors were farmers. The island as refuge is at the base of British consciousness—"… this precious stone set in a silvery sea." The island threatened from without and surviving has been a theme in our history from the Spanish Armada to World War II.

Every evening, BBC radio broadcasts a shipping forecast, a recitation of the names designating different segments of the seas around the British Isles—Viking, Forties, Cromarty, Dogger, German Bight, Humber, Biscay, FitzRoy. I remember hearing this nightly litany throughout my childhood, almost like a prose poem, a daily inventory of the anatomy of our island home, enclosing us, keeping us safe. Sole, Lundy, Fastnet, Shannon, Rockall, Malin, Hebrides, Bailey, Fair Isle, Faeroes. There are more than 6000 islands in the British Isles, every one of them special in some way. It feels like a miracle that I have found the one that is precious to me.

Some say that, long ago, Iona was a place of initiation for the Druids. Potential members of the priestly class were set adrift in an oarless boat and the currents brought them to this part of the island. If the boat drifted into the eastern part of Columba's Bay, known as Port of the Coracle, the man was deemed ready for initiation. If it drifted, instead, into the western part, known as Port of the False Man, he was rejected. Maybe it is a myth, but I like to think it is true.

I walk around Lookout Rock and into the next bay, Port an-Fhir-Bhreige, Port of the False Man, where the shingle stretches much farther inland. My booted feet crunch up the steep pebble slope that marks the year's highest tide. I walk inland and am astonished to find bluebell leaves peeping up between fat rounded rocks, no soil in sight, no other plants. I lift a rock to find a bluebell blooming beneath, deformed in shape but unmistakably a flower. I lift other rocks nearby, releasing the blooms from their impossible struggle to move the shingle on their way to the light.

A hundred yards inland and I am in a totally different landscape: a close-cropped greensward dotted with brown pellets of sheep dung. Ewes and lambs graze peacefully, bracken fronds emerge from the grass

like curled fists opening to many-fingered palms. I feel safe in this place, among my own kind—benign mammals raising their young. Looking back, I see that the late-afternoon sun, partially screened by clouds, has burnished the distant surface of the sea into a silver platter.

❧ ❧

At night, more dreams bring their stories. Talking on the phone with Barry, I make some sense out of two that I remember most clearly. In one, I am supposed to be helping a boy of fifteen or sixteen with his homework, but instead I keep seducing him.

"Yes, at fifteen or sixteen," Barry says, "it seems you made the decision to follow your intellect (do your homework). It was a path that served you in your career, but at some cost to the rest of your life."

Yes, indeed. I need to seduce that part of me away from books and into the sensual, the erotic. Walking the landscape of Iona—listening, looking, feeling, absorbing—I am saying farewell to academia and doing my homework.

In another dream, I look down through several floors of a mill and see many people tied up. There has been some kind of mutiny: "good guys" versus "bad guys." One man—a "good guy"—starts to determine which of the others are with him. He does this by shaking hands. While doing this, he slips each a flat round tin of shoe polish. The recipient looks at it and, if he figures out the password is "one o'clock and four o'clock," he is released.

I look up "mutiny" in the dictionary: "Open revolt against constituted authority; refusal by five or more members of the armed forces to obey a superior officer." My ego, my "superior officer," must indeed see what I am doing here as some kind of desertion, a mutiny. My presence and purpose on Iona are a revolt against academia and my past, just as cancer was a revolt, a mutiny, against the order of my body.

The scene is set in a mill. It could be a place of grinding and dismemberment; it could be a place of weaving substances together into a new pattern. I think it is both. And both are driven by water. I am harnessing the forces of nature, the force of life, to dismember and reweave myself.

"A winnowing process, a sorting out, is going on in the mill," Barry points out. "It is like the immune system, which decides: This one is good; this one is bad. In the dream, everyone is temporarily immobilized, tied up, brought to a standstill, just as the cancer brought your life to a stop. But a good guy starts to release the others. The way out is to know the password that distinguishes good guys from bad guys: what is healthy for you, and what is not. If those immobilized think the password is shoe polish—the obvious answer symbolizing keeping up appearances—they are not released. The persona, how we present ourselves to the world, is not the answer. But if the answer is one o'clock and four o'clock—connoting the passage of time, the living of life—they are set free. Living a psychologically aware life is the route to freedom and health."

An unexamined life is not worth living. I sigh as our conversation ends. I am learning so much from my dreams, so much about the reasons for paths taken and not taken in my life. These weekly conversations, often laced with deep emotion, sometimes with tension as I resist the implications of a dream-message boldly communicated, are a lifeline to me, so far away from the close companionship of old friends. Barry is a wise and loving soul-mate accompanying me on this journey into wholeness. If he had not come into my life, I fear I would have drifted back into the comforting world of academia, my intellect buffering my psyche from insistent reminders of unacknowledged feelings. Dreams bypass the conscious mind. Dreams cannot be denied.

Barry leaves soon to conduct workshops in North Carolina, then to lead other seekers at the Temagami Vision Quest in Canada. I feel envious of those who will be in his presence, others to whom he will give his loving attention. I will miss him.

ॐ ॐ

I take an evening walk down to Sandeels Bay. A perfect interconnectedness of life occurs in the shallow waters off Iona's beaches. Sand eels, which prefer shallow water over a sandy or gravelly bottom, live much of the year buried. With growing light and warmth in March and April, they emerge to feed on the plankton thickening in the sea. The sea birds arrive to make their nests and prey on the adult sand eels. In late May, just as the sea birds need to collect protein-rich fish to nurture their young, the next generation of sand eels, born in March, are just the right size for catching and pushing into the yawning throats of puffins, kittiwakes, shags, guillemots, and gulls. The cycle of life continues.

ॐ ॐ

No wonder the 1920s school of Scottish artists known as the Colourists chose the north end of Iona as their outdoor studio. Rocks of rosy pink and dark gray veined with green; a turquoise sea, its shallow depths floored with sand; gently sloping white beaches strewn with high-tide markings of brown seaweed; rock pools, layered strands of cumulus clouds, green and brown landscape of Mull in the distance, and farther away, on the horizon, the soft blue outline of the Cullins of Skye. I long to be able to paint this scene, yet nothing recorded on paper—in colors or words—can reproduce the sensuality of this place: the ceaseless roar of breaking waves, the call of a herring gull, the stroke of the wind on my cheeks, hot tea from my thermos slipping down my throat, shadows in the damp sand formed by my footprints walking up to meet me.

Above all, this is an erotic landscape. Sprawling on the warm sand, I feel the desirous waves as soft hands caressing me. I let consciousness slip into my loins. The sea here is not a place of danger, but a lover.

Aroused by joy. No need for a human partner. Alone on this beach, nothing but rocks, sand, and sea before me, I feel wrapped around with love, merging as one with all that is pouring in deliriously through my senses.

❧ ❧

Sitting on top of Dun Bhuirg, Hill of the Fort, looking south, I can see the whole expanse of the Machair, the Bay at the Back of the Ocean, and the stream bed slashed deep into the white sand that empties into Port Ban. From this vantage point, I can see the rocky track that leads up to Lock Staonaig, and the fence row marking the road that leads back to the village on the eastern side of the island. I can see both sides of the island at this, its narrowest point, squeezed between the Sound of Iona and the north Atlantic. It is a place for getting things into perspective.

Last night, I finished reading Ruth Picardie's *Before I Say Goodbye.* I feel weighed down with sadness and fear of my own death. She would have no sympathy for me; at sixty-five, I have lived twice as long as she did and have seen my children grow up. It is hard not to feel guilty for being alive.

Thinking about my own experience with cancer and then reading of someone else who had a very different attitude and outcome in similar circumstances is perhaps not wholesome for me. Reading Picardie's book has me rattled; it has jolted me out of my restful-island-retreat frame of mind. She dealt with cancer by shopping and getting facials and consulting bizarre alternative healers whom she quickly labeled as charlatans. Perhaps I might have done the same if my cancer had progressed as rapidly as hers did, or if, like her, I had been in the prime of life. Looking at pictures of her small children losing a mother so young, my heart grieves for them. And for the writer herself, a gifted journalist who wrote of her ordeal without rancor or self-pity, knowing there was little chance she would survive.

I need to stop, to be present in this place and to stop obsessing about someone else's story. A pair of ravens perched nearby alternately squawk at me and engage in gentle pecking at each other's beaks, as if in love-play. More and more, I am aware of birds on the island: seagulls everywhere; oyster catchers and sanderlings along the shore; skylarks hovering in song over the sheep pastures; corncrakes hiding in the long grass, their raucous cries betraying their presence; lapwings near Jane MacFadyen's croft, agitated that I may get too near their nests; rooks incessantly arguing in strident tones in the sycamores; a sparrow, dull brown with an inelegant cheep-cheep-cheep, perched on the gutter of the Argyll Hotel, chattering, it seems, to passersby; and the bird I have fallen in love with, a thrush with beige speckled breast who sings morning and evening in the village and has a range of songs so melodious, so honey-sweet, so inventive, that I am stopped in my tracks every time I hear him. I want to call out in a language he can hear: "Thank you, thank you for the gift of your song, which reminds me to cease what I am doing and be thankful that I am alive."

As I climb down the hill and walk across the green sod of the Machair, there—out on the waters of the Bay—are four white swans. What are they doing here? They are fresh-water birds and seem quite out of place amid beds of kelp and peeping oyster catchers. They float serene, their hooked necks like four big question marks.

It is getting cold. I keep turning to look back at Dun Bhuirg, concerned at what a rocky eminence it appears to be from a distance and how I was perhaps foolhardy to climb up it alone. Two young cows are grazing in a field beside the road. I stop and lean over the fence, making noisy out-breaths as cows do to each other. One becomes curious, approaches, and licks my hand with her thick raspy tongue. I pull some grass to feed her, but she is more interested in licking me. Perhaps it

is the salt. In a field that was ploughed and sown a week ago, twenty-seven seagulls are hunkered down, close together, all facing into the wind, like a collection of porcelain ornaments carelessly left outdoors. I begin to notice that seagulls at rest seem to cluster in groups of twenty to thirty, seldom more or less. Was it the visualization with the seagulls that made the difference; is that why I'm alive? Or was that just the frosting on the cake after chemo and radiation, the Big Guns, had done the real work? I will never know, cannot ever know. Some mysteries are best left unanswered. Why am I even asking these questions? I am here. I am alive. I am tired.

Approaching a slight rise in the road that marks the watershed between the eastern and western shores of Iona, I look back to the west and see what appears to be a string of unfamiliar islands on the horizon. They are rounded, dark gray against the lighter gray of the sky. Then I realize they are slightly above the horizon and are actually clouds. For an instant, they seem to be the Tir na Og—the islands in the Western Ocean which, in Celtic mythology, are thought to be a paradise, the Otherworld, the Land of Eternal Youth. In this place of thin veils, the distinction between mythical and real evaporates like a nighttime dream in the early mists of morning.

Closer to the village, I come upon two young thrushes breaking snail shells on the concrete steps of the village hall. And in the field behind Mrs. Gully's house, a jackdaw sits on the back of one of the old rams, pecking luscious morsels out of his wool. He flies over to the other ram, which is, as usual, kneeling to graze. The bird lands on the upended rump and slithers down to the head like an avian skier, pecks away, and then flies off replete toward Sandeels Bay.

❧ ❧

A herring gull is cackling on the roof as I wake from a deep sleep. A dream begins to fade like an ancient photograph. Barry has an apple tree that has been badly damaged by snow. There are only three apples left on it. He is going to pay 255 dollars to an arborist to see if the tree can be saved.

I note down the dream, then wander to the store to buy a loaf of bread before they are all gone. Later, with toast and tea at my side, I ponder the dream. What do I associate with apples? Once, when staying in Glastonbury—an ancient spiritual site in western England—I climbed the seven-layered labyrinthine path up the hill known as Glastonbury Tor. Descending the hill, I found a wild apple tree at its base and reached out to pick some fruit. But some strong inner voice commanded: "No! Don't pick it." So I did not. That evening, I read that the apple was sacred to pre-Christian people, including the Druids who lived in this part of England, which is known as Avalon, the Place of Apples. To eat an apple was to partake of the food of the dead and know no return.

Later, scanning the bookshelves in Highland Cottage, I move some ornaments and pull out a volume of Scottish fairy tales. One of these tells of Thomas the Rhymer, who is spirited away to the land of the fairies, a place full of fruit trees and other good things. There he is told he must not eat any of the fruit until they come to a tree of red apples. The Fairy Queen gives him one and says: "This I can give thee and do it gladly for these apples are the Apples of Truth, whosoever eateth them gaineth this reward, that his lips will never more be able to frame a lie." It is told that Thomas took the apple and ate it; and for evermore, the

Grace of Truth rested on his lips. And that is why men called him True Thomas.

The apple as a source of truth and as a source of death. The tree in the dream has been damaged by snow; on a mammogram, a tumor appears white, like snow. But this tree is not dead. It bears three beautiful red apples, perhaps the trinity of Christian thought or the trinity of Celtic Welsh belief —the underworld, the earth, and the upper world. For a fee (a price to be paid, the cancer itself?) this tree may be saved.

❦ ❦

Something strange is beginning to happen. On several occasions, I have had a dream or daydream and then, a day or two later, something similar actually happens. Or I am reading a book and find a story parallel to what I have recently dreamed or experienced.

After a late afternoon walk to the north end of the island, along the Strand of the Seat and back across Calva, I eat, go to bed early, and dream that I am making love with Phil, a former colleague. People see us through the windows. Phil draws a curtain, but we're still visible to people at an outdoor café, where a woman gestures and says, "Carry on—what you're doing is only natural." Six days after this dream, a couple comes into Highland Cottage (the door always left unlocked) looking for a place to make love, out of sight. I awaken, startled out of a deep sleep by my bedroom door opening and the light coming on. And there stands a young man with curly auburn hair, his eyes wide with astonishment.

"What are you doing here?" I stammer, half sitting up.

The man, as startled as I, says something like "Mrs. D. said we could stay here for the weekend." (Since it was a Wednesday, I wonder if they were late for last weekend or early for the next.) He quickly leaves the room and starts back down the stairs. I jump out of bed and glimpse a young woman preceding him. She stumbles briefly on the bottom step. Opening the front door, the man calls out: "Maybe she meant us to stay in Rose Cottage."

Through a darkened window, I see them switch on the lights of a cottage at the back. I keep watching. The lights go off. I am overcome with feelings of loneliness and longing. I return to my bed filled with an empty presence.

I start to think of former lovers and the unlikely places we frantically sought out to make love: the hard, hot bench in a sauna in Berkeley; the couch in the director's office at International House; the back of a camper van at Esalen; in a hammock in Oregon; at a deserted beach in California; on a ferry from Russia to Japan. What became of those men? One became my husband (for a while); one disappeared soon after our coital rapture; one was killed in an automobile accident just as we made plans to live together; one moved on after a relationship of several years; several of them I abandoned; one I sometimes still see professionally and we both pretend "it" never happened; one ran away like a startled rabbit, frightened by the intensity of my emotions.

I sigh and turn over in bed. Those relationships happened long ago. I feel envious of the couple in Rose Cottage, still young and full of sexual energy. If only I could, like the woman in my dream, gesture toward the dark-windowed cottage, saying casually: "Carry on. What you're doing is only natural." But I cannot. I wish I were that young again.

What of the dream of the couple making love? Why would I dream of something and then, a few days later, have it really happen? It feels as if I am slipping into some kind of parallel world or altered state. When I sighted the four white swans on the Bay at the Back of the Ocean, I was startled by such an unusual sight—swans at sea? But I had an inkling some explanation or parallel story would present itself. Two days later, I read in a Celtic story, *The Children of Lir*, of a King and Queen who had four beautiful children—Fionuala, Conn, Fiachra, and Hugh. On the Queen's death, the King married her sister, Anoife, who grew jealous of the children because she remained childless and they were so beautiful and loved. She took the children on a journey and, in a lonely spot, ordered her servants to kill them. The servants refused and, when she tried to do it herself, she could not. Instead, she transformed them into four white swans. She laid on them the following curse: They must spend 300 years on the waters of Lake Derryravagh, 300 more on the Straits of Moyle that lie between Scotland and Ireland, and 300 more on the Atlantic by Erris and Inishglory.

After this time, when the Woman of the South is betrothed to the Man of the North, the enchantment would end. Their father, King Lir, was heartbroken. He eventually found them on Lake Derryravagh and, to his great joy, discovered they could still speak with human tongues and make wonderful music. People came from far and wide to converse with them and listen to them, and peace and harmony prevailed in the land.

Later, on the Straits of Moyle and in the Atlantic, they suffered greatly from cold and loneliness. Eventually, as the curse foretold, a woman of the south, Princess Deoca, was betrothed to a man of the north, a chief named Lairgnen. She asked him for the four singing swans as a wedding present. When they were brought to her, their swan plumage fell away, revealing four withered, white-haired humans of vast old age. The couple fled; a hermit-monk baptized the four, who then died and were placed in one grave, from which their spirits ascended to heaven.

I think of the four young men from Iona who drowned in December 1998 returning from a Christmas dance on Mull, their small boat overwhelmed in the darkness by a freak, rogue wave. The street lights in Fionnphort were extinguished that night in a power outage, so if the men had tried to swim to shore, there was nothing by which they could get their bearings. Only one in the group of five survived. It was a tragedy of mythic proportions for this island of barely 100 souls: four of its own, four who had decided to stay on and become crofters and ferrymen, four who would father the next generation of children on the island and keep the tiny primary school from closing down. Four young souls who hover near their place of birth; four white swans floating serenely on the western ocean, their hooked necks asking the ultimate question.

CHAPTER 15

❧

Island Consciousness

I am not sure whether there is no time here
Or more time, whether the light is stronger
Or just easier to see. That is why
I keep returning, thirsty, to this place
That is older than my understanding
Younger than my broken spirit.
—Kenneth G. Stevens[49]

More and more, specific places on the island seem to call to me. An image of the place appears in my mind; a gut feeling urges me to pay attention. I always heed the call. One day in June, I sense that I need to go to the Sacred Hollow, Coire Sianta, located between Loch Staonaig and Columba's Bay. As I approach the long valley where Sacred Hollow is marked on the map, I have a distinct feeling that this is a place to be entered with caution. While the north end of the island feels welcoming and sensuous, and Columba's Bay feels austere and down to earth, this valley—part of which is called Hollow of the Big Mouth and is formed by a geological fault—feels bleak and unwelcoming. Cut off from the sound of the ocean and from sea-borne winds, it lies silent and still. There are no familiar bird calls, no gulls or oyster catchers, lapwings or skylarks, only the faint peep-peep-peep of a tiny brown bird I cannot name that perches on a rock protesting my approach.

As I step over the heather-covered remains of an old wall into the Hollow, a startled rabbit leaps up at my feet and bounds away, its long brown ears flattened against its back. The boggy ground squelches

under my boots and white tufts of bog cotton hang low over the landscape like flurries of snow. I feel a little fearful, like an intruder—and
then I see the orchids. "Oh, how beautiful!" I speak out loud, as I see
dozens of pale pink and mauve heath-spotted orchids punctuating the
water-logged ground at my feet. In a garden of cultivated flowers, these
modest blooms might be lost from view, but here, in this seemingly
bleak and inhospitable landscape, they appear like a miracle. I feel their
presence as a gentle welcoming.

I step up onto a low mound and lie down spread-eagled on a
bed of dried heather. There is no wind; the sun is warm. I feel a deep
sense of relaxation. Breathing deeply and slowly, I seem to merge with
the ground beneath me. Suddenly, I have a flash-image of the snow-
covered apple tree in my dream. This time, in my imagination, I shake
the tree and find it is covered with apples underneath the snow. I wonder if there is some link between the Hebrides and the Hesperides. The
latter were nymphs in Greek mythology who tended a bissful garden in
the far western corner of the world. In that garden was a tree bearing
golden apples that were said to bestow the gift of immortality.

Later that day, as I browse through Elinore's books at Highland
Cottage waiting for the kettle to boil, I find one entitled *Celtic Christianity and Nature* by Mary Low. I skim the pages and come upon
another story of an apple tree shaken into life. In a Latin text probably
known in Ireland as early as the eighth century, it is said that Adam
sent his son Seth to Paradise, to the tree that had died when Adam and
Eve sinned. As he approached, he saw a beautiful child shaking the
apple tree, which then became alive and healthy, covered with leaves.
Adam prophesied that that same child would one day die on the dead
tree, be crucified in order to revive it into life once more.

That evening, I walk north to the White Strand of the Monks. The
tide is receding. Dark clouds beneath the green sea slowly emerge as
slanting gray rocks—dreams from the unconscious peeking through
into the waking day to be warmed by the sun, exposed to human scrutiny until the tide returns. Farther out to sea, some dark dreams are
never uncovered.

‰ ‰

Hiking with Elizabeth along a trail near Carsaig on Mull, I realize how much I miss trees. In and around the village on Iona, there are sycamores and ash trees able to withstand salt-laden winds. There are a few wind-shaped hawthorns clinging to rock faces near Sandeels Bay. But the rest of the island is grass, bog, and rock—too exposed or too much cropped by sheep and cattle for trees to grow. On the southern shore of Mull, however, a sheltered trail snakes through groves of birch, past ash and hawthorn, Scots pine and larch, through the delicate fronds of sword fern and sturdy clumps of waist-high bracken. I feel the textures of leaves, the patterned shadows at my feet, the enclosure of a leafy tunnel-walk melting into my body like honey. Memories of trees from my childhood float into consciousness.

The grand driveway leading to the mock-Tudor Rothschild mansion was lined with horse chestnut trees. In spring, their branches held aloft pinnacles of white and pink blooms; in the twilight, they appeared as ghostly candelabra. In the autumn, we gathered glossy brown chestnuts from under the trees and strung them on pieces of string to play conkers, a traditional children's game where you hit one against another until all but the winner had been reduced to pulp.

In 1942, we heard the news that a method had been found to transform horse chestnuts into badly needed cattle fodder. "We could make a lot of money!" Ronnie said excitedly. "Let's get some sacks from round back of the stables and fill them up."

Ronnie, Shirley, and I filled three sacks with shiny chestnuts and, telling our mothers we would be playing with Gregory the goat in his field (a lie), we walked slowly into Leighton Buzzard, the sacks balanced on the saddles of our bicycles. We knew our way to the government depot near the High Street because my Auntie Jean had taken us there with bags of rose hips, which they bought for making Vitamin C. We received two shillings and sixpence for the rose hips, but the chestnuts were much heavier. We would be rich!

The old man at the depot had whiskers growing out of his nose and ears. I stared, fascinated. Would my Daddy have whiskers growing out of his ears when he came home? I hoped not; they made me feel frightened.

The man looked at us, puzzled. "We've brought conkers ... horse chestnuts ... you know, for cattle feed?" Ronnie volunteered.

The man scratched his head, then broke into a smile, a big black gap where two front teeth were missing.

"Oh that! Sorry kids. That was some stupid rumor. It's not true. We can't use chestnuts."

Our faces fell in disappointment, visions of visits to the cinema, with fish and chips afterward, faded quickly away. We turned back toward home without speaking and poured the chestnuts out onto a weedy patch beside the glinting rails of the London and Midland railway—three glossy pyramids like mysterious dolmens left by a prehistoric tribe long gone from these parts.

Horse chestnuts, ash, beech, oak—so many trees from my childhood. I remember the joy I felt in springtime when trees dormant through the long winter months began to uncurl into life: the rosy-tinted, pleated leaves of sycamore; yellow-green of oak; red-tipped fingers of hawthorn. A weeping willow in the formal gardens at Ascott had been trained over a metal framework so that, when you sat beneath it, you felt as if you were sitting under a lacy, green inverted basket. Each spring, glowing yellow aconites broke through the frosty ground beneath that tree like a sprinkling of priceless golden coins. There was a magnificent copper beech near our cottage whose dipping branches hung so low we could sit astride them and ride them like bucking broncos. Not far away was an exotic redwood whose crumbling bark we once made into "cigarettes." We smoked in secret, out near the boiler house. We all felt sick and Paul threw up in the bushes. We never tried smoking again.

Then there were the trees on the edge of Round Spinney, trees we hadn't noticed before. We were chasing parachutes that day. These were white squares of glossy fabric held by string to a small metal canister. The canisters contained flares that were dropped by our bombers to light up nighttime targets in Germany. The flares were made at a small factory in Linslade where my mother worked. Every few weeks, some of them were fired off in a test.

Whenever we saw them floating above us, we ran through the fields trying to catch them as they fell to earth. The fabric was precious— soft, shiny. Could it have been nylon? Had it been invented then? No, I think not, but whatever it was, we knew our mothers would be pleased. My mother took the squares and cut and sewed them together on her sewing machine to make fancy underwear for herself.

One day we ran all the way to Round Spinney to retrieve the flares. And then we saw something we had never seen before: small round plums catching the sun like Christmas lights. Some were low enough to pick. We held the four corners of a parachute together and filled it with plums.

"Mum will be pleased," I said. "She can make pies and jam."

We started eating them as we walked home. That's when we made up our special name for them—Paul, Ronnie, Naomi, Mary, and I. We called them *peplerries:* "pe" for "peach," because the yellow-pink skin looked like a peach; "pl" for "plum," because they were the shape of a plum; and "erries" for "cherries," because that's what they tasted like.

In a wood close to our house, we fashioned a hut between four trees that formed a rough square. It was Paul's idea to make the walls out of flattened, discarded petrol cans that were left behind after the army had occupied the fields and woods around our house for field maneuvers. I don't remember how we flattened them, but they made good solid walls, and we created a stove out of an old, cast-iron lavatory cistern. When we lit a fire inside it, it gave off a smell of hot metal and burned leaves. Around the hut, we made a perimeter fence of dead branches. One tree was designated the Lookout Tree and someone was posted there while we played, to watch out for The Enemy. Whether the enemy was the Germans (who had not yet come), or the Rothschild children (who might tell their parents we had lit a fire), I don't remember.

The hut was the biggest and most elaborate of our dens. But there were others. We dug a pit and covered it with branches and leaves to make a sort of underground bunker. It was dark and mysterious; entering it was like crawling into a rabbit's burrow. We talked in whispers, although the nearest grown-ups were far away. One hot day in June, we hid away in our burrow to eat alpine strawberries stolen from the rock garden at Ascott. They were sweet and delicious, and we sucked our fingers and giggled at the amazing heist we had carried out without being caught.

But my most poignant memories are not of the hut we built or the bunker we dug, but of a place we just found. At first, the clump of low trees and bushes in the middle of a field of potatoes appeared to be just that—a clump of trees and bushes. But when we got closer, Mary and I found it was an overgrown quarry with steep sides and, in the middle, a small conical hill. This became our favorite place to go in the summer when we were eight, nine, and ten (our birthdays were just one day apart). We called it Happy Hideout. My mother would give me a screw-top jar of vegetable stew and some bread; we stored the food in our saddle bags and took off on our bicycles.

We collected wood, started a fire on top of the conical hill, and poured the stew into an old saucepan we kept hidden there under an elderberry bush. Sometimes, we snuck into a field nearby and dug up new potatoes to roast in the ashes, our hearts pounding for fear Mr. Watson, the farmer, would catch us stealing and tell our mothers.

Many, many years later, I returned to that childhood landscape and started to walk across the field to visit Happy Hideout once more. But before I reached it, I stopped, turned, and retraced my steps. Now, through adult eyes, it would probably look small, overgrown, nothing special. Better to retain the memories that are in my heart.

Best of all the familiar trees of my childhood was The Falling Down Tree, which grew close to our house. It was a tall yew that grew on the edge of a wood, its strong layered branches all growing out in one direction, searching for the light. My friends Ronnie and Shirley and I would climb to the top, then, taking a deep breath, launch ourselves fearlessly onto its branches. Like loving outstretched arms, they held us, passing us layer by layer down, down, down to the ground, where we lay breathless, our bodies quivering with excitement, cradled in a deep bed of fallen leaves smelling richly of damp earth, decay, and slow, slow transformation.

⁂

I sit on the beach at Sandeels Bay, the wrinkled blue-green womb of the island throbbing rhythmically against the shore. Three eider ducks float by on the sunlit water, calling woo-woo-woo to each other (or perhaps to me). Just offshore, the red-brown rocks of Eileann Carrach, Rough Skinned Island, lie like a gnarled and ancient sea creature, basking in evening warmth. From the west, a narrow rocky gully opens into the bay and, in its mouth, amazingly, stands a lone hawthorn tree covered with white flowers.

Beyond the village, trees are so rare on Iona that finding one unexpectedly is cause for rejoicing, even awe. How did this lone specimen manage to survive? Its trunk is twisted; its limbs are covered in green lichen; its whole shape bends toward the south and east. One of its three main branches has been wrenched off by the wind and lies decaying in a narrow stream bed. It feels right that I should find this tree, surviving against the odds. Don't believe the odds, it seems to say. Decide to survive—and you will. But be sure to choose an auspicious environment as I have done. Sheltered from the cold north winds, looking out to sea, listening to the sea's breathing, I am content in this place. That is why I have survived. Choose a place that supports and protects you; select it wisely; allow yourself to bend with the wind, but put down deep roots. Trees may not have the freedom to move around like humans or eider ducks, but we have learned to be content in one place.

I return to the village, with its leafy sycamores, its rowans and fuchsias, its gardens and songbirds. It is said that more than half the

sacred trees in the folk tradition of Ireland are hawthorns. The lone hawthorn at Sandeels Bay seems like a hermit-tree in its cell, withdrawn from the world into meditative stillness. Like me, it is a bit misshapen. One of its branches is missing, yet it is still beautiful in its summer blossoming.

❧ ❧

Each Thursday, a doctor comes over from Mull to a health clinic on Iona—a neat white building next to the school. With a letter from my oncologist in California, I go in for a check-up. The doctor draws some blood to send to the mainland for testing. I am not worried. Cancer rarely enters my mind any more.

As I leave the clinic, I hear a chorus of ewes and lambs bleating with expectation and excitement as they trot down the rough track from Maol and turn into a field by the village hall that hasn't been grazed for several weeks. Across this field runs the ancient route of Straid nam Mavbh, Street of the Dead, now no longer visible. It was the path followed when the bodies of Scottish and Irish kings were brought to Martyr's Bay, then carried overland to be buried in Reilig Oran, St. Oran's Churchyard, next to the abbey. As the sheep and lambs graze hungrily on the lush new grass, their voices fall silent. I stand watching them with deep pleasure. The sheep are assured ample pasturage; the invading crabs have been vanquished; the Street of the Dead has faded from view.

❧ ❧

As I walk west one morning, I meet a group of khaki-clad men and women, some carrying curious Chinese-style "hats."

"What are those?" I ask a short man with gray hair peeking out from under the rim of his tweed cap.

"They are microphones. We are recording birdsong," he replies, gently stroking the "hat" in his hand.

"Oh, you must be looking for corncrakes" I offer, proud of my ornithological knowledge.

"That's right. We think there's one nesting over there in the tall grass."

"Yes, I've heard it. You may also want to go to a field of wild iris below the abbey, and an area of un-mown grass behind the parish church. There are corncrakes there too."

I begin to feel like an old-timer, instructing these day-trippers in the natural history of the island. The man and a few of his companions who had gathered around seem grateful for the information.

"Oh, and there's another bird you may want to record. It's a thrush in the village. It sings so exquisitely every evening."

The group turns away, obviously not interested. Bird recorders, like stamp collectors, are looking for the rare and the distinctive. No matter that the commonplace has a sweeter voice.

I leave them fiddling with their recording equipment and walk on across the Machair, over a stile, and thus to the beach at Port Ban. I settle down to eat my lunch. The tide is coming in, pushing gently up the beach in white-fringed ripples of brine. I pick up some sand and am startled to see it is composed of minute fragments of shell. I had vaguely imagined it to be weathered sandstone, but the rocks of this island are much older than that. It is impossible to conceive of the time it has taken to create a beach like this one out of the broken and pulverized skeletons of myriad sea creatures. To the general sweep of the eye, the beach appears white. But when I pick up a handful of sand and look at it closely, I see a host of colors—brown, ivory, orange, black, flecks of blue and purple—like a pointillist painting viewed close up through squinty eyes.

Through various gates, around wire fences, I find my way to the Little Fair Mound, Sithean Beag, its pyramidal shape eroded by rabbit burrows and sandy niches where sheep lie and shelter from the north wind. Spread-eagled on the hill and glad that no one can hear me, I ask permission of the fairies to be here. An island legend tells of a woman who went at night to cut open a fairy hill and was found dead there the next morning. To the Celts, each balanced human being had a fairy and an animal ally, thereby forming a triune. As I lie on the Little Fairy Mound, strong images of the corncrake and the hawthorn tree from Sandeels Bay return.

In this part of the world, a pre-Celtic fairy tradition was handed down through stories and songs within families. It was recorded in medieval texts from the eighth to 15th centuries, and survived as a living practice into the 20th century. Such fairies are wholly different from the Victorian literary tradition of tiny winged creatures that look like butterflies. This Celtic tradition is of a race of beings that live within the sacred body of the land, are human-sized or larger, and gifted with a level of consciousness and intelligence we don't have. Some are hostile to humans, some friendly. They often protect special places, trees, or stones. Their sense of time is different from ours; they appear to be immortal.

On a recent visit to Iceland, I learned that, there, this tradition of beings that live within the body of the land is still very much alive. Road and tunnel projects through sacred places are often stalled by mysterious accidents to men and machinery. Sometimes a local shaman is called to contact these invisible beings and ask permission for a project to continue. Sometimes the engineers have to re-route the road

I return home via the Glen of the Temple, skirting the first two fields, which are thick with grass being grown for hay and dotted with wildflowers—pale pink milkweed, nodding plantain, ruddy dock, buttercups, and clover. I climb a gate and cross a field cropped close by ten shorn, horned sheep that move away nervously, not used to seeing humans in this part of the island. As I cross a stile and move into another cropped field, I immediately have the strangest sensation that I am only three feet tall. I feel that I am not much taller than the leaves of the wild iris around me, but, checking my shadow, I see that I haven't really shrunk. Perhaps I have indeed entered the fairy realm.

❧ ❧

Day after day, an image of some particular spot on the island insistently appears in my mind and, with pen in hand and pad of paper propped on my knees, I try to capture the *anima loci,* the soul of the place. But, like a wild spirit, it eludes capture and squirms free into the breaking waves. It is said that, when Felix Mendelssohn visited the west of Scotland in 1829, his sisters asked him on his return to tell them something about the Hebrides. "It cannot be told, only played," he said. Seating himself at the piano, he played the theme that afterward grew into the *Hebrides Overture.*

Many have come here to write, to paint, to compose poetry. In a slim volume I bought in the village, *An Iona Anthology,* I find that writings about the magic of the island span fourteen centuries, from the sixth to the 20th. On the verge of the 21st, I am also drawn to record some of what I sense here—to be a mediator between the essence of place and human experience. I write, not to urge others to travel from afar to this remote island, but to encourage them to experience deeply their own sacred place and to access the kind of deep peace that I have found on Iona.

Drawn to particular places on the island, I trust the call; this is an exercise in surrender. Such places feel achingly alive, as if they, too, yearn for human contact. Ecologist and philosopher David Abrams also maintains that mountains and animals, the entire non-human world, is struggling to make contact with us. It feels as if I am living at some level of consciousness for which I have no name. It is neither busy, social, alert awakeness; nor is it nighttime dreaming. It is somewhere in between. I call it island consciousness, daytime dreaming. In this place, it is as if time and space do not exist and I have entered another dimension only fractionally apart from the material world.

One evening, the Sound is the color of bluish skimmed milk, its surface flat with just the faintest dimpled overlay. As I stare at the water, its calmness enters my being, drowning memories, smoothing out perplexities, submerging thought itself. My breathing slows down and deepens. There is no place to be but here, no time but now.

Could I have this experience somewhere else—on some other island, in some other landscape? Perhaps. But for me, it is Iona—its history, people, topography, flora, fauna, weather—that seems to invite me to relax into the deepest part of my being. Iona has become a mirror for my soul. I imagined I had come here to process my experience with cancer, but that goal seems less and less important. A pile of journals from the last five years sits on my bedroom floor in Highland Cottage, mostly unread. I sense that the full import of my stay here has yet to be revealed.

༄

CHAPTER 16

Intellect versus Heart

Concentration is the art of forgetting our own subjectivity in order to be fully available to what presents itself. When the activities of personal thinking and personal feeling are stilled, the subjectivity of the outer world expresses itself … The heart says yes there is something here to behold beyond what I think or feel about it. The heart does not strive after meaning but rather allows the things to disclose themselves. —Robert Sardello[50]

It was a big mistake. Why did I contaminate my stay on Iona by agreeing to take time out to go to an academic conference? Well, "agreeing" is not quite the right word, since I offered to go. And "academic" is not quite the right word either. Conferences at the Findhorn Foundation are a mix of talks by inspiring spiritual teachers, community rituals, periods of meditation, and discussions in small groups of eager participants. The fact that this conference was entitled "Love of Nature" is what drew me. I couldn't resist the thought that I might have something to offer and something to learn. The appeal of being in a large group after so much time alone was equally tempting.

Now I am on my way home. Alighting from the bus at Fionnphort, I wait for the ferry to arrive from Iona. I sit on some rocks in the evening light and close my eyes. Sounds meld into each other: the liquid strands of a blackbird's song; the gentle slap-slap-slap of water meeting the concrete ramp; the hum of the slowly approaching ferry's engine. There is something inexplicably perfect in the joining of these, like a melodious song of the world that is ignored by the insistence of our eyes to pay attention only to what is visible.

The ferry draws close, its black jaws opening to reveal cars, passengers, and crewmen standing inside the green-painted hull. I sit on deck and watch Iona drawing closer, immensely happy to be returning to my home by boat. It is a chilly evening. Smoke curls from the chimneys of the Argyll Hotel and Frieda's cottage.

Did I think I would learn new ways of being with nature at this conference? Yes, I learned some new terms, some conceptual structures on which, perhaps, to "hang" my experiences. Perhaps my own presentation on healing gardens opened a few eyes to the therapeutic benefits of nature. But at this time in my life, I—this little pin-point of human consciousness that appears to be me—must immerse myself in nature and landscape without thought of concept, theory, or outcome.

At one point in the conference, I found myself in tears. I struggled with the tension between Berkeley "researcher" and Iona "poet." I presented myself as researcher as I spoke about the therapeutic benefits of nature, yet in my heart, I yearned to be gone from the ego-bolstering, name-dropping, theory-defending posturing that accompanies so many conferences, even in as un-academic a milieu as the Findhorn community. I yearned to be back on Iona, in a place and mind-set that pre-dates any cognitive discussions of how and why we relate to the natural world. Iona is teaching me all I need to know. To stay put, alone and mostly silent, in one place for a long time, that is the path for me, not lengthy discussions of eco-psychology, deep ecology, and the like. Such discussions would have been stimulating to me at a different period in my life, but not now.

However, the trip was worth it to hear just one presentation, that of Jane Goodall on her work with chimpanzees. Here is a woman, not formally trained in science, who went alone into the forests of Tanzania simply to observe. What she saw and recorded has changed our views on primates and how field studies are conducted. Her understated passion, her modest but compelling presentation, her deep compassion for chimpanzees now in captivity in zoos and scientific labs, brought tears to my eyes. It takes courage to "go into the forest" and just record what you see and feel. I come home to Iona inspired by her example.

❧ ❧

It is early July. Summer has come full-blown to the island. As I walk south past fields of tall grass and flowers where the nesting corncrakes shelter, I am aware for the first time of sweet aromas in the air—from clover and lady's bedstraw, cow parsley, plantain, ragged robin, silver weed, and bird's-foot trefoil. I walk the rocky track past Ruanaich, Place of Red Flowers, and up onto the trackless high moors at the south of the island. I lie back against clumps of heather just beginning to flower and see butterflies. It feels so good to be back.

The next morning, I sleep late and wake to the chatter and laughter of a group of tourists passing the cottage on their way to the abbey. I turn over and remember a disturbing dream. A woman who shares a house with me is making changes to my garden and I'm furious. She has widened a path by digging up the lawn on either side of it and is planting flowers. I don't like the aesthetic of it—a straight path bordered by little flowers—and I'm incensed that she has invaded my territory. I yell at her. My father stands to one side looking helpless.

"It's *my* garden. What the hell are you doing here?" I am very angry. The woman (I think it is Helena W.) responds that she lives in the house too. "Yes, but in one and a half years, you've never shown any interest in the garden. It's as if I decided to claim your piano, never having previously played it."

"Which is the part of you that owns this garden and wants to keep it just as it is?" Barry asks when we speak on the phone later that week. "Which part of you is the 'invader' wanting to widen the path?"

There was certainly some tension at the Findhorn conference between those of us (well, actually, only me) representing the field of environmental psychology, which emerged in the 1960s initially in response to concerns about urban renewal and now embraces research on the restorative power of nature; and the relatively new approach of eco-psychology, which appeared in the 1990s when some psychotherapists expressed concerns about humanity's divorce from the natural environment. We are both "widening the path," making connections to nature and community more accessible. The one who "owns" the garden is angry at the intrusion of the newcomer who has never shown any interest before. Yes, that feels right, for I surely left this conference with some anger and frustration at an "upstart" field not acknowledging, intellectually, what had preceded it and those who had laid out the path in the first place. Academic ego lays claim to the garden.

"But a dream is also about the inner," Barry reminds me. "What, in you, is like the invader of the garden? Perhaps cutting into your time on Iona by going to the conference was like an invasion of the garden. You had to change hats from the Iona-you to the Berkeley-you, and the Iona-you is angry about the intrusion. You spoke about healing gardens, but now, back on Iona, you are immersing yourself in a healing landscape that is natural and undesigned—no lines of flowers bordering the garden path!"

"But in one and a half years, you've never shown any interest in the garden …," I said angrily to the intruder in my dream. Barry asked me what happened one and a half years ago. I could think of nothing, but later, turning back to a journal of that time, two things resonated. I wrote of my concern, even anguish, that I couldn't get the whole of my garden under control, that parts of it were still wild and overgrown. Within six months, that area was cleared and, before I left for Iona, I planted azaleas and ferns suited to the semi-shade and made a winding pathway leading to the site where I plan to have a greenhouse.

Also, eighteen months ago, I had a dream in which the names Palmer and Cooper occurred—both family names. In the dream, I ran excitedly to my mother: "We're both Palmers and Coopers!" I like the balance. Coopers make barrels that are round containers; they produce things. Palmers were pilgrims who carried a palm leaf indicating they had been to the Holy Land on a pilgrimage; they went places. The Coopers are pragmatic, the Palmers intent on a spiritual life. In the eighteen months since that dream, the Cooper in me helped to produce a book on healing gardens; the Palmer in me has come on a pilgrimage. These Coopers and Palmers are learning to live together.

But learning to live together is not easy. A few days later, I wake up from a dream that, unlike some that immediately fade away, remains stark and clear. I'm packing up to leave my academic job, sorting through piles of papers in my office. I hear something rustling and am startled to see two large lizards, each two feet long, like Komodo dragons, slithering through my papers. I'm afraid as they come toward me, but ward them off with a chair. I continue to go through papers and find a copy of the *San Francisco Chronicle* with a long article on the design of campus entries. I am jealous that I'm not the author. A former colleague, Joe, appears and, as we talk, I'm amazed to see he has a crack through his head—front to back, from his eyebrows to the back of his skull so I can see light at the other side, like a fissure through rock. He tells me the lizard-dragons are dangerous.

I sigh. Even after all this time (five years since formal retirement), I still haven't closed the doors on academia. Dangerous dragons, primordial nature hiding within the sheaves of intellectual verbiage. I still want to see my name in print; I don't want others to take my place. It is probably a common human emotion, but not one I want to admit to. Joe appears. In reality, he is a friendly, supportive colleague—"an image of your sensitive animus," Barry suggests when we discuss the dream a few days later. "Living and dreaming on Iona, you are light-years away from Berkeley and your academic life. Intellect versus emotion. Everything in your life story that you've tried to control and express through your academic career wants to break loose. I think that may be the meaning of the fissure through Joe's head in your dream."

The next day, I wake to a cloudless sky, pack a picnic lunch, fill my thermos with green tea, and walk across the island to Port Ban. I settle into my favorite place, a niche in the rocks above the high-tide line, and notice how profusely the rocks here are splintered with fissures. There is a maze of narrow, straight lines, as if a knife had been dragged across the rock, soft as butter. There are wider cracks where wind-blown sand has come to rest; deep fissures where the beach laps inland in soft white murmurs; triangular cavities holding tidal pools shaped like inverted pyramids; low-lying gaps between bare rocks where soil has slowly formed, providing niches for swathes of grass and pink-nodding sea-thrift. And in one place, there is a crevasse you can walk through—steep, black-splattered walls, linear pools where, between tides, seaweed rests like fine green hair. The sky is visible at the far end where a multitude of incoming waves have eroded softer strata and found their insistent, watery way into a secret, wider cleft beyond.

Even the rocks that have been here longer than time itself, longer than we can comprehend, are not impervious to change.

What is the fissure I saw passing through Joe's/my head in my dream? Something softer, something ready to surrender to the passage of time is being washed away. It is nothing to be frightened of. It is an opening through which light can penetrate, where flowers can grow, where the tide can flow. It is a gap where change is happening.

※ ※

Once a week in summer, staff at the abbey lead a pilgrimage walk through the landscape of Iona. It is an opportunity for those spending a short retreat on the island to learn about its history and visit the places associated with St. Columba. I have never felt drawn to join the chattering crowd who, armed with backpacks and walking sticks, stride toward the western shore. To talk and laugh while exploring the landscape is not my way.

But perhaps I am missing something. I run into Rosie Turnbull near the post office as she returns from the pilgrimage; she is exuberant. "It was wonderful—both an inner and outer experience. There were more than 100 of us, but it didn't feel like a crowd. Everyone was, to some degree, a seeker on the path. There was a quality of celebration, of community; people helped each other over the muddy bits of the path, sharing their life stories—just like in the Canterbury Tales!"

For a brief moment, I feel envious of her experience, but not for long. Whether it is my introverted nature, my re-working of childhood explorations, or my yearning for time to reflect, I need to see and sense this place in solitude.

※ ※

I come in from pulling weeds around the front door of Highland Cottage and make myself a pot of tea. On the table, a vase of flowers is content just to be. Roses, stocks, pink campion, and hedge parsley are calmly and fully themselves. What else can they be? I sink into the

chair, vaguely conscious of a lace curtain pulsing in the warm breeze and the soothing sounds of the waves at the bottom of the garden. My eyes graze lazily over titles in the bookcase, an icon of Christ, a photo of the Dalai Lama, a fabric wall-hanging of two monks sailing an ancient Hebridean craft on waves whose crests break into traditional Celtic designs. This room, this house, this island are continually teaching me all I need to know: to let go, be silent, and be fully in the moment. Environmental philosopher Shierry Weber Nicholsen describes it thus:

> What one finds in nature's silence ... is a sense of pure presence in the intangible present moment.... When we enter the silence, we return from the exile that is our ordinary state of mind. To become receptive to the natural world in this way is to come home.[51]

In the evening light, I amble along the shore at Traigh Mor, Big Strand, beach-combing. The sand is decorated with drifts of tiny shells that look like orange-brown berries; the conical shapes of whelks cast long triangular shadows. I pick up pieces of sea-smoothed glass and fragments of blue-and-white china transported through time from long-ago kitchens and tumble-washed by the waves into tiny seashore jewels.

Here, the rocks are a muted black and gray—unlike the multicolored strata at the north end or at Columba's Bay. But nature has splashed across these somber rocks the most extraordinary display of lichen—gray, white, gray-green with tiny fissures like the scales of a crocodile, ochre-yellow splotches, gray-green brittle tentacles a half-inch high, like tiny maritime cacti. The colors bleed across the rocks and into each other like an infinitely varied, slow-growing abstract work of art, here for the viewing, no entry fee required.

Low tide at Martyr's Bay. Water trickles down the gentle slope of the beach, etching the sand into delicate tree-like patterns. Meanders of minute rivulets of water have created intricate designs: tiny tendrils and fern-like fronds where water first emerges from the sand; wider, waving rills like braided locks of hair farther down the slope; a maze of branches merging into channels like tree trunks where they meet the incoming tide. Patterns like these can also be seen in huge river systems, only visible from the air; in the branching of our nerve cells, invisible to the naked eye; in stones called dendrites with tree-like markings; in the growth of trees themselves. Animal, vegetable, mineral. Patterns from three kingdoms, appearing as ephemeral tracings on the evening sand, soon to be washed away by the midnight tide.

❦ ❦

A dream. I'm in a large room at a party. There are lots of people there; I feel comfortable, happy, at ease—which is strange, since, introvert that I am, I often hover on the periphery, intimidated by large groups. The fire in the party room needs more wood; I go into another room to find some logs. I am startled to see a former colleague (I'll call him Matthew), sitting there alone.

"Matthew! Is that you? Is that really you?"

I am surprised, because Matthew died several years ago.

"Is it you?" I ask again.

"It is—and it isn't," he replies.

There is a burst of laughter from the party behind the closed door.

"Can other people see you?" I ask.

"Yes—but most will tell themselves it's not Matthew, just someone who looks like him."

I turn over in bed and slowly emerge into consciousness. Why would I dream about Matthew? Why now? I haven't thought about him for years.

Matthew and I both arrived in Berkeley in the early 1960s, he as an Assistant Professor, I as a graduate student. We were about the same age. I remember thinking how handsome he was, with a slim figure, fair hair, blue eyes, and ridiculously boyish good looks that he retained into his fifties. At a summer party somewhere in Marin County, he sprawled on the lawn in his open-necked shirt and crisp white pants as if he'd just come in from a game of cricket, or stepped out of the pages of *Brideshead Revisited.* We started going to parties together; I guess there were no restrictions back then about male faculty dating their female students.

Matthew taught a design studio in which I was a student. Although I'd barely picked up a pencil or paints since grade school, I found I had some talent for it. I had looked at landscapes all my life, but never in this way, examining places that had been consciously designed. My eyes were opened.

When it was time to write a thesis, I decided to find out if people living in a housing project near Berkeley looked at their environment in the same way as the architects who had designed it for them. I had a hunch that they didn't. I was right, or at least partially so.

Matthew encouraged me to teach; I owe him a lot. "You're asking questions no one else is asking. Students need to learn from you." Academic friends later marveled that I was hired at Berkeley without a Ph.D., without an interview, without a selection committee. Back then, in the Sixties, such things were not apparently required.

Matthew and I enjoyed many years together as colleagues. But the dating had long since stopped. One evening after a party and a few too many drinks, I became a little too amorous. Matthew froze; his body became stiff (well, most of it did). This man seemed to be asexual. For the rest of his life, I never heard of him linked to a woman, or to a man.

Now, in a dream, Matthew has returned. The academic animus lingers; it is there and not there. Matthew seems gender-less, not able to acknowledge his sexuality, just as I felt in the halls of academe. Those few of us who were women on the faculty learned to be efficient, competent, smart, but (most of the time) to keep our sexuality strictly within bounds. In an atmosphere that was the opposite of Hollywood, we were there for our brains and God forbid we should use any womanly wiles to succeed in our careers. I sacrificed my femininity and never let people see the full person that I am. The Matthew-in-me is still present, but has become a shade, a ghostly presence in the process of transformation.

In the dream, I pick up some logs and return to the life-filled, energy-driven, libido-drenched party, closing the door to Matthew's room quietly behind me.

❧ ❧

Gray monochrome sky. The red-splashed fuchsia hedge outside my window nods gently in the almost-windless air. It is tempting to stay inside on such a day—not because it is raining or cold or windy, but because the lack of sunlight casts a gloom over both landscape and in-scape. It is as if there were some element of the Other that is closer on such days, and my reluctance to venture outdoors is an expression of a vague inner fear. Yet, as always, a place on the island enters my consciousness and seems to whisper: "Come to me." On this day, the call comes from Port Chlacha Geal, Port of the White Stones, on the other side of the island.

As I walk west, I stop to watch hens scratching for morsels at Clachancorrach, Rough Stones, marveling at the way their neck feathers smartly telescope as their heads bob up and down, and how they deftly defecate without soiling the soft feathers on their rump. Just before the track meets the east-west road to the Machair, reeds and purple-tinged grasses have grown to five feet tall in a burst of summer growth. These reeds, along with heather, were once used to thatch the houses on Iona.

A flock of sheep approaches and I stand to one side of the road as they are herded by a fat-tired, all-terrain vehicle with two sheep-dogs perched on either side of the driver. The ewes have all been shorn, the path of the clippers marked by slight ridges across their bellies and flanks. The March and April lambs that trot alongside are now almost as big as their mothers. It is a blessing they cannot know that their days are numbered.

A flock of starlings clusters on the roof of Lagnagiogan chattering, preening, twittering. As I pass by, they take off, whirl overhead, and come to rest in a nearby field, falling to earth in patterned sequence, like a black-dotted silken shawl draping itself across the landscape.

I walk across the springy turf of the Machair and down onto the beach. Just off-shore, I see a shag, its black head and long neck appearing periodically above the waves. It dives, reappears gulping down some fishy morsel, looks around briefly, and dives again. It is said that the shag, or something very like it, flew over seas in which ichthyosaurs swam. The oldest fossilized shag was found in rocks laid down sixty million years ago. With all our technology and forays into virtual reality, we will never know what memories this ancient bird carries in its genes or how it experiences its watery world. Our human perceptions, filtered through memory and language, record such a minute portion of this house of treasures in which we live.

It is low tide. Seven black-faced sheep, horns curling around their ears, straddle beds of kelp on the shore. They munch on the wet, salty seaweed, brown strands drooping from their mouths like long moustaches.

Settling against a rock, I take my lunch from my pack. I bite into a whole-wheat roll filled with sardines and cucumber; cold cucumber tastes like the watery essence of earth. Tomato, slightly acid on my tongue, molars biting through sun-ripened skin. A bite of raw carrot pushed to the back left corner of my mouth, teeth mashing a soft, sweetish pulp. Hot green tea from my thermos slips down my throat and warms a passage down, down, down, falling like summer rain.

Smell of the sea. I slide my tongue over my upper lip; taste of salt, flesh caressing flesh. I bite into a ripe plum; the purple skin is slightly bitter; the orange-pink flesh is sweet and soft. I suck on the wooden stone, then throw it into a patch of yellow seaweed near my feet.

Eat slowly. Nowhere to be but here. Waves curling over half-submerged rocks break into lips of cream and disappear. One unique watery event in the life of the planet, repeated until the end of time.

I take out a knife and cut into an apple—Cox's Orange Pippin. We had such a tree at the house where we lived after the war. The flesh is firm, somewhere between tart and sweet. The sound of crunching reverberates through my jaw and into my inner ear. I bite into a ripe pear and close my eyes, the better to taste its sweet flesh, its gritty skin. Opening my eyes, I examine the marks of my teeth in its pearly-white body. Chocolate biscuit: the sound of chewing is softer than an apple. I run my tongue across my front teeth and delve into the pockets of my mouth to seek out the last vestiges of chocolate.

Another drink of tea. I fold up my sweatshirt to make a pillow, arrange it on the rock behind me, and lie back in the sun. One arm across the warm pebbles by my side, the other across my chest, ris-

ing and falling. Eyes close. Sea sounds flow through me. No body; no mouth; no ears; no nose. Just the sea rising and falling; rising and falling; rising and falling, falling … falling.

🙶 🙶

The next day, I wake up thinking of Grandma Cooper, my father's mother. Strange that I should think of her here, now. Before the war, and then later when we were back in London, she always had us over for tea on Sundays. The polished mahogany table in her dining room was covered with a white lace tablecloth. The teacups were Royal Derby china with a dusky brown glaze decorated with blue and yellow flowers, and a gold rim where you placed your lips.

First, we had sandwiches made with thin slices of white bread spread with salted butter and Shipham's fish paste. Grandma always cut the crusts off and, after tea, I was allowed to put them on a ceramic platter on the lawn for the birds. The platter had a family of ducks walking along one edge and I really wanted to have that platter when Grandma died, but it went to my Uncle David and then to cousin John. He has it still.

After sandwiches, we had cakes baked that morning by Grandma and her daughter, my Auntie Enid, who taught mathematics at the Royal Masonic School for Girls. She never married, though sometimes she wistfully referred to a man she had met on a student trip to Budapest in 1927. She lived with Grandma—I think they even shared a bed—until Grandma died when she stepped out from behind a bus without looking and was hit by a motorcycle. The doctor said she didn't suffer; it was instantaneous.

I especially remember the cakes we had at those Sunday teas. They were arrayed on large decorated plates and a three-tier arrangement of silver platters. They probably weren't really silver, more like silver plate, but I thought they were very grand. Under each arrangement of cakes was a lace doily made by Grandma, who crocheted in the evenings as she listened to a play or a boxing match on the wireless. She loved listening to boxing matches. Maybe it titillated her, listening to an activity so different from her proper Victorian upbringing.

And the cakes. There were flapjacks and rock cakes, jam tarts and Bakewell tarts, sometimes a Victoria sponge, and always seed cake, because she knew that was the favorite of my brother, her eldest grandson, Paul.

After tea Grandma let us open a wooden chest on her upstairs landing where she kept a lot of games—Lotto, Snakes and Ladders, Draughts. But best of all, I liked it when she let me unlock a special glass-fronted china cabinet with a tiny gray metal key. On the second shelf from the top was a family of three carved wooden bears with "Made in Bavaria" stamped on their flat bottoms. I took them out very carefully and made up stories about their adventures as I arranged and re-arranged them on a low footstool covered with needlepoint. Grandma did needlepoint as well as crocheting and knitting. She was always making something, looking down intently at needles and wool, or crochet hook and yarn, or large-eyed embroidery needle and colorful thread. I inherited a needlepoint fire screen she made. Fire screens are for putting in front of the fireplace in summer. Where is it now? My summer screen now is a huge square pottery vase bought for me by Al Schwartz at Nepenthe, when we met and fell in love at Esalen in the Sixties. It is more appropriate to my current eclectic California living-room decor than Grandma's needlepoint. But I still have her footstool, too low to rest my feet on, but just right for balancing a tray with dessert and a cup of tea as I put my feet up to watch the evening news on TV.

⁂ ⁂

It is Tuesday morning; time to roll out the wheeled plastic rubbish bins on Iona. The blue garbage truck drives off the ferry and up the steep concrete ramp onto the island. Vulture, the name emblazoned across its front, seems particularly apt. I am dismayed by how much more I have to throw away here compared to where I live in California. No doubt many Scots see Americans as profligate wasters of materials, but the truth is that our curbside recycling program in Berkeley—established in 1973, the first in the U.S. and probably in the world—is so comprehensive that all I put in the rubbish each week are a few plastic food wrappers. On re-cycling pick-up day, one sturdy plastic container holds the week's newspapers, office paper, junk mail, and magazines; others contain glass, tins, and plastic. With kitchen and garden waste consigned to the compost bin, there is little left that is rubbish. In an urban setting, recycling of almost everything is economically feasible; in as small and remote a place as Iona, it is not. There is a Bottle Bank near the jetty, but whether its contents truly go to a recycling center or to a landfill is anyone's guess. And if recyclables are hard to dispose of on the island, what of defunct machinery and builders' rubbish? To dispose of the latter, an Iona resident has to rent a skip and have it driven to the landfill at Tobermony on Mull. Few can afford the expense, so old concrete and bricks are dumped in remote ravines, while defunct farm machinery is left to rust away in the fields as it has for generations.

⁂ ⁂

On a day out on Mull, I bend over a garden wall to smell the dangling pink flowers of a wild currant bush. Every time I smell the indefinable sweet-tart scent of these tiny pink flowers, I am jerked back to some childhood event I cannot quite recall. Every time, that smell whispers "childhood—wartime—England," but whatever happened by or on or inside the wild currant has slipped from my memory like a figure walking just ahead of me into a plume of smoke. I can never catch up to see who or what the figure is. Then, on this particular day, a memory surfaces of an old retired soldier. There were hundreds of these veterans (as they would be known in the United States), or Chelsea pensioners (as retired soldiers from the Royal Chelsea Hospital are known in England) evacuated from their sprawling 17th-century barracks in London to live for a while, away from the bombing, in the ornate Rothschild mansion. Somehow, somewhere, one of them invited me—a naive eight-year-old—to sit on his lap. I remember the stale smell of his breath, ruddy cheeks pock-marked with tiny bomb craters, hairs coming out his nostrils like thistle-down, but not as pretty. I didn't want to be there, my bare legs sticking to his blue serge trousers, one hairy hand with calloused fingers stroking my arm. He was a grown-up. How could I say "Don't do that. Stop it, stop it!" He had done nothing wrong, but it didn't seem right.

Was he yearning for his daughter? His granddaughter? Or was it more devious? Did he hope for an erection in the crotch of his blue serge pants—a little girl sitting right on top of him, only her cotton underpants, her summer dress made of pink-and-white seersucker, and his blue serge pants separating the most private parts of their two bodies? Did I think that then, or is this the adult woman trying to understand why this brief and, in the end innocent, encounter sticks in my memory? Was there a wild currant bush near where we sat? I stoop to smell the flowers again, sweet-tart smell traveling to the seat of memories in my brain and half opening the door to reveal something that did or didn't or might have happened sixty years ago.

ঽ৯ ঽ৯

I hear that Marv and Nancy, friends in northern California, have discovered severe problems in the septic system of a property they have just bought, rendering it virtually useless. They are in a quandary over what to do. I have a strong intuition I should write and ask them if they have had their "personal sewer systems" checked. I apologize for being so personal and send the letter. The day before my letter arrives, Marv is diagnosed with colon cancer. We talk on the phone and he is almost in tears as he speaks of this amazing synchronicity. He is reassured by my query and the sense that we are not alone in our states of anxiety.

On the day of his surgery, I sit on a rock at the north end of the island and pray for his recovery. A little later, I climb the rocky hill just outside the abbey thought to be the site of St. Columba's cell and pray again. Is it prayer? I don't really know. Perhaps it is a healing meditation. I don't suppose it matters. Breathing in, I sense the word "healing," drawing energy from the rocks beneath me. Breathing out, I envisage Marv and sense love pouring down from above, over and through him. While doing this, I am vaguely aware of a chorus of bird song from the village. Occasionally, the rasping cry of a corncrake slices through the air—the jarring message of cancer.

⁊⅌ ⁊⅌

Centuries ago in the spiritual practice of the Celtic church, people were encouraged to find in life an *anamchara* or "soul friend," someone to whom they could open their inner lives, hiding nothing, in order to know and explore the feelings in their hearts. Barry has become that person for me, hearing my dreams, listening non-judgmentally to the ramblings of my soul. There seems to me no greater gift than that one person should listen quietly to another and nurture the discovery of the soul. No doubt the early fathers of the church would be incredulous that such deeply personal conversations can be carried on now via telephone with a soul friend thousands of miles away.

I call Barry to talk about a dream. I'm in a workshop group with Barry as the leader. He sets us a task. People produce interesting drawings and insights. I go to Barry and confess I don't understand what it is he's asked us to do. He's surprised, but tells me again—and again, I don't understand or don't hear him.

What can this mean? The Barry-in-me, the wise healer, has set myself a task: to come to Iona and reflect on the experience of cancer, healing, and the magic presence of this island. I have produced some writing and perhaps some useful insights, but part of me thinks that I don't understand what I've come here to do.

Barry comments: "The dream seems to say: 'What is it I'm supposed to get from this?' That's the eternal question. You're writing about a mystery. Can you live with that? You're in some relationship with the mystery and the mystery has touched you. In the dream, I, as Barry, stand for someone who, from time to time, helps to mediate a contact with the mystery. The deepest meaning of the dream is that you're supposed to become fully aware that you can't—and never will—fully 'get it.' Life is a mystery! It's as if, in your case, cancer came to help you face up to the mystery of its healing. Perhaps that's its function in the world. Surviving may not be the way to 'get it'—unless by doing so, you *do* get it!"

PART IV

Dreaming with Eyes Wide Open

❧

CHAPTER 17

Words I Never Told My Father

You may little suspect the fullness of someone's character just from reviewing your memories. Your father's character, say, goes on unfolding and you go on learning about him, from him. He returns to mind in flashbacks and reveries. As you age, and you become more like him, he often feels nearer. A glimpse in the mirror, a dish in a restaurant, a joke in an old movie, and traits of his light up, never having been noticed before. Under scrutiny, the images reveal more and more, revising the obituary, nuancing impressions, teaching still. —James Hillman[52]

Hoof prints of cows and sheep pattern the damp sand down to the water's edge. What is the shore to them? Do they lap at the incoming salty tide? Are they, like us, mesmerized by the rhythm that echoes their own breathing, their beating hearts?

Off shore, the sea is painted in shades of turquoise and brown. Breaking waves pick up sand and fling it up the slope in milky-edged swells. Seaweed-covered rocks are gradually submerged and transformed from something material and touchable into abstract pulsating shapes, fragments of dreams slipping away as we emerge into consciousness.

Are we awake or dreaming on this earth? On this island, it is easy to dream with eyes wide open. Days merge like drifting clouds. Birds sing to the earth in ways we have lost. The ardent sea makes love to the shore with salty-tongued caresses at my feet.

I move up the beach, above the high-tide line. Dune grass invades the sand in wiry, quivering patches. The wind bends their fronds downward, pointed ends inscribing faint patterns in the fine sand. Back and forth, back and forth, like tiny persistent styluses, the plants etch circles around themselves, as if marking as sacred this, their dwelling place.

I lie full-length on the sand, hat over eyes, head resting on my pack. Breathing slowly, I vaguely keep time with the waves, falling into a half-sleep. Flickering memories of my father in the last weeks of his life appear. He is propped up in bed at the Royal Free Hospital in London while I sit beside him doing embroidery—a cushion cover in somber colors of dark green, dark blue. Eyes down, needle piercing the canvas, I avoid eye contact with my father while we sit in each other's presence, often in silence.

My mother insisted he not be told he was dying of cancer. His father, my grandfather, on being told he had colon cancer but that, with surgery and a colostomy, he would live, turned his face to the wall and died within a few days. The family story goes that the thought of a colostomy was too much for this dignified Edwardian banker to bear; he would rather die.

"We mustn't let Daddy know he has cancer," my mother insisted, "or he will just give up like Grandpa Cooper." Returning to this family drama from my newfound California independence, I was outraged. To prevent this man, my father, from sharing his fears with his family went against everything I had embraced in the heady stewpot of Berkeley in the Sixties: be honest; share your feelings; don't hold back. But I didn't feel able to go against my mother's wishes. And so, on my daily visits to the hospital, my father and I talked of world news, the weather, and how he would soon be home. Later, I realized that my mother had instigated this conspiracy of silence as much to avoid her own feelings of impending loss as to protect my father from the truth. In her nineties, twenty years later, she told me how much she regretted that decision.

As my father lay dying, why did I not ask him questions about his life—about growing up in Stoke Newington, working at Rothschild's bank, his time in the army, his feelings about retirement? But it was not part of our family culture to ask each other personal questions or encourage self-disclosure. We lived in our own private worlds,

going about our daily activities—work, school, shopping, recreation—recounting our observations, but barely sharing our feelings except at a most superficial level. That is what I tell myself, recalling those bedside encounters with some sense of guilt. Perhaps I am more like my mother than I think: fearful of death, avoiding painful conversations.

I recall photos of my father in the family album: Cyril Clement Cooper, his mother's first-born son, perched uncomfortably, unsmiling, astride a donkey at a seaside resort somewhere in England in 1903. Years later, a picture of a handsome young man of eighteen sitting self-assured, his delicate hands on the keys of an upright piano. In a fading sepia print, he is a tall man in his twenties posing beside his bicycle on a tour of France with his best friend, Bertie Dale. A formal portrait of my father-to-be beaming beside his smiling bride, Christine Duncan, in her daring knee-length 1920s wedding dress outside a Methodist Church in north London. My favorite is a picture of him as a young father, crouching on the grass in Uncle George's plum orchard

in Edelsborough, pretending to bite a clover flower from its stem, to the obvious delight of his young son, Paul.

A few years later, a picture of my father in a striped, knitted bathing suit with shoulder straps shows him towering above me, his hand reaching down to hold mine while my mother, in revealing swimwear, holds my other hand. We were at Minehead, a seaside resort on the north Somerset coast. It was August 1939, a month before England declared war on Germany, and the last time we were together on a happy family holiday. There is a picture of my father standing in the driveway at Ascott in an ill-fitting uniform with a rifle by his side. Probably it was taken when he joined the Home Guard. Sometime in 1940, we sat in a photographer's studio in Leighton Buzzard and posed for a family photo. We all look so serious, so somber. Perhaps it was taken because Dad was going off to war—a last picture together, just in case.

❧ ❧

I remember very little of my father from when I was a small child—those years before the war, before he left in his army uniform, before we moved to the country. Was he tender? Did he read to me? Did he play with me? There are photos from those years, but I don't actually remember the events or places.

There is a picture of my father in the family album—very tall and wearing corduroy breeches, wheeling a bicycle with firewood roped to its frame, and Paul and me looking impossibly small walking beside him. My face holds just a half smile, as if I am not quite sure if I am happy or not. Mum must have taken that photo; maybe as early as that summer our relationship was fraught by something not quite said, a love not quite believed.

That picture was taken when we went on holiday, not long before the war, to a rented cottage in Dorset near Poole Harbour. There was no water or electricity and the walls were three feet thick. There was just one small window facing the water, a marshy inlet of the sea. Someone told us that light from an oil lamp in that window sent signals to boats running contraband. Or maybe that was just a story Dad made up. I remember nothing of the interior of the cottage—just Paul and me walking to the edge of the inlet to collect drinking water from a pump or well, and the evocative smell of the pine forest where we went to gather firewood.

Water and wood, the basics of life—that's what I remember. Why don't I remember sitting round the fire when we burned the wood, or standing in the kitchen drinking the water? My memories are always of the outdoors: the rushes near the edge of the inlet, the smell of pine resin in the forest. What happened indoors that I don't want to remember?

Later, as an adult, I felt proud that my father had volunteered for the army in 1940. But at that time, when I was six, I felt confused and frightened that he was going to leave us. The grown-ups talked of Hitler, rationing, clothes coupons, air raids, and bomb shelters. Children separated from their parents were being evacuated from expected bombing and stood misery-faced on railway platforms with labels round their necks like stray dogs.

We were going to move to the country for safety, Mum and Paul and I, but my father wouldn't be with us and that filled me with an empty, un-nameable fear. For the next five years, I barely saw him; my connection with him stretched out like a worn rubber band, getting thinner and thinner, likely to snap at any moment. When he came home on leave, often without warning, an unexpected knock on the door would wake us in the early hours of the morning. No telephones in those days. I remember my mother on the doorstep, sobbing into the rough khaki threshold of his chest while Paul and I hovered nearby, shivering in our pajamas, hesitant to approach this almost-stranger.

One leave I remember more clearly because of a story he told us. Dad was stationed in Liverpool, searching ships that came into port. Instructed to prepare a fire in a waiting room for disembarking refugees, he jumped on a log and fell, breaking his leg. He was transferred to a military hospital in Chester. One day on a bus, with his leg in plaster and wearing hospital blues, he was told his fare had been paid by two elderly ladies sitting nearby. "One of our men, home from the front line. Wounded in battle ... we want to express our thanks." That's what they seemed to be saying with their sympathetic smiles and gently nodding white hair. "No, no. I'm not a hero. Just a stupid accident jumping on a log," he wanted to say. But instead he smiled back and mouthed "Thank you." Later, the same thing happened in a café in Chester; an unknown person paid his bill, grateful for the opportunity to express their thanks to the Wounded Soldier.

Why does this story stick in my mind? Perhaps because soldiers on leave were cautioned to say very little about where they were stationed, what they were doing. Government posters on buses and in railway stations declared: "Keep it under your hat," "Walls have ears," "Careless talk costs lives." We knew better than to ask questions. Perhaps, in the privacy of the bedroom, he told my mother. Later, as an adult, I could have asked, but I didn't and now I regret it.

When Dad was stationed overseas, we speculated about where he might be going. Perhaps the Azores, since he had learned Portuguese while working at a bank in Lisbon as a young man. But no, the army in its wisdom sent him to Italy where he didn't know the language. He had a flair for languages, however, and soon spoke Italian so fluently that, out of uniform, people took him for a native.

Letters came via the army censor to my mother, but rarely to us. My father was fading away like a figure walking off into the mist. I do remember once when the post came bringing something addressed to

Paul and me. Inside was a piece of paper neatly folded into triangles and covered with a spidery script in black ink. We turned it this way and that, but couldn't figure out what it was. A note in the envelope told us that one of my father's mess-mates had made it for us. Then Paul squinted at it and discovered the mystery script was our names—Paul and Clare—only decipherable when held at a particular angle. We were enchanted. Our father had sent something specially made for us! He had talked about us to a friend. Why wouldn't he? We were his children; he loved us. But the long separation had sown seeds of doubt in my mind, flickers of doubt that never entirely disappeared.

The second special package I remember was a small square box. We opened it excitedly and inside, carefully wrapped in newspaper, was a perfect yellow lemon. I didn't remember ever having seen a lemon before. By 1943, 3000 ships bringing food and supplies to Britain had been lost in the North Atlantic. Citrus fruit was not high on the list of priorities. We took our spoonfulls of free, government-issued rose hip syrup after breakfast each day and almost forgot that oranges and lemons had ever existed.

I stroked the slightly pitted skin of the lemon and ran my fingers down lines that seemed to mark the division between segments of the fruit. I pressed it against my nose and closed my eyes, sucking in the delicious foreign smell of a fruit ripened in the Italian sun. A lemon! We had our own lemon!

Mum said it was precious, that we needed to share it. She arranged to raffle the lemon to raise money for the Spitfire Fund. We sold tickets at sixpence each. There were lots of takers. Ultimately, we didn't get to taste the lemon. The raffle was won by Mrs. Bond in the village and we had to be content with the knowledge that we had raised needed money for the war effort. We dutifully handed fifteen shillings and six-pence to a teller at the Midland Bank in Leighton Buzzard for the Spit-fire Fund, money to help build another small fighter plane to engage German bombers as they flew across the English Channel. Our fifteen shillings and sixpence may have bought a crucial switch on that plane, but I didn't care about the Spitfire Fund; I wanted to taste that lemon. A lemon from my father.

One day, a small parcel arrived with the usual army postmark. It was for me! I could barely contain my excitement: a parcel, a parcel! I pulled off the string and paper, and there was a box of wooden Swiss *Caran d'Ache* crayons. I didn't remember having had crayons before. It was wartime: no dolls or crayons. Making toys had ceased long ago. Factories were making bombs, building Spitfires and Hurricanes. Appeals went out for old pots and pans to melt down for precious steel. Even the iron railings around elegant London squares in Bloomsbury and Kensington were sawn down to provide for the war effort. At such a time, who cared about children's crayons?

My father did; he remembered me! Although where he found a box of Swiss crayons in occupied Italy I'll never know. I took them to school, so proud. Some of the younger children had never seen a crayon. It must have meant he loved me, mustn't it? He had taken the trouble to send me such a special gift.

By this time, perhaps it was 1941, the Rothschild children, Evelyn, Renée, and Anne, had been sent to Canada for safety. In June 1940, when the threat of invasion seemed imminent, the government instituted a program to send evacuees overseas to the United States, Canada, South Africa, Australia, and New Zealand. By July of that year, more than 200,000 applicants were received for children to leave. One ship, the SS Volendam, en route to Canada, was hit by a torpedo, but miraculously, all of the children on board took to the lifeboats and were saved. A month later, in September 1940, the SS City of Benares was also torpedoed in the Atlantic and 256 people died, eighty-one of them children on their way to safety in North America. After that tragedy, the program was closed down. As a child, I knew nothing of that tragedy, just a lingering suspicion that, if you had the money, you could buy your way to safety—not true, as it turned out, as the children's passages were free.

After the Rothschild children left, some of their possessions were distributed to the children who lived on the estate. I was given a rabbit and a dress—soft cotton with tiny pink and pale-blue flowers and intricate smocking across the front. Best of all, I received a pencil case of Renée's. It was red leather, shaped like a big flat letter "D" with a zipper around the curved sides and Renée's name scratched in ink on the grosgrain lining. When you opened it and laid it out flat, there were little red-leather loops for pencils. I took the crayons my father had sent me and pushed them into the loops, arranging the colors like a rainbow: red, orange, yellow, green, blue, purple. I don't remember what I drew with them, what pictures I composed. But I used them sparingly, sharpening them carefully with Paul's penknife, until at last they were such tiny stubs I could no longer hold them in my fingers.

❧ ❧

I remember the day my father came home. We were back in our London house. It was a Sunday afternoon in the summer of 1945 and I was eleven. Grandma Cooper, his mother, had come to tea. My mother had saved up our rations of butter and sugar and made a cake. There was a knock at the door and there he was, in uniform, sergeant's stripes on his arm and a dirty off-white kit bag slung over his shoulder, his name stenciled on the side: "Sgt. C. C. Cooper 10350865." I still have that kit bag somewhere in the attic and the medal he was awarded: the Italy Star.

The atmosphere around the table that afternoon was tense, brittle as winter leaves. Later, when I went to bed and left the grown-ups, I kissed everyone except my father—Mum, Grandma, Paul—and ran out of the room filled with frozen questions and loud, silent answers. "Aren't you going to kiss your father?" my mother called out to me. Awkwardly, I turned back from the door, crossed the room, and quickly brushed his cheek with my lips, quivering like quicksilver. Then I ran upstairs to bed, where I lay sleepless, my head jangling with questions into the numbing night. I know that I must have hurt my father's feelings, not wanting to kiss him. But I didn't remember him; I didn't know who he was.

Being stationed in Italy gave my father a chance to live a life so different from that of a lowly London bank clerk—its climate, its food, its women, its expressive language gave his soul a chance to sing. I remember the day my mother told me what had happened in the war, why she often sobbed in the night when letters came from Italy. It is a scene etched in my memory like the jagged crack across the floor of our front hall.

I was twelve or thirteen, preparing to meet my friend Mary in the West End to go to the theater. It was a hot afternoon and I was ironing a dress in the kitchen. It was a seersucker dress, small pale-blue and lavender flowers on a white background. The window was open; the sounds of a lawn mower drifted in, a dog barked in the distance.

"You know Dad just went to Lisbon on business ..." my mother queried.

"Yes," I said, gripping the handle of the iron more tightly.

"Well—long ago, before he met me, he worked there for a while and fell in love with a Portuguese woman, Zita. He wanted to marry her but Grandma Cooper strongly objected, Zita being Catholic and the Coopers being Methodists. So reluctantly, he broke off the engagement."

My mother took a sip of tea and, thankful that I could avoid eye contact, I focused on steering the iron in and out of the ruffled bodice of my dress. Where was this conversation leading?

"Last week when Dad was there, he saw Zita and found he still loved her."

I sucked in my breath and felt a trickle of sweat slide down between my newly emerging breasts.

"That's not all. I have to tell you what happened in the war. He had a woman in Italy, maybe more than one. He wrote and asked me to send clothes for her. As desperate as we were for food and clothes, things in Italy were even worse." I held my breath. The iron rested in one place, then I quickly picked it up as I smelled scorched cotton.

"Later he asked for money to pay for an abortion."

How could she be telling me this? No-no-no—I don't want to hear any more. My mother shouldn't be telling me this. This is between Mum and Dad, not me, not me. I brushed tears away with the back of my hand.

"I'm sorry, Clare. I'm sorry. I've kept it all inside. I had to tell someone."

I stood staring down at the dress. I heard desperation in my mother's voice, but couldn't bring myself to look at her.

"I thought the past was over, the war, everything ... but it's all come back again because of Dad going to Lisbon and seeing Zita."

Mum stared down at the kitchen table. I caught a glimpse of her—jaw clenched, shoulders slumped—then quickly turned back to ironing my dress.

"After the war, Dad proposed bringing this woman back from Italy. He wanted us to live as a *ménage à trois*. That's when I put my foot down. It's her or me. Either you come back to the family without this woman, or I'll ask for a divorce."

A divorce? My parents had come close to a divorce? At that time, it was a word you hardly ever heard. No one in our family was divorced. No one I'd ever heard of was divorced.

There was sudden rat-tat-tat at the front door. We both stiffened. It was my brother. He had gone on a errand and forgotten his key.

"I'm sorry I had to tell you. I shouldn't have told you all this …" My mother's voice trailed away as she pushed her cup to the center of the table and stood up stiffly. I didn't know what to say. I picked up my dress and left the room.

I took the underground into London, the afternoon's conversation roiling around in my stomach. I met Mary and we had a quick supper at Lyon's Corner House at Piccadilly Circus. I don't remember what we talked about, but I remember we ate mushrooms on toast, the cheapest item on the menu.

We settled into our seats in the theater gallery to see Laurence Olivier and Vivienne Leigh in Shakespeare's *Antony and Cleopatra*. The air was hot and stale. The dialog washed over my head as if in a foreign language. In the Intermission, I went to the Ladies Room and vomited half-digested mushrooms into the toilet bowl—black spongy shapes racing into an inky whirlpool as I stared disbelieving into my future. Men could betray you.

Ultimately, there was no divorce. Slowly, the family re-established itself. In 1947, my parents went on a spring holiday to Italy. One afternoon, during a thunderstorm over Lake Como (Mum later told me), they went back to their hotel room and made love, and Anthony was conceived. He was named after the patron saint of Italy. In the place of great wounding, a healing took place.

❧ ❧

There were times in my teen years when Dad and I did things together. They were good times, as I slowly let down my guard and came to know him better. He introduced me to so many things: art, music, maps. He took me to a Van Gogh exhibit at the Tate Gallery, the first major art show in London since before the war. My eyes began to open. I loved listening to him play the piano—pieces by Albeniz and de Falla hinting that his yearning for something in the Latin soul was there long before the war, long before his time in Italy. He patiently accompanied me on the piano when I practiced the violin—something that must have been excruciating to his musically sensitive ear.

My early interest in the violin was squashed, however, by an insensitive conductor at a summer music camp while I was at university. While rehearsing a piece by Mozart, the conductor suddenly tapped on the lectern and pointed his baton at me. I looked behind me, hoping he was signaling to someone else.

"No, you!" he shouted impatiently. "Play a scale in C-minor."

I froze under his harsh gaze. I could read music, but had never learned much about theory, and certainly wasn't prepared to play a scale on command. I stared at the floor, examining the knots in the wood and wishing I were anywhere else but there. I had never experienced such a public humiliation. I went back to the converted garage where I was living, bent over the toilet, and vomited until nothing came up except bitter yellow phlegm. I never played the violin again. I don't think I ever told my father why.

When I think of the music my father and I shared, I remember especially an open-air concert at Kenwood House, where we sat near the top of a sloping lawn, looking down at the orchestra beyond a small lake. I don't remember Paul or Mum being with us, but perhaps I so much wanted Dad's full attention that I've erased their presence from my memory. The orchestra played Beethoven's *Pastoral Symphony*, the most exquisite evocation in music of the miracle of nature. As we listened in the fading evening light, birds in the trees around us began to sing. I believe that evening was the start of our coming together again as father and daughter, music and my childhood memories of nature healing the wounds we both had suffered in the dark days of the war.

On many occasions, my father took me with him to lectures at the Royal Geographical Society. (Despite the grand name, anyone could belong by paying a fee.) We shared a passion for maps and exploration and stories from strange lands. Over tea and biscuits after the lecture, we mingled with what seemed to me like an ultra-sophisticated crowd. Perhaps I fantasized we were a couple; Mum never came with us. Dad so handsome, his six-foot-four-inch frame towering over the crowd; me negotiating the stormy passage of adolescence, hoping he would think me attractive. On the drive home from Kensington to Finchley, we talked about the lecture as street lights flashed by and agreed to look up details of the geography of Nepal or the Sudan in the old family atlas when we got home.

The happiest memories I have of us as a family were Sunday evenings at home in my mid to late teens. I don't remember any family meals together from before the war and, during the war, when it was mostly just Mum and me (after Paul left to go to school in London),

I don't remember ever sitting down to eat together, though we must have done so. I guess that's why I have such fond memories of meals together after Dad came home.

Lunch on Sundays was always a classic English roast—lamb, pork, or beef with roast potatoes, peas, Yorkshire pudding, gravy. With tea and cakes at four o'clock, we were quite full by the evening, so we just had a light supper. Dad always took care of it, arranging cheese, crackers, celery, fruit, and coffee on a tea trolley and wheeling it into the living room where we sat by the fire reading the theater and film reviews in *The Observer*.

After supper, we played bridge on a folding card table with a green baize top inherited from Auntie Edith. Actually, I hated the game and only learned it reluctantly so that Mum, Dad, and Paul had a fourth to make up a game. When I was dummy, my father urged me to watch so I could learn something about strategy, but I didn't care about strategy and turned instead to reading the Sunday paper.

One of the most important things I shared with my father, just the two of us, was gardening. Dad hadn't much cared for gardening as a young man with a growing family in a London suburb. But after the war, perhaps spurred on by my enthusiasm, he discovered a love for gardening that lasted the rest of his life.

When Mum and I returned to London from Ascott, I persuaded her to let me have an allotment in a local park that had been subdivided into vegetable plots to encourage city dwellers to "Dig for Victory." By the time my father returned, it was planted and thriving. On Saturday mornings, Dad and I walked the half mile to the allotment with our dog, Raq, carrying our tools. Dad did the heavy work, as I remember, spading and forking. I weeded and sowed rows of lettuce, radishes, and carrots, pressing the damp soil down with my fingers, sometimes freezing still when a robin perched on the handle of a fork nearby.

It wasn't until later, when I returned from my first trip to America, that I understood another side of my father. On a family holiday to Florence, we stopped at the border between Switzerland and Italy. I got out of the car to stretch my legs while Dad conversed with the border guards. Suddenly, he seemed like a different person. As he started speaking Italian, his voice rose several registers, his arms flew out in unfamiliar gestures, he touched me tenderly on the arm. We all need to find that place in the world that makes us whole. Inside the reticent English banker was a passionate Italian, screaming to get out.

❧ ❧

How incomparably all our lives were changed by the war—my father, discovering and then relinquishing a life and a culture that touched his heart, and returning with some ambivalence to the life of a city banker, responsible husband, and father; my mother, embracing the role of victim and "wronged woman." Not till years later did she outlive the bitterness of those years. And I, bewildered and bereft by my father's absence—necessary though it was—conflicted in my subsequent relationships with men. Fearful of abandonment, I found refuge in a life of the intellect. My father left with a rifle on his shoulder and returned to find a daughter with a pen in her hand. No, I did not become a famous novelist or poet, but I entered a career where thinking, research, and publishable writing are essential to success. And in some ways, unconsciously, I used those activities to erect a barrier of protection around myself.

After graduate school at Berkeley, I went through years of indecision about staying in the United States. Dad and I both opened up and found ourselves in a country far from home. I plunged into the human potential movement of the Sixties and worked on my relationship with my father. As a sexually active adult, I came to understand the dilemma he must have faced in Italy during the war—yearning for physical contact with a woman, so far away from his wife.

Some time ago, I had a dream in which I have to arrange a funeral for a soldier who has died in a war; I am to phone his widow when all the arrangements are made. But before I can do so, the funeral party shows up, the widow in her husband's uniform. They sit somberly around a large square table waiting for the coffin to arrive and the ceremony to begin. I frantically look for the number of the funeral director, but when I phone, no one answers. A funeral without a body; I am worried and embarrassed.

I think that dream is about me and my father. It is "as if" he died in the war and yet there is no body. He did come back, but we had all changed. The widow/daughter decides to put on his uniform, to become the breadwinner, the protector, the "masculine" adventurer, the academic. I will never forget or stop loving my father, but my psyche says the time has come for a funeral, for a ritual parting. It is thirty-three years since he left this earth; I need to let him go.

⁂

When I was sick as a child in the war—the occasional cold, chicken pox, mumps—I used to sit up in bed with a pad of paper and draw maps of an island. I think it must have been my father who taught me how to read contours, pouring over his collection of Bartholomew's maps with the topography colored in subtle shades of green and brown.

It was a secret island I drew, with an indented coastline, cliffs and valleys, a jetty where boats landed, a trail to the highest point, smugglers' caves, and sandy beaches. And now I am on that island! How could I have known, fifty-odd years ago, that an island like the one I kept drawing as a child would become a significant place of healing for me, a window into my soul?

My father so loved maps and exploration and travel; perhaps these were the voices of his soul. Yet he ended up a foreign-exchange dealer in Rothschild's bank in the City of London, a career at which he excelled, yet one that was far from what might have been. In Italy, far from home and family responsibilities, he experienced for a while the "might have been" of his life. It is as if his soul came alive there in that land of sunshine, sensuality, and lemons.

Ultimately, I became fascinated with that part of my father's soul-life that was most accessible to me: his love of maps and a yearning for travel and adventure. I began to live his unlived life, diving deep into the field of geography, learning to read the history of the landscape through the study of maps, garnering prizes, even falling in love with my high school geography teacher. For a while, it became the driving force of my career.

Much later, cancer appeared in my life, as it did in his. It took me to a place, this island, the island I constantly drew as a child when my father was far away—a place where I have been able to access deeper and deeper levels of my psyche. In the process, my body has come into balance and been healed. The life of the psyche is so very, very complicated. I am struggling with moving away from my mind's need to understand things in concrete terms and approaching the mystery of the Self. I wish that, when my father was alive, I could have accessed a tenth of what I now vaguely understand.

But just as the Mormons believe they can save the souls of the deceased by having them baptized into the church, perhaps we who are alive can heal family wounds by exploring the interconnected psyches of both the living and the dead. For me, my parents are not "dead." Although I can no longer access their physical presence, their souls feel very much alive.

❧ ❧

Something extraordinary is happening to me here on Iona. Something about living here and sharing my dreams with Barry—a loving male figure to whom I can open my heart; a wise counselor who has helped me understand the complexities of my relationship with my father. I think I am reaching a state of resolution: the bewildered little girl has matured into an independent woman.

The other night I had a dream in which I am on a railway platform with a group of academic colleagues waiting for one of our number to arrive on a train. Across the tracks on the opposite platform, I see a group of friends and family waiting for Dad's arrival. He is returning from the army, but it is long after the war; he is older and I am now an adult. I am torn: should I stay with my colleagues or go to greet him? I quickly make my decision, run down some steps, through a tunnel (a symbol of the unconscious), and up some steps to where a crowd is greeting my father. I've missed a short speech he made, but I watch as people gather round, then start to leave the station. Dad is to drive me home.

"I have my own home now" I tell him. He seems a little surprised.

"Oh—your own home?"

"Yes."

"Your own home? ... Well, that's good ... that's good."

"Yes, it is."

We smile at each other, as if both recognizing a separation that is essential, that is timely and appropriate. I smile again at my father and then at the road ahead as he drives me safely home.

I wish I could have shared all these memories with him; asked him the questions I never asked; thanked him for the many thoughtful ways he showed his love, even if, in all our life together he never once said "I love you." And nor did I.

☙ ☙

A seagull cries overhead; I am back on the beach on Iona. Eyes drifting shut, I become aware of both my parents smiling down at me. Not exactly smiling—no faces, just an over-arching presence of love. Because of their love, I am here. It is a miracle: to be incarnate, to be, however briefly, on this beautiful earth. I relax into my breathing, hearing the waves getting closer. I get up and walk down to the sea. The waves breaking cold on my bare legs remind me that I am here.

CHAPTER 18

❧

Turtle Shell Breaking

You are not
a troubled guest
on this earth,
you are not
an accident
amidst other accidents
you were invited
from another and greater
night
than the one
from which
you have just emerged.... —David Whyte[53]

Strong winds rattling the windows disturb me several times during the night. Waking to calmer weather, I write down a dream before it slithers away. People are breaking apart a turtle shell, a large shell of a rare species. They are using the shell as building material for a new hotel. I am outraged, since this hotel is being built for tourists who will come to see this rare turtle in its natural habitat—the very turtle whose shell is being broken to build the hotel!

As I bite into my toast and tangy tart marmalade, I think about the dream. I usually try to write down some thoughts about a dream before I call Barry, but this time I am stumped. A turtle shell? A tourist hotel? Although it would be easy to dismiss these puzzling nocturnal dramas as mere nonsense, the psyche's sloughing off of unwanted material, my conversations with Barry have taught me to see them as sources of insight, as powerful messages that I can hear no other way. I start to think of dreams as the compost of the psyche, a rich medium promoting future growth.

The line to New Mexico is alive with static. I dial several times before I can hear Barry's voice clearly and he mine. We exchange a few pleasantries, talk of my anxiety about returning to Berkeley, and then discuss the dream. After trading ideas back and forth and speculating about its meaning, Barry says:

"Perhaps some personal protective shell, some encasement of the vulnerable-inner is being broken apart. This shell has allowed you to live. The fragments of what once protected you are now being used to build a new structure. Your stay on Iona is the breaking apart of the shell, an initiation. The fragments being used to build something new are the words you're recording that people may one day visit in order to contemplate their own protective shells, their own turtle-selves."

I sigh. Dreams cannot be ignored. Something in me is changing, breaking apart.

❧ ❧

The only constant is change, the Buddha taught. As I live my quiet life on this island, I am constantly aware of change: the tide ebbing and flowing; spring flowers dying, summer flowers pushing up through the long grass; lambs growing fatter, moving unknowingly toward inevitable slaughter; the weather changing overnight from a sea smooth as rippling silk to a cauldron of wind-lashed waves biting the shore.

Everything around us speaks of change and yet the rocks of this island seem to tell a different story. They were formed long before mammals appeared on the earth—before birds, before turtles, before plants, before insects, even before the appearance of oxygen. The age of these rocks and any changes that have occurred to them cannot be comprehended by the human mind, so we cling to the notion that perhaps something in this world is unchanging. This place seems to reassure us through its geology, the sound of waves and call of birds, that there is an essential essence we can depend on.

For several centuries, the Reilig Oran—a graveyard next to the abbey and terminus of the Street of the Dead—was the preferred burial place for the kings and chiefs of Scotland. The soil of the island was considered sacred and it was predicted that Iona alone would survive the end of the world. Among many prophecies from that time is one that says:

> *Seven years before the Judgment*
> *The sea shall sweep over Erin at one tide,*
> *And over blue-green Islay;*
> *But the island of Columba*
> *Shall swim above the flood.* [54]

❧ ❧

As I walk past the Heritage Centre, my attention is drawn to a sycamore that has lost a large branch. Perhaps it happened years ago; the gaping wound in its trunk seems softened by many seasons of rain, wind, sunshine, and bird-song. As I draw closer, I am astonished to see a tiny sycamore seedling growing inside the scar. How had a seed from the parent tree landed and germinated *there*, in its very place of loss and dismemberment? No matter "how," it speaks to me of death and rebirth, of seeking new growth in the very place of our deepest wounding. How many times have I walked this way before and never seen it?

❧ ❧

I climb to the summit of Dun I. This is where my healing journey began, clambering up the rocky hillscape in my imagination to lie on the greensward, picturing the seagulls picking off the crabs that were invading the island, my body, my peace of mind. Now, healthy and grateful, shielded by rock from a gusty west wind, I sit and stare at watery wrinkles on the surface of a pool known as the Well of Eternal Youth. It is triangular in shape—two sides bounded by rock faces, the third opening up to a cleft that looks out to the north, to views of Mull, Staffa, the Treshnish Islands, and Dutchman's Cap. This little pool of fresh water, caught up in the rock of Iona, has been seen since antiquity as a place of healing and perpetual youth.

A young blond man interrupts my thoughts—probably a participant in a workshop at the abbey this week. He bends down at the pool and splashes his face with water. "Now I'll be young forever," he says, smiling at me.

"You look pretty young already. But there are some interesting things to learn as you get older."

"Perhaps I can stay young and still learn them," he says, smiling. He runs his fingers through his hair, clambers up the rocks out of sight.

A rain storm blows in from the west. I try to go on writing, but give up, put on my jacket, and start to walk across the summit of Dun I. Just as suddenly, the rain abates. I settle against a rock to eat my lunch. A seagull wings by and then alights a few feet from me. I throw it pieces of bread; it comes closer. I talk to it quietly, thanking it for its help in my healing, in ridding the island of crabs.

I scramble down the hill, thinking about the rainstorm, the seagull. It seems almost like the story of the cancer (the storm) and its healing (the seagull) in microcosm. Just as I am musing on this, I look down and see forget-me-nots. I've never seen this flower anywhere else on Iona, but there they are, just a small patch with tiny blue flowers. It seems almost staged, almost hokey—but there it is—nature seemingly saying to me: "Don't forget." As if I could.

※ ※

I look out of the cottage window at the Sound of Iona. The ferry is making its way through the white-flecked swell to the ramp at Fionnphort. All is quiet, just the rhythmic breathing of the waves against the shore. Herring gulls, in contemplative mood, hunker down on the rocks, all facing south. The sky is overcast; the weather, as the forecasters like to say, is "uncertain."

I recall a quote from Karen von Blixen on the nature of the soul, which she says refuses to be caught in our net of words, but rather "swims away like a fish." Indeed. This small rocky eminence set in a vast sea is like the conscious mind full of sights, sounds, thoughts, feelings—encompassed by a vast unconscious whose secrets are sometimes fleetingly revealed and then, just as suddenly, washed away by the next incoming wave. And yet I keep trying: I speculate on messages from dreams; I note moments of awe, when time and space dissolve; I ponder the mystery, a tantalizing hair's-breadth away.

I pick up a book from a shelf in this book-rich dwelling. In a Foreword by Christopher Bamford to *The Dove in the Stone: Finding the Sacred in the Commonplace* by Alice O. Howell, he writes:

> Iona is ... an ensouled place. Columba and his Saints, who knew the wisdom of God in creation and worshiped it continuously, have made it so. Iona's power is such that it instructs all who walk there in the arts of ensoulment. It is a place of soul and of imagination, sacrament and the feminine.... Grace descends gently there; it is in the very atmosphere, invisibly fertilizing those whose hearts are opened.... But Iona can be any place where the heart is open. For when the heart is open, we enter the realm of the imagination, that active mirror in which spirit takes form in images and matter is immaterial.... This is the soul realm which we have lost. [55]

Cancer was the jolt in my life that jettisoned me into the soul realm I had lost. My logical mind throws up a counter-argument. If cancer has something to do with loss of the soul, then why did holy men (undoubtedly ensouled beings) like Suzuki Roshi, who founded the Zen Center in San Francisco, or Cardinal Basil Hume, beloved head of the Roman Catholic Church in Britain, die of cancer? Illness comes with different messages. For some, it comes as a wake-up call; for others, it is their means of slipping away—as it may, eventually, be mine.

Alice Howell, a Jungian scholar and poet, journeyed to Iona when she was entering what she called "the youth of my old age" and recorded: "Somehow, when I stepped onto Iona the first time, the inner landscape suffused the outer, or the outer embodied the inner ... some inner conviction took hold: there is an inner beauty in each of us hungering to be matched in outer experience. When this happens in truth, some great affirmation leaps up within us and for a moment out of time, we move from hope and belief to certainty."[56]

Iona is, for me, that great affirmation. Whether the day is sunny or gray, its atmosphere seems to enfold me in a gentle embrace as if to say: Be here. Be yourself. All is well. Its wisdom, half hidden, has to be approached in silence lest it slip away into the realm of the Other. But if it does, it will always reappear at another time, in another guise. As Alice Howell wisely reminds us, the wisdom hidden in nature is like a small child playing hide-and-seek; now you see me, now you don't.

As I walk toward the north end of the island, it occurs to me how much I have been steeped in the feminine aspects of reproduction and mothering since living on the island. Lambs were being born when I arrived. By midsummer, they are almost as large as their mothers, who still allow them to suckle occasionally, or sleep up close on a chilly day. Birds, too, are raising their young all around me. I have followed the fortunes of a blackbird family that made its nest in the fuchsia hedge opposite Highland Cottage. On the Bay at the Back of the Ocean, families of eider ducks paddle around close to the shore.

Mothering and the feminine also mean knowing when to push your children out into the world. One day, in a field below the abbey, I watch a starling searching for food in the close-cropped grass. A youngster almost as large as its parent and quite able to eat on its own follows its mother, impatiently jabbing her in the back to remind her of her mothering duties each time she finds a worm. She, I am pleased to observe, ignores his pleas: "Time to find your own food."

ᕥ ᕥ

My days of solitude on the island are tempered by social events, all the more enjoyable because they are of a kind I never encounter in the city: Quiz Night at the Pub, a *ceildh* (pronounced "kay lee") at the village hall. In times gone by in this part of the world, people visited from house to house and each contributed a song or a poem. Now, in many parts of Scotland, people gather at a community hall for a dance or a local talent show—a ceildh.

A bagpipe band comes over from Mull on the 7:00 PM ferry and warms up, playing on the pier. At 8:00 PM, they walk up to the village hall, a crowd of visitors and island residents following. The hall is packed. We listen to a concert of traditional music: pipers play, a women's choir from Mull sings, a little girl plays her flute, another sings "Gathering the Thyme," a man plays the accordion. Small girls squeeze their way along the rows selling raffle tickets. Children sit or sprawl on the floor near the performers, remarkably well behaved and watching wide-eyed as father, uncle, or older sister plays the pipes, and mothers and aunts sing traditional songs in Gaelic. After the concert, the short solid master of ceremonies who has come over with the pipers from Mull calls on a little girl with flaming-red curls to come up and draw the winning raffle tickets. The first winners have their choice of bottles of Scotch or wine; the later ones choose from less exciting prizes of chocolates or shampoo.

Finally, after tea and sandwiches, the dancing begins: the Gay Gordons, Strip the Willow, the Boston Two-step, the Dashing White Sergeant. Carole and Ian demonstrate the steps. Soon the floor is alive with dancing couples—small children and white-haired oldies, teens and plump matrons, women dancing with women, men with men, men with women—it doesn't matter. People miss their steps and get tangled up with the couple next to them; a cat wanders in from outside and quickly retreats; those not dancing sit along the sides of the hall, tapping their feet and clapping in time with the insistent rhythm. In times gone by, before telephones or TV, this human togetherness provided an essential balance to the loneliness of life on distant crofts in the long winter months.

Windows are flung open to let in more air, people pull off sweatshirts and jackets, a person falls in the melee of the dance and is helped to a seat by the door. When all seem near exhaustion, the MC calls a break and three children get up on stage, giggling, to perform an action song about a frog. The next dance is announced. More and more people join in. I get up to dance the Gay Gordons with Peter from the hotel, then, barely catching my breath, the Dashing White Sergeant with Niels from Traigh Bhan. Onlookers are dragged half reluctantly onto the floor. Three little girls skip and hop excitedly on the stage.

Sullen-faced boys, barely in their teens, refuse to join in the dancing and look faintly embarrassed at this display of adult exuberance.

It feels good to see so many people I know, even though they may not know me: Crawford, the postmaster; Mark, the postie; Ian Dougall, the owner of the croft named Ardionra; people who work at the abbey, the Argyll Hotel, the St. Columba Hotel. However peripherally, I am part of this island community. It is impossible to imagine a concert and dance in Berkeley where I see the man who delivers mail to my house, the woman who serves me at the grocery store, neighbors and friends, white-haired ladies and small children—all dancing, laughing, and enjoying a simple good time together. In the field next to the hall, four rams graze quietly as darkness falls, music and laughter pouring out through the open windows into the balmy night air.

⁊ ⁊

Summer is here. I walk past the beach at Martyr's Bay and stop briefly to watch two naked toddlers scream with delight as they run in and out of the shallow water. It triggers a memory from childhood of the place we called the Bare Bridge.

It was very hot that summer. So hot that dogs lay panting in the shade, tar oozed up between roof tiles, and men on the farm sweated profusely as they swung sheaves of wheat up onto the wagons. Mary and I decided to go to one of our favorite places—the brook. I wonder if it had a name? It was probably too small and unimportant to be worthy of a name on a map, but to us, at the age of nine, it was as exciting as the Nile or the Amazon. Some days, we walked through the water to an island that was our secret place. We raised a flag there and claimed it as our own and wouldn't allow any other children to go there with us. Once, we allowed Mary's younger sister, Margaret, to come with us, but she kind of spoiled the secret, so we never invited her again.

On that particular very hot day, we splashed around in the brook for a while, grateful for the cool water running between our toes. Then we decided to take off all our clothes and lie down so we could get wet all over. The brook was not deep enough for swimming, which was a good thing, because I don't think either of us knew how to swim at that time. We lay in the water where the bottom was sandy, looking up as distant cumulus clouds drifted overhead.

"Look—that one looks like a sheep!" I said. "Over there," Mary countered. "That's a castle. Ooo—it's changing—now it's more like an elephant." We could see wildflowers along the banks, drooping in the heat: figwort, marsh marigold, milkmaids, and cow parsley. A flash of rainbow colors and a kingfisher shot over the water. Somewhere in the distance, we could hear the sound of a tractor. "I'm getting hungry," Mary said. "Let's go home now."

"How are we going to dry ourselves? We don't have a towel."

We stood up, water dripping off our bare bodies, glistening in the sunshine.

"The footbridge! Let's run back and forth on the bridge and shake all the water off."

And that's what we did. It was a simple bridge of two wide planks. We screamed with delight at what we thought was very daring and outrageous behavior. When we were almost dry, I glanced across the meadow that bounded the brook on one side. We both saw him at the same moment—a man leaning against a gate in the steel fence that ran around Grimstone Furze. His eyes were wide, his mouth half open—at least, that's what we told ourselves after the event.

Terrified, we ran into a nearby field and lay down panting in long grass not yet mown for hay. The dry stems tickled our thighs, but we were too scared to move or stick our heads up to see if the man was coming after us. A skylark sang above us, exuberant on this perfect summer day and oblivious of the human drama enacted far beneath her.

Eventually, we peeked above the swaying heads of grass and meadowsweet. We saw the man turn and walk away, scratching his head and whistling to his dog, who had been enjoying a brief nap at his feet.

We crawled back to where we had carelessly tossed our clothes, quickly put them on, and ran all the way home. We never told our mothers. Ever after that, we called it the Bare Bridge.

Forty years later, I returned. The bridge was still there, as well as the fence around Grimstone Furze and the gate where the man had watched amazed as two happy pre-pubescent girls danced in the summer sunshine. It was the first crack in the fine glass of our innocence.

≈ ≈

Low tide at Traigh an t-Suidhe, Strand of the Seat. I sit on a rock and watch water from a previous high tide, trapped in limpid pools behind sun-warmed boulders, cascade toward the sea, turning in wide rippling meanders and spiraling down a steep rock channel at my feet. It flows first in a smooth quick descent through which the rocks shine clearly in patterns of buff, gray, and white. Then, caught in a small pool, the water chatters in a clockwise spiral, turns across a lip into a second pool, and reverses direction, sloughing off strands of bubbles that quickly dissolve as the water moves faster, noisily, down another steep descent onto the sandy beach.

The fast-moving channel now becomes a slower stream, carving a shallow passage through the sand, noiselessly sculpting its bed into abstract patterns that shift, collapse, and re-emerge. Nearing the sea, the stream divides around rocks, stroking strands of seaweed—brown, olive-green, lettuce-green—until, close to journey's end, the water becomes suffused with sand, its color gray and murky like aged eyes. Two channels divided by a narrow spit of sand slowly encroach on each other until the spit collapses and the two become one. A shallow wave at sea's edge breaks with a gentle sigh—and the stream dies in its arms.

I sit for an hour watching. The flow continues, unchanging. Individual drops of water emerge from the deep pools behind me, race through the channel at my feet, reach the sea, and disappear. Yet the stream remains—glinting, chattering, bubbling, turning—like a great up-welling never-ending on-rush of life energy.

I look out to the horizon, strangely exhilarated. I remember my son when he was perhaps five or six, looking down at our cat one day and saying, in a moment of existential wonder: "She's alive! She's *alive!*" I feel caught up in a cauldron of boiling aliveness. All I have to do is stop—and look.

It was Kafka who wrote so wisely about the experience of the aliveness of the world. His words—as I remember them—went something like this:

> You do not need to leave your room. Remain sitting at your table and listen. Do not even listen, simply wait; be quiet, still, and solitary. The world will freely offer itself to you to be unmasked—it has no choice; it will roll in ecstasy at your feet.

It is said that the membrane between the material and the spiritual worlds is particularly thin in this place. Yes, I can feel that now. It is as if the rocks, the landscape, the waves, the birds invite me—entreat me—to look beyond their material form and open my consciousness to deeper meanings below the surface. It is as if this whole island were a dream and, looking at it with soft eyes, I allow it to reveal answers to questions I didn't even know I had asked.

※ ※

I take a walk to the abbey gift shop; maybe they have some new books in stock. But I find nothing I want to buy. I open a little gate and walk down a narrow gravel path toward the abbey itself.

It is said that there were once many stone crosses on Iona, but that, at the time of the Protestant Reformation, most were demolished or thrown into the sea. Or perhaps that is just a fiction. In any case, now there are only three. The oldest of these, St. Martin's Cross, has stood outside the main entrance to the abbey since the eighth century.

I walk over and look at the cross more closely. On the top, a ring of stone encircles a cross. This is the classic Celtic cross, thought to symbolize the earth and sun as venerated in Celtic lands encompassing the Christian cross of redemption—a simple design symbolizing two strands of belief woven together. I stare at the Celtic knot design on the tall shaft of the cross and follow its swirling pattern—round, up, down, under, over; no place to begin, no place to end. Perhaps it is a symbol of an individual life moving through an infinite variety of experiences,

pains, sorrows, and wonderments, the whole forming a perfect, unend-ing pattern. No birth, no death, just being and becoming. Surely it is also a symbol of the inter-connectedness of all matter, all beings woven into one exquisite, complex web of life without end.

On one side of the cross are carved biblical scenes, teachings made manifest in images from a time when most people were illiterate. Some are now hard to decipher. Gray-green lichen has colonized the surface and more than a thousand years of rain have smoothed the mason's handiwork. I step around to look at the other side, at what is known as a serpent-and-boss design: snake-like forms twisting around protruding spheres. Snakes, which can shed their skins, are symbolic of the Resur-rection. Some think this design also relates to a pre-Christian reverence for the serpent and its egg. Two sides of the same coin; two sides of the same cross. I think about this juxtaposition of nature imagery and Christian symbology. It seems altogether apt in this place, which has been inhabited for more than 6000 years and where present-day Christian services in the abbey give thanks for the sun behind all suns, wind over the flowing water, the moon and the running tide. In the medieval manuscript, *The Book of Kells,* images of nature—plants, birds, earthly creatures—twist and weave in glorious, colorful patterns through the words of the Bible. The written word and images of nature—two sources of learning sacred in Celtic Christianity. Iona, redolent with spirit, was—and still is—a place where people come seeking insight into the great unanswerable questions of life.

❧ ❧

It is a wet and blustery day. Walking back from the retreat house of Traigh Bhan after a noon meditation, I pull the hood of my jacket tightly round my face and stop by the Iona Pottery to watch the waters of the Mill Stream swelling, mounding, breaking over rounded rocks, weaving between the sword-like leaves of wild iris.

We live on a water planet; we live in a water-filled body. Rain, mist, fog, snow—obeying the laws of gravity—settle gently into the landscape. Water seeps down, percolating, hydrating, cleansing, sweeping through my body, carrying out toxins. The tide rises; salt water embraces the land. My blood responds in its salinity, my tears, the water of my womb. I am water; I need water. I need its sounds—fountain, freshet, waves, waterfall, beck, burn, brook, rapids, spring. I need its smell, its touch. The soul of the world is wakened in watery dreams. It was the British poet Philip Larkin who wrote:

> If I were called in
> To construct a religion
> I should make use of water."[57]

By the time I return to Highland Cottage, the rain has stopped and banks of cumulus clouds drift across the sky. I sit near the window savoring my lunch of barley soup and hot buttered toast, my eyes never tiring of the view of the sea.

We sail the sea, we dive beneath the waves, we climb mountains and cross deserts, but we cannot explore clouds except with our eyes. Wondrous beings, creatures of vapor, sun, and wind, how can we comprehend your vastness, your peaks and valleys and canyons of mist-filled air?

Over the mountains of Mull, a huge cloud drifts slowly south. Soundless explosions of white are lit by the sun above, silhouetted against a sky of milky blue. Below are shadows of blue-gray, dove-gray, where the sun's rays cannot penetrate—or is it just that the vapors there reflect the blue of the sea beneath? Changing before our eyes, clouds are messengers of surrender. They let go, melting into never-repeated shapes and patterns until, eventually, they dissolve and return to earth as fog and rain, once more to swell the sea. They swirl in river meanders and settle into bogs and swamps to feed seagull and asphodel, cattle and sea thrift. Then, drawn skyward again by the lure of the sun, they replay an endless story of watery reincarnation. Can I accept that we, too, may enact a parallel story?

❧ ❧

In his wonderfully titled book, *After the Ecstasy, the Laundry,* California Buddhist teacher Jack Kornfield writes:

> It is the goal of spiritual life to open to the reality that exists beyond our small sense of self … In awakening, our whole sense of identity shifts. We let go of our small sense of self and enter the unbounded consciousness out of which we come. What becomes known with absolute certainty is that we are not and never have been separate from the world. It is as if our heart, our knowing, expands further and further until we contain everything, until we are the world.[58]

He continues to describe three of the most powerful ways of entering this realization: through meditation or prayer; through encounter with another person—teacher, priest, or "ordinary" person who has reached this insight; or through entering a period of solitude.

As I read this, I begin to wonder: Can there be enlightened places, as there are enlightened people? Are there places whose very presence and whose every inter-connected sparkling detail encourage us to let go of our small sense of self and surrender into the certain knowledge of the oneness of everything? Iona is such a place for me. It feels as though I have apprenticed myself to this place, as others might seek a teacher in human form. My childhood bonding to nature; my whole career exploring the connections between people and place; my passion for healing gardens. It is small wonder that I have sought spiritual understanding in and from a place, and not from a specific guru or teacher, religion or sacred text. My spiritual practice is, and always has been, rooted in the here and now of the natural environment. It is not everyone's way. But it is the way that is comfortable for me. The great variety of religions and beliefs in the world demonstrate that there are myriad pathways to the one Truth.

⁊⦑ ⁊⦑

I wake in the night to yet another dream. I find an overgrown garden. Tall thistles grow in what were once flower beds, the purple flowers catching the light, white thistledown from spent flowers drifting by like flotillas of tiny parachutes. I start to walk through the garden, my feet squeezing the gravel underfoot in weedy pathways so that, with each step, I seem to be claiming this space as my own. I smell the scent of lavender, the peppery aroma of cow parsley—garden flowers and wild flowers intertwined in a lush galaxy of growth. Then I come upon some fruit trees: apple, I think, and plum. They need care—pruning and fertilizing. I will bring in compost, rich compost and mulch. I will make this garden my own.

Suddenly, I become aware of a tall, concrete building looming to my right. I tilt my head and count nine stories, nine rows of identical steel-framed windows, nine floors of cubicles and file cabinets, studio desks and telephones, corridors and computer terminals. I draw in a short breath, something between a cry and a strangled gasp of recognition. It is Wurster Hall, home of the College of Environmental Design on my old campus at Berkeley. It is the building where I worked for thirty years—scene of academic tensions, budget struggles, cliques and back-biting, ego trips and ego wounding, anxiety and last-minute, nail-biting, lecture-preparation stress. Yes, there were good times too: camaraderie, socializing, student rapport, intellectual excitement. But for me, they were often overshadowed by the anxiety that I didn't quite belong, didn't quite measure up in this stew-pot of brains and ambition. Nine floors of offices, nine elevators opening, nine graffiti-scrawled stairways, nine doors beckoning—who will be on the other side? Nine, nine, nine-in-one. 9-9-9, 9-1-1. I'm calling for help; there's a crisis here. Can you hear me? Will you answer the phone?

I am out of the building and in the garden! The trees of my soul need to be cared for, perhaps to blossom and bear fruit once more. This garden is Iona itself, the unattended aspects of my life—the deep feminine, the intuitive, the spiritual. I will tend this garden of mine with the nutrients it needs, with compost made from dying aspects of earlier growth, with the broken fragments of turtle shells. It was Carl Jung who said: "In the final analysis, we count for something only because of the essential we embody and if we do not embody that, life is wasted."[59]

CHAPTER 19

☙

Moving to Greenbank

*Many people miss out on themselves as they journey
through life. They know others, they know places, they
know skills, they know their work, but tragically, they
do not know themselves at all. Ageing can be a time of
ripening when you actually meet yourself, indeed maybe
for the first time … a time for visiting the temple of your
memory and integrating your life … a vital part of coming home to yourself.* —John O'Donahue[60]

Elinore phones to say that she and her family will be returning in late
July and will need Highland Cottage. Can I find alternative accom-
modation for my last month on the island? I am momentarily taken
aback, a little angry. I thought the offer to stay here extended through
August. But I recall Elinore telling me a story about a man she allowed
to live in a cottage at the back of hers until he got his life together. He
hung on and on, and eventually she had to ask him to leave. Perhaps
she worries I will do the same.

I call Barbara to ask her advice and an arrangement is quickly
made. I will stay in a room in her house until I leave the island. I pack
up my clothes and books and quite an accumulation of rocks and shells
that I have collected in the last few months. Barbara comes for me by
car and thus I move to Greenbank.

Unlike Highland Cottage in the heart of the village, Greenbank
stands alone in a field and is almost the southern-most dwelling along
the eastern shore of the island. Walking the half mile from the village,
you open a small iron gate and cross a field, carefully avoiding the

sheep droppings that litter the grass. Barbara lives in one half of the house, and I (and any others who may be here on retreat) live in the other half.

I move into a large upstairs room with a comfortable double bed, a desk, chair, wardrobe, and sink, and deep window sills where I put books, papers, and my favorite rocks and shells. One window faces east toward Mull and the Isle of Erraid; the other faces north across the Sound of Iona to another craggy, pink-gray rocky shore of Mull. In the distance, on clear days, I can see the slopes of Ben More. I sit close to the window watching clouds move imperceptibly across the distant landscape. A gray heron perches like a sentinel on the rocks below Greenbank; silvery stems of dune grass dance agitated in the wind.

As I become familiar with my new home, I find a favorite space to sit and ponder. It is an enclosed porch facing east, morning sun stream- ing in through its glass roof. There are red geraniums on the window sill, pots of basil growing in a corner, outdoor jackets hanging on pegs, boots and walking shoes lined up on an old piece of carpet near the door. Here, I do the dishes and wash my clothes, watch the ferry plying between Mull and Iona. Here, I sit and write, alternately absorbed in words, the slow tracings of my pen, and then staring out with soft day-dreaming eyes at sea and rock and passing seabirds. Here, I can sit and stare—and do nothing. (Why can I seldom do that in my own home?) A perfect environment for aging—that time of life when it is right and proper to sit and stare, to contemplate what has been, to make sense of a life which—if not over—has run much of its course.

"How can older people sit and do nothing?" I used to think when I was young and full of energy. "Quite easily," I now reply, only it isn't "nothing." Sitting and thinking at my age is akin to coming out of an enthralling play or movie with a complicated plot and needing time to reflect on the story, the ins and outs of the narrative, the paths not taken. We need time, silence, solitude to consider what it all meant—to look back, not with regret, but rather with curiosity. A lifetime is a complicated plot to unravel. It was, I think, a character in one of Virginia Woolf's novels who recalled, at such a time as this, that he had outlived certain desires, was not as gifted as at one time seemed likely, and that certain things lay beyond his scope. Indeed.

There are many things I shall never understand, like economics, literary theory, and the stock market. I have never understood them, never really wanted to. There are many things I still want to understand, but probably never will, like capturing a fleeting moment in a seventeen-syllable haiku, how to play the piano, and why love comes and goes in our lives like the vagaries of the weather.

I lean back in my chair, cradling my head in my palms, elbows akimbo, just like my mother. With a jolt I recognize this as a way she often sat in her old age, her feet up, staring lovingly out at the walled garden of her London house. It was a garden my father created from a weed-filled, rubbled patch of ground after they moved in retirement to a neighborhood in a less fashionable segment of Hampstead. At the bottom of that garden was a tree planted by Auntie Jean. My mother insisted it was a black walnut; I think it was a form of acacia. No matter; my mother loved that tree and, when she went into a nursing home for the last eighteen months of her life, I gave her a framed photo of it to place on her window sill.

Thinking about that time fills me again with guilt. Why did I not leave California and go back to care for her in her last months of life?

It was a poor decision and I live forever with the repercussions in my heart.

Why didn't I go? Because there was such a deep ambivalence in our relationship that was never resolved? Because her narcissism—she always needing to be the center of attention—left little room for me? I know the reasons why mothering was difficult for her. Sent away to a boarding school of almost Dickensian frugality when she was only eight; being desperately unhappy there; trying to cut her wrists in a bathtub when she was sixteen; having a nervous breakdown during final exams at college when she was twenty-one. Never receiving much love or tenderness from her own mother, she shied away from expressing feelings or demonstrating the love I know she had in her heart for her children. I know the reasons, but they don't erase the yearning for closeness I felt in childhood.

❧ ❧

It is a good drying day: intermittent sun and a gusty wind. I wash my clothes at the sink. Letting myself out through the garden gate, I pick my way between sun-dried sheep droppings to the washing line flapping with Barbara's sheets. It gives me such deep pleasure to know that the wind and the sun will soon dry my clothes; no mechanical drone of a steel-drum dryer. The wind has turned to the north and is cold for a summer day. I look back: the legs of a pair of pants are dancing a mad fandango. I return to the sun-warmed porch and make my lunch of Brie spread on thick Orkney oat cakes, a tomato, a carrot, ripe plums, a chocolate biscuit, and hot green tea. My life is full of silence, solitude, and simple pleasures. I am happy.

In the evening, I sit in the porch and watch as the sun picks out the row of former lighthouse-keepers' cottages on the Isle of Erraid, the island which formed the basis of Robert Louis Stevenson's *Treasure Island,* and where his father was himself a lighthouse keeper. As the light dims, Harold, a retired minister, walks by along the pebbly track between Greenbank and the sea. He is taking his black cat, Pavarotti, for an evening stroll. The cat darts in and out of the dune grass, disappearing for a moment, then racing after the slow-moving man who holds his jacket tightly around his body against a cold north wind.

Patches of sky in the east become rosy-pink. I go upstairs to the bathroom, one of the few rooms with a window facing west, and there—over the Bay at the Back of the Ocean—is a startling sunset: high stratus clouds layered in rose, blue, and mauve; low cumulus clouds like explosions of dark gray smoke; the roofs of Clachancorrach and Cnoc Oran silhouetted against the flaming sky. Sheep settle onto the hilltops, facing west. If, as Jane Goodall maintains, chimpanzees express emotions akin to awe when watching a waterfall, may not sheep appreciate the beauty of a sunset?

Dreams are coming thick and fast again. In one, a scheme is being inaugurated at a hospital whereby each staff member will adopt a child, pay attention to it, and give it gifts. A rather serious unemotional administrator starts announcing who will get which child. As he does so, one by one, the hospital staff start to cry. "What's going on here?" says the administrator in an exasperated tone, as if he can't understand why there's so much emotion.

I am happy this is the day I talk with Barry. Much as reading and insights from nature enrich my life, it is my dreams that provide a depth of understanding I can find in no other way. I tell Barry about the dream and we are both silent for a while.

"In many ways, we all live parallel lives: part of you immigrated to California and had a successful career, but the English child in you stayed in the old country. What you left behind has deeply affected you. Now, in Iona, you're in touch again with your abandoned child-in-nature. You've deeply dramatized the split in your life by going to Iona and staying there a long time, not just for a one-week retreat. The dream says boldly: Here is your split."

I sigh deeply. The anguish of the ex-patriot, the voluntary exile. Much as I feel my house—and especially my garden—in Berkeley is my home, the broader expanse of California and the whole United States is not. On many trips "home" in the past thirty years to see my mother, I tacked on a walking holiday somewhere in England: the Cornish Coastal Path, the Cotswolds, the Coast-to-Coast Trail, the Pennine Trail, Dorset, the Isle of Wight. I laughingly tell my friends I am going to get a "fix" from the English countryside. That's what it feels like: I am re-injected with something of deep value to me, something that puts me in a state of near bliss. A landscape high.

But what about the pragmatic administrator in the dream? That side of me is also present, necessary to "get things done." The caring staff at the hospital who have emotions are like the energies that carried me along in the research and writing of *Healing Gardens,* which described how hospitals can be empathic to the side of life that is childlike, natural, nurturing.

"The healing garden is the story of your life!" Barry exclaims in an excited tone. The line is a little crackly between Iona and New Mexico. I strain to hear his voice. "The garden as your childhood landscape where you found the nurturance not experienced in the family; the garden as therapy in your own garden in Berkeley when you had cancer; the garden as re-introducing nature into hospital settings; the garden that is Iona. You are paying attention to the child-in-nature and it's a deeply emotional experience for you … the caring staff are weeping. You have re-immersed yourself in the natural world, far from your friends and your usual support system. In everything we do, we dramatize the inner situation. Going back to Berkeley may well be causing you some anxiety. Intellect versus the earth; you've retired from one and immersed yourself in the other. This is what seems like the unbridgeable gap."

I sigh and reluctantly put down the phone at the end of our conversation. I stare into space, seeing and not seeing. I feel numb. This is a lifetime's work.

❧ ❧

As I leave the Spar shop with a bag of groceries, I stop to pat a dog that is tethered outside. Memories of a favorite childhood pet come tumbling back.

Judy was a mongrel, part Bedlington, part Dandie Dinmont—two semi-obscure canine breeds that, in Judy, produced a dog about the size of a small sheep, with sheep-like, soft, curly, gray wool on the top of her head, and beige-brown hair on her back and legs. I don't remember where she came from or whether we had her first as a puppy. I know she lived with us at 27 Arden Road in London before the war, because there is a photo of me kneeling on the lawn peering intently at two rabbits in a wire-enclosed run with my right arm draped casually around Judy's shoulders.

When we were evacuated to the country, Judy, of course, came with us. But country life introduced all kinds of temptations she had never encountered in London. First, there were a neighbor's chickens that Judy loved to chase. She didn't actually kill them; it was more like canine harassment.

"You'd better curb that bitch of yours, or I'll come after her and give her a beating she'll never forget."

What to do? We didn't have a fenced yard or garden where she could be kept from roaming. We didn't want to keep her chained up. We consulted Mr. Bielby, the Ascott gamekeeper, who wore stained corduroy breeches and had legs that bowed out like two letter Cs. He had a solution. It was a brutal one, but it was effective. He put Judy and a big rooster in a large, scratchy burlap sack, tied the top closed, then beat it with a carpet beater, the two terrified animals squawking, barking, and struggling inside. When he finally stopped and opened the sack, Judy and the rooster took off in different directions, feathers and hair flying in their wake. Judy never chased chickens again.

Another recurring problem involved Judy's unwanted suitors. When she was in heat, dogs from near and far came calling, sitting outside the house at night howling. My mother put something on Judy's genitals that was supposed to solve the problem. It had a very particular smell that comes back to me when I wash my hands with rose-petal soap. But rose petals on the genitals didn't work. Rather it seemed to drive dogs mad with desire. Judy had puppies, one of which, I remember, we called The Professor; he sat off alone looking pensive in a doggy sort of way.

But the chickens and the unwanted suitors were relatively minor problems compared to the sheep that grazed in fields near our home. One day, I came home from school and called out to my mother: "Where's Judy?" I wanted to go roaming in the woods and it always felt better to have her along.

"Clare—sit down. I have to tell you something." I knew it was bad; my mother never spoke like that.

"You know Judy started chasing Mr. Watson's sheep? Well, two of them had miscarriages and he told me yesterday that if he caught her at it again, he was going to shoot her."

I caught my breath and felt sweat seeping out from under my fringe. "So you see, there was nothing else I could do. I took her to Mr. Armstrong, the vet, today and he put her to sleep."

I sucked in my breath and held tight onto the seat of the kitchen chair. How could she have done this? My Judy, my friend. How could she do this?

"I'm so sorry, Clare. I didn't know what else to do."

"But you could have told me...."

I got up, stormed out of the kitchen, slammed the front door, and ran until I was out of breath. I climbed to the top of a swaying ruddy-barked beech tree, holding on tight as the wind moved the branches and I let the tears run down my cheeks into the wool of my favorite sweater decorated with clusters of round red cherries.

Judy was a casualty of war, albeit a very minor one, but huge in my childhood memory. A dog raised in the city who could not adapt to life in the country, as was true for so many human evacuees. Food from sheep and chickens was far more important than the life of a domestic pet. It is said that hundreds of thousands of dogs and cats were put to sleep in wartime Britain because their owners were unable to feed them.

❧ ❧

Walking home from the north end of Iona, I am lured into the abbey coffee shop by the thought of a piece of flapjack—crunchy squares of oatmeal, flour, butter, and syrup, just like my mother made, even better. Ahead of me at the counter, I see Niels, the present custodian of Traigh Bhan. I join him at a table by a window that looks out at the abbey. I ask Niels about his first visit to Iona.

"It was 1991. I came here on a week's retreat and felt an overwhelming sense of 'coming home.' I sensed that, here, I could be all that I am; I didn't need to pretend any more. I walked into Traigh Bhan and fell in love with that house. I went home to Denmark and quit my job. Then my father died. It felt as if all the ties were being cut. And in 1995, I became the custodian of Traigh Bhan!"

How is it we are drawn to a place? How do we recognize the place that will allow us to be "all that we are?" So many of us are placeless, wandering. "How is it for you—observing the many people who come to Traigh Bhan on retreat?" I ask.

Niels smiles, wistfully. "I love the simplicity of my life here: taking care of the house, taking care of the guests. Some people sleep for the first day or two. I see subtle shifts taking place. Sometimes, people recognize it when they're on the island; sometimes, it happens later. I've seen a few people get terrified, wanting to leave immediately, not wanting to face whatever it is in their lives that needs to change."

We sip our tea in silence. I take the last bite of flapjack, and then, licking the tip of one finger, I pick up flakes of oatmeal left on the plate and place them deliciously on my tongue.

⁂

I sit in the porch at Greenbank and put a cherry into my mouth. It has come straight out of the fridge. I let it rest there, the cold of its skin seeping onto my tongue, the cherry stalk sticking out of my mouth like the tongue of a gecko waiting for unwary insects.

I let my front teeth sink into the flesh. It is warm now and the sweet taste of cherry juice slips around my taste buds. I crunch the peel between my back teeth until there is nothing left but the clean, hard stone, unyielding, holding a secret in its core to which my teeth and tongue have no access.

My Great-uncle George had a fruit farm in a village named Edelsborough in Bedfordshire. I think he raised cherries, but I know he raised plums—greengages, damsons, Victoria plums hanging from trees in his orchard like glittering Christmas tree ornaments, Christmas in July. I don't remember Uncle George, but I do remember visiting Aunt Emily—Auntie Em, we called her—after her husband died, after the war. I remember the shallow stone sink in her kitchen at Chiltern View and how you had to pull the black steel arm of the pump up and down, up and down, to get the water to flow. It seemed thrilling to me as a child, so much more exotic than those identical chrome taps in London that disgorged hot and cold water at the flick of a wrist.

When you wanted to go the loo, you had to pick your way along stepping stones to the garden's cold wooden outhouse and sit on a wide wooden seat with a hole in it. There were spiders in the outhouse. I didn't mind the spiders, but I did mind the long drop under the hole in the seat, and the sound of pee falling on sodden paper and mounds of shit sprinkled with lime from a rusty bucket by the door. You had to wipe your bottom with newspaper and I worried that the words would come off on my skin. Would they be the right way round, I used to wonder? Or would they be backward and I'd have to hold a mirror under my buttocks and squirm around to read the headline from the Daily Mirror.

Auntie Em began to lose her memory and didn't know who we were when we came for Sunday tea. Paul and I ran under the long rows of plum trees, catching flower petals in the spring, jumping up to pluck ripe plums in the summer. One Sunday, Auntie Em brought out some letters and began to read to us. They were letters Uncle George had written to her from the trenches in France in the First World War. "I don't know who George is—but he wrote such nice letters," she said wistfully. "He must have cared for me, I think. He always wrote 'Love from George' at the end of each letter."

My father and mother exchanged glances. Should they remind her George was her husband? But then she'd also be reminded she was losing her memory. "Yes, George must have loved you a lot," my father finally said, always the one to smooth things over, to make people feel good.

"It's so kind of you to visit," Auntie Em said, cutting slices of Victoria sponge with a strawberry jam filling. "Here, do have some more cake. George will be home soon, but there will still be plenty for him."

Auntie Em has gone now; probably the house and the outhouse and the orchards are all gone too. I sigh, and catch a whiff of the basil growing in the porch at Greenbank. It is 9:30 PM, yet still light. Outside the window, the sea is totally, inexplicably, flat, like the proverbial mill pond. Three seagulls float on the water close to the shore; seventeen more perch on a rock that runs like a large elephant's head and trunk out into the still, salt water.

❧ ❧

I wake suddenly in the night and switch on the bedside light to write down a dream. I see my late cat, Pushkin, on top of a nine-story building, peering over the edge, wondering how to get down. To my amazement, she jumps and, with legs splayed, falls like a bird and lands safely. But she is now on a podium on which the tall building rests; she is still not on the ground. She goes to the edge and jumps again, and, three more stories down, lands safely on the ground. I am amazed at her pluck and keep pointing at the building and telling people what has happened.

Is this the story of my survival from two bouts of cancer? The first, the most fearful and shocking, is the leap of six stories; the second, less of a shock because I know I can survive it, the three-story jump to the ground. Now I am on the ground. I am healthy; I have survived the Long Fall.

As I discuss this dream with Barry some days later, he asks: "How did Pushkin end up on top of a high-rise building? And what is the question to which this dream is the answer?"

I often dream of cats. They are usually, for me, a symbol of sensuality, instinct, and, in this case, survival. Pushkin jumps off a nine-story building and, having nine lives, she survives. As I think more about the dream, I realize the setting is again Wurster Hall, locus of my academic career.

"And at the end of your career, you were at the top," Barry comments. "Your intellect got you to the top of the building, but your body needed to get down to earth. Perhaps that's why you got cancer; you were too high, too inflated. The descent from the heights was death-defying, dangerous—but you handled it. You had to fall to get back into your body and femaleness. Part of you is a cat-like survivor. And now you're on Iona, truly on the earth and dealing with earthly things."

Yes, that feels right. A life close to the earth, loving and learning from the earth, is what I've always wanted. When I was a child and people asked me: "What do you want to do when you grow up?" I always answered: "I want to be a gardener." But I allowed myself to get diverted—to the top of a high-rise building. I had to take a death-defying leap to return to earth. Like the cat in my dream, I survived.

The hour talking with Barry goes by all too quickly. I long to be with him, physically—to see his eyes meeting mine, to feel his arms hugging me, my head on his shoulder, if only for an instant. The intimacy of the analytical relationship is excruciating for what it appears to offer, and for what it does not, cannot, deliver. I stare out the window and continue talking to Barry in my imagination.

Do you remember the first time I came to visit you in Taos and how you emerged from your house as I came back down the hill? You had suggested I might want to take a walk in the forest and I had readily agreed. My heart was so full of emotion, a heart held tight like a ball clenched in the anxious hand of a child. My mind was racing, trying to make sense of our conversation, words pouring out—sometimes clear like sunlight on a mountain stream, sometimes slow and awkward, as if I were just learning to speak. Often, there seemed to be a filmy veil between us, something I wanted to tear away but couldn't. At times, there seemed to be two men in the room—you and a ghost that hovered between us so I couldn't tell to whom I was talking. I tried to look through the ghost directly at you, but it was impossible. Either I saw the ghost, or I saw you. But sometimes, just for an instant, the body of the ghost was superimposed on your body and I saw you as one being—tall, masculine, half-smiling—drawing love out of me like a hive of voracious bees sucking nectar from a thousand summer blooms.

When you suggested that I take a walk that day, after we had talked for so long, I climbed a grassy hill, peered through the windows of an empty house, listened to the aspen leaves, and eventually made my way back past tall yellow flowers of mullein. Then I saw you stepping out of your house. You must have been waiting for me to return. Perhaps you wanted to be sure I was safe.

A whole lifetime of yearning was encapsulated in that moment, like that of an insect trapped in golden amber. In my mind's eye, I have played that scene over and over: me coming down the hill, you stepping out of your house, you stepping out of your house, you stepping out of your house. How often before that had I come down the hill, any hill, all the hills of the world, hoping someone would step out of their house, thankful that I had safely returned?

❧ ❧

I sit close to the window in my room. How beautiful the sight of a sailing boat—black-hulled, tan-sailed—slipping through the water like a silent, three-winged moth. I, viewing the boat through my window; the boat's passengers viewing this gray-and-white, shore-side house a half mile distant; each of us perhaps distractedly thinking, "Who lives there? … Who sails by?" But we will never know, never know. The boat disappears beyond the window frame, and out of my consciousness.

As dusk falls, the shadow of the house in which I sit lays itself across the field between this dwelling and the sea, muting the colors of quivering buttercups, extending its rooftop chimneys across fence posts, creeping, as the sun falls lower, toward the waves. A fishing boat moves north along the Sound, a trail of sea birds following in its wake like a shower of white confetti.

The shadow of the house is now so large and distant-spread that it no longer resembles a dwelling place. It has dulled the colors of flowers, fence posts, and dune grass, but not the beach beyond, where two elderly women stroll in the last rays of the sun—dark-blue jacket and pale-blue jacket—their faces framed by crowns of shimmering white hair lit up like frosty halos.

In a tidal pool, a gray-bodied, white-necked heron stands motionless, eyes toward the water, waiting, waiting.

CHAPTER 20

❧

Remembering Stephen

*Sometimes when I enter a familiar room or street, I
think I see a past self walking toward me ... I used to feel
impatient with her: Why was she wasting time? Why
was she with this man? at that appointment? forgetting
to say the most important thing? Why wasn't she wiser,
more productive, happier? But lately, I've begun to feel
a tenderness, a welling of tears in the back of my throat,
when I see her. I think: She's doing the best she can. She's
survived ... Sometimes I wish I could go back and put my
arms around her ...*

*We are so many selves. It's not just the long-ago child
within us who needs tenderness and inclusion, but the
person we were last year, wanted to be yesterday, tried to
become in one job ... in one love affair or in one house
where even now, we can close our eyes and smell the
rooms.*

*What brings together these ever-shifting selves of
infinite reactions and returnings is this: There is always
one true inner voice. Trust it.* —Gloria Steinem[61]

I awake slowly to the sound of waves. No alarm clock here. No need
for any kind of clock. No place to be but here and now.

I pull the covers up under my chin and arrange the pillow more
comfortably under my head. Memories of Stephen, my ex-husband,
float into my mind. Iona seems to be my place of resolving problematic
relationships, of healing wounds from the past.

※ ※

Stephen was an exuberant child of the Sixties and Seventies who helped open my life to experiences I never dreamed of. He played such an important role in my life, bringing me out of my reserved Englishness and into the freer, self-expressive atmosphere of the Hippie generation.

I'll never forget that fall day in 1969 when he arrived at my campus office with Chester, his half-feral dog, in tow. Chester, with his sleek black-and-beige coat and his long wolf-like muzzle, was an amazing animal. He came from the banana belt of Colombia, where Stephen served in the Peace Corps. He got to know Stephen's graduate-student schedule, leaving him in seminars to wander the Berkeley campus, only to reappear just as the class ended. Once, when I was giving a lecture on social issues in urban parks—littering, vandalism, crime—I began to discuss controversies over dogs. Right on cue, Chester got up and left, sending the back row of students where Stephen always sat into titters of laughter. Not knowing what was going on, I imagined I had said something stupid.

Stephen began coming regularly to my office hours—sometimes with a genuine question about a class assignment, sometimes with information he thought I should have on the wonders of goats' milk or the evils of eating white sugar. He was really into health foods. But in the end, that didn't save him.

I remember the first time I saw Stephen as someone other than one of my students. I was driving through the intersection of College and Ashby Avenues in Berkeley on a sunny November day. He was standing on the corner, handsome in his 1960s Guatemalan shirt and beads, with long reddish hair and beard, like pictures of Jesus in my Sunday School class. But Jesus was far from my mind when, shortly after that, I invited him for Thanksgiving dinner at a friend's house and, that night, ended up in bed with him. Who seduced whom? I think it was mutual.

At first, we kept our relationship a secret. The issue of sexual harassment on college campuses had not yet emerged in society, but I knew that sleeping with a student was not something to brag about. Not so Stephen. He was always outrageous and outspoken. I think that is why

I was attracted to him. He was so different from my English veneer of reticence and mock-modesty. I was mortified when, at his annual student review in front of my faculty colleagues, he casually told them we were living together. Their startled academic eyes practically popped out of their heads. Well, there goes promotion and tenure, I thought. But, to give them their due, my colleagues never held it against me. Nor did they when, a year or so later, I became pregnant.

Stephen didn't want us to marry, even though we were in love and I was expecting his child. I hauled us both off to see Leo, maverick Berkeley therapist, buddy of counter-culture gurus Ram Dass, Timothy Leary, and Alan Watts. I was adamant. "Married or not, I am having this baby." Stephen relented and we were married in San Francisco City Hall with good friends Al, Michael, and Nancy as witnesses.

Stephen took such care of me during my pregnancy, feeding me yeast and vitamins, yogurt and black-strap molasses. We went to Lamaze classes at French Hospital in San Francisco, bought goodies at a Russian bakery on Clement Street, and then picnicked in a remote area of Golden Gate Park where Tasmanian tree ferns cast feathery shadows on our outstretched legs. I exposed my breasts to the sun because Stephen had read that it prepares the nipples for nursing. I smile as I remember the day when a mounted policeman arrived and we tried to explain what we were doing. He told me to cover up and rode away shaking his head in disbelief.

Jason was born with a half-smile like Buddha's on his lips. He did not cry, although I did, with the joy of seeing my first-born son. How did we manage it anyway? Making love in a Colombian hammock slung between two Douglas firs in an Oregon campground is no mean trick. I guess Jason was ready to incarnate. Stephen shocked the hospital staff by asking to take the placenta home. We buried it ritually at a ceremony in Al's garden when Jason received his name. The redwood tree planted over it is now two stories high and Jason is six feet tall.

The birth really "freaked Stephen out"—there are no other words to describe his reaction. After he helped me through the delivery, he was furious when the hospital staff asked him to leave so I could catch up on my sleep. It had been a sixteen-hour labor. He drove around all night, then phoned to say: "I'm not ready to be a father. I'm moving out. I'll ask Nancy to come and get you." I was devastated. All the new fathers came to the hospital bearing flowers and gifts, but Stephen never came. Later, I heard from psychotherapist friends that this is not an unusual reaction. Women go through nine months of hormonal changes to prepare them for motherhood, but fathers are less prepared and sometimes cannot cope with the sudden responsibility. Nancy told Stephen to pull himself together—or words to that effect—and, reluctantly, he came to collect us.

As soon as we were back in our Berkeley apartment, everything changed. Stephen became a devoted, besotted father. He had read that men in some remote Melanesian tribe suckle their babies and that, if an infant is kept on a man's nipple long enough, he will produce milk.

He tried it, to no avail. Instead, he insisted on getting up at 6:00 AM to feed Jason with a bottle so I could sleep while he lay close and "suckled" our newborn son.

At Jason's naming ceremony, Stephen passed around pieces of squash from our garden as a symbol of our son's American roots. I passed around a glass of mead (Where on earth did I find it?), symbol of his British heritage. Jason kept crying until Ed, priest-turned-therapist, invoked his name and we all chanted "Jay-son. Jay-son." Jason stopped crying in astonishment. My mother had traveled to California for the ceremony and made a traditional English christening cake. She decorated it with frosting and Jason's name, then looked around our sunny balcony for some feathery green leaves to complete her culinary composition. At the ceremony, people smiled knowingly at each other as they saw the cake. We hadn't the heart to tell Mum she had festooned the cake with marijuana.

The year we spent in Australia with baby Jason was a special time for us. I was teaching at the University of Sydney; Stephen worked for an architectural firm, helping to re-design the city's waterfront. We taught workshops together in Tasmania, Adelaide, and Brisbane. We were young quasi-hippies and had some wild times. On one occasion, we had been to the Atherton tablelands in Queensland and were driving our rental car back to Cairns airport. Stephen had learned to distinguish psychedelic mushrooms from other, more dangerous, varieties at the wild Aquarius Festival in Nimbin—the Australian version of Woodstock. He picked some he found growing in cow pats on the tableland.

"Take some with me," he urged, smiling. The open car windows gulped in hot fetid air, taking me back for an instant to a childhood visit to the tropical glasshouse at Kew Gardens.

"No, I can't. I'm scared. I'm nursing Jason; it wouldn't be right," I protested. Cane fields flashed by in the heat; a mirage ahead looked like a deep black pool in the road.

"It won't hurt him," Stephen insisted. "Anyway, we'll soon be in Cairns. You won't feel the effects till we're on the plane. Just think of it: you can look down on the Great Barrier Reef while you're high!"

I resisted and resisted. What if Stephen had picked the wrong mushroom? I watched for signs of impending death, but he seemed healthy and relaxed. Finally I gave in, chewing a piece of mushroom that tasted like wood and smelled of dry leaves.

Then a mini-disaster struck. When we got to the airport and turned in our rental car, we found our flight to New Guinea had been delayed by more than an hour. As a result, I reached the peak of my magic mushroom trip staring at aluminum-legged chairs and waiting-room decor, not at watery images of coral formations far below in the Great Barrier Reef. When it came time to board, I walked unsteadily to the check-in counter, holding Jason tightly in my arms.

"Name?" asked the neatly uniformed Qantas employee.

"Name?" I asked myself, sensing the clerk getting impatient. "Name? What's a name? Who am I? What's in a name?"

"What is your *name?*" she repeated slowly and clearly.

I stood frozen. I couldn't understand her question. And I didn't know the answer. Luckily, something, somewhere in the far recesses of my brain must have clicked, because I pushed my passport toward her.

"Clare Marcus?" she asked.

I nodded yes. She looked at me quizzically and handed me a boarding pass.

We stumbled onto the plane giggling and, throughout the flight, kept asking the stewardess for more snacks. We were in the munchies phase. Those were good times.

⁂

Stephen was the most wonderful father to Jason, and then to Lucy, born two years later. What an eventful week *that* was: in one seven-day period in late April 1974, I got tenure at Berkeley, celebrated my fortieth birthday, gave birth to Lucy, and we bought the house on Stuart Street where I still live. Again, Stephen asked for the placenta and we planted it under a pear tree in our garden at Lucy's naming ceremony. The tree bears fruit every year and is now tall and healthy, just as Lucy is a tall and healthy young woman.

Stephen was so much more skilled than I at cooking, at making a room look beautiful, at arranging a table to look attractive, and at welcoming to our guests. I remember how I tried to keep Grandma Cooper's china and silver "for special occasions," and how he protested, asking "Aren't *we* special?" And he was right. I tried not to let these "feminine," homemaking talents of Stephen's feed into my insecurities as a woman. But I found that it *did* matter. I was the breadwinner; he was the homemaker.

Not long after we moved to Stuart Street, things began to unravel. I had always known Stephen was bisexual. Soon after we started dating, he told me he had given up a black male lover to be with me. I suppose I felt some sense of smug pride that I had lured him away from a male partner. And it reinforced my sense of sexual attractiveness when he told me he'd once lived with a former mistress of the poet, Pablo Neruda, and had had an affair with a popular counter-culture guru. Well, not an affair exactly—more like a one-night stand in a New Mexico campground, but I elaborated on it over the years. To be in the company of such illustrious former lovers gave me a titillating sense of celebrity and worth.

When Jason and Lucy were both toddlers, Stephen started having affairs with both men and women. My sense of self-esteem crumbled and fell away like the sun-cracked paint on our newly purchased house. I turned a blind eye to obvious clues, desperate to keep our family together. I choked down my mounting resentment, just as my mother had a generation earlier. My silence prompted Stephen to drop hints that just couldn't be ignored. Eventually, he left.

My grief was intense, diabolical—like an unexpected hurricane sweeping away everything in its path. My childhood fear that I would be betrayed and abandoned had come to pass. Sleepless in the now half-empty bed, I stiffened at the sound of every heat contraction in the roof, every murmur of midnight-walking strangers passing by. Inexplicably paranoid, I imagined someone entering the house to kill me, just as I had when imagining the arrival of the dreaded enemy in my wartime childhood. Our house—the symbol of our marriage—was no longer a refuge or haven.

It was time to ask for help. The psychiatrist I turned to stared impassively as I blurted out my grief. I had no handkerchief; there was no box of Kleenex. I felt increasingly distraught as I mopped up my tears with a wad of paper I found in my pocket. I never returned for a second appointment. I resigned myself to becoming a single mother and primary breadwinner and, for many years, put my own emotional and sexual needs aside.

❧ ❧

The judge at our divorce hearing sneered at our plans for joint custody—"Kicking the children back and forth across the Bay" were his actual words—but I think we both did the best we could for our children. They had their own rooms, clothes, toys, and pets at each of our houses, which were just half an hour apart. They seemed equally at home in both places.

Lucy came home one day after playing with two little friends in my neighborhood and said with surprise, "Do you know, Mummy, Hans' and Frederic's mommy and daddy live together in the *same* house!" I hadn't the heart to tell her that many families lived that way and that we were something of an exception. In those days, there were no children's books in which the parents were divorced, let alone in which one of them was gay. We were ahead of the curve and did the best we could raising our children, shielding them from the problems we had with each other. For that, I am grateful.

The saddest thing for Stephen about the divorce was what happened to Chester. For a long while after we separated, Chester stayed with me, wandering the streets of Berkeley and displaying an uncanny ability to find his way home. People even reported seeing him cross the road at green lights or via pedestrian crossings. Finally, when Stephen had settled in a group house in Haight-Ashbury, Chester went to live with him and was allowed to roam as he always had. But, unused to San Francisco, he got lost. Stephen repeatedly called the Dog Pound to see if he'd been found and they always said no. Finally, he insisted on seeing their records and discovered that Chester had been there all along, but had been put to sleep only a few days before. When Stephen came to Berkeley tell us, Jason, Lucy, and I knelt in the driveway and held him in our arms as he sobbed and cried out his pet names for his beloved wolf-dog—"My foozle-woozle. My fito-weeto."

Equilibrium slowly returned with the passing seasons. Stephen— volatile and charismatic as ever—opted for a gay lifestyle and, after many lovers, found happiness with Jack, who became the dependable, responsible anchor in his life. For a while, I found some measure of joy with a new lover, Bill. Through all this turmoil, Stephen never ceased to be a loving and attentive father. We once agreed wryly that we had come together to bring forth our two wonderful children. We both thought the other was the best possible parent. Clearly, we were just not meant to be life-long partners.

I smile when I hear about conservative views on the "horrors" of gay parenting. If only they knew. Stephen was so much more loving and nurturing a parent to our children than my own father—straight, undemonstrative, and raised in a very different culture—ever was to his.

For a while, I resented the emergence of the Gay Freedom Movement; it gave Stephen the courage to leave me and follow the path he'd probably been destined for since childhood. He had grown up in a working-class Jewish neighborhood of St. Louis. He once sent away for flower seeds from a catalog and transformed the family's dusty backyard into a garden. His father chided him—"Flowers are for pansies," and pushed him toward a major in architecture at Washington University—a "manly pursuit"—and away from garden design, which was his real calling. Later, at Berkeley, Stephen took a Masters Degree in Landscape Architecture. He designed parks and playgrounds, and eventually started his own business creating beautiful gardens for wealthy clients in Hillsborough and San Francisco.

In the end, I accepted Stephen's gay-ness and went on Gay Freedom Day parades with him and our children, marching down Market Street in San Francisco under the Gay Fathers' banner. The children grew up knowing their father was gay, but barely comprehending what that meant. Once, at a party, four-year-old Lucy sat on the knee of one of my colleagues—a married man with children. "You're a nice man," she said, looking up at him, smiling. "Are you gay?" A chip off the old block.

When Lucy was in high school, she became aware of a growing homophobia among the teenage boys. She volunteered to be part of a forum in which she spoke of what it was like to have a gay father. She was popular; the boys respected her. So they began to think twice about telling "faggot" jokes. Jason spoke at World AIDS Day gatherings at college about the necessity of using condoms. I was so proud of them both.

Our children have become such fine young people. I remember one day, when looking at Jason sweetly sleeping in his crib, I said to Stephen (hippie and iconoclast that he was), "What will we do if he grows up and wants to be a bank manager?"

"Kick him out of the house!" he replied, and we both laughed.

Well, Jason didn't become a bank manager, but he did become an entrepreneur. At thirteen, he installed a drip irrigation system in my garden, and then went on to turn irrigation installation into a business. After learning to be a pilot and river-rafting guide, he took a Masters in

Business Administration at Northwestern University in Chicago and is doing good things in the world. Stephen would be so proud of him.

And proud of Lucy, too—artist, snow boarder, scuba diving instructor, fanatic about filming underwater life, with a Masters in Marine Biology from an Australian university near the Great Barrier Reef. Stephen started them both on the paths they have followed, taking Lucy scuba diving at eleven in Hawaii, and giving Jason 100 dollars to invest when he was a teenager.

Can I forgive Stephen for the pain he brought into my life—the infidelities and deceits? It is easier to forgive someone when they are gone from your life and memories of the hurt begin to fade. Yes, I can forgive him when I remember the wild and wonderful times we had together: tripping on peyote in Oaxaca one New Year's Eve and watching the cathedral floor oscillate in waves; marching in anti-Vietnam War protests in San Francisco; sprawling on the grass at flower-power concerts in Golden Gate Park; smoking marijuana at wild Berkeley parties (though I never did get the hang of inhaling); exploring red-rock mesas in New Mexico; buying clay figurines in Acoma; planting tree saplings in Berkeley's People's Park, now grown into a woody grove where homeless people sleep; molding the shape of my pregnant body and our unborn child in the damp beach sand at Zihuatanejo in Mexico. Yes, I can forgive him.

ȝ‍ɕ ȝ‍ɕ

When we separated, Stephen complained that I put my work first, the children second, and him last. I protested, but to some extent he was right. I am still working that one out—the power that ambition, my work, the striving of ego have over my life. Perhaps there was something about my devotion to my work—my teaching, my writing—that attracted him to me. I was the dependable anchor to which he temporarily moored his tempestuous, drifting self. Later, Jack fulfilled that role and remains faithful to Stephen's memory.

When Stephen learned he had AIDS, he went into therapy with Jason and Lucy to talk about his approaching death. That was a courageous and compassionate act, one that helped our children deal with their anguish at the thought of losing their father. He did so well for a while; his design business flourished as never before; his body responded to medication. But we all knew that it—and he—couldn't last.

When Jack phoned with the news of Stephen's death, I ran screaming from the house, as if being in the garden would take away the pain, as if the fruit trees he had planted—lemon, plum, pear, persimmon— would suck the grief out of me. Those last few weeks, he had barely been able to eat, so I took him ripe persimmons (his favorite fruit) from the garden. I scooped out the thick orange flesh with a teaspoon and fed him like a baby.

"I'm all packed and ready to go," he said softly, licking a smear of tangy fruit from his upper lip, his humor intact until the end. "But I think I've forgotten my toothbrush...."

"Don't worry," I said, scraping the last of the persimmon from its orange globe shell. "I don't think you'll need one where you're going." And we both laughed.

As we left the house on the night of his death—Bill, Jason, Lucy, and I—I saw that the orchid plant he had given me for my fortieth birthday, which had been flowerless for more than a decade, now bore a long arching spike of magenta buds ready to burst into bloom.

As we drove over the Bay Bridge, I rocked back and forth in disbelief, rubbing my legs to reassure myself that my body was still intact. Bill, silent at the steering wheel, leaned over and stroked my hand. The children, fifteen and seventeen, sat in the back seat and talked incessantly of a ski trip they were to take the following weekend. I wanted to scream: "Don't you realize your father is *dead*?"

As we made our way up the steep stairs to his Noe Valley apartment, familiar faces stared down over the banister. I stumbled and someone ran to catch me. Stephen lay peacefully, dressed in his favorite Guatemalan shirt with wide blue stripes, a woven floral band we had bought together in Mexico tied tightly across his forehead, and a bouquet of winter flowers from his garden across his chest. I had never seen a dead body before; it did not frighten me as much as I had expected.

"Tell Clare I am sorry about all the fights," Stephen had whispered to Jason not long before he died. Now it was over. I bent down and kissed his cold cheek, the color of straw. "It's okay to go now," I whispered. "It's okay to go."

At the memorial gathering on a warm January day in Alice's garden, Jack and Rosie, Stephen's mother, were too grief-stricken to speak. Along with many others, I talked about Stephen and his life, cut short at forty-eight. The ex-wife of the deceased. What did that make me— the kind-of-widow?

The other day, I was back in Wurster Hall on the Berkeley campus and I walked past my old office on the third floor. There, unmistakably etched in the shiny wood of the door, were scratch marks made by Chester when he came looking for Stephen so long ago. He has left his mark on the world, as Stephen has certainly left his mark on me.

❧ ❧

I sit in my room on Iona, thinking about Stephen and the long, loving, agonizing journey we took together. Yes, the parallels between my relationship with Stephen and my relationship with my father are more and more clear to me: both were loving men who were, at times, painfully unfaithful. Now, in the state of peace I have found on Iona, I can view these betrayals of long ago in a curious state of acceptance. Events happened. I feel the need neither to grasp them as victim, nor reject them in denial. Both men brought great riches into my life.

I stare out to sea and the shadows on Mull, a mile away. There is a reflection of my room in the window. Through the reflection, I see waves breaking on the black and gray rocks below. Waves caress my bedclothes, surging down beneath the sheets, foaming over pillows, stroking their languorous fingers across my body. Here, on Iona, I am a willing partner to the sea's seduction.

CHAPTER 21

✧

Look around You

Put down the weight of your aloneness and ease into
the conversation. The kettle is singing
even as it pours you a drink, the cooking pots
have left their arrogant aloofness and
seen the good in you at last. All the birds
and creatures of the world are unutterably
themselves. Everything is waiting for you.
—David Whyte[62]

On a cloudless day, I set out to walk the southern reaches of the island. My boots slap against the wiry grasses disdained by grazing sheep in the field beside Greenbank. I stare down at the sandy furrows carved by the beck that runs across the beach at Traigh Mhor, Big Strand. Then, in the valley above the beach, I come across a lone thistle, strangely twisted out of shape.

Thistles are what I eventually chose as a symbol for cancer cells when the tumor appeared in my colon and I embarked on a second round of healing imagery. I imagined thistles invading the pastures of Iona, more and more of them, rendering the grass inaccessible for grazing animals. Then moles came to the rescue. Maybe I chose them because the colon is an underground tunnel, like the home of this earthy, burrowing creature. I imagined the moles as the chemo eating away at the roots of the unwanted thistles, rendering the plants above the ground soft and sapped of life-energy, their prickles harmless. Then the sheep—my white blood cells—were able to eat them without injury to themselves and the pastures sprang to life again. And here I am on a warm August afternoon, three years later, faced with one strange, misshapen thistle in the valley above Sandeels Bay.

There are three kinds of thistles growing on Iona: creeping thistle, tall with small mauve flowers I've seen cattle eat—evidently a delicacy; marsh thistle, tall with small leaves, that grows beside running water; and spear thistle, symbol of Scotland, a more spiny plant with large purple flowers that no animals will touch. That is the thistle now before me, one foot away from my sandy boots. Its stems are twisted like corkscrews; its prickly flower buds bend down unnaturally toward the earth. I count seven of them; none are turned toward the life-affirming warmth of the sun.

"What has become of you?" I ask, but there is no answer.

I continue down the soft fold of the valley that leads to Sandeels Bay and see another stunted thistle, then another, then another. And then it hits me. Of course, they have been sprayed with herbicide. Their growth has been stunted by man-made chemicals. It comes as a shock. Somehow, I expected this place to be free of such poisonous intrusions. But here they are: the natural flora of this island habitat, twisted out of shape, injured so it cannot flower. One zap and they are gone—not dead, exactly, but unable to reproduce.

I recall a book by a young woman scientist about the links between pesticides, herbicides, and cancer. The evidence seems irrefutable and yet official bodies blather on about "the war on cancer" as if the answer, or at least a large part of the answer, were not staring us in the face. We "race for the cure" instead of exposing the cause.

I continue my walk up over Moal nan Manach, Hill of the Monks, and along the wet and rocky track past Ruanach, Place of the Red Flowers, thinking about the stunted thistles and the need for all of us—particularly those who have had cancer—to do something politically about harmful chemicals in the food chain. I feel so helpless. Where to start?

Eat organic produce; that is a start. Support the farmers who raise food without the use of pesticides and herbicides. Grow some of your own food, as I do in Berkeley and Barbara does at Greenbank in the small walled garden to the west of her house. Lobby for truthful food labeling. Boycott companies that produce genetically modified crops, that patent seeds and manufacture harmful chemicals. In services at the abbey, there are, amazingly, prayers for those who build and farm sustainably. Yes, yes—that is a start.

ॐ ॐ

Today, at eleven minutes past eleven AM on the 11th of August, a solar eclipse occurred over Britain. Unfortunately, on Iona, clouds covered the sky—the first overcast day in almost three weeks. Disappointed, I glance out the window at 10:50, and there it is: through a hazy break in the clouds, a distant sun appears as a curved new moon. Then—it is gone.

Later, in the sanctuary at Traigh Bhan, where fourteen of us are present for the noon meditation, I see an image in my mind of a total eclipse—the light blocked out by a black disk. But around the disk, bright shafts of light flare out like volcanic eruptions, like a vast phoenix rising out of the darkness. Perhaps the disk is our blindness to what is around us in our busy, competitive, resource-consuming lives—and our blindness to what is happening as a result to the sacred planet on which we live. And the flares of light? Perhaps they are the glimmerings of hope that change is happening, that we are in the midst of what Buddhist teacher Joanna Macy has termed the Great Turning. It is also the light I have sensed as a radiance pouring out of the landscape of Iona—out of the rocks, the waves, the birds, the sheep, the wildflowers, the grasses, the sand. The radiance of a divine presence that can only be seen when we stop and look around us.

Later, as I walk along the beach of Boundary Strand, it is as if an eerie pall of stillness has fallen over the world. The sea is between tides, its glassy flatness not even marked by ripples. Green-and-brown seaweed is draped over the rocks like a soft, briny cape. No sounds of sea birds; no calls of sheep; no distant hum of a fishing boat's outboard motor. Just the low, low hum I always hear at this place when the air and sea are still. I used to think it was a boat hidden behind an offshore island, but now I think it is the hum of the earth.

I walk the length of the beach in bare feet, sinking into dry sand above the high-tide mark, walking down to the lower sand still damp from the sea. Imprints of treaded boots, the mounds and valleys of high-arched bare feet, the ambling claw prints of a wandering sea bird.

Silent rivulets of water meander down to the edge of the sea, bearing their gifts of sand. I stand in one and watch the water make new paths around my feet.

※ ※

The space within the ruins of the 13th-century Augustinian nunnery in the village comes as close as anything on Iona to a small park. It includes mown lawns, flowerbeds, and benches where people stop to rest, read, or eat their picnic lunches. It is a designed and cultivated landscape. A gardener employed by Historic Scotland comes over from Mull once a week to cut the grass and deadhead the flowers. It has a gentle, contemplative presence, as if the sisters of long ago still walk invisibly in prayer. Grasses grow atop the walls of the roofless refectory; ivy-leaved toadflax with tiny pink-mauve flowers has taken root in crevices in the walls of gray and rosy-tinted stone. People talk in hushed voices and curb their children from running too wildly. Despite their ruined state, the buildings murmur their ecclesiastical origins.

I surreptitiously pick seedpods from rosy-colored lupines to take home to my Berkeley garden. A couple with matching yellow T-shirts

eat their picnic lunch and throw crumbs to a gathering of sparrows at their feet. A young man with a red knitted cap looks for a place in the shade, settles with his back against the refectory wall, and opens the day's *Scotsman.* Cries of rooks and sheep drift in over the walls. A couple settles onto the narrow ledge seats of the ruined chapter house, where the sisters assembled daily to discuss nunnery business. The man opens his pack and takes out a black plastic cell phone.

It is evening. Long shadows of broken walls fall across the grass in sharp-edged patterns. Gulls cackle and argue from rooftops in the village. A lone bee collects nectar from white clover blossoms near my feet.

I feel deeply content in this place, deeply content as evening falls on the day and eventually on my life. I recall a photo on the book jacket of *The View in Winter: Refflections on Old Age* by Ronald Blythe. An older man sits in a deck chair looking out onto the world, apparently reflecting, ruminating. Now I am that person. No longer pressured to achieve, to produce, to be "of use," I reflect on pivotal relationships in my life; I sit and write about what I see and hear around me. That is enough. A thrush sings. A Red Admiral butterfly lands on a rock and opens its gaudy wings to the sinking sun.

⁂

It is now the height of summer on Iona. The rooks that noisily claimed territory and made their nests in the leafless sycamores in April are now silent or departed, their nests masked by thick summer foliage. Hogweed stands three and four feet tall along the roadways. Snails inch slimily up its rough stems. Children dig in the wet sand and catch small green crabs when the tide goes out. Every half hour, the ferry from Mull empties another crowd of day-trippers onto the island. Humphrey the horse waits patiently in the shafts of a carriage to carry those who are unable to walk across the island. Sheets and towels slap in a warm breeze behind the cottages and crofts that offer bed and breakfast. A woman in a skimpy pink bikini, followed by two small children clutching plastic buckets and spades, ambles through the ruins of the nunnery on her way to the beach.

I walk across the island and sit on the Hill of the Angels, surrounded by flowers. The grasses here, now six to eight inches high, have not been cut for hay and apparently not grazed for a while. Among them, a great variety of wild flowers bloom exuberantly in the noonday sun: purple and white clover; pale-blue harebells; purple self-heal; yellow hawk's head, lady's bedstraw, and bird's-foot trefoil; yarrow and the pale-pink heads of wild carrot. In the distance, the rasping call of a corncrake. The sky is cloudless; the horizon of the western ocean is a dark blue line beyond which lies—North America.

My heart feels full in this place. They say the origin of the word "pilgrim" is the Latin word *peragrum,* which means "across the field." Indeed, I am a pilgrim as I walk across the fields of this benign place acknowledging the sacred in the dense matter of the earth, in the birds and creatures of this island, in the people I meet (or just glimpse from a distance), in the flowers that surround me on this summer day— flowers that sing a silent song of creation only the bees can hear.

I eat my lunch at Columba's Bay sitting on a rock and enjoying the cold insistent tide as it reaches farther and farther up my bare feet and legs. Shifting a few feet upslope, I dig in the deep stony beach for half an hour searching for rounded pebbles of Iona marble, known as Mermaid's Tears. It is said that, long ago, a mermaid fell in love with one of the monks at the abbey and each night prayed that she might be given a human heart and soul. But her prayers were never answered, and each night she returned to the sea weeping. Each of her tears turned into a green pebble flecked with white. Sailors who keep these pebbles in their pockets are said to be protected from drowning. I push the larger rounded rocks aside, dig deeper, and find several small green pebbles, perfectly smoothed by countless tides and winter storms. I put them in my pocket and gather up my things..

Starting homeward, I take short steps as I climb the steep track inland from Columba's Bay. I draw in a quick breath. Close to my feet is a dead rabbit, almost totally eviscerated. Nearby are its intestines in a neat, ridged coil, rendered brown and leathery by the sun. It feels like a gruesome omen. In a phone call from home, I heard that a friend has stage-four colon cancer, too advanced even for chemotherapy. Two days later, a call from Marv tells me he will soon start chemo for stage-three colon cancer. I think of them both and then, on a whim, I go to a place known as Sacred Hollow to lie down.

I ask permission of the wee folk who reputedly live in this part of the island. Receiving a half-hearted "Yes," I proceed, and promptly fall (or almost do) as my foot gets caught between two rocks. I ask permission again and, this time, the response feels more positive. I lie down on a mound of heather and relax into the ground, aware of the eerie call of a buzzard, then two of them, to my left. I feel frightened as, inexplicably, I experience tingling in my fingers and become short of breath. I start breathing through my mouth to pull in more oxygen. A voice seems to say, "Look around you." So I do, and all looks as it did before I lay down.

Balancing on rocks, I cross a small beck and return to the trail. A dead rabbit. I think of the rabbits that surrounded me in childhood. Wild rabbits that my mother shot for food with the double-barreled shotgun my father left her as defense against the enemy should an invasion occur.

As a child, I felt so helpless in the life-and-death struggle we faced. Sometimes, I imagined myself as a man, like my father, with a uniform and a rifle going off to war. At other times, I saw myself sitting astride the roof of our house with a machine gun in my hands, picking off helmeted enemy soldiers as they approached up the driveway.

But these were fantasies. In reality, one thing I *could* do was to help produce food. Close to our house, near the edge of a wood, were the hutches where I kept my rabbits. I bred them for food to supplement our rations. I don't remember anyone teaching me how to care for them; it was something I just seemed to know. They were chinchillas, with soft gray coats that revealed patterns of black and white and gray in ascending, concentric circles if you blew into them. When I picked one up by the loose skin on its neck and held it against my shoulder and stroked its back, its little heart beat wildly against my own. I knew which wild plants they liked to eat: dandelions, sow thistle, cow parsley, clover. I snuck handfuls of hay from haystacks in nearby fields to provide for their bedding, never taking too much from any one stack so Mr. Watson, the farmer, wouldn't catch on.

I don't remember suffering through the embarrassing and titillating Sex Ed classes my American friends describe from their high school memories of the Fifties. All I ever needed to know about sex I learned from my rabbits.

"Before you start back to school, we need to talk about where babies come from," my mother began in a faltering voice as we finished breakfast one morning.

"I know all about it," I interrupted. "I've watched my rabbits."

That was the end of the discussion. My mother looked surprised, then relieved. I took my dishes to the sink and left the room.

When it was time to breed one of my does, I lifted her gently into the hutch of a buck—never the other way around or a fight would ensue. They sniffed around each other for a while, then the doe crouched and the buck, aroused, clambered on her back, front paws pinning her to the ground. The mating was over quickly in a frenzy of thumping and thrusting, ending with a scream as the buck catapulted off onto his back. If I heard the orgasmic scream, I knew the mating had been a success. It didn't take much imagination to assume that humans "did it" in much the same way. Country children don't need Sex Ed classes to inform them of the facts of life.

We couldn't buy film during the war and, in any case, my father had donated our camera and binoculars to the government when they appealed for them (along with picture post cards of the French coast) to help in the war effort. As a consequence, I have very few pictures of myself between the ages of five and eleven. There is one, however, that I cherish. In it, I am sitting holding one of my rabbits in my arms like a baby. It is lying on its back, its long ears hooked over my bare arm, unafraid, its soft belly-fur exposed. I never cared much for dolls, but I loved my rabbits. I kept their hutches clean, decorated the edges of their bowls of bran with carrot treats, and gave them the names of operatic characters—Carmen, Tosca, Rigoletto—and of war heroes— Gort, Wavell, Monty.

Given how much I loved my rabbits, it is all the more astonishing what I allowed to happen to them. I still feel pangs of guilt. When they were the right age, I told my mother it was time for Tosca or Monty "to go." She told Mr. Cook, an elderly neighbor, and he carried out the deed while I was at school. That evening, we had rabbit casserole for dinner and I tried to dissociate the food in my mouth from the animal I once had nurtured. "Hard-hearted Clara," some friends at school called me.

That hurt. I couldn't explain to them, or indeed to myself, that sacrificing what I loved was my small contribution to the war effort, to our survival. I kept a little account book. In the "Out" column, I entered what I paid for the bran rations I bought at a feed store in Leighton Buzzard; in the "In" column, I entered the money my mother paid me for the meat.

One moment, I was having rabbits killed; the next, I was saving them. There were wild brown rabbits that lived in burrows in the side of Happy Hideout, the old overgrown sand quarry where Mary and I often played. Mr. Bielby, gamekeeper for the Ascott estate, set cruel steel traps at the entry to each burrow; the rabbits ate the crops, he said. The first thing we did each time we arrived at our magic place was to take a large, thick stick and whack at the traps so that no rabbit would be caught while we were playing there. One day, we arrived too late. We heard the screams as we clambered down the steep sides of the quarry. I found a rabbit writhing in panic, caught in a trap by its hind leg, which was bloody and raw to the bone. I knew it couldn't live much longer. Shaking with fear and guilt, I found an old brick and threw it at the rabbit's head. It was the first and last mammal that I knowingly killed.

૨Ꮐ ૨Ꮐ

I stub the scruffy toe of my right boot against a rock and return from daydreaming about childhood. I follow the track down to the Machair and notice a young man in faded jeans and a navy sweatshirt on a hillside sloping down to the beach. A young red-headed woman sits nearby; the man is digging.

"Definitely not a tourist," I think. "But what is he doing?"

As I come closer, I notice a red plastic container and a piece of black rubber tubing. I approach, trying not to appear too curious. The young man starts filling in a number of entries to rabbit burrows, ramming the earth down firmly with the back of his spade. Then he pushes the rubber tubing down the last burrow and packs earth around it. The young woman hands him a white tablet. I am close enough now to see the man drop the tablet down the tube, then pour some liquid after it. He is poisoning the rabbits.

I turn my head away as I come close, pretending I haven't seen this act, that I don't care. But inside, I am outraged. My breathing becomes shallow, my mouth dry. I think of the rabbits breathing in the noxious fumes, feverishly climbing over each other, gasping, trying desperately to escape. The young man pulls out the tube, throws another shovelful of sandy earth onto the tiny air hole, laughs as he says something to the young woman, picks up his gear, and whistles to his dog on the beach below.

I want to run after them, to protest, to pull the sand out of the burrows with my hands. But I do nothing. This island is my place—and it is not. I do not own land or a house here; I do not raise sheep or comb the hills on frosty nights seeking newborn lambs abandoned by their mothers; I do not mend the barbed-wire fences or oil the rusty hinges of farm gates. Rabbit burrows riddling the hillsides are hazardous for the sheep; rabbits eat precious grass the sheep and lambs need for grazing. I was once a rabbit killer too. Just keep walking, I tell myself.

I kick at some loose rocks as I walk down the steep track—frustrated, angry, sad. The couple, with their black-and-white collie, are some distance away now, heading home. The track peters out and I emerge onto the flat sheep-cropped sod of the Machair. No more rocks; no need to watch where I place my feet. Easy going. "Look around you," the voice had said. And then I see them: dozens of rabbits, heads down, alive, and quietly eating. Like the push and pull of the tides, like night and day, like breathing in and breathing out, life and death co-exist. One moment, an eviscerated rabbit on the trail; another moment, the rounded shadows of live rabbits patterning the grass as the sun slips low into the Atlantic. I pull in a deep breath and head for home.

CHAPTER 22

♥

The Spirit of Place

It is time for us to take off our masks, to step out from behind our personas, whatever they might be: educators, activists, biologists, geologists, writers, farmers, ranchers, and bureaucrats—and admit that we are lovers, engaged in an erotics of place. Loving the land. Honoring its mysteries. Acknowledging, embracing the spirit of place— there is nothing more legitimate and there is nothing more true. That is why we are here. It is why we do what we do. There is nothing intellectual about it. We love the land. It is a primal affair. —Terry Tempest Williams[63]

I sit in the choir stalls and look across at the stones of the abbey, at people assembling for the Sunday morning service. White beard, gray hair; gray rock, white mortar; lines of aging furrow from nostril to chin; shadows of fissures between stones, marks of the stonemason's trowel, fractures from ancient cooling; red hair, Celtic child of the north, blond ponytail, fair curls framing tired face; rosy-pink quartz, black-and-gray granite, oxide staining; flushed cheek, downcast eyes. Faces and rocks, subject to the passage of time—erosion, weathering, disintegration, pulled by gravity back into the earth.

As I wait for the service to begin, I think about my childhood exposure to organized religion, which was not a happy experience. During the war, my mother took us each Sunday to the morning service at All Saints Church in Wing, the village near our home at Ascott. I think she did it partly out of duty, feeling we needed to be exposed to the religion of our forebears. Perhaps for her, the ritual, the psalms and prayers, were soothing at that time of anxiety and loneliness. But for me, those Sunday mornings were excruciating. I didn't understand the sermon; I hated that some people genuflected to the altar—it seemed like idolatry—and I resented the fact that Madame de Rothschild, French and Roman Catholic, worshipped alone in a side chapel separate from the rest of us.

I did enjoy the hymns, especially one that became my favorite:

> All things bright and beautiful
> All creatures great and small
> All things wise and wonderful
> The Lord God made them all.[64]

If God was in nature, then religion was "OK" by me; it was the Jesus part that was more difficult to swallow.

To distract myself during the boring parts of the service, I examined a marble plaque on the wall near where we sat.

> Sacred to the memory of William Theed Esq., of Crafton in this parifh; a moft worthy gentleman, who fulfilled all the duties of thif life with the utmoft integrity, and the moft Christian Benevolence. He dyed in Grays Inn, London, on the 15 of February, 1757, in the 58th year of hif life.

I liked to say the words under my breath, especially "moft" and "utmoft," which sounded so funny.

Not far away, another wall plaque:

> Sacred to the memory of William Fynes Esq., late of London Merchant ... By industrious Application joined to an extensive knowledge in Trade and Businefs, He acquired an affluent Fortune....

With his "affluent Fortune," he could apparently afford a more elaborate memorial. Above the inscription was a tearful cherub raising a marble curtain to disclose a funerary urn. Underneath it, a marble skull with empty eye sockets and stumps for teeth both intrigued and frightened me.

In the north aisle was a 16th-century monument to Sir William Dormer and his wife, Dorothy. The knight and his wife lay rigid on a plinth, their hands clasped in prayer, a small dog at their feet, four children kneeling beneath them. Were their actual bodies there, I used to wonder, inside the stone? I fantasized that, at night, in the silent darkness of the church, they arose and danced, their little dog joyfully yapping at their feet, ecstatic at his nightly release from stony death.

The only good part I can recall from my early Christian upbringing was going to Sunday school. Each week, we were given a small pictorial stamp—Jesus in the manger, Jesus raising Lazarus, the Sermon on the Mount. Each week, I licked my stamp and pasted it carefully into a little book. Since there were no toys for sale during the war—no foreign stamps or coins to meet our childish urges for collecting—these stamps took on great importance.

Centuries before, someone had left a bequest to the church stipulating that every child who attended Sunday school should be given a bread bun. By the 1940s, the bequest was somewhat depleted. The buns, now sticky with frosting, were given one week to the boys, the next week to the girls. So, despite the allure of the stamps, I started to skip Sunday School every other week. I only went when the girls got their buns, and I ate mine as I ambled home across the field named Pound Piece, sucking the sugar from my fingers, happy in the bird-singing summer sunshine. On the alternate Sundays, I played in the woods instead of taking the footpath into Wing. My mother never found out.

Unlike my childhood experience with churchgoing, it has become deeply pleasurable to me to attend abbey services on Iona. A deep bell tolls, reminding those on the island that the service will soon begin. In my childhood, the church bells were silent, to be rung only in the event of the Germans landing by parachute, or to call people to assist in their capture. The Sunday ritual in early August at the abbey is especially moving. Chris leads the service, Brian is the celebrant, and Jan gives the sermon. That I know these people's names and have often seen them about their work makes this service even more meaningful. Since the abbey has no organ, music for the hymns is played on a grand piano.

As people assemble, the pianist plays pieces by Schumann, pieces my mother used to play. My eyes fill with tears.

In the sermon, Jan talks about light: the importance of light in our lives, the wonder of the night sky when the light of the sun is gone, seeing things in a new light. August 6th marks the Feast of the Transfiguration, when Peter, James, and John saw Jesus suffused in radiant light on a mountaintop and heard the word of God from a cloud. August 6th is also the anniversary of the dropping of the first atomic bomb on Hiroshima, a different and deadly cloud. It is also the five-year anniversary of my diagnosis of breast cancer, a disease both treated and perhaps caused by radiation. Medical statistics seem fixated on five-year survival rates. What it actually means that I have reached this auspicious date, in remission and feeling healthier than at any time in my life, I am not quite sure. But it seems right to be in the abbey on this day. I feel as if something new and at the same time archaically old is opening in my heart. It is impossible to write about it. It just is.

Later that day, glancing out of the bathroom window at Greenbank, I draw in a quick breath. Liquid orange light spatters the skyline. High stratus clouds are layered in pink and lavender; a long slice of sky is blue, almost turquoise, like the sea. Sheep on rocky hilltops are silhouetted against the sky. They chew their cud and merge with the sod. And they and I watch as the fiery globe of the sun slips once more into the waves of the western ocean.

❧ ❧

The southern one-third of Iona is uninhibited—by people, that is. I decide to walk across parts of this wild landscape I have never explored before. The day is sunny and warm, and the sky cloudless—a good day for crossing terrain that might be problematic in the rain or mist. I can see on the map that, by following a long fence across the Blar nam Manach, Plains of the Monks, and Sliabh Siar, Western Moorland, then turning west along Garadh Dubh Staonaig, Black Dyke of Staonaig, I will encounter a track near Staonaig that I know well.

I did not expect to find a trail on the Moorland—none is shown on the map. But there it is, perhaps ten inches wide, snaking through tussocky grass and heather-covered hillocks, through low-lying bog and

across areas of exposed rock. Was this made by humans or animals, or both? No matter; it gives me unexpected joy to find it. I was prepared to slog across country, keeping the long fence in sight. But here is a path; beings have walked this way before.

Why am I surprised? I'm well aware that, even where the way is expansive and clear, on the flat, clipped greenswards of the western and northern grazing lands, sheep follow specific paths, their feet treading the grass into a slightly different color. I see no sheep or cattle on my outward journey, but clearly they have been here. The landscape reflects back to us what we barely know. The unexpected path tells me subtly that, even in difficult circumstances, a path will open up, a way will become clear.

Am I reading too much into everything I see? It seems as if the answers to questions we ask are constantly being presented to us if we only trust and take the time to look around us. We've lost the art of letting the land call to us. In a book about the Australian indigenous peoples' deep connection to the landscape, a Dutchman, Frans Hoogland, recounts an element of tribal knowledge taught him by Paddy Roe, an aboriginal elder in the Kimberley region of Western Australia.

... We have to walk the land. At a certain point for every body, the land will take over. The land will take that person. You think you're following something, but the land is actually pulling you. When the land starts pulling you, you're not even aware you're walking—you're off, you're gone. When you experience this, it's like a shift in reality. You start seeing things you've never seen before. I mean, you're trained one way or other and you actually look through that upbringing at the land ... And all of a sudden, it doesn't fit anything. Then something comes out of the land, guides you. It can be a tree, a rock, a face in the sand, or a bird ... And then another thing might grab your attention, and before you know it there's a path created that is connected to you ... that is the way you start to communicate with the land, through your path experiences. And that path brings you right back to yourself ... When you're walking the path, it's coming out of you. [65]

The night after I found a path I didn't expect to be there, I have a dream that seems entirely appropriate. I am driving a car quite fast on a freeway leading to Los Angeles. I don't know the way and the freeway signs are too dirty to read, so I just keep guessing which fork in the road to take. I drive on different sides of the road, not sure which one is correct. I'm not certain where I'm going but, somehow, I get there. I hardly need help interpreting that one. The dream just about sums up my journey to Iona—maybe my whole life.

꙳ ꙳

I walk into the village and Bruce, a retired builder well into his seventies, sails by on his bicycle, the wind at his back, his black beret pulled low over his forehead.

"Morning!" he calls out as he passes.

"Morning!" I reply with a smile, two souls on the road acknowledging each other's presence.

I walk past Carraig Beig, Little Rock, the house next to Martyr's Bay that was once a church. In the added-on glass-roofed porch, three people sit around a low table, a flask of coffee between them, sun glancing off the furniture. A gentle scene; it causes me to smile. These glimpses, these brief meetings, are so touching and important to me here because, in the urban environment where most of my life is lived, people rarely make eye contact, let alone say "Good morning" to those they meet while walking.

I stop in the Spar shop for a newspaper. I'm in luck; there is one copy of *The Guardian* left. I treat myself to a decaf coffee and a piece of shortbread at the Argyll Hotel. St. Teresa of Avila insisted that there are five basic human needs that have to be met if we are to live a fulfilled life: good prayer, good work, good relationships, good sleep, and good food. The last four create the necessary conditions for the first, which, in turn, energizes the other four. How wise she was.

The sun is streaming into the plant-filled hotel porch where I sit. Along the window sill are geraniums, white-and-blue lobelia, rosemary, scabious nodding its lavender blossoms where a breeze wafts in through an open window. I sip my coffee; Fifties' music drifts in from the kitchen. White wicker furniture casts shadows on the red tile floor. Mark, the postie, walks by carrying two parcels. The expanse of sea between Iona and Mull appears to flow like a river, driven by a strong wind from the north. The water quivers; wind and sun weave a tapestry of shimmering hues.

Simone Weil called prayer "attentiveness." If that is so, then the slow pace of my life here and the beauty that surrounds me have indeed lured me, all unawares, into a state of prayerfulness.

❧ ❧

I wake up from a dream in the middle of the night and, after much resistance—Who cares? I'm too tired—I sit on the edge of the bed and write it down. In the dream, I'm with a group of academic colleagues on a field trip to look at the latest designs for student housing. We stop at a café to eat, but the service is slow, so I leave the group to go home and change. While there, I become fascinated with a mottle-skinned toad who has settled on some warm pebbles almost the same color as it is. I get down on my knees to look more closely; I touch its back and make it jump. The toad eases its way between the pebbles, buries its head, and virtually disappears it is so well camouflaged. I realize I'm keeping the group at the café waiting. On my way back there, I call out to a scooter driver to put on his lights as he's barely visible. It's getting dark; I must have been looking at the toad for a long time, but, when I check my watch, I see it's only 2:15. I haven't been gone that long.

I finish recording the dream, unaware until a few days later of all that it implies. I settle back under the covers, now wide awake but unwilling to get up and start the day. Strange that I should dream about a toad. Some people are scared of mice, or spiders, or moths; I am terrified of frogs and toads. If I walk past a pond or an area of marsh and hear the familiar "rivet … rivet" of frogs, I am frightened and want to run. My mind drifts back to an incident from childhood.

I am about eight years old. I am walking down Well Lane in Wing, about half a mile from our house, on my way to a dairy to pick up some milk in a lidded can. It is summer. I remember cow parsley perhaps three feet tall growing beside the thick hedgerows that bound the lane on either side. A woman I don't recognize peddles slowly toward me on a bicycle with a rusty frame and fat tires. As she comes closer, I hear her breathing heavily, her head bent over the handlebars. Suddenly, from the lush summer greenery, a toad jumps out onto the asphalt and methodically hops across the road right into the path of the bicycle. As I watch in horror, the fat black tires roll over it, squashing it flat— blood, sinews, skin, fine brittle bones leave a gruesome design on the roadway as the woman rides on, oblivious to what has happened. For a minute or so, I cannot move as I stare at the bloody corpse of a creature so full of energy a moment before, its life force rising in a steamy cloud from the pulpy remains of its body.

And then I run. Forgetting my errand, I open the white-barred gate by the lodge, run down the Long Walk, skirt the lily pond, leap through the tall grass in the daffodil field, and so reach home—sweating, fearful, trying to erase the bloody image from my mind.

But it never was entirely erased. In the ensuing sixty years since that incident, I have been terrified of frogs and toads. The fear is not that they will harm me, but that, inadvertently, I will harm them, perhaps stepping onto a soft vulnerable body and splaying its guts upon the earth. Amphibians are masters of camouflage; with mottled skin and abstract hues that mimic their habitat, they hide from their enemies, but not from hurrying human feet or rubber bicycle tires.

Camouflage, from the French *camoufler,* to disguise. In an empty garage opposite our house during the war, we made camouflage netting used by military posts and airfields to drape over tanks, artillery, and planes. Someone in an army vehicle delivered huge pieces of open-weave fabric and hung them from the ceiling of the garage. From a large sack of materials, we pulled long strips of hessian in dark green, brown, light green, and black, and wove them in and out of the hollow squares in any way we pleased. When we were done, the dark-hued netting was bundled up and taken away and we started again. It was something that we children could do to help the war effort. We felt so proud to be doing something. From the sky, military targets draped with the netting were perceived by roaming German bombers as innocent patches of woodland or clumps of evergreen shrubs. Perhaps our fumbled weaving saved some lives and precious planes.

But sometimes camouflage can be too effective. In 1943, some troops in training were stationed in a field not far from our house. Most of the men slept in tents, but one night—perhaps it was unseasonably warm—three of them settled in their sleeping bags on top of a ground sheet in a slight dip in the field. For warmth, or perhaps out of habit, they pulled a rough piece of camouflage netting over where they lay. In the early morning hours, an armored tank practicing for maneuvers perceived the netting as vegetation and drove right over them. The news of the accident spread quickly. It is possible that, in my child's mind, the episode of the toad and of the three crushed soldiers fused in my psyche. Hiding your presence can equal death.

Half a century later, I dream of a toad and I am not terrified—but fascinated. A few days after the dream, I call Barry in New Mexico.

"What do you associate with toads?" he asks, and I recount the episode from my childhood.

"Why would I find a toad so fascinating when I seem to have connected it since childhood with death—with being killed?"

"In what way have you been looking at death?"

"Well, it's certainly been there in the background, sometimes very much in the foreground. Two bouts of cancer. How could I *not* look at death?"

"And what did you do to help yourself through cancer?"

"I went into nature! I gardened; I picked flowers; I imagined myself on Iona. And now I'm living here!"

"Exactly!" Barry responds, excitement in his voice. "To assist yourself in healing from cancer you turned to the mystery of nature. And suddenly, in a dream, here it is again. The thing that most frightens you—the toad associated from your childhood with mortality—is now what fascinates you."

I sigh. "It's amazing. I would never have imagined myself getting on my knees to study a toad, even touching it to make it jump. In the dream, I was totally absorbed, completely fascinated with this animal."

We are both silent for half a minute, taking it all in.

Barry starts speaking again. "You know, fascination in a dream is a powerful word; the language of archetypes. I think the toad contains something of the numinous for you, some magical quality. All your attention is drawn to a creature as lowly as a toad. The dream says: Here is where life is." I sigh and remain silent.

"What do you make of the scene at the café?" I ask Barry.

"What do you think?"

"Well—I'm with my architecture colleagues and then I leave. Sounds like my retirement!"

"I think so. And you become fascinated with the toad when you 'go home to change.'"

"Oh, yes! I leave my colleagues to go home and *change.* I certainly did that—and then some! What about the man on the scooter?"

"I don't know." We are both silent again; I scribble some words in a notebook on my lap. Barry draws in his breath audibly. "Look what happened. Nature, the toad in the dream, is so fascinating to you that there is a disjunction in time. It has grown dark—the man on the scooter needs to put his lights on—yet when you look at your watch, little time has passed. The temporal time of life and eternal time have, for an instant, touched. A fabulous dream."

Another silence. I sit quietly staring out the window. The tide is out; rocks that appeared as quivering dark patches of sea a few hours ago are now naked and exposed to the afternoon sun.

※ ※

In Deborah Tall's *The Island of the White Cow: Memories of an Irish Island,* a young American woman recounts her sojourn on a remote island off the west coast of Ireland, beautifully expressing the change of consciousness that happened to her there.

> Life has become vivid to me as it never was before. It's as if everything I've done up to now has been a step removed from reality, veiled. A bank of machines stood between me and experience. What did clean clothes ever mean? Now when I boil water, soak, scrub, wring, and hang out my clothes to dry, I feel I have washed clothes! … Weather asserts itself, defines the day. All the casual facts of life have been dissected, discovered, made real for me. Because everything is foreign, laid bare, I am forced to rethink and feel it as if for the first time. [66]

Yes, life for me on Iona has also become more vivid. It is so easy, in a familiar place, to allow the environment, the daily habits of living, to disappear into the murky reaches of consciousness. We live our days on auto-pilot. It is comfortable, but numbing to the soul. On Iona, as for Deborah Tall on the Island of the White Cow, I am forced to rethink the seemingly mundane aspects of my life: shopping, washing clothes, buying a newspaper, the weather. It feels as if I have woken up from a long sleep. Or, as English poet Kathleen Raine so beautifully expressed it: As dreamers wake from sleep, we wake from waking.

Living here, I have been thinking a lot about the places in my life. This Scottish island that has enlightened the recesses of my soul; Lincoln, Nebraska, where I first experienced being a foreign student and felt alienated in the arid Great Plains landscape; the beautiful landscape of the Peak District in Derbyshire, where weekend hikes allowed me to escape the grim environment of industrial Sheffield; the streets of London, which, in my young working life, I came to love as much as my father did throughout his life; New York, such a lonely place for a new immigrant; Berkeley, where both my wild side and my intellect were allowed to flower; Stockholm, where I spent one of the most romantic years of my life, with David; Australia, where our young son took his first steps and Stephen and I were happy together; New Guinea, where we were the first white guests ever to stay in a village in the highlands near Mount Hagen, and where Lucy was conceived; and of course, the English countryside and the bittersweet memories it imprinted on my soul. We learn as much from our relationships to place as we do from relationships with our fellow humans, if we but pay attention and look around us.

In childhood, we develop critical human relationships, but we also relate to physical places—crawling on the floor, pulling a wagon around the block, daring to climb an impossibly high tree, venturing alone into the half-feared, overgrown, abandoned quarry. These places enable us to explore our courage and emerging ego away from the protection and familiarity of the parental home. Without such explorations, we would never grow up.

At the other end of life, in the quieter, more reflective time of our middle and elder years, place again becomes profoundly important. With the strivings of making our way in the world, with child-rearing and the development of a healthy ego mostly behind us, we may seek a place for repose and reflection. We "settle down" into the earth; we "put down roots." It is essential that we do so somewhere, for that place—whether a city, a country village, a foreign land, or the neighborhood of our birth—has much to tell us. If we care about self-reflection—if we have any inkling that there is a human urge toward wholeness that will continue until our last breath, whether the impetus to look deeply into life is a particular traumatic event or a slow, persistent awareness—we must allow place to nurture and heal us, even if the means of that transformation will always remain a mystery.

Are some people more attached to places than others? For those who are not, do they live a diminished life? To become attached to a place, we need to perceive it, to know it, to understand it—then to engage in effective action, to preserve and steward it. When we love a place, does it love us back? When 19th-century English nature poet John Clare had to move from the village of Helpstone where he had spent his whole life, to Northborough in the fens, he grieved for the place he was leaving behind—not only because of how well he knew and loved it, but because the place had known him. He referred in a poem to the settings that had touched his heart as "... sweet spots that memory makes divine."

Years after her stay in Ireland, Deborah Tall, married with children and an academic career, moved to upstate New York. Once again, she found herself ruminating on place, on finding the right place.

> If we find it, do we know to stay? Is it right for a lifetime? I can't be sure. I thought I'd found my place once, in Ireland; now I'm wondering if I can find it here.... Maybe we need different places for different phases of our lives. Maybe cherished places remain alive inside us even if we have to move on—our attachment to the earth not thinned, but widened.[67]

❦ ❦

The cherished place that remains most alive in my heart is Ascott, the Rothschild estate, whose wild and overgrown expanses were a children's paradise. Here, we barely acknowledged the war as we explored and hid and climbed and crawled. No other place, not even my garden in Berkeley after thirty-five years of tending, will ever come close to evoking the emotions embedded there in the fields, the trees, the flowers, the birds of my childhood terrain.

Not all my memories of that place, however, are of emotional connections to the land. Some are of childhood escapades that we thought very daring, even risqué. A particularly memorable event is what we did one day to the Birth of Venus. The pond within sight of the stately Rothschild home was perfectly round and had a neat concrete edge. This, in turn, was surrounded by a circle of lawn and by a circular yew hedge, the kind with yellow leaves. In the middle of the pond was a statue we liked to peer at and giggle—Paul and Burt and Ronnie and Shirley and Mary and I. It was a statue of a naked woman, Venus, riding on a conch shell drawn by prancing bronze horses. The Birth of Venus, it was called. But we didn't care about all that Greek mythol-

ogy stuff. We just cared that she was naked—stark, not-a-stitch-on-her naked. This was long before magazines like Playboy, or a glimpse of a porno movie as you surfed the fifty-seven channels on a hotel TV. We had to take nudity where we could find it and the Birth of Venus, transported at great expense from Venice by the present Mr. Rothschild's father, was where we found it.

The pond, in those days, was covered with slimy green duck weed because almost all the gardeners were away fighting the war. The three gardeners left behind were old and arthritic and took long tea breaks with cracked mugs in a shed behind the greenhouses.

One day, as we gawked at Venus and her upturned breasts, Paul pulled out some pond weed and started massaging it into a green drippy ball. While we watched, fascinated (older brothers always seemed smarter), he threw it with a resounding thwack against her thigh. No sooner was this done than we were all scooping out wet weed and fashioning it into green, mush-missiles. Thwack—on the conch shell. Thwack—on the head of the horse. Thwack—Oh no it missed. Thwack—on her shoulder. And then thwack—most glorious thwack of all— right between her legs. It hung there, a dripping green mound of pubic duck weed, pouring liquid down her voluptuous thighs. We fell on the grass in hysterics, almost coughing up breakfast in the thrill of this daring escapade.

A day or two later came the first frost of winter. Venus' green hair stuck to her like a lover. By the time the weed fell off with rising temperatures next spring, the statue was stained irreparably. Twenty years later, Paul and I returned. The Rothschild estate was now maintained by the National Trust and open to the public on specific days each week. The gardens were mown and clipped and neat again, no longer the enchanting wilderness of our childhood. Or perhaps we too had become mown and clipped and neat. We passed through the yew hedge and stood before the familiar statue. And there stood Venus—and on the mound that bears her name, the unmistakable stain still proudly born. Yes, we had once been children here—Paul and Burt and Ronnie and Shirley and Mary and I.

❧ ❧

I unfold my map of Iona, now worn along its creases after much use. It is a beautiful map at a scale of just over six inches to the mile, with the details and place names noted, derived from books on Iona history and interviews with island residents. All the names are shown in English and Gaelic; there are detailed plans of the village and the abbey, and a round map of the horizon in all directions, so you can recognize far-off islands by their shape on the skyline.

Most of all, I love the evocative names on this map: Hollow of the Otter, Hill of the Herdboys, Dog Fishes Meadow, Port of the Dead Man, Place of Red Flowers, The Old Woman's Fold, Bed of the Grey Horse, Cliff of the Marten Cat, Mary's Yellow Slab, Young Hector's Garden, Port of Ivor's Cornfield, Gully of Little Bran's Lad, Hump of the Monk, Meadow of the Dead Goose, Hill of the Frog, Pigeon's Cave, Luke's Island.

The names speak of people and incidents long past, when every field, every rocky eminence, every gully penetrated by tongues of the sea had a name and a memory. Who were Ivor, young Hector, Mary, Luke, and little Bran's lad? What became of the dead man, and how did the gray horse meet its end? We name our thoroughfares 17th Avenue and High Street, then wonder why our cities have no sense of place.

The Greeks have two words for place: *topos* and *chora*. *Topos* implies position or the objective features of a place, as in topography. The term relates to map-making, measurement, mathematics, and logic. *Chora* is an older term used in emotional statements about places—places of experience, imagination, mythic memory. Gradually, the pictorial cues that suggested how we might feel in a place, what we might experience—the sea monster, the shipwreck, the flaming volcano—were banished to the margins of maps and then eliminated altogether. The logic of space and the spirit of place became divorced.

Alan Gussow, a conservationist and landscape artist, once wrote:

> There is a great deal of talk these days about saving the environment. We must, for the environment sustains our bodies. But as humans we also require support for our spirits, and this is what certain kinds of places provide. The catalyst that converts any physical location—any environment, if you will—into a place, is the process of experiencing deeply. A place is a piece of the whole environment that has been claimed by feelings. Viewed simply as a life-support system, the earth is an environment. Viewed as a resource that sustains our humanity, the earth is a collection of places.[68]

Our ability to recognize and celebrate the spirit of a place has been stunted by our over-dependence on rationalization. The philosopher Thales is reputed to have said: "Of all the things that are, the most ancient is God, for he is uncreated. The most beautiful is the cosmos, for it is God's workmanship. The greatest is place, for it holds all things."[69]

Philosopher E. V. Walter tells us that Plato considered place "the nourishing receptacle of experience, keeping everything astir, exciting continual vibrations in her contents, filled with the powers of what she contains. 'She is herself shaken by the entering forms, and by her motion, shakes them again in turn.'"[70] Was St. Columba attracted to Iona because it contains some ineffable spirit of place, or did he and centuries of monastic worship imbue it with that spirit? Plato tells us that it is not either/or —but both. Place and human experience in that place are the yin and the yang, continuously evoking and absorbing each other.

To comprehend the meaning of place—*chora* rather than *topos*—Plato argues that it is a "knowledge that must be 'grasped' ... for it is outside both reason and sensation, to be apprehended by a kind of sensuous reasoning ... reasoning that renders chora intelligible is matched by an exceptional mode of perception—dreaming with our eyes wide open."[71]

That is what Iona has taught me to do: to dream with my eyes wide open. One evening, as I walk back from the Peace and Justice service at the abbey, it seems as though everything is suffused with light: honeysuckle blossoms growing over a garden wall, the tall flower-heads of reeds bending in the wind, a lone gull on a rock, sheep on a flat-topped hill silhouetted like shadow-puppets against the soft lemon-gray of twilight. I finally sense what I have resisted much of my life: that an immanent God permeates all matter. Once there was doubt; now there is none. We are cradled in a divinely created universe that is love, Buddha-nature, Christ, God, Allah. It cannot be otherwise.

ↄ

The World Turned Upside Down

There is a whole portion of reality which is offered to us without our making any special effort beyond opening our eyes and ears ... But there is another world ... which though hidden, is none the less real. If this other world is to exist for us, we need to open something more than our physical eyes and to undertake a greater kind of effort ... The deep world is as clear as the surface one, only it asks more of us. —Ortega y Gasset[72]

I borrow an audiotape from Traigh Bhan and listen to a mystically inclined architect, Peter Dawkins, describe what he believes to be the seven chakra points of Iona. The skeptic in me initially dismisses the whole idea: energy points in the body derived from Hindu thought applied to the landscape of a Scottish island? It seems far-fetched. But something about the idea intrigues me. That night, I have a dream. A huge figure crouches beneath the island. It looks like a giant sleeping, or praying, or not yet born.

"I cannot be seen; I can only be known," it says. "I am waiting."

"For what are you waiting?" I ask.

"For the world to be turned upside down; then you will know me."

The next day, I take out my map of Iona, trace it onto a sheet of paper, and draw the giant, crouched under the island as I had sensed him in the dream. Head, brow, throat, heart; the chakra points of the island begin to make sense. But this isn't a place where things have to "make sense." I pull on my boots, put a water bottle and a sandwich in my pack, and set off for Columba's Bay.

In the flat grassy area just inland from the bay, a lamb calls, bleating; mother responds, deeper voiced. Lamb, elated, runs across the cross-cropped grass; mother feeds impassively. Lamb butts its head into tasty warm udders, lifting the ewe's hind quarters off the ground. Mother moves on.

As I walk onto the shore, dense with sea-rounded stones, my feet strike chords of sound: deep bass notes where the rocks are large; higher notes as the rocks become smaller; piccolo notes from the smallest pebbles.

Yes, I can accept that this solid base of the island where St. Columba and his monks landed after their voyage from Ireland is the root chakra of Iona. The root chakra in the body is associated with the adrenal glands which prepare the body in times of stress for the classic fight-or-flight response. Fight or flight. In my dealing with cancer I took a firm stand somewhere between them—neither running away in denial, nor taking up arms in angry outrage. On Iona, I have returned to my animal nature, to sweet communion with the earth.

I lean back against the base of a rocky cliff, close my eyes, and hear a voice: my own, or the rocks'? Does it matter?

"Be in touch with every element each day," the voice says. "Feel the warmth of the sun. Be conscious of the air you breathe. Dig your fingers into the earth and feel its nurturance. Listen to the sounds of water; let them soothe your body. Be conscious of the elements in which you live and surrender to the power they have to create balance in your soul and in your body."

I scramble up the steep slope that leads inland from Columba's Bay and make my way along the Hollow of the Big Mouth, up to the rocky eminence that Dawkins suggests is the sacral chakra of the island body: Carn Cul ri Eirinn, Cairn of the Back to Ireland. A myth first recorded in the 18th century, and probably apocryphal, tells how, when St. Columba was banished from Ireland, he vowed he would settle on the first island he encountered from which he could no longer see

Ireland. He climbed to this point and, not seeing Ireland, determined this was the place.[73]

A wind has sprung up. I pull the hood of my jacket around my face and settle with my back against the pile of rocks, a cairn, that marks this place. The sacral chakra: the seat of sexuality and relationships; the center of movement—motion, emotion; letting things flow like water.

My emotions are aroused by this place, by the sensuality of all that surrounds me. Tides pulling in and out; birds gliding on invisible pathways of air; grass heads bending, sand shifting, flowers sighing. The sights and sounds and shapes of this place pour into my body like the taste of good wine. I surrender to its love.

"I am yours," I whisper to something ineffable, invisible, beyond the material world. "You have seduced me and I willingly give you all of myself."

The next morning, I walk to a cluster of rocky hillocks on the edge of the Machair, said by Dawkins to be the solar-plexus chakra of Iona. They are called The Bed of the Earthnuts, Uiridh nam Braonan. Earthnuts?! What a wonderful name. These rocky protuberances exploding through the greensward do indeed look like huge geologic walnuts. I approach down a winding valley: a tiny stream cuts deep into the peat, three small birds crossing and re-crossing in front of me, seemingly protesting my presence.

Climbing one of the earthnuts, I can see the broad green expanse of the Machair before me. A wind is blowing off the sea; the rock beneath me feels warm and benign. The solar-plexus chakra: seat of vitality, resentment, anger, moral outrage, transformation. Before me is the bay where the bodies of drowned sailors washed up in World War II. This is the chakra of my own shipwrecks. I'm sure that held-in resentments had a part in my susceptibility to cancer.

Yesterday, as if to test me, news arrived that provoked my emotions. A highly qualified scholar who had applied for a position at Berkeley and could have taught the courses I used to teach was turned down. The appointment of someone else, in a different specialty, was a political done-deal. I spent a sleepless night. It feels as if the courses I created, which brought some kudos to the college, are now seen as unimportant. All my buttons of fragile self-worth are being pushed. Now, in the light of day, I attempt to put some emotional distance between this event and who I am now. I have left academia behind, with all its petty cliques and political deals. It's an environment that breeds resentment and I won't fall into that trap again. If I've learned anything from cancer, it is the need to let things go, to release anger, to avoid taking everything personally. I cannot keep judging my self-worth by what I achieved in the past, by a career that was a painful struggle in a sometimes less-than-supportive environment. That is not who I am now. The person I am now—sitting writing on a hot summer day on Iona—is someone I am proud to be. I am a survivor. I have turned my creativity in other directions. Cancer has helped me turn my life around and goaded me into letting go of the past.

The solar-plexus chakra is also the seat of moral outrage and empowerment. Certainly a lot of my professional work was generated from this place—questioning the decisions made by architects and planners in clearing so-called "slums," re-housing the inhabitants in soul-destroying high-rise buildings; arguing for the environmental needs of those who rarely have a voice—children and the elderly. Moral outrage was a way of taking anger and turning it into positive social activism, constructive muck-raking. But what the world needs now is not just environmental activists, but also quiet observers and poets of the environment whose words and images speak to people in ways that will arouse deep emotions about nature and, in turn, perhaps trigger their own moral outrage about what we are doing to our planet-home. People do not change by being told that they are wrong, but by being moved to see the right path from personal experience. I want to use my own sense of empowerment and imagination to remind people to look closely at what is around them, and to see how we can look to the environment for healing even as we seek to celebrate and protect it, and so become healers ourselves.

I close my eyes and follow my breath. "Stay centered," I hear from within. "Imagine your solar plexus like a magnet—like the sun—always pulling you back to the center. Do not be distracted by resentment, fear, judgment, doubt. They are like demons on the path, dragging you away from what is essential. Name them and let them go. Return always to the center, for that way lies the path of balance and healing."

I open my eyes. The sea is the color of blue ink streaked with green; sheep graze quietly; a skylark sings high and invisible above; I can see the hazy outlines of Coll and Tiree on the horizon. I am startled to see a seagull perched just behind me. "Thank you. Thank you!" I whisper. The seagull looks quizzical, backs off, and flies away.

I walk across the soft turf of the Machair, through a gate and over a fence, and settle into a sandy scar in the gentle green slope of the Hill of the Angels, Cnoc man Aingeal, thought to be the heart chakra of the island. The story goes that, one day, St. Columba left the abbey community he had founded on the other side of the island and told his monks not to follow him, as he wanted to find a place to be alone. He settled on this low hill facing the western ocean and started to pray. Despite Columba's instructions, a young monk followed and observed him from a distance. To his amazement, he saw a host of angels hovering around Columba's head; frightened, he ran back to the abbey. When Columba discovered who the monk was, he swore him to secrecy and it was only after the saint's death that the monk told the others in the community of this astonishing encounter.[74]

Because of this story, I am always cautious when I approach this place; it feels sacred, the heart of Iona. I lie back on the grass and close my eyes. I feel the heart of the island. It is beating in the waves; it is beating in soft footfalls; it is beating in the dance of grass heads; it is beating in the distant song of sheep. The giant sleeps, but his heart is beating; my own heart beats in harmony. The wind from the west feels like the on-rush of breath, the island's lungs expanding and contracting. Air is the element associated with the heart chakra. I feel it caressing my skin, moving my hair, streaming into my lungs. We are continually bathed in air—inside and out—just as we inhabit an invisible womb of love.

"Let your heart open," a voice seems to say. "Accept yourself unconditionally. The seagull's fear and caution are also within you. As your heart is open to yourself, so it will be to others and to all of creation, which surrounds and caresses you like a loving mantle."

I sigh deeply. Why do we find it so difficult to accept ourselves, to let go of the inner critic, to just be? I stare out to sea for a long time, then continue walking across the Machair and up the steep-sided valley known as the Glen of the Temple, Gleann an Teampuill. What temple was here? The island is full of mysteries.

Soon the sounds of the sea are far away. Rock walls enclose a flat-floored valley; a tiny stream is made visible by the reeds that mark its course. Some distance from the sea, the valley forks on either side of Hill of the Signal: a Y shape—three valleys meeting, an auspicious number in Celtic lore.

Breathing heavily, I climb up the steep flanks of Hill of the Signal, following sheep paths—zigzagging, tacking between rocks and clumps of sleeping heather. What a wonder it is to be here, to be alive, incarnate in this world. I look down onto the green trough of the glen, afternoon shadows painting faint lines of long-ago furrows. The rocky sides of the valley are smeared with patches of brown and lavender where the heather is just coming into bloom. A cluster of eleven domestic ducks that have been drinking in the beck climb up its bank, flap their wings in the drying wind, and move slowly across the grass. A gull flies overhead; I see its shadow skimming across the rocks in front of me before it comes into view.

I feel pure in this place. It is as if there were no separation between my living, breathing, perceiving body and my soul-nature. No posturing, no pretending. I am who I am—no more, no less. A serene inner calm embraces me. We don't look at nature and think, "If only that tree bent the other way." The landscape is what it is. This island invites us to view ourselves in a similar vein, not through the lens of complacency or arrogance, but through a loving gaze of self-acceptance.

What were the signals sent from this hill? Who sent them? Who received them? This is said to be the throat chakra of the island, a place of communication, half way between the heart and the mind. This is the chakra that seems to have been most alive and accessible to me throughout my life: the chakra of communication where, through speech or writing or art, we transcend the ordinary limitations of the body.

I lie back on the grass, aware of a skylark pouring out her song like a love-chant to the landscape. Another joins her and then, out of nowhere, the sound of an unseen jet scraping across the sky. Moments later, only the skylarks remain.

"Speak softly," I hear a quiet inner voice say from within this place of the throat chakra. "Your time of speaking to large groups is past; let others do that. You must look in the shadows, lift the veil, and communicate what you sense is there. Be patient; your task, like the places you are discovering, is not clear; it is not brightly illuminated with the light of logic. Take a candle; be cautious; move quietly and, in time, more will be revealed than you thought possible. Rest your throat and your power of speech. Be gentle on yourself. You have more to communicate, but it may be difficult for people to hear."

I sit up and—whoosh—a large gull lands on a rock to my right. I start to feed it a half sandwich left from lunch. A mist slowly engulfs the west of the island, pouring down the hillsides in gentle white drifts. The mouth of the glen grows fainter; rock outlines grow blurry, like drops of water on a half-finished painting.

I start for home, following a broken wall up a valley that runs east toward the village over rocky domains of bog cotton, peat, and sphagnum. Each time I look back, the gull remains, standing where I had sat, eating the bread I left, which he was too fearful to pluck up in my presence. Just as a rock face is about to obscure my view, the gull launches into the west wind, sails up over my head, and disappears to the north.

The mist has quickened, swirling around my body like elfin smoke. This is true Scotch mist—not rain, not fog, not drizzle, but a damp white presence shrouding the distance from view, muting the cries of birds, thrusting the island's eyes inward. Eventually, I am gladdened to see the outline of a building below me. Then the stone walls along the road and people moving like gray ghosts toward the sea. I kick my boots against a rock to knock off the mud, then step onto the road, and walk to the village and buy a book at the Craft Shop near the ferry landing—*Iona*, by Fiona MacLeod. After so many hours out on the island, I am anxious to settle into a warm, comfortable place—and read. It is time for afternoon tea at the St. Columba Hotel.

I sit in a corner of the lounge in a deep armchair and read the book from cover to cover. Fiona MacLeod was a man who assumed a female pseudonym. Ironically, while George Sand and George Eliot had to assume male pseudonyms because they wrote of "manly" passions, power, and conflict, William Sharp (19th-century Scottish writer) assumed a woman's name for his "dream self." Writing poetry, dreams, visions, myths, and prophecies inspired by the landscapes of Scotland, Sharp chose to use a woman's name, perhaps the better to be heard.

> I have nothing to say of Iona's acreage or fisheries, or pastures: nothing of how the islanders live. These things are accidental. There is small difference in simple life anywhere....
>
> There is another Iona, of which I would speak. I do not say that it lies open to all. It is as we come that we find. If we come, bringing nothing with us, we go away ill-content, having seen or heard nothing of what we have vaguely expected to see or hear.... None can understand it who does not see it through its pagan light, its Christian light, its singular blending of paganism and romance and spiritual beauty. There is,

too, an Iona that is more than Gaelic, that is more than a place rainbow-lit with the seven desires of the world, the Iona that, if we will it so, is a mirror of your heart and of mine.[75]

 intricate ornamental glyphs

The following day, I walk north and rest against a rocky knoll, Cnoc an Suidhe, Hill of the Seat. A north wind has sprung up; grass heads quiver at my feet. Below me, the beach known as Strand of the Seat is just out of sight. I lean against a rock splashed with yellow, gray, and black lichen; two snails nestle in a crevice near my shoulder; dark green moss forms abstract cushions near my feet. Across the water, the sheer cliffs of Mull reach up to rocky outcrops bathed in cloud. A distant tour boat moves silently on its way to Staffa.

Here, little has changed since St. Columba's day: a gate, a fence row, a distant boat. Otherwise, these were the sounds he heard, the view he saw. Of all the islands—seven visible from this spot—why did he choose this one?

I can't accept Dawkins' description of the brow chakra as Cnoc nam Marbh, the Hill of the Dead, near the abbey. This rocky eminence where I now sit, said to have been St. Columba's meditation seat, feels more to me like the brow of the island, the chakra of intuition and creativity, of seeing, both inner and outer. The brow chakra represents the coming together of the right and left brains, focused thinking and diffused awareness; it is said to mediate between the personality and the soul. When we resist the connection between soul and personality, a mental or physical illness is said to result, helping to restore the balance. Apparently, my stubborn ego needed the threat of death to begin to soften and relinquish control over my life. "Question with your heart," the evening light seems to say, "and intuition will answer you."

Shifting my shoulders into a rocky crevice, I close my eyes. My breath finds a pattern in tune with the distant sound of waves. "Do not be afraid to speak what you know. People need to connect with the sacred in the landscape. It is something that many sense, yet few have words to describe. By writing of your experience on Iona, you give others permission to embrace and acknowledge their own sacred connections to the land. Do not hesitate. The world is in pain. As others recognize the place that nurtures their souls, each may be moved to protect it in his or her own way."

With my eyes still closed, I become aware of the sounds around me: waves pounding, distant, melodic; lamb calling, mother lost; shrill birdcall, sheepdog bark. A seagull lands nearby. Startled to see me, it stares, orange-eyed, then wings away. It wheels around and returns, settling on the ground not far away. Alternately looking around and preening its wings, the gull tucks its legs beneath its body and settles its full white breast into the grass. It is secure in this place; its eyelids start to droop.

❧ ❧

I join a retreat group for a half-hour meditation at Traigh Bhan. We sit in a half circle under the roof of the sanctuary, warm-colored wood embracing us. Outside, heavy rain. As the bell sounds for the end of meditation, I open my eyes to the sea and see wind carving its surface into wrinkled patterns of green, gray, white, black.

The sea is unknowable, unfathomable, but I feel comfort in its breathing. Beneath the waves are mountains and valleys, kingdoms undreamed of. It is the world turned upside down.

I glance out the window to the south. Three horses stand below a rocky hillock, completely still, heads down, forefeet firm. Sheep don't stand immobile in the rain: they feed or walk or, more likely, lie down. Above a nearby hillock, the heads of two black-faced sheep appear like dusky butterflies—ears akimbo, noses into the wind, bodies hunkered down into the rock bed.

I leave the sanctuary, pull on boots and rain gear, and set off for the summit of Dun I, the crown chakra of the island. I start to climb. The turf is water-logged; rocks glisten; the air is pregnant with moisture. Careful where you place your feet; balance your weight, stay alert. No wonder monasteries provided cloisters for thought-free, mechanical, contemplative walking. When your feet lift automatically—lift, step, lift, step—your mind can wander, your heart can pray. Not so climbing Dun I.

The rain stops; the sun breaks through the clouds. I can see the islands of Dutchman's Cap, Staffa, Barra, Rhum, Eigg, South Uist, Skye. Below me is an expanse of green punctuated by swellings of rock, like immobile calcified sheep of monstrous proportions. Around them graze real sheep, the size of white maggots, inching their way across ghosts of fields imprinted in the landscape. Behind the sights and sounds of Iona is a mystery—a secret just out of reach. "Go within," the island seems to say. "And trust."

I find a sheltered crevice in the rock, lie down, and sense the power of the land seeping into my body. I imagine my body encompassing the whole of the island—feet at Columba's Bay, head on Dun I—as I did so many times in my healing imagery. I imagine dolphins swimming round the island, no longer able to find any crabs. I take off my hat and feel the sun's warmth on the top of my head.

"Feel the sun on your crown chakra." The air whispers. "Drink it in and let it flow through your body. Be one with all living beings: the sycamore leaves, gannets diving for fish, meadowsweet in the Glen of the Temple, the long hair of Highland cattle, the silver notes of skylarks. Let them enter you. Appreciate and love them, for you are all one, no separation, just ego's imagining. Your body is healed. Keep your spirit open to the world around you; drink in the land through all your senses."

I start to walk north, looking for the Well of Eternal Youth. I always have trouble finding it. Is this a message? I unfold my map. If I line up the corner of the geological survey post on the summit of Dun I with an offshore island and follow the line, I will find it; it is there on the map; maps can be trusted. I follow the line as best I can and—yes, it is there. A rock face looking east, slabs of gneiss; water pouring down into a deep, dark, rectangular peat-laden pool. Twenty streams of water—some screw-shaped, twisting; others straight glass rods linking turf and pool. In one corner, a maze of linked bubbles jostle for space, some large like glass domes, others tiny like drops of dew. As one bursts, another is born. Peering closer, I see the silhouette of my body reflected in each one. Not my body, but Every Woman. "Fear not death—the life force falling creates life after life," the cascades sing. "Joined yet separated by vaporous membranes, our bubbles burst and are replaced. Think of the falling water and not of the bubble; be attached to the process and not to the form."

I touch the water, drink a few drops, and start down the mountain. I meet a man and a boy on their way up. They part. The man takes the easier, but longer, route; the boy clambers up a steeper path. "See you at the top, Dad!" he calls and then, amazingly, starts to sing a hymn in a dazzling soprano voice. Is it a girl? I look up. No, definitely a boy.

Walking carefully down the rocky track, I become aware of a rotting, acrid smell. Then I see a long-dead sheep mired in a muddy pool below me. Wool gone, its taut white skin is still stretched across its ribs; its head, half-submerged, displays lips, teeth, and one empty eye socket. No, not empty; maggots are moving in place of eye and brain. Perhaps it was caught in last winter's snow and lay frightened, slowly weakening. Death is all around us, reminding us to make the most of our time on this beautiful earth. Seize the day. Live—while you have the chance.

CHAPTER 24

ℰↄ

The Height of Summer

I believe that the universe is one being, all its parts are different expressions of the same energy, and they are all in communication with each other, therefore parts of one organic whole.... The parts change and pass, or die, people and races and rocks and stars; none of them seem to me important in itself but only the whole. The whole is in all its parts so beautiful ... that I am compelled to love it, and to think of it as divine. —Robinson Jeffers[76]

It is the height of summer. Sheep, panting with the heat, shelter in the shade of rocks and houses. Black sparkles of tar melt in roadway wrinkles. In fields of newly cut hay, seagulls doze in contented clusters.

I sit on the sand at Port Ban. The tide is lapping inward over hot sand. Wading into the sea, I am immersed in the womb-water of this island, floating beneath high cirrus clouds and a huge colony of gulls on Pointed Stack, which scream and mew and chatter in animated conversation. The sea is warmer here, thanks to the Gulf Stream, and much more appealing for swimming than the waters off San Francisco, cooled as they are by the Alaska current and susceptible to dangerous undertows. People don't believe it when I tell them. Europeans equate California with palm trees, tropical seas, strange cults, and Hollywood. Californians hear the word Scotland and think of rain, wind, porridge, kilts, and bagpipes. How little we truly know of each other.

The end of my stay on Iona is approaching. As the beaches become decorated with sun-bathers and plastic buckets, it feels like the right time to depart. Perhaps I am becoming too much of a recluse.

Certainly I have not spent a great deal of time talking to people. I seem to be an observer rather than a participant. It is enough for me to know that Donna, who serves me with a cheerful smile at the Spar shop, comes from New Zealand and is here for the summer; that Mark, the postie, has a sailing boat with tan-colored sails named Freya; that Amy, the baker at the St. Columba Hotel, won a first prize for her baskets made of Iona grass at the Highland Show; that the son of the McCormicks will go to the high school in Oban next year; that Davey Kirkpatrick, whose son, wee Davey, drowned last December, has another young David working for him on the boat trips to Staffa; that people are lining up for the chance to rent the house named Arnish when it is transformed from its now derelict state by the National Trust for Scotland. I don't need to know the life stories of these people. I am just grateful to have shared this place with them, to recognize their faces, to see them going about their lives. In Anne Morrow Lindbergh's *A Gift from the Sea,* she describes her time of seclusion on a beach in New England, where she too spent little time reflecting on the people she encountered, preferring instead to contemplate sand and shells and the meaning of her life. "People, too, become like islands in such an atmosphere, self-contained, whole and serene; respecting other people's solitude, not intruding on their shores, standing back in reverence before the miracle of another individual. 'No man is an island,' said John Donne. I feel we are all islands—in a common sea."[77]

❧ ❧

Returning on the ferry from a shopping trip to Oban, I'm aware of seagulls as they wheel overhead and my eyes brim with tears. "Thank you," I say again and again, in my heart and out loud to the sea, to the seagulls, to the sheep and the landscape. In my meditations on the other side of the world, something of the ineffable essence of this place enabled me to surrender and supported me in my healing. How can I express my thanks sufficiently?

It is here that I have experienced the Other; the subtle presence of something indescribable yet more real than the material world. When I stop to watch two seagulls dancing for worms; when I experience the

breaking of waves on the shore as the breath of the world; when I pick up a rock and am astonished at its multi-colored beauty, I am for an instant released from the time-bound suffering of the ego-self and surrender into the eternal essence of creation. Is that at the core of healing, of wholeness? Is it this surrender to the ineffable that releases us from internal conflict? "Thy will be done," I have prayed, though scarcely conscious to whom my words are addressed.

❀ ❀

An evening amble along the beach. I think again how wonderful it is that we have so many words to connote walking: to putter, to shuffle, to amble, to stroll, to saunter, to walk, to stride. I definitely ambled, moving slowly, arms behind my back, eyes down searching for the telltale glint of sea-washed glass lurking in the wet sand. It is low tide. Perhaps it is at that magic point—between tides—when the sea is flat, soundless. Seaweed hangs brown and parched on exposed rocks.

At Traigh Mhor, Big Strand, the sand is ridged in corrugated furrows, the fossilized remnants of waves thrusting landward at the last high tide. A lone gull rides serenely on its mirror image. Farther out to sea, a heron stands motionless on a rocky islet. Or is it the crane that strayed to Iona from Ireland and was nursed back to health by St. Columba? Howard's boat—gone for two weeks—is back at anchor. Sheep call to each other, far away. A seal eyes me from offshore. How will I find such tranquility in the future?

※ ※

A hot day at Port of the White Stones. I close my eyes to narrow slits and pull my sun hat down to my eyebrows, shielding myself from the white sand's glare. At the other end of the bay, Lotte is swimming, her black dog, Dram, standing hesitant on the shore with an orange Frisbee in his teeth. A flock of herring gulls glide up from the hills behind me, calling plaintively.

Just offshore, a promontory of rock is rhythmically washed by the incoming tide. The gray-and-pink strata have eroded into soft undulations that mirror the shape of waves breaking around and over them. Water falls back into the sea down softly eroded valleys. The humpbacked peaks at the tip of the promontory disappear beneath land-seeking waves, and reappear like glistening mountain ranges after the Ice Age. Foamy tongues penetrate deep into softened clefts and pour out again in gray-green, silver-streaked waterfalls.

This rock is in love with the sea and she with him. Over millennia, innocent of human history, sea and rock have coexisted and shaped each other, parting and reuniting in tidal coupling. Together they sing, while each without the other would be mute. And poor, weak mortals, fragile in our split-second life spans, can only look on in wonder and give thanks for the miracle of being alive.

※ ※

At the Wednesday noontime meditation at Traigh Bhan, I feel so deeply calm and centered that I don't want to leave the sanctuary. I sense the presence of my parents pouring over and through me. But for them, I would not be here, incarnate on this beautiful earth. But they are gone. Gone forever. I feel a wave of deep sadness.

I sit staring at the sea through the east window, reluctant to join the others. Eventually, I go downstairs and, after apple cake and tea in the porch with Niels, Barbara, Maria, and Michaela, I pull on my shoes and walk slowly down to the White Strand of the Monks and settle in my favorite spot, looking out at the Island of Storm. The sea looks so incredibly blue, the sun so welcome after four days of rain. I eat my lunch, then lie back on the sand. As my breathing slows and I relax, I experience the sound of the sea passing through me—no ears *hearing* the sea, no me *and* the sea—just the sound. A breeze blows across my face, the sun shines on my cheeks and forehead. For a moment, they seem to penetrate my body. Then, they just are. My body ceases to exist. No Clare or ego or a specific person, but a manifestation of divine energy just like everything around me—sand, rocks, sea, wind, sun, birds, seaweed, dune grass—all joined in a sacred dance, our separateness just an illusion.

❧ ❧

It is late August. A heat haze has hung over the island for several days. The sheep pant in the fields; lambs that have not gone to market are almost full grown. They doze close to their mothers and cast a wary eye at me as I walk by. I follow the road to the north end of the island. A flock of rock doves peck around in the stubble of a field recently cut for hay. A collection of starlings rests on the top of Hill of the Seat, like untidy black stubble on the upturned chin of the rock.

Out at sea, the islands that recently seemed like gray silhouettes are now almost dissolved in haze. A Hebridean cruise ship is anchored off the Isle of Staffa, looking like one more misty island, its passengers probably now ashore exploring Fingal's Cave. What would Mendelssohn think? Could he have imagined cruise ships pausing to view the black, basaltic cavern he made so famous in his music?

I have come to this sprawling, white, shell-sand beach—Traigh an t-Suidhe, Strand of the Seat, and Traigh-na-Criche, Boundary Strand—because it is one of my favorite places on the island. Sitting on a rock close to the water's edge, I close my eyes and hear soft splashes, watery surges, trickling, gurgling—how inadequate are our words to describe the omnipresent breathing of the waves. Nobody comes to a beach and sits with their backs to the sea. We are compelled to face it. It is the environment from which we first emerged, our long-lost home, the great unknown. It can soothe us with its heartbeat and kill us with a rogue wave. It is the life force itself—essential, unstoppable, ungraspable—seducing our senses into submission. Numerous tiny rivulets of water, trapped in the sand at the last high tide, runnel down to meet the waves in elaborate branching tree-like patterns. The gulls are quiet, resting on offshore rocks. The sheep grazing up above the beach are silent in the still evening warmth. This place and time feel like a pause in the breathing of the world. Surely God is here and everywhere.

⁂

It is early morning in the abbey. Light streams through the west window. The sound of a lawnmower drifts in through an open door. It is good to be here before the tourists arrive and without the distraction of a service. My attention is caught by several sea spleenwort ferns, incongruously growing in the rough stone wall near the altar. At the top of a pillar nearby, a worn stone carving shows soldiers on horseback apparently riding to meet or slay a dragon-like creature—the medieval symbol often used to represent pagan beliefs and the veneration of nature. How wonderful to find this juxtaposition in a Christian stronghold. The ferns might easily have been pulled out when they first took root, their growth perhaps loosening the mortar between the stones. Somehow, they were left, nature taking root within the very body of the church that once found its veneration threatening to orthodox beliefs. Here in the abbey, nature is without and within.

In the healing chapel to the south of the chancel, the sun casts light and shadow onto a Gaelic bible. There is a bowl of roses on a window ledge beside a small sign that reads: "Ally, Logie, Robert, wee Davey. In life and death we are in God's hands." I look through the window at the expanse of water where they all drowned in the accident last December. I have thought of them often during my stay on the island: when looking out at the Sound of Iona, when seeing Logie's mother tending her lambs; when seeing Ally's blue-eyed father on the ferry, or his mother walking her black-and-white collie in the evening; Robert's mother at the Heritage Centre; wee Davey's father skippering the boat that took us to Staffa. I did not know these young men; I do not know their parents. But I feel, in minute proportion, the sense of loss and outrage they and the whole island community must feel. I think of my own children—it is hard to do otherwise—and cannot conceive of the hole in my heart that such a loss would create.

In a corner of the chapel, people have pinned onto a wooden cross notes for help and healing in a tangled mass of paper:

"Watch over my children."

"Thinking of Little Campbell, aged 3, who is waiting to undergo brain surgery."

"Pray for peace in Northern Ireland."

"May peace come to the people of Kosovo."

"Our twin boys—loaned to us for one day. You would be one year old now. Lots of love, Granny."

"Dear God—Please look after my Dad and help him have a happy life, and try and let me see him quite soon." Beside this is a stick-figure drawing with an arrow labeled "My Dad."

And in similarly childish writing, a note with a happy face beneath it: "Dear God—thank you for everything. Amen."

I always feel nurtured by the stone walls and wooden roof of this quiet place. When I attend services, I sense that a subtle shift has occurred within me. This change has happened because of time spent in the abbey and time spent walking the landscape. It is impossible to separate them. As I have experienced God immanent in the natural world—in rock and greensward, sheep and herring gulls, wild flowers and clouds—so I have, in the abbey, begun to experience God as transcendent, existing beyond the material world I encounter through my senses.

I begin to sense that my life matters, that I am here on earth for a purpose, and that I am loved. It is not some startling epiphany, but rather a feeling that has crept into me. This shift has been aided, not by specific words spoken in the abbey, not by readings or sermons, but by the presence around me of so many believers. Just by breathing the same air as they, something has entered my soul; my heart has opened and some ineffable energy has poured in. All my resistances have melted and I have allowed a path to open up before me. If cancer came into my life to bring me to Iona, to permit this to happen—so be it. Evidently, I could hear the message in no other way. I am deeply grateful to the abbey and the community around it for letting me slip in, anonymous, a skeptic—and be carried along as if in loving arms, until I have learned to believe that I live in a God-filled world.

⅋ ⅋

I sit in the porch at Greenbank and open a book, but this evening, the printed word does not entice me. A pale gray cloud caps Ben More, on Mull, then slips slowly down its creased flanks. Far above, cumulus towers are painted white by the sun. Higher yet are clouds like lenses—gray-blue below, white-gray above—layer upon layer, with glimpses of the sky between, sky of the lightest transparent blue that forms an unassuming backdrop for the drama taking place center stage. I glance back at my book, but the sentences seem irrelevant. I look back at the slowly evolving cloudscape before me, always subtly moving, lenses merging, shades deepening, edges spilling, shapes changing slowly, slowly, like a multi-hued celestial gavotte. The sun gradually dips in the west and its dying rays are reflected in the sky, rose and lavender now, like the smooth interior of a vast, earth-caressing oyster shell.

The sun has gone. Gray upon gray the sky, and ever inward turns the eye.

As my sojourn on Iona draws to a close, I'm beginning to understand, at a deeper level, why I was drawn here and why I came to this island in my imagination in difficult times. The landscape, the writing, the reading have brought me back to my roots, have helped me make sense of the passions in my life, and have opened me to a spiritual heritage that I can now totally embrace. I thought that the purpose of my journey here was to come to terms with cancer; it turns out that it was also to come to terms with my whole life.

⅋ ⅋

I lie awake, then reluctantly pull myself up to sit on the side of the bed to write down a dream before it fades away. I go to a hospital to give birth. I shower, put on a gown, and am shown to a bed by a nurse. I wait and wait, but nothing happens—no labor pains; no one comes to check up on me. Finally, bored with waiting, I set off with another woman to go for a walk. It is an elaborate journey. We walk through many neighborhoods, in and out of many houses, through a university campus, and into a downtown area. We browse in a bookshop, then realize we should get back to the hospital. But we get lost several times and have to ask the way. On this rambling journey, I fall and am injured several times. When I get back to the hospital, I can't decide whether to get my wounds treated first, or just to wait for the birth. Finally, I'm back in bed waiting for the birth. No one has noticed I've been gone. Only one hour has passed, although it seems much longer.

I am thankful that I will talk with Barry the next day. As we talk about the dream, I stare through the window of my room at the sea, a cup of tea at my side. Later, I write down the gist of what he has to say:

> This dream is the story of your life, of your analysis. You're waiting for a birth, for some level of transformation, but nothing happens. You set out on a journey, spending time in different houses, on a campus, becoming familiar with books. You are injured on this journey—emotional hurts, abandonments, cancer. These hurts are what everyone experiences in life. In the dream, you wonder: Should I get the wounds treated, figure out what caused the wounds? Or should I wait for birth/transformation to occur? In the dream, you arrive back where you started and only an hour has passed.
>
> You see, you had to *live* your life in order to get back to where you started. Like the legend of Parsifal. He sees an archetypal ritual at the Grail Castle about healing, about the meaning of life. But he is too young and naïve to understand it. He has an experience he doesn't comprehend and journeys through life "doing" his life, on a quest, always searching for that meaning. Then the Grail Castle reappears—and he *gets* it!

From the psyche's point of view, life is little more than an hour. Not that it is unimportant. Unless you have this life, you can't find your way back. Life is what happens while you wait to give birth. The lesser birth is being born; the Greater Birth is transformation. Therapy treats the wounds; analysis aims for transformation. Not everyone gets to that place of Greater Birth—or needs to.

❧ ❧

I walk along the shore below Greenbank picking up limpet shells for some vaguely planned art piece I will create at home. Traversing the beach at Traigh Mohr, I clamber up a short rocky ravine and walk out into the valley that leads down to Sandeels Bay. Rabbits feeding in the evening light scurry away, white tails flashing. There is no one around. I follow a sheep track down to the bay and then step into Tinker's Gully to look one last time at the hawthorn tree—such a brave, lone being in this almost treeless environment. To my consternation, I find a dead seagull spread-eagled on the grass at the base of the tree, partially eaten away; and on the beach, fragments of the skeleton and fleece of a long-dead sheep uncovered in the sand. Two dead creatures. The seagull and the sheep—archetypal inhabitants of Iona and the very creatures I chose in my imagination as metaphors for the white blood cells in my immune system, ridding the island of cancerous crabs and invading thistles.

We are here for such a short time. I survived cancer with the help of healing imagery, but it is only a temporary reprieve. The island reminds me that my body will eventually fail and return to the earth. I should not become too inflated. Just because I have survived cancer, I have not become immortal.

The two bodies at Sandeels Bay remind me of a task I have been pushing to the back of my mind. After leaving most of my mother's ashes in her garden in London, I took the remainder back to Berkeley to put under my roses. But that done, there were still more left. I put them in a corner of my clothes closet. From time to time, I remembered they were there and asked myself: "What am I holding on to?"

I have held on to her ashes just as I have held on to my guilt about not being with her when she died, not being the expressive and loving daughter she must have wanted. It is time to let go of those feelings, to acknowledge that we both did our best, which is all that two people can do—mothers and daughters, friends, lovers, partners. "You were always a very independent little girl," my mother often told me. Longing for tenderness that wasn't there, I busied myself in seeming indifference and retreated into nature. My mother, observing me, assumed that was my preferred way and rarely intruded. Thus we distanced ourselves from each other, saddened by unfulfilled expectations, unable to express the truth.

I have brought her ashes back again across the Atlantic and plan to leave them somewhere in Iona. My mother never came to this island, but it feels right—for me, the living, to leave something of her here, in the ocean that stands between my home country and the continent where I now live. The sheep and the seagull have jolted me back into thinking about death.

CHAPTER 25

❧

Memories of My Mother

*The heartbeats I felt in the womb—two heartbeats, at
once, my mother's and my own—are heartbeats of the
land. All of life drums and beats, at once, sustaining a
rhythm audible only to the spirit. I can drum my heartbeat back into the Earth, beating, hearts beating, my
hands on the earth—like a ruffed grouse on a log, beating, hearts beating—like a bittern in the marsh, beating,
hearts beating. My hands on the Earth beating, hearts
beating. I drum back my return.*
—Terry Tempest Williams[78]

In the course of my growing up, my mother and I lived in the same
house, but it never felt as if we were "together." I have often wondered
if that feeling of distance had its roots in the prevailing culture of child-
rearing in the 1930s. Long before Dr. Spock's humane approach to
the needs of babies, Dr. Truby King promoted a disciplined approach,
insisting that babies must be fed on a strict four-hour schedule, encouraged to have regular bowel movements, and be left in their cribs to cry
if they wouldn't go to sleep. A strict regimen was supposed to build
character; cuddling was to be avoided.

I never asked my mother if she followed Truby King's advice, but it
seems likely since it was the prevailing belief at the time. She certainly
told me that, when I was born, they paid little attention to me, since
Paul had just come home from the hospital after surgery and they didn't
want him to feel "replaced" by a new baby. Also, my father's father was
dying at the time, so the family had plenty to cope with.

Once, when I was visiting my mother with my own two children, she heard me praise them for pictures they had brought home from school. Later, on our own, she cautioned against "too much praise," saying it would make them "swell-headed." I quickly replied that I would praise my children as often as I could and tell them every day that I loved them. Clearly our views on child-rearing could not have been more different.

I remember very little about our life in that house at Ascott in the war. As a child, I left the house as often as I could to climb trees, dig in my garden, tend my rabbits. Sometimes, I picked bunches of violets and primroses, milkmaids and cowslips to bring home for my mother. I can still draw a map locating every field and copse, every track and hiding place within a mile of our house, but, try as I may, I don't remember one detail of the bedroom where I slept.

Where did we eat in that house? I don't remember a single meal; not one. That's not quite true. I remember Sunday evenings when my mother invited young convalescing soldiers from a local military hospital to come and have sandwiches and coffee with us and enjoy a game of Monopoly. Two of them were so grateful that, when they returned to their unit, they gave me a money order for ten shillings and sixpence so I could buy a garden spade at Coopers the Ironmongers in Leighton Buzzard. I was so thrilled with that spade: the first garden tool of my own.

I don't remember much family time from those days. My mother cycled off to her job at the munitions factory in Linslade. And later, when painting the flare canisters made her ill, she moved to a job in a quantity surveyor's office in Leighton Buzzard that she liked much better. Before Paul returned to live with Grandma Cooper in London, he and I cycled off to our respective schools. When we came home, I remember listening to Children's Hour on the radio each day, 5:00 to 6:00 PM, with Uncle Mac reading stories while Mum cooked supper; or we listened to Dick Barton, Special Agent; or to the reassuring voice of Alvar Lidell reading the nine o'clock news; or to comedy shows on the BBC (Tommy Handley, Arthur Askey, Richard Murdoch) that kept our spirits up in those dark times. But I don't remember where we sat down for dinner or what we ate.

What I remember is my mother's sadness. I felt such confusion, hearing her sobbing in the bedroom next to mine when a flimsy blue air letter, stamped in red—"Army Censor"—arrived in the post. I knew it was from my father, but there never seemed to be a message for me, just something that made her cry. I didn't know how to ask her what that "something" was, didn't want to ask her. Better to just hold on tight to my pillow—a life-raft in a stormy sea. Better to stare at the cracks in the ceiling, lit up by moonlight, and imagine I could see a camel, a mountain, a five-barred gate. Better to think about tomorrow—feeding my rabbits, cycling to school—and imagine everything was back to how it was before the war.

Every night after I went to bed, my mother played the piano. It was her source of solace as gardening was mine. I listened to Chopin and Beethoven as I drifted off to sleep and wished that she would come upstairs and hug me good-night. Even today, over fifty years later, I cannot hear Schumann's *Scenes from Childhood* without dissolving into tears. It was her favorite piece.

As an adult, I can understand why she was depressed and deeply worried in those years. I remember one summer evening in 1940 when we went for a walk and ended up outside Mr. and Mrs. Bielby's house. He and my mother liked to talk politics. I recall my mother leaning on one side of the white five-bar gate, and Mr. Bielby on the other, talking about Dunkirk. I didn't understand what it was all about; I just played around with Judy, our dog. Now, decades later, I have an insatiable need to understand everything that happened in the war, to fill in the gaps of my childhood. By that date, in late May 1940, German forces had taken Denmark, Norway, Holland, and Belgium, and had reached the French coast, only twenty-one miles from our shores. Seeing no hope, Churchill ordered the total evacuation of the soldiers of the British Expeditionary Force, who had been fighting in France and were trapped on the shore at Dunkirk. The appeal went out for help and thousands of fishing boats, private yachts, pleasure steamers, lifeboats—the "Little Ships," as they came to be known—crossed the English Channel and rescued more than 330,000 men in eight days. The traumatized, rescued troops expected the worst on their return to England, but, Julia Gardiner tells us something different:

> The reception was ecstatic, the defeated army was accorded a heroes' welcome ... the railway tracks all the way back to London lined with people on both sides clapping and cheering.... Hitler had hoped that after the fall of France, Britain would sue for peace, leaving him free to pursue his conquest of Eastern Europe. But Winston Churchill, in a speech to the House of Commons, made it clear that: "We shall go on to the end ... We shall defend our island whatever the cost may be. We shall fight on the beaches, we shall fight on the landing grounds, we shall fight in the fields and in the streets, we shall fight in the hills, we shall never surrender. We shall defend our island whatever the cost shall be ..."[79]

Even now, as I read those familiar words, they bring tears to my eyes. I am proud to come from a country that, even in the worst of times, never gave up.

Later in the war, there were times when Mum and Paul and I lay rigid with fear on our bunks in the cold cellar listening to the hum of rockets passing overhead. Scarcely able to breathe, I prayed that the engine wouldn't cut out: "Please God—Mummy, Daddy—not here, not here ... don't let it land here." V1 rockets, sometimes called flying bombs, were launched from a secret site in occupied Holland. (The V stood for *vergeltungswaffe,* or reprisal weapon.) They droned across the North Sea, timed to land and explode in London. The twenty-five-foot-long, cigar-shaped missiles flew without a pilot on a pre-set course for a pre-set distance. Their engines then stopped abruptly and they fell to earth in an eerie silence, exploding on impact. Sometimes the timing mechanisms failed and the rockets continued on their way, humming over fields of sleeping sheep and quiet villages unthreatened by foreign invasion since the Norman Conquest of 1066. Humor is at the core of British culture and, in defiance of this new and deadly menace with its droning engine, the populace began to refer to them as annoying insects, "doodlebugs," or "buzz bombs."

This was Hitler's last desperate attempt to break the will of the British people. Between June and September 1944, almost 8,000 of those rockets were launched over London; 12,000 people were killed; 23,000 houses were destroyed. Trains leaving London were crammed with people seeking safety. By early September, the number of flying bombs had diminished and people assumed that it was over. But on September 8, the second of Germany's deadly secret weapons, the V2, came down on Chiswick. Although fewer V2s fell, their impact was even more devastating. They flew at ten times the speed of the V1 and made no sound. There was no possibility of defense. These were the first ballistic missiles. With no warning, they could demolish a whole street of houses and leave a crater fifty feet wide. One fell on a Woolworth's store in London and killed 160 people. At the end of the war, Werner von Braun and Walter Dornberger, two members of the German team that developed the V2, surrendered to the U.S. and became part of a group of scientists that paved the way for U.S. manned space exploration.

In total, during those war years, more than 60,000 British civilians were killed. Of those, nearly 8,000 were children. While these numbers were minimal compared to what happened on the continent—1.2 million Jewish children died in the Holocaust; 400,000 children died in the siege of Leningrad—as one author writing of this time has wisely said: "There can be no balance sheet for death."[80]

⁂

Out in the country, we were the lucky ones. When the siren sounded and we spent the night on bunks in the cellar, my mother seldom spoke of what had happened—or not happened—in the night. The next day, she set off to work on her sit-up-and-beg bicycle; on weekends, Paul walked across the fields to Mr. Watson's to see if there were any farm chores he could do to earn a few shillings; and I took off into the woods, climbed a tall beech tree, and looked out over the countryside. In daylight, outdoors, I felt safe. But our house was filled with unspoken fears and my mother's muffled sobbing in the night.

Once, my mother allowed Paul and me to go up to London for the day with Paul's friend, Burt. Somehow, we ended up in Regents Park. I remember there were trenches dug into the grass, bounded with sandbags and barbed wire. There were a few barrage balloons floating overhead, looking like silvery fish or swollen pigs. It is hard to believe in this day of drones and interceptor missiles that the long steel cables tethering these balloons to the ground were effective in deterring German dive bombers.

Burt picked up a girl in the park and soon they were on a bench, necking ("snogging," we called it then). Paul and I sat a distance away, embarrassed and getting worried as we realized we had missed the afternoon train. It started to get dark; the air-raid warning went off. Searchlights came on, crisscrossing the sky, seeking enemy planes. We made our way to the rail terminus at Euston, carried along by a crowd that seemed to know its way—which was fortunate, as most of the street lights were dimmed because of the blackout. I remember sand bags piled around the entrances to buildings, buckets of sand, and stirrup pumps in case of incendiary bombs. I was scared and took hold of Paul's hand.

People with cushions and mattresses were queuing to enter the underground station at Regents Park and spend another uncomfortable night in the relative safety of the platforms. Nearing Euston, we saw a building sliced in half by an earlier raid, flowered wallpaper in the bedrooms and a claw-footed bathtub still intact. Scrawled on the walls of what had been the kitchen were large white painted letters that spelled out: "London can take it" and "Business as usual." There were lots of soldiers at Euston station, carrying kit bags and rifles. I thought of Dad, but I was beginning to forget what he looked like.

Our train spluttered north, the blinds drawn as they always were after dark—in trains, as in our homes—so that we wouldn't be spotted by German bombers. The compartment was illuminated by a blue pinpoint of light and I could just make out Paul's and Burt's taut faces, sitting opposite. I pressed my face against the window and peeked round the edge of the blind to catch a glimpse of the Ovaltine factory at Kings Langley where Auntie Jean worked. I loved the painted image on the factory facade of a smiling young woman holding a sheaf of wheat and a basket of eggs, an image from an era before air raids and bomb shelters. Auntie Jean supplied us with Ovaltine for hot drinks and Ovaltine tablets to suck. Too bad I didn't like either.

Just before Berkhampsted station, we passed a ruined castle that had always intrigued me. Portions of walls built of chalk and flint—some high, some low—enclosed a flat area of grass where famous statues stood, removed from their plinths in central London to protect them from the bombing. Evacuated, just like us. I recognized Oliver Cromwell, George Washington, and Richard the Lionheart, sword held aloft, seated majestically on a horse with one leg uplifted, its head stretched forward, its nostrils flaring. I used to imagine that at night, when we were all asleep, they walked around, conversed, and commiserated with each other about how tiring it was to stand motionless all day in the damp, un-mown grass.

The train juddered to a stop. Where were we? Maybe Cheddington? There was no way to know. All the signs on railway stations, all the signposts on roads, had been removed long ago to confuse the enemy were they to invade. Bernard Miles, a much-loved British actor, used to recite a comic monolog about a railway journey in these times when the station announcer couldn't say the name of the place. He ended the piece in his thick Buckinghamshire accent: "All right! All of you as was comin' 'here, you've arrived, so get orff!"

When our train finally arrived at Leighton Buzzard, I glimpsed Mum standing with her bicycle looking frantic, scanning the faces emerging from the train.

"Thank God," she said. "Where have you been? I was sick with worry."

Paul and I shrugged. "We missed the train," I said, shuffling and looking down at my scuffed and dusty lace-up shoes.

"You've no business missing the train when I was waiting for you and worried to death you were caught in a raid."

I looked away into the darkness feeling guilty.

"Sorry, Mum," Paul mumbled, twisting the hem of his gray zippered jacket between his fingers.

"That's the last time I let you go up to London on your own. Paul—you were in charge; I just don't understand how you could be so irresponsible."

I sighed deeply and began to shiver. I was cold and I just wanted to be home in bed. "Here," Mum said gently, pulling a red thermos flask out of her bicycle basket. "I've brought some hot chocolate. Have a drink—and then we'll ride home."

Decades after this event, I read Vera Brittain's *England's Hour*, a moving account of her memories of living in London during the war. "Day after day," she wrote, "men and women working in offices, in factories, or in their own homes, fight their human fears with a brave show of human indifference. Even the children sing in the shelters, subjecting themselves prematurely to adult self-control, with what long term effects on their nervous systems we do not yet know."[81] Though I did not spend time in the shelters as so many other children did in the war, that period of my young life forged in me such a profound sense of attachment to, and pride in, my homeland that, only after decades of living in the United States, when it had clearly become my permanent home, could I take the enormous step of becoming a U. S. citizen. It felt, at some level, like a form of betrayal.

᪐ ᪐

I wish my mother and I could have talked about our fears, but the stiff-upper-lip attitude of the British that forbade it was also what kept us, and the whole country, from falling apart in those terrifying times. I admire how my mother kept going, and kept *us* going, despite all the pain and fear that surrounded us. I admire, too, how she kept us fed despite our pitiful rations of one to four ounces of butter (depending on supplies) and three ounces of cheese per person per week, one egg, two ounces of tea, eight ounces of sugar, and four ounces of bacon. Of course, we had eggs from our own chickens, the rabbits I reared, and vegetables that the Rothschilds generously gave to all of us on the estate. I remember the pamphlets from the Ministry of Food with tips on how to cook with dried eggs and dried milk, and how to make a passable replica of mashed banana by sprinkling banana essence on mashed parsnips. Once, when Jason and Lucy were studying World War II in middle school, their teacher asked me to come and speak to a history class. I phoned my mother and she remembered exactly what our rations had been. I put together what would have been allowed for a family of four; it barely filled half of a Safeway bag. Those California children sat silent in disbelief. Perhaps it helped them put into perspective for a moment the incredible abundance in which they live.

I have to say that I never remember being hungry in the war. Bread was never rationed; I guess we filled up on that. The bread we could buy, the so-called "National Loaf," was so disliked that people began to call it "Hitler's Secret Weapon." The government fostered rumors that it had aphrodisiac qualities to encourage people to buy it. It is said that the cohort of children raised in Britain in World War II were particularly healthy because we did not eat much fat, sugar, or red meat, and we certainly had no candies or ice cream. Whatever our deprivations, we were infinitely better off than people on the continent—in Germany, occupied Holland, France, the death camps.

❧ ❧

June 6th, 1944. How that date resonates for members of my generation. The allied landings in Normandy to liberate mainland Europe from Nazi occupation. There had been months of secret preparation and deception—"a bodyguard of lies," as Churchill called it—to distract the Germans from the real location of the invasion. In the early hours of June 6th, 4000 warships bombarded the Normandy coast. American, British, and Canadian troops waded ashore and landed behind enemy lines by parachute. By the end of the day, 150,000 Allied troops were on French soil. It was the largest single-day amphibious invasion of all time.

I remember my mother running to tell the news to Shirley's and Ronnie's mothers. There was an air of excitement, of smiles and hopefulness the like of which I didn't remember ever seeing before. Even the dour faces of our teachers at The Gables looked more relaxed, almost happy. I don't think we children understood the full import of what had happened, but I remember that we danced in circles outside school, kicking up the gravel like excited young ponies just put out to grass. Perhaps our fathers would soon be coming home!

I remember so well the day my mother and I moved back to London. It was August 15th, 1945—VJ Day (Victory over Japan Day). The final day of the war. Mum had saved the dividends from years of shopping at the little co-op store in Wing and we had just enough money to pay for the move. The end of the war! I was so excited, sitting up high in the cab of the moving van. As we drove by flags and bunting and Union Jacks and street parties with big signs saying "There'll always be an England," I pretended the parties were all for us, celebrating our return home, welcoming us back to London.

We moved back into 27 Arden Road and Mum and I worked like beavers, cleaning and painting our house, which had been commandeered by the government for essential war workers when we left to live in the country. Six separate households had taken up residence—air-raid wardens, firemen, factory workers needed in London—and it was quite a mess: grease-stained counters, dirty floors, a gray rim around the bathtub, the garden overgrown with elderberry bushes. A jagged crack had appeared in the mosaic tile floor of the front hall, the result of a bomb that destroyed a house a few doors away.

My mother took up painting and sculpture after the war, when she was in her forties, and found she had talents that had long lain dormant. She painted in oils and acrylic, and Dad answered an ad for an abandoned railroad shed, which he set up at the bottom of the garden as her studio. He encouraged her new-found passion—which was strange, because, earlier in their married life, when she had indulged in her considerable talent for writing, he had belittled it. She told me many years later that she had once submitted a story to a magazine. The magazine liked it and said they would publish it if she made a few changes. For some reason, Dad squelched her excitement with two simple words: "That's ridiculous." She never followed up on the magazine's offer and rarely did any creative writing again.

Was he jealous? Did this bring up an unspoken issue—that Mum had been to university and Dad had not? What happened between this event and my mother's discovery of painting twenty-five years later—which he gladly supported? Perhaps he had matured. Perhaps the war and the near-collapse of their marriage rendered him a wiser and more compassionate man.

Now they are both gone. I have several of my mother's paintings in my house in Berkeley, but nothing that she wrote. At the top of my stairs is a semi-abstract painting of a mother and child in the style of Diego Rivera. The colors are rich, like those of a garden; the brush strokes are sensuous, like languorous caresses on the canvas; the

mother's arms cradle the child in a moment of infinite love. Did she imagine herself the mother in that picture—or was she perhaps the child?

❧ ❧

My mother could never stand not being the center of attention. When her own mother focused on caring for a blind and dying husband, her upbringing was turned over to older sisters—Jean, Ella, Elsie, Daisy, Annie—who spoiled her and primed her to recite poems she had learned by heart at family gatherings. As long as she was the center of attention, she felt loved. Without such attention, she was not even sure she existed. With such narcissistic tendencies in my mother, I had a hard time embracing my own femininity, my very embodiment.

"Don't draw attention to yourself or Mum will feel uncomfortable," an inner voice cautioned me. In her last illness, when friends and relatives dropped by and inevitably asked me about my own recent illness, she interrupted with: "I've had breast cancer too, you know!" When I was old enough, I immigrated to another country to become my own person. I had to do it to survive. And at least I ended up living in a place and culture where therapy and self-exploration are condoned and encouraged. My mother never had that possibility.

Was my mother jealous of my career? I once asked her that and she responded "No," but without much conviction in her voice. "You lived the life I never lived," she said, and I resented that. I lived *my* life. My life was not a substitute for what she didn't have. But I felt the sadness behind those words; as for so many women of her generation, the roles of wife, mother, and daughter were the only ones deemed appropriate. For me, there was a choice, and she championed my going to university and worked at Selfridges department store to help pay the fees when Dad's view was that girls could be secretaries, nurses, or teachers, nothing more.

In many ways my mother *was* a supportive parent, but it hurt that she was so often not present, not demonstrative, not affectionate. She complained that, in all their life together, my father only once told her that he loved her—on their wedding day. But I wonder: did she ever tell him? We were a family in which those crucial words were never spoken, and, in our different ways, we were all diminished by it.

It saddened me that she never read my book, *House as a Mirror of Self.* It felt like the work of a lifetime. She read several books a week, right up to the end—library books, mysteries, novels—but not mine. I was disappointed, too, when I returned from Iona or Findhorn and she showed no interest in what I had found so compelling there—the spiritual journey I was drawn to undertake. But then, I know I disappointed her as well.

When staying with my mother in her early nineties, I borrowed a tape recorder and asked her to tell me about her life. She balked at first, and we had a hard time getting started.

"Why would anyone be interested?" she asked.

"I would. Your grandchildren! Your great-grandchildren! You have lived through most of the 20th century."

Finally, prompted by a simple question—"Tell me about the first house you can remember and what you ate for breakfast"—we were off. We talked for three long evenings, but when it came to 1940 and the war, she refused to go on. "I don't want to talk about it; it's too painful. And the years after the war—well, you can remember that part. Let's stop here." And so we did.

∂⊱ ∂⊱

A year or so later my brother Anthony called from London to say Mum was very ill and I flew from Berkeley to be with her. It was nine months after my cancer diagnosis; treatment was finished and I was regaining my strength.

She lay on her bed in her London apartment, breathing heavily, a plastic oxygen tube in her nostrils leading to a throbbing machine nearby. Her cat, Jerry, thin and aging himself, was sprawled at her side.

My mother was ninety-three and appeared to be dying. I had been reading *On Death and Dying* by Elisabeth Kübler-Ross and surmised that she was in the last stage of emotional preparation for death—that of acceptance. She told everyone that she wanted to die, that she hoped each night would be her last. She dozed and slept while I sat nearby. In a brief period when she was awake, I gave her a foot rub, smearing cool peppermint lotion over her paper-like skin, working it gently into the dry arches, the corn-callused toes. Later, the doctor came to give her a shot of morphine "to make her comfortable." She slept, the cat sprawled across her right arm. I felt numb though not especially sad since I knew she wanted to go.

But, as it turned out, this was not her time. Despite her expressed wish to die, yet again some inner force brought her back. She listened to Schumann tapes and looked out at her beloved garden. Bridget, a young Irish nurse saving up for her wedding, moved in to care for her and I took off for a few days of hiking on the Isle of Wight.

There were a few more false alarms—my mother calling Anthony and his family to her bedside to say good-bye, then a message coming the next day saying she was fine, sitting up in bed watching TV. The summer before she died, we had a mellow time, a time of soft, almost intimate communication. We played Scrabble together—and she always won. I pushed her in a wheelchair to the park several times, and I remember how delighted she was watching families walk by, stopping to look at flowers, feeling the sun, listening to the liquid song of a yellow-beaked blackbird in the hawthorn tree above us.

Finally, a fax arrived from her doctor in London reporting that she was "very ill/terminal." I hurried to make arrangements to leave Berkeley. On the day before my flight, I went down the garden to hang out some washing in a brief respite between torrential El Niño rains. A large butterfly suddenly appeared, fluttering near me and then settling on a torn piece of blue tarpaulin. I was amazed—we just don't see butterflies in February, especially during the wettest winter on record. So many times around death and transformation an insect has appeared to reassure me, to bring a message. At Auntie Jean's funeral, a lone bee appeared and hovered over a wreath. It was mid-winter in England and bees are just not around at that time, but she had been a passionate beekeeper all her life and one had found its way to the ritual of her parting. When my long-ago boyfriend Al Schwartz died in a car accident and I sat at a friend's house in shock, a pure white moth flew through the window, settled on my arm, and stayed there motionless for over an hour. Al was always a tease, a joker. That a white moth would bring a message of reassurance from Schwartz seemed entirely appropriate.

On arriving in London, I took a taxi straight to the hospital, but as I asked for her room, I knew I had come too late. "I'm so sorry—your mother passed away last night." I went in to see her. It was a shock, her face half covered in purple bruises from a fall at the nursing home, her hair pulled back, her mouth, without false teeth, fallen open. I won't remember that face but rather her face when alive and animated, when looking out at her garden, when playing the piano. I sat by her bed for a while, talking to her, stroking her forehead, and telling her it was okay to go, to float away, to let go. Did she know that I was there?

In a state of jet-lagged shock, I turned my chair and looked out at the hospital garden. I felt nurtured by the green, a tree in blossom, people hurrying to work beyond the garden wall. And then a magpie flew by carrying a twig in its beak—early nest-building. "One for sorrow," I thought, remembering the traditional English rhyme we say on seeing magpies, alone or in twos, threes:

> One for sorrow,
> Two for joy,
> Three for a girl,
> Four for a boy.

Close on the tail of the first magpie, came a second: "Two for joy!" The sorrow of death, the joy of a spirit released. My mother's body didn't serve her any more. I sensed she was floating free as a bird on that unseasonably warm Februrary day.

❧ ❧

I felt a range of emotions at my mother's death—the stunned realization that, with both parents gone, there was nothing between me and the grave. The stark realization of my own inevitable death came sharply into focus again. It was too late to ask questions about mysterious figures in sepia prints from the 1930s in the family album; too late to say those things I always meant to say, but never could. "What happened between us in the war that was never repaired? Despite my seeming aloofness, I do love you."

At the forefront of my emotions, like some snarling, lip-curled beast, stood guilt. Guilt that I didn't arrive in time to sit with her through her dying, that I didn't arrange things faster so I could be with her at the end. But the bitter truth is that I didn't want to be there; I was afraid. I am not comfortable with death. Is anyone? I hear stories from friends and relatives about how they sat with someone dying, holding their hand until the last breath. I have never done that, probably never will. It is a cowardice of which I am ashamed. "I hope I am not alone when I die," she sometimes told me. But in the end, she was; I failed her. "Last minute Annie," Mum used to call me: late for my birth, the opposite of premature; late for appointments, for classes, always on the run. Yes, I was even late for her death.

At the memorial service, I spoke of her life and many accomplishments: the gold medal she received for being the top student at the Royal Masonic School for Girls; her skill as a pianist; her discovery in middle age of latent talents as painter and sculptor. It was not an unexpected death. She was ninety-three when she died and there were few tears in the church except for Anthony, her youngest son, with whom she had the most tempestuous relationship.

After the service, we gathered for a reception at a nearby hotel, people chatting and smiling as the tensions eased a little. As at many funerals, it was also a reunion—with family friends, old neighbors, long-lost cousins. The waiters were all Italian, recent immigrants to London. One of them whispered to my sister-in-law Mary in broken English:

"What are you celebrating?"

"Oh, it's a funeral."

"A funeral?!" He looked wide-eyed. "In Italy, we cry at funerals."

"Oh, we cried at the church," Mary explained. The waiter moved away, shaking his head in disbelief at these unemotional natives of northern Europe.

I moved among the guests, thanking them for coming. I greeted Jim, the Irish handyman who had helped Mum out with household repairs in the years after Dad died.

"Your mother loved you, you know," he said quietly in his Ulster brogue—and I turned to brush away the tears.

The rabbi of a synagogue where Dad had worked part-time as an accountant after his retirement came to his funeral. "Your father was so proud of you," he said, patting my arm as we stood outside the church. "He often talked about you." The Irishman and the rabbi conveying messages of pride and love, messages that were never spoken face to face. Perhaps the Italian waiters were right to look at us in disbelief.

The cremation at Golder's Green Crematorium took place on a brilliantly sunny day. As we emerged from the chapel, the lawns of the memorial garden were vibrant with white, orange, and purple crocuses. The sight took my breath away. It was as if the world were rejoicing, not weeping. A few days later, when I went to collect the ashes, it was cold and windy.

Sitting in the crematorium office, I felt anxious, picking at my nails. How would they present the ashes to me? What would they look like? They brought me the ashes tied up in a plastic bag, inside an anodized "urn," inside a cardboard box, inside a large green carrier bag. I took the tube to Belsize Park, walked down the long avenue lined with leafless trees and let myself into her flat. It was sprinkling rain. I went into the garden and started digging the ashes lightly into the ground under the tree she loved so much—the one Auntie Jean had given her. It was leafless now, but as spring came, I imagined her spirit suffusing its bursting buds. I put more ashes under the pear and apple trees Dad had planted; under each of many roses; around some daffodils and hyacinths just coming into flower. The ashes looked no different from those I rake out of my fire after burning wood—gray, powdery, fine. Ashes to ashes. I felt some sense of relief doing this after the tension of the previous two weeks. Bringing her home.

The next day, I remembered a fragment of a dream. I come to a church and, since it is full of people singing, I assume I've arrived too late for the service. But I look at my watch and find that I've actually arrived too early—it is 5:30 PM.

I had been thinking that I arrived in London "too late," but the dream tells me I came early, in plenty of time for the service I came to perform—helping arrange the funeral, speaking in the church, laying her ashes to rest in the garden. What I did in London was what I had come for. My mother's story (the other service) was ending. I was there to be a part of another story—a story that began as I arrived, that began with her death, that began at 5:30, the start of the quiet, relaxed evening of my life.

Here on Iona, my mother's ashes weigh heavily on my mind. I have brought the last of them with me. Can I let go of the sadness and guilt I feel, the unfulfilled expectations, the words not spoken? All I can think of is that we came together—mother and daughter—for some purpose we will never understand. I want to honor her, her life and struggle, and lay her remains to rest in the most beautiful place I know. *That* I can do, and perhaps she will know it and be glad.

❧ ❧

"You look just like your mother!" cousin Des said as we sat down to dinner last year in Devon. "I thought it was Chris coming in."

I was shocked. I look just like my mother? I don't want to look like her. I want to look like myself. But, from her, I have inherited my love

of words and music, and what little talent I have for painting (though she had so much more).

How will my daughter react when she enters a room in her middle age and someone says, "You look just like your mother!" Will she, like me, recoil in disbelief and not a little displeasure? Or will she laugh and toss her sun-bleached hair and say: "We were always close; why wouldn't we look alike?" Perhaps it helps when mother and daughter have such different personalities and talents that they can only look at each other in wonder. Lucy: snowboarder, scuba diver, rock climber, daredevil. Clare: introvert, dreamer, scaredy-cat, loner.

Now that I am getting old, what might my children write about me? That I always read them bedtime stories, but sometimes let my thoughts stray to tomorrow's lecture? That I never taught them how to cook, but I took them hiking in Cornwall, where we picked blackberries in the soft October sunshine and I taught them how to read maps and hypnotized a cow by blowing up its nostrils? That I didn't know how to make a Halloween costume (didn't even know what Halloween was), but I took them with me to live for a year in the Findhorn community, where I worked in the garden, they went to local Scottish schools, and we learned circle dances and lived in a tiny mobile home like an aluminum shoe box?

When I experience what a mother-daughter relationship can be—loving, sharing confidences, giving advice each to the other, like mine and Lucy's—I realize how far apart my own mother and I were. There was a gulf between us that was rarely bridged, a gulf that had its beginnings in her childhood when her own mother was distant, unavailable, absorbed with the care of her ailing husband. She told me so many times of the grief and betrayal she felt at being sent away to boarding school, something that none of her eight brothers or sisters had to endure.

Does every mother learn to be a mother from her own experience of being mothered? I believe so, and I forgive my mother for what I experienced as a lack of mothering when I was a child. In some ways, I learned not to expect or want it. I knew times were hard: the war, fear of invasion, Dad far away, the factory work she hated, no friends to confide in. So I hope she can forgive me for seeming distant, independent, unaffectionate. I did not give her the love that mothers yearn for from their offspring. I did try—with therapy, with counseling—to pull down the barriers I had erected to protect my child-self, but I was never entirely successful.

After my mother died, I took most of her clothes to an Oxfam charity shop in West Hampstead. All her dresses but one—a dress made from a length of blue shot silk I had brought her from China. She loved that dress and I couldn't bear to part with it. Back in Berkeley, my friend Carolyn had started to make quilts. I gave her that dress, some Marimekko pieces left over from Sixties dresses of mine, and some little-girl dresses of Lucy's I had saved. Carolyn made them into a beautiful quilt of blues and mauves and purples. I sleep under that quilt each night, warmed by the clothes of three generations of women: Christine, Clare, Lucy. Part of my mother is close to me still.

I sit on the beach at Port Ban—late afternoon, no one around. Shallow waves ripple landward in gently hissing tremors. The tide is slipping out, each ripple barely reaching the edge of the wet sand moistened by the wave that came before. A skein of fresh water moves in quiet meanders, carving miniature sandy cliffs in its slow descent toward the sea. Above the rocks, a grassy slope slumps seaward like aging skin obeying the call of gravity.

Small rocks punctuate the expanse of sand, each with a trail of bright green seaweed, sun-parched, abandoned by the receding waves. At water's edge, the same delicate green rock-hair moves languidly back and forth, back and forth, as lazy waves stroke it seaward and landward in salty caresses. All is calm; just the sea's breathing. Nowhere to be but here.

My mother's body was conceived, born, nurtured. It grew, knew passion, swelled, bore children, matured, aged, crumpled, fell, let out its last breath. Now its remnants are in my keeping, ready to be consigned to the womb of the western sea.

"You lived the life I never lived," my mother said. That life—of work, achievement, books, promotions—is fast slipping away. The present is my life, no one else's. On Iona, I have become fully and truly myself. I was born of two mothers: the one who gave birth to my body, the other who released my soul. Biological mother and Mother Earth, now you are one. And I—this brief flicker of consciousness, this skin-trapped child-woman—can only look on in wonder. A line I once read echoes in my head: When we are born, we cry and others rejoice; when we die, others cry and we rejoice.

I pour my mother's ashes into a cup and wade far out until the sea is up to my knees, all the time quietly weeping and whispering: "I love you Mum." In letting go of her ashes, I am letting go of her expectations of me, my expectations of her. We both did our best.

I immerse the cup in a wave. Ashes flicker down in the sunlit water like a shoal of tiny, glistening fish, in their natural element once more. This feels like the right place, among fragments of a billion creatures of the sea. Every being, upon death, becomes part of the living whole once again.

I move back up the beach and huddle into a crevice in the rocks to seek some shelter from the wind. I look up and, to my amazement, see words spelled out with rocks placed on a sandy bank far above the high-tide line. "Praise God for this place."

I sit for a long time staring out to sea. Dark clouds are massing in the east; the sun still shines brightly from the west. Slowly, as light rain begins to fall, the complete arch of a rainbow paints the sky. (An internal skeptic interjects: "What is this—some kind of spiritual theme park?")

How few words we have to describe happiness adequately. The tide has turned and slowly laps toward me; shadows lengthen; towering cumulus clouds swell, burst, and merge as if the earth were on fire and steam were painting the sky. Iona has taught me that there *is* a divine Creator, whatever name—or no-name—we choose to give it, and that we are deeply loved, as we who come here love this divinely created place.

❧ ❧

The following evening, I have dinner with two friends at the Argyll Hotel. It is a glorious evening: the sun tints the rocks of Mull pink, the Sound of Iona shimmers dark blue. We are chatting and laughing when I become aware of a child, a girl of perhaps eight or nine, standing at a window of the dining room staring at the sea. She has short, bobbed hair and a pink-and-white dress with a bow at her back. Something about her, perhaps a sadness, perhaps a longing for the world outside, pulls at my heart and, for a few brief moments, I *am* that child. The conversation around me fades to an indecipherable murmur. Then, the child turns, walks back to where her family is dining, and I, suddenly conscious of my absence, re-join the conversation at my table. Sometime later, looking to my left, I see the girl curled up on her mother's lap, leaning against her breasts while the older woman's hand gently strokes her back. An emptiness washes through me, and I turn away.

❧ ❧

I sit in the sunlit porch at Greenbank and stare at a photo of my mother I brought with me to Iona. She is sitting at her kitchen table in London. Behind her is an electric kettle and a coffee percolator that reflects the back of her head in its shiny chrome surface. On the wall is the electric can opener Paul gave her when arthritis made it too difficult for her to open cans of food for her cats, Tom and Jerry.

On the Formica table in front of her, with its glowing brown fake-wood panels, there stands a white teapot with an aqua lid, two jugs, and a large open tin, slightly chipped around its rim, with half a fruit cake inside. My mother always made fruit cake when I came home—fruit cake and chocolate shortbread, my favorites.

There are two mugs on the table, both with white-patterned exteriors and glossy brown interiors. What a good choice, those brown interiors. I'm always scrubbing away at my white mugs stained with tannin from my tea. I learned to drink tea without milk when I first went to live in America, but when I came to visit, my mother often forgot and poured milk in first, as we do in England.

In the photo, she wears a patterned blouse and a cotton jersey cardigan (that's a word I never hear in America). It is aqua in color, matching the lid of the teapot. Her right hand holds the handle of the mug as if, any moment, she will raise it to her lips and drink. Her left arm is propped on the table, her left hand cradling her face as she looks directly at me, a wistful smile hovering around her lips and eyes. On the little finger of her left hand is the silver-and-turquoise ring she bought at an art fair in Live Oak Park one summer when she came to visit me in Berkeley. She loved that ring—modern, arty—so different from her formal diamond engagement ring from the 1920s. I now wear it on the little finger of my left hand and often think of her when I glance at it.

In the photo I can just see the door to the cupboard where Mum kept her cups and saucers, jars of jam, vases for flowers, egg cups, and a sugar bowl. Perhaps I took the picture the year I bought new decorated paper to line the shelves of that cupboard. I threw away the old paper, spattered as it was with drips of hardened marmalade and grime from a dozen years of slowly falling dust. Mum was annoyed with me for doing that—putting in clean new paper without asking her. I thought it would be a surprise, but she took it as a criticism of her housekeeping ability. There was so little I could do that she would accept with just a gracious, "Thank you." No, that's not quite true. I liked to re-fill the boxes and pots on her balcony with fresh flowering annuals and with that she seemed pleased. Once when I planted pansies, she sat in her favorite chair looking out at them through the tall French windows—and started to cry. I asked her why, but she couldn't say. When I took that photo in the kitchen, she protested, "I look so terrible in photos. I've grown so old." But I urged her just to look down at her mug and, when I was completely ready with the camera, I said—"Now"—and she looked up, her white hair framing her lined face.

What were we talking about that day when I took the photograph? My children, perhaps, or her other grandchildren. Gossip from the neighborhood; how boring it was now to talk to some of her old friends, all aches and pains; how she missed Richard Truss, the minister at her church who had been assigned to a new parish in a poor neighborhood south of the Thames.

And so we sat at the kitchen table on a summer afternoon, talking of this and that, my mother's head cupped in her hand, she staring at me, with something akin to love in her tired, blue eyes. I hope my eyes, in turn, expressed something of my love for her. But neither of us was ever able to say those three deep-in-the-ocean words we both so longed to hear: "I love you."

CHAPTER 26

ℰ🙰

Sauntering

Never did I think so much, exist so vividly, and experience so much, never have I been so much myself ... as in the journeys I have taken alone and on foot. There is something about walking which stimulates and enlivens my thoughts ... The sight of the countryside, the succession of pleasant views, the open air ... all these serve to free my spirit, to lend a greater boldness to my thinking....
—Jean-Jacques Rousseau[82]

On a hot and hazy day shortly before I leave the island, I set out to visit the Hermit's Cell. I don't begin until 4:00 PM, when most of the day-trippers are making their way back to the ferry. Following the Ridge of the Causeway from near the Macleod Centre, I walk across country into the interior of the island. Despite more than a week of hot, dry weather, the boggy areas are still wet and I am glad I have worn my boots.

The Hermit's Cell is a circle of stones, maybe two feet high and twelve feet across, that marks the site of a hermitage where a monk, perhaps St. Columba, came to engage in silent prayer and contemplation more than a thousand years ago. It has a doorway facing south and is protected from the north wind by a rocky eminence, Big Hill of the Querns. I settle comfortably against the turf that now covers the first layer of rocks that form the walls of the cell. The air is still, no calls of birds or sheep, but I can hear quite clearly the sound of the recorded safety message on the ferry almost a mile away.

I close my eyes and think in turn of many people I know who are sick or in remission from illness: Katie, Linda, Frances, Kirstin, Marv, Anita, Vivienne, Paul, Michael, Vicky, Alistair. I think about the many people at home who helped me in my recovery from cancer. Breathing in, I envisage healing power pouring out of the earth, out of Iona, up through their feet, through their bodies, and passing out to the sky. Breathing out, I imagine love pouring from the sky through their bodies and back down into the earth. I want to share the power of this island, so healing for me, with others in need, with those who are healers. Is this prayer? I don't know. It's what I can do. It feels right.

I open my eyes, aware of the song of a skylark above me, invisible against the heat-laden sky. I look around at the grass, rocks, mounds of heather about to bloom, and start walking again. I look for the Well of the North Wind that is marked on the map and soon find it—a small pool at the base of a rock with tiny forget-me-nots growing in the damp soil. Indeed, I will not forget—either this place or what has happened to me here.

I had planned to return home by the same route I followed to the Hermit's Cell, but when I check the map against the terrain before me, I realize that, if I walk northeast across Calva Meadow, I will come to the small, rusty gate I approached from the other direction some weeks before. I walk in a more or less straight line. With my boots already covered with mud, it doesn't matter where I step. I pass through the gate, walk across the Hill of the Herdboys, and see a patch of white ahead, as if a flock of gulls had been preening. Drawing closer, I find two feathered wings of a young gull, their colors not yet matured from the brown-and-white flecked pattern of youth to the pure gray-and-white of adulthood. One animal's death brings needed calcium and minerals to the living. A year from now, the seagull's wing feathers will have melded into the earth, bringing sustenance to yellow celandine and sticky sundew, hairbell and asphodel.

As I walk the length of Boundary Strand and Strand of the Seat, I pick up old plastic bottles, as I often do, and put them in my pack to deposit later in a litter container near the ferry ramp. I didn't used to bother to pick up pieces of plastic string on the beach, but some time ago, I saw a gull with a long blue strand trailing behind it, perhaps caught in its claws or around a leg. Even then, I didn't particularly look out for string, until I saw the same gull again, weeks later, the blue trail of plastic still attached. Now I pick up pieces of string and rope along with empty bottles of mineral water and Lucozade. "Messy picnickers," I used to think judgmentally, until I realized that perhaps these bottles came in on the tide, tossed overboard from yachts or ferries and floating to rest on Iona's shores.

I think back to when I lived with Stephen, Jason, and Lucy at St. Francis Square—a housing co-operative in San Francisco. We shared an inner courtyard with a hundred other families, with lawns and trees and a playground where I sat with Lucy in my arms watching Jason digging in the sand. Over the year we lived there, I became very protective of that space, picking up litter or broken glass, taking care of a place that had become partially my own. As I left our apartment one day on its more public side, stepping onto Laguna Street, I remember asking myself: "Why don't you pick up litter here, beside the street, as you do in the courtyard?" My answer was: "It is public and not my responsibility." Now, on Iona, I realize that this place has become partially my own, my responsibility. I can no more pass by a discarded bottle on this beach than I can ignore litter on the front steps of my house.

I leave the beach, walk up the path through the dunes, and rest on a bench thoughtfully placed on higher ground with a view over the sea and distant islands. The bench has an inscription on its back: "In memory of Hugh D. B. Morton, who loved this island. The family."

The sun is sinking. The surface of the sea glimmers with countless silvery shards of light. The Celts feel a special sacred affinity with the liminal, that sense of threshold between one place and another, one season and another, one time of day and another. Twilight, the gloaming, was thought to be a time of special numinosity, when the boundary between the known and the sought-after becomes the thinnest of veils. It is good to sit in this place in the gloaming, looking out to sea without any particular thoughts, just a soft awareness of all that lies around and before me.

I start back along the road. Long shadows of fence posts are cast across the tarmac with taut wire between them and a strand of barbed wire across the top, so that I seem to be walking across a shadowy score with demi-semiquavers marking my beat. It is getting late, but—no need to hurry, nowhere to be but here. I digress from the road into the graveyard next to the abbey, ambling slowly along the pebbled paths, reading names and dates, conscious of many lives that ended in early adulthood, others—particularly of women—that stretched into distant old age. I am grateful to the souls who people this place. I want to be reminded of death, lest I let my life slip by barely lived.

I walk on past the St. Columba Hotel, glancing down into the kitchen where Mark and Alistair are setting out desserts for the dining-room guests. Approaching the ferry slip, I see other friends from the hotel—Amy, Hanne, Corine, and Dawn—waiting to greet Alexander, who is returning from the mainland after a period of illness.

As I leave the village, a little drama plays itself out. A male thrush is perched on the phone line opposite Dun Craig. A foot away sits its mate, a beak full of worms, waiting to feed them to yawning mouths in a nest, presumably, nearby. But on the garden wall of Dun Craig sits Baby, a black-and-white cat notorious for leaping through the open windows of any house he chooses, settling on a stranger's bed, or depositing a headless rabbit on a doorstep. "Come along, Baby," I say, scratching him behind the ears. "How about a walk?" And he, ecstatic at receiving some attention, bounds along beside me like a dog. Looking back, I see the female thrush has disappeared and the male is following us, flying from one garden wall to the next until we are well and truly out of his territory.

And so to my home at Greenbank. I have been gone more than four hours. I am hungry. I have sauntered, a word derived from the French *sainte* and *terre* to describe the journey of those who went to the Holy Land. No great insights. No consciousness-riveting epiphany, but I have, indeed, been to the holy land.

❧ ❧

I watch from the ferry as Iona recedes into the distance, the sun picking out the white of Highland Cottage, the beige stones of the abbey, the gray shape of Greenbank, white sand beaches, sheep-dotted grazing land, the rocky skeleton of the island. I feel a tinge of sadness, but mostly I feel a great sense of calm—of deep, belly-filled contentedness; of gratitude.

This island entered my life as might a wise and loving friend. As I struggled with the meaning of abrupt changes in my life, I slowly came to terms with what happened, with critical relationships past and present, with what I have embraced in life and what I have unconsciously rejected. Iona has become a powerful ally in my search for soul. As I surrendered to the teachings of this place of healing, it whispered to me in countless different ways, reminded me, sometimes commanded me, in a firm but loving voice: "Don't go back to sleep." Indeed, I will not.

On the train rocking south from Oban to Glasgow, I talk with a young fair-haired woman whose children sit opposite doing crosswords and playing Hangman. In yet another of those synchronicities that have punctuated my life, I discover that she has traveled to the United States to seek out Native American healers—in the Lakota Sioux tribe at Rosebud, South Dakota, at a Crow Reservation gathering in Montana. She hands me a green business card: "Secrets of Nature—Healing for humans and animals." In line with the beliefs of her teachers, she does not charge for her services. In modesty, her name does not appear on her card. Why does this Scots woman travel to North America for

answers? Why did I make the long journey to Iona? Is it the call of the exotic, the distant, the Other? There are no answers. But if a place, a culture, an island keeps recurring in your dreams, appears unbidden in pensive moments, you can be sure it has something to tell you that you need to hear. Heeding the call, your life is changed.

The speed of the train arouses the bracken beside the track into a feverish dance. The distant hills, remote and silent, are indifferent to our passing. As I stare out at the landscape—sheep-grazed fields bounded by rough walls—I recall the beginning of a poem by Thomas Merton:

> Be still
> Listen to the stones of the wall
> Be silent, they try
> to speak your
> Name
> Listen
> To the living walls.
> Who are you?
> Who
> are you? Whose
> silence are you?[83]

Epilogue

I was never a pre-Raphaelite beauty,
Or anything but pretty enough to satisfy
Men who need to be seen with passable women.
But now I am in love with a place
Which doesn't care how I look, or if I'm happy,
Happy is how I look, and that's all.
—Fleur Adcock[84]

It is the summer of 2001 and I have returned to Iona for a month. Nothing much on the island has changed. A new house is being built near Martyr's Bay; Uncle Davey's house, Seaview Cottage, now has wooden flower planters and a neat edging to the lawn; a couple new to the island is living at Lagandorain and has a flock of black Hebridean sheep; the abbey coffee shop has become a gift shop; the post office now has a computer and a photocopying machine for use by customers.

As I approach the small ravine at the western end of Sandeels Bay, I am dismayed to see that the hawthorn tree has fallen. The trunk still stands to a height of perhaps six feet, but its crown has snapped off and lies on the ground amid grasses and yellow-flowering iris. Momentarily, I feel deeply saddened; this little tree, surviving against all the odds, afforded me such a message of hope when I came upon it two years ago.

I approach the dead tree, picking my way between rocks and find— it is still alive! Short, leafy sprouts are growing out of the trunk and around the roots. A new cycle of growth has begun. This tree, breathing salt air and harboring snails in the twisted creases of its trunk, speaks of survival and persistence in the face of loss.

"I am here," the tree seems to say. "That is all. I carry no message, no teaching. It is you who see that in me, but I am happy to be a mirror for your soul. We are all here—you, the rocks, the sea, the birds—to reflect the innermost thoughts of others who meet and ponder on us. Write what you have to write. Do not delay. My days are numbered; so are yours. Have faith in what you feel and do. You have come to Iona for a purpose. Live it."

In a new book, *Iona Portrayed: The Island Through Artists' Eyes, 1760–1960,* published since my last visit to the island, I find an illustration by an artist named W. C. Crawford—a watercolor of Sandeel's Bay painted in 1920 with the hawthorn tree silhouetted against the beach. This tree is more than eighty years old.

I set off to walk the uninhabited southern portion of the island, up and over the rugged moorland—Plain of the Monks, Big Hill of the Strangers, following the narrow sheep trail I was so happy to discover two years ago. Approaching the southern shore, I decide to go somewhere I've never been before. It is tempting, now that I know the island so well, to keep going back to familiar places, but here—as anywhere—familiarity lulls us into inattention.

I follow a narrow canyon toward the rocky inlet knoen as Port of the Young Lad's Rock. No person in sight; no sheep or cattle; no sound of birds. As I approach the small bay, two black shags fly across its narrow entrance. I feel a little uneasy. There is a strong smell of rotting seaweed. "Perhaps I'll just turn back," I think. "This place feels as if it doesn't want humans to intrude." But something urges me to continue.

I lean against a boulder. Huge sections of rock as big as cars are piled up on the western side of the inlet, sheared off from the cliff face above. When did this happen? A hundred years ago? Ten thousand? Yesterday? Some are bare, with sharp edges; some, more muted in color, are coated with a rich growth of gray-green lichen.

I watch the waves, still not feeling comfortable enough to sit down. Then, on a partially submerged rock, I see the dark body of what appears to be a seal, licking its back. It disappears into the sea, then reappears dragging seaweed onto the rock, and behind it—a long tail! It is not a seal; it is an otter. The unexpected sighting of this shy creature dissolves all feelings of discomfort I sensed in this place. On many visits to Iona, I have never before seen an otter. It comes back and forth to the rock for about five minutes, eating shellfish it pulls out of the kelp.

I remember that other otter I met when, in my imagination, I dived into the waters of Loch Staonaig. It told me that I didn't have to swim against the current. Perhaps I needed to see an otter again today to remind me. Otters, at home in the water, are an ancient symbol for the feminine, the unconscious, the creative forces of life. When we allow ourselves to follow the path less traveled, the world reminds us and offers us something extraordinary.

I make my way inland again, back up the canyon, watching where I place my feet, aware of bog asphodel, heath-spotted orchid, the small blue flowers of wild scabious. Following an old, overgrown wall, I come at last to Loch Staonaig and feel a mild sense of relief on encountering a familiar path. I need to balance the exhilaration of exploration with the comfort of coming home.

Approaching Columba's Bay, I am surprised by something new in the landscape. On the close-cropped grass above the beach, a labyrinth has been marked out with rounded rocks. I slowly walk the seven-fold path and feel a profound sense of peace.

I eat my lunch and am about to start for home when I remember a custom on the abbey pilgrimage. People are invited to select a rock and heave it into the sea as they think of some trait or feeling they would like to let go. I find a large, rounded rock—a pinkish color flecked with white. It is about the size of the breast I lost. It is now seven years since my diagnosis of breast cancer. It is said that the whole cell structure of the body is renewed every seven years, leaving no cell as it was. If so, my body is not the same entity it was when cancer appeared. It is time to let go of what happened.

I walk to the water's edge: "I let go of identifying myself as a cancer survivor. That phase of my life is over. I am no more a cancer survivor than I am a survivor of adolescence, of birthing, of working, of retirement, of life itself. It came. It went. It was a gift." I throw the rock far out into the waves, pick up my pack, and start for home.

On the greensward up above the bay, a herd of cattle rests. They are all lying down—cows, calves, heifers, bullocks—a peaceful extended family. And in the midst of them, a large bull: not rampaging down a street; not standing over bleeding figures crying in pain, but softly

chewing its cud, contented eyes squinting shut in the afternoon sun. The bull in me has found its voice in this place of salty silence.

 ⁂

I have returned to the island every summer but now, in 2008–9, I am here for the first time in winter. Gales and rain often persist for two or three days, sometimes making it impossible for the ferry from Mull to run. Bitter winds from the north comb the dune grass into silver waves. I am less inclined to walk to a favorite beach, more ready to stay inside my room at Greenbank—reading, watching a lone heron fishing in the rock pools on the beach below my window. I have started to write poetry. It began with a dream in which I was to attend a workshop where Dylan Thomas would teach us how to talk to animals. Now I try to capture fleeting insights, feelings, incidents in as few words as possible. It is a welcome challenge in this quiet, inward time of year.

With few visitors travelling to this remote place, the facilities that serve them in the summer are all closed: the two small hotels, the café near the jetty, the craft shop, the second-hand bookshop. Only the few services essential to island life—the Spar grocery, Finlay Ross shop, the post office—are open. These are the places where residents casually meet, and where I see people that I recognize and stop to chat.

There have been many changes to the manmade landscape of the island since I lived and wrote here ten years ago. Ten new houses have been built. Some defunct farm buildings have been transformed into a collection of craft stores. A handsome new fire station has been constructed, Celtic knot decorations at its entrance made by an island wood carver. There is a youth hostel at the north end of the island; there are solar panels on the roof of the St. Columba Hotel.

There are changes to the population as well. More people have come here to retire. Some young people who met here have stayed, married, and had children, while some who grew up here have gone away to university and found careers in Glasgow, Edinburgh, or beyond. Others who went away to study agriculture have returned to the island to maintain the family tradition of raising livestock. The primary school has eight pupils—enough to keep it open—and the many babies and toddlers coming along will keep it viable into the future.

In 1999, Mark, the postie, delivered the mail on his bicycle. Now a young woman delivers letters and parcels in a smart, red Royal Mail van. Near the jetty, beside the container for recycling bottles that was there ten years ago, there is now a container for recycling cans. Every second Tuesday, a truck comes to pick up recycled paper from the blue bins outside each house. The *Oban Times* reports that the manager of the St. Columba Hotel now uses biofuel distilled from the oil used to cook fish and chips to run his car.

In this season, when the weather rarely encourages long walks on the island, I find myself much more engaged in social events than I was in my more reclusive frame of mind in the spring and summer of 1999. Once a week, I go to a Tai Chi class held in the fire station (with the fire engine removed), the only public building that is warm enough. On Thursday evenings, I join a small group of women for line dancing in the unheated village hall, our energetic steps to cowboy music soon enabling us to peel off some of our four or five layers of clothing. The paucity of visitors and the lack of heating preclude services in the large sanctuary of the abbey. I now enjoy attending services in the small parish church where the congregation consists primarily of permanent island residents.

I feel particularly happy that this visit to Iona coincides with Christmas and its various holiday events. At a craft fair, islanders sell items they have made—pottery, silver jewelry, knitted hats, candles, matted photographs, sesame toffee, grapefruit marmalade. A crowd enjoys tea and mince pies around the fire in the common room at the abbey; some days later, a group goes caroling around the village on a crisp starlit Christmas Eve, returning to the abbey refectory for hot cocoa and more mince pies. An island women's group hosts a Christmas dinner at Bishops' House in mid December. A sign on the village notice board invites "All resident ladies." I make discrete inquiries. Am I a resident? (Am I a lady?). I find I am welcome to attend and help a neighbor prepare forty pounds of Brussels sprouts for the traditional turkey feast, followed by a choice of six luscious homemade desserts. The traditional American apple pie and ice cream just doesn't cut it here. Say what you like about British cooking, people in these islands really know how to make delicious desserts.

I now know many more islanders by name, and almost all of them by sight. Some probably wonder why I have chosen to come and live here in the winter; I think I am the only one to do so. I have relished the short days and even the bleak weather. I have gone inward—reading, writing, thinking, dreaming—as never before. It feels, also, as if the islanders are more welcoming than they are in the summer months when most are too busy with their gardens and their bed-and-breakfast businesses to get to know strangers who are on the island for a day, or perhaps just a few hours. Or maybe I have changed.

In my spring and summer visits, I was very aware of the rebirth of life—birds nesting, lambs being born, wild flowers blooming, gardens springing to life, days when the light lasts until 10 or 11 PM. In December the sun doesn't rise until 8:30 AM and sets again at 4:00 PM. In this dark season death is more apparent. I have found dead seals, their eyes pecked out by hungry crows; I have watched a buzzard tearing apart a curlew, white down scattered on the grass like scraps of paper. The birds whose songs I relished in summer—lark, blackbird, robin, thrush—are silent now. The raucous cries of corncrakes, now wintering in sub-Saharan Africa, are absent, and a disturbing piece in the *Oban Times* reports that their overall numbers may be declining. Yet some birds are present in even greater numbers than before. A flock of more than 100 graylag geese has always wintered here, but now more are staying here year round. Fewer fly north to nest in Greenland and Iceland, perhaps a result of global warming. This concerns island residents, since the birds are voracious consumers of grass needed by the sheep. One notorious island resident, Baby the cat, who often leapt through windows and settled on the beds of strangers is with us no more—much to the sadness of his owner, but to the relief of more than a few island residents.

In the often-overcast days of late February, there are a few signs of spring: clusters of snowdrops beneath the sycamores where noisy rooks will soon build their nests; spear-like leaves and tight buds of daffodils piercing the cold ground between the graves near the abbey.

The most significant internal change that has happened to me is that I have substantially recognized, and worked successfully to take back, the projections I put on Barry. It was his qualities of wisdom, compassion, insight, love which first drew me to him with an almost magnetic force. How could I possibly have these qualities in myself? In our analytical work together, he mirrored back to me what I was unwilling, unable, dare not see and own in myself. He patiently held those projections for me until I was able to retrieve and reintegrate this gold – my true nature – back into myself. The qualities that make Barry a remarkable psychoanalyst, are – in lesser measure – also part of who I am. I no longer feel the helpless–child–in–nature–looking–for–the–lost–father. Our relationship, as supportive and loving as it ever was, is now more balanced.

As on many other visits and during the long sojourn that forms the core of this book, my life slows down. Dreams emerge from a deeper place. My soul is soothed. I have relished the short days, even the bleak weather. I cannot say why this particular place nurtures me as no other, what particular resonance draws me back. Yet I know this is my place of healing. That is enough.

ENDNOTES

1 Deena Metzger, *Writing for Your Life* (San Francisco: Harper San Francisco, 1992), p. 71.

2 The official name of the community is the Findhorn Foundation, to distinguish it from the nearby village of Findhorn. Throughout this book, however, I refer to the Findhorn Foundation as the Findhorn community, or just as Findhorn, as that is how it is referred to colloquially by those who have visited or lived there.

3 James Hillman, *The Force of Character and the Lasting Life* (New York: Ballantine Books, 1999), pp. 129, 130.

4 James Hillman, *The Soul's Code: In Search of Character and Calling* (New York: Random House, 1966), p. 4.

5 Jelaluddin Rumi, trans. Coleman Barks and John Moyne, *Open Secret* (Boston: Shambhala Press, 1984), p. 7.

6 Doris Grumbach, *Life in a Day* (Boston: Beacon Press, 1996), pp. 119 -120.

7 Sharon Butala, *The Perfection of the Morning: A Woman's Awakening in Nature* (St. Paul, MN: Hungry Mind Press, 1994), pp. 63, 64.

8 Keith H. Basso, *Wisdom Sits in Places: Landscape and Language among the Western Apache* (Albuquerque, NM: University of New Mexico Press, 1996), pp. 126–127.

9 John Fowles and Frank Horvat, *The Tree* (Boston: Little, Brown and Company, 1979), no page number.

10 Mike Brown, *Evacuees: Evacuation in Wartime Britain 1939–1945* (Stroud, UK: Sutton Publishing, 2000), Introduction (no page number).

11 James Hillman, "Epigraph in Lieu of Preface," *The Soul's Code: In Search of Character and Calling* (New York: Random House, 1996), p. xi.

12 Sigmund Freud, *Origins of Psycho-Analysis*, quoted in E. V. Walter, *Placeways: A Theory of the Human Environment* (Chapel Hill, NC: University of North Carolina Press, 1988), p. 101.

13 Philip Sheldrake, *Living between Worlds: Place and Journey in Celtic Spirituality* (London: Darton, Longman & Todd Ltd., 1995), pp. 7, 8.

14 Sheldrake, *Living between Worlds*, p. 59.

15 Sheldrake, *Living between Worlds,* pp. 30, 31, 59.

16 As quoted in Shierry Weber Nicholsen, *The Love of Nature and the End of the World: The Unspoken dimensions of Environmental Concern* (Cambridge, MA: MIT Press, 2002), p. 39.

17 Adam Nicolson, *Sea Room: An Island Life in the Hebrides* (New York: North Point Press, 2001), pp. 3–4.

18 Confucius, in *Wisdom For the Soul: Five Millennia of Prescriptions for Spiritual Healing,* ed., Larry Chang (Washington, DC: Gnosophia Publishers, 2006), p. 427.

19 Joseph Campbell, *The Power of Myth* (New York: Doubleday, 1988), p. 5.

20 Dom Helder Camara, *A Thousand Reasons for Living,* trans., Alan Neame (Philadelphia: Fortress Press, 1981), pp. 52, 103.

21 Etty Hillesum, *An Interrupted Life: The Diaries of Etty Hillesum* (New York: Pantheon Books, 1983), p. 196.

22 Arthur W. Frank, *At the Will of the Body: Reflections on Illness* (New York: Houghton Mifflin, 1991), p. 1.

23 Arthur W. Frank, *The Wounded Storyteller: Body, Illness, and Ethics* (Chicago: University of Chicago Press, 1995), pp. 17, 53.

24 John Fowles and Frank Horvat, *The Tree* (Boston: Little Brown and Company, 1979), no page numbers.

25 Quoted on *The Writers' Almanac,* American Public Media online newsletter, June 9, 2009.

26 Alain de Botton, *The Art of Travel* (London: Hamish Hamilton, 2002), p. 59.

27 Kathleen Raine, *Farewell Happy Fields* (London: Hamilton, 1973), p. 24.

28 Pat Barker, *Regeneration* (New York: Penguin Books, 1993), p. 184.

29 Kat Duff, *The Alchemy of Illness* (New York: Pantheon Books, 1993), p. 70.

30 Carl Jung, *Memories, Dreams, Reflections* (London: Collins, 1963), pp. 35, 59.

31 Richard Goodman, *French Dirt: The Story of a Garden in the South of France* (Chapel Hill, NC: Algonquin Books, 2002), p.160.

32 Dom Helder Camara, *A Thousand Reasons for Living,* trans., Alan Neame (Philadelphia: Fortress Press, 1981), p.51.

33 John Muir, "1913," in *John Muir, John of the Mountains: The Unpublished Journals of John Muir,* ed., L. M. Wolfe (Madison, WI: University of Wisconsin Press, 1979), p. 439.

34 Mary Oliver, "The Journey," from *Dream Work* (New York: Atlantic Monthly Press, 1986), pp. 38–39.

35 Kat Duff, *The Alchemy of Illness* (New York: Pantheon Books, 1993), p. 74.

36 Duff, *The Alchemy of Illness*, pp. 93–94.

37 Ian Bradley, *The Celtic Way* (London: Darton, Longman and Todd Ltd., 1993), pp. 35, 59, 191.

38 Bradley, *The Celtic Way*, p. 59.

39 Bradley, *The Celtic Way*, p. 103.

40 Bradley, *The Celtic Way*, p. 103.

41 Robert Van der Weyer, *Celtic Fire: The Passionate Religious Vision of Ancient Britain and Ireland* (London: Darton, Longman and Todd, 1990), as quoted in Bradley, *Celtic Way*, p. 113.

42 John O'Donohue, *Anam Cara: A Book of Celtic Wisdom* (London: Bantam Books, 1997), p. 136.

43 *Meditations with Meister Eckhart,* trans., Matthew Fox. (Santa Fe, NM: Bear and Company Inc., 1983), p. 48.

44 Shierry Weber Nicholsen, *The Love of Nature and the End of the World: The Unspoken Dimensions of Environmental Concern* (Cambridge, MA: MIT Press, 2002), p. 20.

45 R. S. Thomas, "Via Negativa," from *Collected Poems 1945 – 1990* (London: J. M. Dent, 1993), p. 220.

46 Doris Grumbach, *Fifty Days of Solitude* (Boston: Beacon Press, 1994), pp. 27–28.

47 Frances G. Wickes, *The Inner World of Man* (New York: Harper, 1963), as quoted in *The Choice Is Always Ours: The Classic Anthology of the Spiritual Way,* eds. D. B. Phillips, et. al. (San Francisco: Guild for Psychological Studies, 2004), pp. 307–308.

48 Adam Nicolson, *Sea Room: An Island Life in the Hebrides* (New York: North Point Press, 2001), p. 141.

49 From "Iona,"in Kenneth C. Stevens, *Iona Poems* (Edinburgh: St. Andrews Press, 2000), p. 18.

50 Robert Sardello, *Facing the World with Soul: The Reimagination of Modern Life* (Hudson, NY: Lindisfarne Press, 1992), pp. 25, 46.

51 Shierry Weber Nicholsen, *The Love of Nature and the End of the World: The Unspoken Dimensions of Environmental Concern* (Cambridge, MA: MIT Press, 2002), pp. 22, 25

52 James Hillman, *The Force of Character and the Lasting Life* (New York: Ballantine Books, 1999), p. 157.

53 David Whyte, "What to remember when waking," from *The House of Belonging* (Langley, WA: Many Rivers Press, 1997), p. 27.

54 Geoff Holder, *The Guide to Mysterious Iona and Staffa* (Stroud, UK: Tempus, 2007), p. 43.

55 Christopher Bamford, Forward to Alice O. Howell, *The Dove in the Stone: Finding the Sacred in the Commonplace* (Wheaton, IL: Quest Books, 1988), p. x.

56 Howell, *The Dove in the Stone*, p. 8, 9.

57 Philip Larkin, "Water," from *Philip Larkin, Collected Poems,* ed. Anthony Thwaite (New York: Farrar, Straus and Giroux: 989), p. 93.

58 Jack Kornfield, *After the Ecstasy, the Laundry: How the Heart Grows Wise on the Spiritual Path* (New York: Bantam Books, 2000), pp. 92–93.

59 Quoted in James Hillman, "Epigraph in Lieu of a Preface," *The Soul's Code: In Search of Character and Calling* (New York: Random House, 1966), p. x.

60 John O'Donohue, *Anam Cara: A Book of Celtic Wisdom* (London: Bantam Books, 1997), pp. 235, 222.

61 Gloria Steinem, *Revolution from Within* (New York: Little, Brown and Co., 1992), p. 322-323.

62 David Whyte, "Everything is Waiting for You," from *Everything is Waiting for You* (Langley, WA: Many Rivers Press, 2003), p. 6.

63 Terry Tempest Williams, "Yellowstone: The Erotics of Place," from *An Unspoken Hunger: Stories from the Field* (New York: Vintage Books, 1995), p. 84.

64 Cecil Frances Alexander, *Hymns for Little Children,* as quoted in Iona Opie and Peter Opie, eds. *The Oxford Book of Children's Verse* (Oxford: Oxford University Press, 1973).

65 Frans Hoogland, as quoted in Jim Sinatra and Phin Murphy, *Listen to the People, Listen to the Land* (Carlton South, Victoria, Australia: Melbourne University Press, 1999), p. 19.

66 Deborah Tall, *The Island of the White Cow: Memories of an Irish Island* (New York: Athanaeum Books, 1986), p. 28.

67 Deborah Tall, *From Where We Stand: Recovering a Sense of Place* (New York: Knopf, 1993), p. 48.

68 Alan Gussow, *A Sense of Place: The Artist and the American Land* (San Francisco: Friends of the Earth, 1971), p. 15.

69 Thales, as quoted in E. V. Walter, *Placeways: A Theory of the Human Environment* (Chapel Hill, NC: University of North Carolina Press, 1988), p. 121.

70 Walter, *Placeways,* p. 123.

71 Walter, *Placeways*, pp. 121, 123.

72 Ortega y Gasset, *Meditations of Quixote*, adapted from a translation by J. W. Jeaffreson. Quoted in Jane Hirshfield, *Nine Gates: Entering the Mind of Poetry* (New York: Harper Collins, 1998), pp. 118, 119.

73 Geoff Holder, *The Guide to Mysterious Iona and Staffa* (Stroud, UK: Tempus Publishing Ltd., 2007), p. 111.

74 Holder, *Mysterious Iona and Staffa,* p. 97.

75 Fiona MacLeod, *Iona* (Edinburgh: Floris Books, 1982), first published in 1910 by Chapman and Hall, p. 15.

76 Robinson Jeffers, quoted in Warwick Fox, "Transpersonal Ecology and the Varieties of Identification," in Alan Drengson and Yulchi Inoue, eds., *The Deep Ecology Movement* (Berkeley, CA: North Atlantic Books, 1995), p. 143.

77 Anne Morrow Lindbergh, *A Gift from the Sea* (New York: Vintage Books, 1965), p. 40.

78 Terry Tempest Williams, *An Unnatural History of Family and Place* (New York: Vintage Books, 1992), p. 85.

79 Julia Gardiner, *The Children's War: The Second World War through the Eyes of the Children of Britain* (London: Piatkus Books, 2005), pp. 65, 67.

80 Juliet Gardiner, *The Children's War*, pp. 65, 67.

81 Vera Brittain, *England's Hour* (Pleasantville, NY: The Akadine Press, 2002, originally published 1941), p. 142.

82 Jean-Jacques Rousseau, *The Confessions*, trans, J. M. Cohen (Harmondsworth, England: Penguin Books, 1953), p. 158.

83 Thomas Merton, "In Silence," from *The Collected Poems of Thomas Merton* (New York: New Directions, 1977), pp. 280–281.

84 Fleur Adcock, "Weatherings," in *Fleur Adcock Poems 1960–2000* (Newcastle-on-Tyne, UK: Bloodaxe Books Ltd., 2000), p. 124.

PERMISSIONS

Fleur Adcock, excerpt from "Weathering" from *Poems 1960-2000*. Copyright © 2000 by Fleur Adcock. Reprinted with the permission of Bloodaxe Books Ltd.

Dom Helder Camara, ["I love flowers more and more"]; ["If you have a thousand reasons for living"]; and ["Do you think land has no feelings?"] from *A Thousand Reasons for Living*, translated by Alan Neame. Copyright © 1981 by Alan Neame. Used by permission of Darton, Longman & Todd, Ltd.

Philip Larkin, excerpt from "Water" from *Collected Poems*, edited by Anthony Thwaite. Copyright © 1988, 1989 by the Estate of Philip Larkin. Reprinted by permission of Farrar, Straus & Giroux, LLC and Faber & Faber, Ltd.

Thomas Merton, "In Silence" *The Collected Poems of Thomas Merton*. Copyright © 1957 by Thomas Merton. Reprinted by permission of New Directions Publishing Corp.

Mary Oliver, excerpt from "The Journey" from *Dream Work*. Copyright © 1986 by Mary Oliver. Reprinted with the permission of Grove/Atlantic, Inc.

Jelaluddin Rumi, ["The breeze at dawn has secrets to tell you"] from *Open Secret: Versions of Rumi*, translated by Coleman Barks and John Moyne. Copyright © 1984 by Coleman Barks and John Moyne. Reprinted with the permission of Coleman Barks.

Kenneth Steven, excerpt from "Iona" from *Iona Poems*. Copyright © 2000 by Kenneth Stevens. Reprinted with the permission of Saint Andrews Press.

R.S. Thomas, excerpt from "Via Negativa" from *Collected Poems 1945-1990*. Copyright © 1993 by R.S. Thomas. Reprinted with the permission of J. M. Dent & Sons, Ltd.

David Whyte, excerpt from "What to remember when waking" from *The House of Belonging*. Copyright © 1997 by David Whyte. Reprinted with the permission of Many Rivers Company.

David Whyte, excerpt from "Everything Is Waiting for You" from *Everything Is Waiting for You*. Copyright © 2003 by David Whyte. Reprinted with the permission of Many Rivers Company.

Photo Credits

Author photo: Barbara Hellenschmidt

Photos on p. 66; 135; 212; 218; 229; 230; 238; 279; 296; 340; 348: Photographers unknown.

Photo on p. 371: Barbara Hellenschmidt

All other photos: Clare Cooper Marcus

About the Author

CLARE COOPER MARCUS is Professor Emerita in the Departments of Architecture and Landscape Architecture at the University of California, Berkeley. She is the Principal of Healing Landscapes, a consulting firm that specializes in researching the effectiveness of restorative landscapes in healthcare settings. She is internationally recognized for her research on the social and psychological implications of design, particularly urban open space, affordable housing, and environments for children and the elderly. Marcus has been recognized for her work with awards from the American Institute of Architects, the American Society of Landscape Architects, the American Horticultural Therapy Association, the National Endowment for the Arts, and the Guggenheim Foundation. She has authored/co-authored/edited numerous publications, including five previous books—*Easter Hill Village* (1975), *Housing As If People Mattered* (1986), *People Places* (1990), *House as a Mirror of Self* (1995), and *Healing Gardens* (1999). She lives in Berkeley, California, holds joint British and American citizenship, is a mother, grandmother, poet, and passionate gardener.

❧ ❧

Is there a specific physical place that you feel has helped you during a period of physical, emotional, or spiritual healing? If you are willing to share the story of your experience with this place, please contact me at:

clare@ionadreaming.com

www.ionadreaming.com